Social and Political Thought of Mahatma Gandhi

During his campaign against racism in South Africa and his involvement in the Congress-led nationalist struggle against British colonial rule in India, Mahatma Gandhi developed a new form of political struggle based on the idea of *satyagraha* or non-violent protest. He ushered in a new era of nationalism in India by articulating the nationalist protest in the language of non-violence or *ahisma*, which galvanized the masses into action.

Social and Political Thought of Mahatma Gandhi focuses on the principles of *satyagraha* and non-violence, and their evolution in the context of anti-imperial movements organized by Gandhi, looking at how these precepts underwent changes reflecting the ideological beliefs of the participants. The book focuses on the ways in which Gandhi took into account the views of other leading personalities of the era while articulating his theory of action, and assesses Gandhi and his ideology. Concentrating on Gandhi's writings in *Harijan*, the weekly newspaper of the *Servants of Untouchable Society*, this volume offers a unique contextualized study of Gandhi's social and political thought.

Bidyut Chakrabarty is Professor in Political Science at the University of Delhi, India.

Routledge studies in social and political thought

1 Hayek and After
Hayekian liberalism as a research
programme
Jeremy Shearmur

2 Conflicts in Social Science
Edited by Anton van Harskamp

3 Political Thought of André
Gorz
Adrian Little

4 Corruption, Capitalism and
Democracy
John Girling

5 Freedom and Culture in
Western Society
Hans Blokland

6 Freedom in Economics
New perspectives in normative
analysis
*Edited by Jean-Francois Laslier,
Marc Fleurbaey, Nicolas Gravel
and Alain Trannoy*

7 Against Politics
On government, anarchy and
order
Anthony de Jasay

8 Max Weber and Michel
Foucault
Parallel life works
Arpad Szakolczai

9 The Political Economy of Civil
Society and Human Rights
G.B. Madison

10 On Durkheim's *Elementary
Forms of Religious Life*
*Edited by W.S.F. Pickering,
W. Watts Miller and N.J. Allen*

11 Classical Individualism
The supreme importance of each
human being
Tibor R. Machan

12 The Age of Reasons
Quixotism, sentimentalism and
political economy in eighteenth-
century Britain
Wendy Motooka

13 Individualism in Modern
Thought
From Adam Smith to Hayek
Lorenzo Infantino

14 Property and Power in Social
Theory
A study in intellectual rivalry
Dick Pels

15 **Wittgenstein and the Idea of a Critical Social Theory**
A critique of Giddens, Habermas and Bhaskar
Nigel Pleasants

16 **Marxism and Human Nature**
Sean Sayers

17 **Goffman and Social Organization**
Studies in a sociological legacy
Edited by Greg Smith

18 **Situating Hayek**
Phenomenology and the neo-liberal project
Mark J. Smith

19 **The Reading of Theoretical Texts**
Peter Ekegren

20 **The Nature of Capital**
Marx after Foucault
Richard Marsden

21 **The Age of Chance**
Gambling in Western culture
Gerda Reith

22 **Reflexive Historical Sociology**
Arpad Szakolczai

23 **Durkheim and Representations**
Edited by W.S.F. Pickering

24 **The Social and Political Thought of Noam Chomsky**
Alison Edgley

25 **Hayek's Liberalism and Its Origins**
His idea of spontaneous order and the Scottish enlightenment
Christina Petsoulas

26 **Metaphor and the Dynamics of Knowledge**
Sabine Maasen and Peter Weingart

27 **Living with Markets**
Jeremy Shearmur

28 **Durkheim's Suicide**
A century of research and debate
Edited by W.S.F. Pickering and Geoffrey Walford

29 **Post-Marxism**
An intellectual history
Stuart Sim

30 **The Intellectual as Stranger**
Studies in spokespersonship
Dick Pels

31 **Hermeneutic Dialogue and Social Science**
A critique of Gadamer and Habermas
Austin Harrington

32 **Methodological Individualism**
Background, history and meaning
Lars Udehn

33 **John Stuart Mill and Freedom of Expression**
The genesis of a theory
K.C. O'Rourke

34 **The Politics of Atrocity and Reconciliation**
From terror to trauma
Michael Humphrey

35 **Marx and Wittgenstein**
Knowledge, morality, politics
*Edited by Gavin Kitching and
Nigel Pleasants*

36 **The Genesis of Modernity**
Arpad Szakolczai

37 **Ignorance and Liberty**
Lorenzo Infantino

38 **Deleuze, Marx and Politics**
Nicholas Thoburn

39 **The Structure of Social
Theory**
Anthony King

40 **Adorno, Habermas and the
Search for a Rational Society**
Deborah Cook

41 **Tocqueville's Moral and
Political Thought**
New liberalism
M.R.R. Ossewaarde

42 **Adam Smith's Political
Philosophy**
The invisible hand and
spontaneous order
Craig Smith

43 **Social and Political Thought
of Mahatma Gandhi**
Bidyut Chakrabarty

Social and Political Thought of Mahatma Gandhi

Bidyut Chakrabarty

LONDON AND NEW YORK

First published 2006
by Routledge
2 Park Square, Milton Park, Abingdon, Oxon, OX14 4RN

Simultaneously published in the USA and Canada
by Routledge
270 Madison Ave, New York NY 10016

Routledge is an imprint of the Taylor & Francis Group

Transferred to Digital Printing 2008

© 2006 Bidyut Chakrabarty

Typeset in Garamond by Wearset Ltd, Boldon, Tyne and Wear

British Library Cataloguing in Publication Data
A catalogue record for this book is available from the British Library

Library of Congress Cataloging in Publication Data
A catalog record for this title has been requested

ISBN10: 0-415-36096-X (hbk)
ISBN10: 0-415-48209-7 (pbk)

ISBN13: 978-0-415-36096-8 (hbk)
ISBN13: 978-0-415-48209-7 (pbk)

Dedicated to
those appreciating the glory
of our noble profession

Contents

Acknowledgements   x

By way of introduction   1

1   Gandhi: the idea of *swaraj*   30

2   The Mahatma at the grassroots: the praxis of *ahimsa* or
    non-violence   56

3   Politics and ideology: critique of Gandhi   84

4   Gandhi's writings in *Harijan*: discussion and interpretation   116

5   Introducing the text   130

    Conclusion   166

    Glossary   178
    Notes   180
    Bibliographical notes   219
    Select bibliography   221
    Index   228

Acknowledgements

This book is written by an individual author but, of course, with the support of a wider collectivity. There are some who always support their friends without being partisan. There are, however, some in this collectivity who tend to belittle the contribution of those allegedly belonging to 'the other'. I owe a great deal to them. Because of their obduracy, I have become resolute in my conviction that my academic effort is not futile. The more they target me the more firm I will be. Thank you friends for having sustained my zeal for creativity despite all odds. This book is the outcome of what I have learnt from Gandhi during my struggle against structural inequalities and institutional decay due largely to the narrow-mindedness of those destroying the system in the name of its protection.

I am thankful to Professor Mohit Bhattacharya who sustained my academic inertia by drawing my attention to the brighter side of our vocation. I am also grateful to Professor Subrata Mukherjee and Dipa Boudi who stood by me whenever needed. Professor Bob Frykenberg and Professor Ronald Terchek were always generous in sharing ideas with me which greatly improved my understanding of the history of ideas in a colonial context. I would like to put on record my gratitude to Dr Amiya Chaudhuri for his support to the project since it was mooted. Without Dipakda's sincere support in my fight against injustice, it would not have been possible for me to concentrate on my academic feat. Professor V.S. Parmar contributed to my creative faculty by way of stories and jokes which were not exactly academic. My gratitude goes to Ashok and Minu for being 'friends indeed' in the campus. My students in the University of Delhi continue to remain my sources of energy. I shall be failing in my duty if I do not record my appreciation for them. Bhuwan, Rajinder and Prakash were always available for help. Despite being busy with her family and professional commitments, Roopinder contributed to this project as much as she could. I put on record my appreciation for Minati, who helped me in tracking the right kind of books from the DSA Library, and Mahinder for typing the excerpts from *Harijan* at very short notice. I am thankful to Mr Gopinath of Routledge-India for his help.

My family, of course, stood by me. Pablo and Barbie remained the most creative distraction during the preparation of the manuscript. Sanchita was always a source of lively debates on various wider issues of human existence and thereby helped me conceptualize some of the basic human values which informed Gandhi. My two Calcutta-based sisters sustained my energy by pampering me whenever I was in this most happening city in India. Without my mother's inspiration, the project would not have taken off. I am grateful to her.

I am thankful to Navjivan Trust, Ahmedabad for *Harijan* excerpts. I express my gratitude to Professor Barbara Caine and the School of Historical Studies of Monash University, Melbourne for having supported my project on Gandhi. I am indebted to Professor Ian Copland for having drawn my attention to some of the most complex dimensions of the Gandhi-led political mobilization in transitional societies.

By way of introduction

Mohandas Karamchand Gandhi (1869–1948), popularly known as Mahatma Gandhi, continues to evoke interest even several decades after his death in 1948. It is true that Richard Attenborough's film *Gandhi* popularized Gandhi immensely all over the world but the Mahatma also remains an important topic of research and discussion among those interested in exploring alternative ideological traditions. The task is made easier simply because Gandhi's own writings on various themes are plentiful and unambiguous. His articulation is not only clear and simple but also meaningful taken in the context of his leadership of the most gigantic nationalist struggle of the twentieth century. He wrote extensively in *Young India* and *Harijan*, the leading newspapers of the era, commenting on issues of contemporary relevance. These texts frequently addressed matters of everyday importance to Indians in the early and middle parts of the twentieth century, matters which may not appear relevant if seen superficially. Writing for the ordinary folk, he usually employed metaphors and engaged in homilies to teach Indians about their abilities and also their strong traditions. This is one of the ways in which he involved the Indians in non-violent struggles against British imperialism, untouchability and communal discord.

There is no dearth of texts helping us to decipher what Gandhi stood for.[1] The problem lies in the language in which his ideas were articulated. The language is so simple that it is notoriously open to diverse interpretations. For instance, Gandhi's critique of modernity and modernization in his *Hind Swaraj* is constantly referred to as illustrative of his obscurantism. And, the only correct way of reading him is therefore to see him arguing that India must return to a simple agrarian economy and simple society. This interpretation appears overstretched and fails to capture the complex nuances in Gandhi's thought, which flourished in a context when India, as part of the British colony, had adopted the path of capitalist development. It is true that Gandhi's insistence on rural economy and uncomplicated life was perhaps logical in his conceptualization of Indian society and economy. Hence his arguments supporting a particular society and economy are not only criticisms of the dominant organizing principles of the era but also provide 'idealized alternatives to them which he wants men and women to enlist in their struggle to protect their own autonomy'.[2] In so doing, Gandhi was simply critical of the contemporary civilization that drew on a total rejection of what he defined as the perennially valid 'traditional values'. His oppositional views upheld a new theoretical enquiry that was meaningful only in a colonial context in which the politically dominant ideas tended to swallow the countervailing ideas with indigenous roots. Gandhi's peculiar genius lay in his understanding of how the complex fabric of traditional Indian society could be 'related to the essentially modern phenomenon of the movement for political independence'.[3]

Furthermore, Gandhi's charisma had 'a cultural referent'. His success as a leader was less due to his 'oratorical or theatrical skills' than to the reputation that preceded him and 'the ideal he embodied'. As the Rudolphs argues, 'the authenticity with which he sought virtue and the highest religious goals through self-control, truth and non-violence re-enacted a familiar but rarely realized cultural model, that of the saintly man'.[4] What he represented was 'saintly politics',[5] which acquired salience in British-ruled India where the indigenous cultural traditions had a natural appeal to the peripheral masses. Many were struck by the contrast between his remarkable physical appearance and the aura surrounding him. In his first meeting with Gandhi, Lord Reading, the Viceroy expressed surprise at his growing popularity among the Indians by saying

> There is nothing striking about his appearance. He came to visit me in a white dhoti and cap, woven on a spinning-wheel, with bare feet and legs, and my first impression on seeing him ushered into my room was that there was nothing to arrest attention in his appearance, and that I should have passed him by in the street without a second look at him. When he talks, the impression is different.[6]

By playing upon a very varied symbolic register, Gandhi was able 'to establish with the Indian public a rapport of profound complicity which often escaped the eyes of the British, who were not very sensitive to the nuances of Gandhian symbolism'.[7] To the Indian masses, he was a renouncer, a *sanyasi* who adopted a lifestyle entirely different from those of the Anglicized politicians until then controlling the anti-British campaign in India.[8] While his lifestyle endeared Gandhi to the masses,[9] those who then led the Congress failed to understand him. As Lajpat Rai commented, 'such of his countrymen as have drunk deep from the fountains of European history and European politics and who have developed a deep love for European manners and European culture, neither understand nor like him. In their eyes, he is a barbarian.'[10] Yet Gandhi gradually became the centre of the nationalist activities in opposition to the typical constitutional means of protest against colonialism. In fact, his rise to the leadership of the Congress in 1920 radically altered its social composition by simply allowing the politically peripheral groups in contrast with the Anglicized elite of the great metropolitan cities. A new middle class – some of whom came from the smaller cities and towns and were prone to express themselves in the vernacular rather than in English – joined the Congress whose membership until then remained confined largely to the metropolitan cities of Calcutta and Bombay. This non-metropolitan middle class with close links to the countryside was 'better-placed to draw rural India into the struggle, thanks to its contacts with an upper strata of relatively rich peasants'.[11] Judith Brown thus argued that Gandhi's rise did not symbolize 'a radical restructuring of political life' or emergence of mass politics; rather it signified the rise of Western-educated and regional-language-literate elites of backward areas, in place of the Western-educated leaders of the presidency towns. It was the loyalty of these local leaders or the so-called 'sub-contractors' that enabled Gandhi to extend the constituency of the nationalist politics.[12] What is wrong in such an interpretation is the failure to comprehend the mass appeal of Gandhi as a leader who could also appeal directly, beyond the ranks of this elite leadership, to the Indian peasantry and draw their support for his struggle against the British.

Gandhi was not merely a leader – he also became a part of the masses. His simple attire, use of colloquial Hindi, reference to the popular allegory of Ramrajya had made him comprehensible to the common people. In popular myths he was, as Shahid Amin has shown, invested with supernatural power which could heal pain and deliver common people from their day-to-day miseries. The masses interpreted Gandhi in their own ways, drawing meanings from their own lived experiences and making him a symbol of power for the weak and underprivileged.[13] As evident on various occasions, the masses 'crossed the boundaries of Gandhian politics and deviated from his ideals of non violence, while believing at the same time that they were following their messiah into a new utopian world of Gandhi raj'.[14] This also suggests that the introduction of Gandhi to Indian politics radically restructured its nature and his effect was not confined to the presidency towns. Not only did he inculcate new styles of political articulation, he also enlarged the nationalist constituencies by incorporating new actors, so far peripheral in the anti-British struggle. So Gandhi was a symbol of radical changes both in the nationalist political articulation and its constituencies, which now expanded beyond the Western-educated elites in metropolitan towns.

Thus he was a man of both thought and action, a rare combination. As a man of thought, he was highly critical of the madness of modernity and articulated 'an alternative vision [combining] the best insights of both the pre-modern and modern world-views while avoiding the naïve individualism and moral vacuum of the currently fashionable post-modernism'.[15] He also discovered a uniquely moral method of political change in the form of *satyagraha*, and provided an effective alternative to violence, perpetrated by the ruling authority. As the Rudolphs put it: 'Indian nationalism had tried the paths of loyal constitutionalism and terrorist violence and found them wanting. Gandhi's answer was *satyagraha* (truth force), expressed through non-violent but non-constitutional direct action.'[16] He also spoke about 'structural violence and the violence of the status-quo'.[17] Poverty was, for instance, violence to him because it was the outcome of exploitation of human beings by human beings. Doing nothing to alleviate suffering when one has the means, as the argument goes, is also a violent act. As a man of action, he led perhaps the most gigantic nationalist struggle of the twentieth century on the basis of what he thought was morally acceptable. Without compromising one's integrity, he also demonstrated how to build a strong political platform drawing upon the moral strength of *satyagrahees*.

That Gandhi was different from his erstwhile nationalist colleagues was evident when he launched his *satyagraha* movements in remote areas of Champaran, Kheda and Ahmedabad instead of the presidency towns, then the hub of nationalist activities. His political strategies brought about radical changes in the Congress, which expanded its sphere of influence even in the villages. As J.B. Kripalani, one of Gandhi's trusted lieutenants during the nationalist struggle, admitted,

> In those days, such was our nationalism that we did not know what was really happening in the villages. We, the educated, lived more or less an isolated life. Our world was confined to the cities and to our fraternity of the educated. Our contact with the masses was confined to our servants, and yet we talked of the masses and were anxious to free the country from foreign yoke.[18]

At Champaran in Bihar, peasants raised their voice against the European planters for forcing them to produce indigo under the *tinkathia* system which imposed the production of indigo in three-twentieths of their land. The movement which began in the 1860s gained momentum even before Gandhi arrived on the scene. Led by the local middle class and rich peasant leaders, the pre-Gandhian efforts, however, failed to involve the actual cultivators. This is where Gandhi's intervention was most effective. A unique political action, the 1917 Champaran *satyagraha* was the first of its kind in India and one which Gandhi led in accordance with his plan and ideology. Gandhi's presence in Champaran represented hope for the *raiyats* of the plantations. His act of civil disobedience and determination to endure prison convinced the peasants that the Mahatma was their saviour. His extreme simplicity had brought him closer to them than all the erstwhile leaders. How he struck a chord with the peasants was surprising. Even Rajendra Prasad, who accompanied him during the Champaran movement, said that 'it is a matter of mystery to me how these people seemed to develop the confidence that their deliverer had come'.[19] Not only did he amaze his co-workers, his arrival in Bettiah in the Champaran region also caught the British sub-divisional officer by surprise, as evident in his report:

We may look on Mr. Gandhi as an idealist, a fanatic or a revolutionary according to our particular opinions. But to the raiyats, he is their liberator, and they credit him with extraordinary powers. He moves about in the villages, asking them to lay their grievance before him, and he is daily transfiguring the imagination of masses of ignorant men with visions of an early millennium.[20]

Gandhi, to the masses, meant a resurrection of hope.[21] His non-violent resistance provided a viable alternative in the struggle against colonialism where force had become both illegitimate and ineffective. The Champaran *satyagraha* forced the government to adopt the 1918 Champaran Agricultural Act, whereby those compelled to let their land for indigo cultivation were given some relief. What Gandhi left was carried forward by local peasants, with Champaran becoming a strong base for non-violent political mobilization, though the Congress leadership never allowed them to organize protests against the indigenous landlords. Despite the peasants' failure to lead movements against the vested interests, the Champaran *satyagraha* articulated the neglected voice of protests. Gandhi emerged as the supreme leader and non-violence gained salience. This was not a subaltern protest, but one in which the subalterns were inducted into the process of political mobilization. In other words, the Champaran *satyagraha* represented 'a battle in which many different levels of consciousness coexisted [presumably because of] the complex perspective of the participants'.[22] Apart from projecting Gandhi as a perfect mobilizer, this 1917 *satyagraha* also contributed to a unique multi-class political platform uniting the clearly antagonistic classes for the battle against foreign rule. Not only did Gandhi succeed in containing the class wrath within a specific limit, he also created a situation in which the struggle against the exploiters coincided with the challenge against colonialism. So Gandhian non-violence, as the Champaran *satyagraha* demonstrated, provided a potent means of legitimate and effective resistance within the new political dispensation in which the Congress was gaining in importance. The Champaran movement was a watershed in Gandhi's political life, not only in terms of conceptualizing *satyagraha* as a device but also in terms of its application to build a political platform regardless of class.

Similar to the Champaran experiment, the 1918 Kheda *satyagraha* was a Gandhi-led no-revenue campaign.[23] Hard-hit by economic hardship due to the destruction of crops by rains, a rise in agricultural wages, the high rate of inflation and the outbreak of bubonic plague, the Patidar peasants organized a movement against the government's decision not to waive land revenue. Launched by Mohanlal Pandya and Shankarlal Parikh from a small town of Kathlal in the district of Kheda of Gujarat, the movement gained momentum as the Gujarat Sabha, an organization under the aegis of the Congress, extended support. Once approached by the Gujarat Sabha, Gandhi arrived in Kheda in March 1918 to launch a *satyagraha* campaign against the government decision to confiscate the properties of defaulters. The campaign lasted for four months and in June the government of Bombay decided not to implement the order, sparing the peasants who failed to pay the revenue. Like the Champaran *satyagraha*, the movement, spearheaded by local Congress activists, continued with local support. Gandhi's presence was more symbolical than anything else. Even his lieutenants, Vallabhbhai and Vitthalbhai Patel, remained insignificant in the entire movement, in which the local leaders became most important. As a cementing factor, Gandhi brought the *satyagrahees* together for the movement that had an agenda set by the local leaders in their own terms. In other words, Gandhi was important in the Kheda *satyagraha* so long as he agreed to support the demands of local leaders. This was evident when Gandhi urged the villagers to join the British army during the First World War and they refused.[24]

During the Kheda *satyagraha*, Gandhi also participated in the Ahmedabad textile mill strike of February–March 1918.[25] This was a different kind of experiment involving the workers. The successful campaign in Champaran had catapulted Gandhi to the centre-stage. When the workers in Ahmedabad became restive, Gandhi was invited by Anusuyya Sarabhai, a social worker who happened to be the sister of Ambalal Sarabhai, the president of the Ahmedabad Mill Owners' Association, to intervene and resolve the crisis. What triggered the strike was the withdrawal of 'plague-bonus' to the workers. Equivalent in some cases to 80 per cent of the wages, this was paid to dissuade the workers from fleeing the plague-ravaged towns. Once the epidemic was over, the mill-owners decided to discontinue the practice. This decision affected the workers adversely simply because of the spiralling price rise due to the outbreak of war.

Drawing on his belief that there was no major contradiction between capital and labour, Gandhi sought to defuse the crisis through dialogues with the mill-owners. The mill-owners appeared to be adamant and characterized Gandhi's intervention as 'unwarranted'. On 22 February, 1918, the mill-owners locked out the weavers despite Gandhi's repeated requests. With the closure, Gandhi decided to champion the workers' demand though he asked them to tone down their earlier demand for a 50 per cent wage increase to 35 per cent. Although the workers agreed to Gandhi's suggestion, the mill-owners did not relent and workers seemed to lose morale. It was at this juncture that Gandhi began the 'first' of his seventeen 'fasts unto death' on 15 March, 1918. This three-day fast appears to have forced the mill-owners, who deeply respected Gandhi, to come to an agreement with the striking workers. As per the agreement, suggested by the arbitration board, the workers demand was partially fulfilled because they got a 27.5 per cent wage hike instead of their revised demand for a 35 per cent increase. So the compromise formula 'looked like a face-saving formula and a tactical defeat for Gandhi'[26] though he forced the mill-owners to accept the principle of arbitration in which workers' representatives had a say along with the employers.

A unique event in Gandhi's political life, the Ahmedabad strike added a new chapter to the history of the Indian nationalist movement. Though critical of Gandhi's 'obsession' with 'passive resistance', *The Bombay Chronicle* appreciated the principle of arbitration as 'a turning point in labour–employer relations in Ahmedabad' in particular and a unique system of 'resolving industrial disputes' in general.[27] Similarly, *The Times* criticized Gandhi for 'blackmailing' the mill-owners who happened to be his 'admirers' by his 'fast unto death', though it hailed his role in articulating 'arbitration' as 'an effective device' to break the *impasse* between the workers and industrialists.[28]

These three movements projected Gandhi as an emerging leader with different kinds of mobilizing tactics. What was common in all these movements was the fact that a) they were organized around local issues; and b) in mobilizing the people for the movements, the importance of the local leaders cannot be underestimated. There is no doubt that Gandhi's appearance on the scene gave a fillip to these movements. Yet, if we carefully chart the movements, we will discover that Gandhi was invited to lead when support was adequately mobilized by the local organizers. By his involvement with these movements at a stage when they struck roots in the concerned localities, Gandhi projected a specific kind of leadership: he was not a primary but a secondary organizer. There is no doubt that the movements gained different heights with his intervention. The masses interpreted Gandhi's message in their own terms and 'rumours surrounding the powers of this messianic leader served to break the barriers of fear involved in confronting formidable enemies'.[29] As evident in Champaran and Kheda, Gandhian intervention in elite nationalist politics established for the first time that an authentic nationalist movement could be built upon the organized support of the peasantry, though its political object was not one which Gandhi endorsed. The peasants were meant to become 'willing participants in a struggle wholly conceived and directed by others', with Gandhi providing 'a national framework of politics in which peasants are mobilized but do not participate' in its formulation.[30] This was also true of the Ahmedabad strike where Gandhi accommodated the interests of the mill-owners even at the cost of the workers since their demand was partially conceded. Based on his belief that capital and labour were not contradictory to each other, Gandhi agreed to the negotiated settlements as probably the best solution under the circumstances. Workers failed to get what they had asked for. Yet Gandhi's role was most significant in articulating a form of political mobilization in which the workers were also decisive. Just like the Champaran and Kheda *satyagrahas* that extended the constituencies of nationalist politics by incorporating the peasantry, the Ahmedabad textile strike was a watershed, for it accorded a legitimate space to the workers in what was conceptualized as nationalism.

These three movements constitute a milestone in what Gandhi articulated as nationalist politics. A leader had emerged to radically alter the complexion of India's struggle for freedom. With his involvement in mass movements in Champaran, Kheda and Ahmedabad, Gandhi 'forged a new language of protests for India by both building on older forms of resistance while at the same time accepting the colonial censure of all forms of violent protest'.[31] Two complementary processes seem to have been at work: at one level, local issues obviously played a significant role in mobilizing the masses for protest movements in the localities; at another, the presence of Gandhi at a critical juncture helped sustain these movements as they were perhaps losing momentum due to the growing frustration of the local organizers. So Gandhi was a missing link that not only galvanized the masses into action but also contributed immensely to the successful conclusion of these protest movements in Champaran, Kheda and Ahmedabad involving completely different constituencies of nationalist politics, namely, peasantry and labour. These movements appear to have set the tone and tenor for future movements which Gandhi was to lead, with the people at large participating in response to his call for political action. Although he was a secondary organizer in all these movements, he appeared to carry with him 'a magic wand' that not only activated those who remained peripheral but also sustained the momentum of the movements despite odds. He emerged as a mass leader who felt the pulse of the people perhaps more accurately than anybody else during the freedom struggle. And the consequence was obvious because it was Gandhi who transformed the struggle for freedom to a wider nationalist campaign involving various categories of people including those who usually remained detached. As Jawaharlal Nehru most eloquently put it,

> [Gandhiji] attracted people. They did not agree with his philosophy of life, or even with many of his ideals. Often they did not understand him, but the action that he proposed was something tangible which could be understood and appreciated intellectually. Any action would have been welcome after the long tradition of inaction which our spineless politics had nurtured; brave and effective action with an ethical halo about it had an irresistible appeal, both to the intellect and emotions. Step by step he convinced us of the rightness of the action, and we went with him, although we did not accept his philosophy.... Gandhiji, being essentially a man of action and very sensitive to changing conditions ... the road he was following was the right one thus far, and if the future meant a parting it would be folly to anticipate it.
>
> All this shows that we were by no means clear or certain in our minds. Always we had the feeling that while we might be more logical, Gandhiji knew India far better than we did, and a man who could command such tremendous devotion and loyalty must have something in him that corresponded to the needs and aspirations of the masses.[32]

Gandhi led three major pan-Indian movements. The 1919–21 Non-Cooperation Movement[33] was the first one that gained significantly, with the merger of the Khilafat agitation of the Muslims against the dismantling of the Khalif in Turkey.[34] The Civil Disobedience Movement was an all-India movement[35] in which Gandhi reigned supreme. Basically a salt *satyagraha*, the Civil Disobedience campaign manifested differently in different parts of India. The 1942 Quit India Movement, also known as the open rebellion,[36] was the last of the three pan-Indian campaigns spearheaded by Gandhi. Like the earlier anti-British nationalist offensives, the Quit India Movement was not uniform in its nature throughout the country, and yet masses drew on Gandhi and his ideas while zealously participating in what was proclaimed to be the final battle with the colonial ruler. Although these movements were organized in different phases of India's nationalist struggle, two features that recurred in all these instances of mass mobilization are as follows: first, Gandhi remained the undisputed leader who appeared to have swayed masses with his charisma and 'magical power'; and second, despite their pan-Indian characteristics, these movements were independently organized by the participants, drawing on local grievances both against the rural vested interests and the government for supporting them.[37] As examples from rural Bengal show, the message of the Mahatma was decoded completely differently by the people during the Quit India Movement.[38] On occasions, they even justified violence in the name of the Mahatma. This was what was unique in Gandhi, who succeeded in infusing a mass zeal for participation in the freedom struggle in contrast with the past when the nationalist movement was narrowly conceptualized and participation was therefore highly restricted.

What the book is (not) about

Writings on Gandhi are plentiful.[39] They fall into three types: a) biographical; b) philosophical (focused on his socio-political ideas); and c) those relating to the role of Gandhi in the Indian freedom struggle. This book is not a straightforward biography, nor does it deal exclusively with Gandhi's socio-political ideas. Rather, it is a work that dwells on the Mahatma as a civilizational character, who provided a well-argued theoretical framework with which to view and conceptualize human behaviour in societies that experienced colonialism. The aim here is not merely to contextualize Gandhi but also to identify those issues in his writings which are also transcendental in nature and content. In order to place this study in relation to the available literature, a twofold strategy will be pursued. First, the prevalent literature will be reviewed selectively by focusing on those ideas constituting the foundation pillars in Gandhi's social and political thought; second, while dealing with the contextualized Gandhian response, the book will focus on the ideas of other leading contemporary personalities who sought to provide an alternative to the hegemonic model devised by the Mahatma. In other words, the book argues that Gandhi's social and political ideas are dialogical and hence need to be grasped in relation to what was conceptualized by others as 'a parallel cosmology' of ideas with different thrusts and different ideological roots as well.

The first part is confined to those works dealing with the ideas that gradually became a significant part of Gandhian cosmology. This is not a review of literature, but an analysis of the ideas that had resonance in Gandhi's social and political thought.

Judith Brown's *Gandhi: prisoner of hope* is a sequel to her earlier works on the rise of Gandhi as a political leader in the context of the Non-Cooperation and Civil Disobedience Movements.[40] On the basis of her extensive research into Gandhi's political life, Brown attributed the Mahatma's success to his perennial optimism, believing in a better life. As a true *satyagrahee*, the Mahatma followed 'a vision of truth and tried to deploy the strength of truth and love in daily life'.[41] Despite frustration and episodes of depression, Gandhi never lost hope.[42] In fact, that was the hallmark of his political philosophy. An essential aspect of this was his firm belief that human beings and the situations in which they were placed were bound to change. Thus he always remained, as Brown argued, 'a prisoner of hope' who never felt insecure in his mission despite uncertainties all around. Whether this left an imprint in his political style is debatable. What is clear is the fact that Gandhi's alternative vision for India and her struggle for freedom certainly galvanized the masses into action in contrast with the loyal constitutionalism of the Moderate era and the revolutionary terrorism of the Extremist phase.

Apart from being an optimist to the core, Gandhi rose to prominence for his 'saintliness', his repute as a Mahatma and as one devoted to the Indian nation and her poorest people. Corroborating more or less what others have already said, Brown reiterated the point by saying that 'it was he who was custodian of the Congress conscience, he who strove to burnish its national image, as it seemed often to come perilously close to disintegration'.[43] As long as the Congress was a movement, it was possible for Gandhi to guide the party in accordance with what he thought appropriate. The situations changed, however, with the acceptance of government by the Congress following the 1937 provincial elections. This put the Mahatma in a great dilemma since he doubted the worth of state structures and had tried to turn Congress into a social service organization. His profound spiritual vision of life as a pilgrimage helped him to adapt to the changed political circumstances in a very forthright manner because 'the new environment provided him with an opportunity to be welcomed rather than resisted with fear'.[44] Despite his unstinted commitment to *swaraj* and *satyagraha*, the Congress zeal for Gandhian ideals seemed to have considerably waned with the acceptance of the ministry. There emerged a hiatus between the leader and the led, for the Mahatma pursued his vision at personal cost, paying the price of ill health, exhaustion, self-doubt, loneliness and misunderstanding by others. A prisoner of hope became a prisoner of his ideals, as it were. By 1946, he realized that his role was neither welcome nor appreciated by his colleagues in the Congress. He sensed his 'ebbing authority'. He thus confessed that 'my voice carries no weight in the Working Committee. . . . I do not like the shape that things are taking and, I cannot speak out.'[45] During this time the Congress had accepted the 3 June partition as possibly the best way out of the communal bloodbath. The Mahatma was not consulted about such a momentous decision. Gandhi never agreed to partition on communal grounds and held strong views on Jinnah's two-nation theory. He was completely disillusioned when Nehru, in response to his query as to why partition was finally accepted, wrote 'now a time for decision has come and mere passing of resolutions giving expression to our views meant little. I felt convinced and so did most of the members of the Working Committee that we must press for this immediate division so that reality might be brought into [the] picture.'[46] Endorsing Nehru's views, Patel, in his communication, also underlined that the decision was taken after adequate deliberations among those who mattered in the Congress, and concluded the letter by saying that 'you are, of course, entitled to say what you feel is right'.[47] This probably shocked the Mahatma to such an extent that he felt that he was redundant politically and hence a burden to the Congress. Expressing his helplessness and anguish, he, in one of his prayer meetings, thus mentioned that

> whatever the Congress decides will be done; nothing will be according to what I say. My writ runs no more. . . . No one listens to me any more. I am a small man. True, there was a time when mine was a big voice. Then everyone obeyed what I said; now neither the Congress nor the Hindus nor the Muslims listen to me. Where is the Congress today? It is disintegrating. I am crying in the wilderness.[48]

He might have reconciled to the changed Congress as probably the most judicious thing to do at that moment. He neither rebelled nor undertook a fast unto death. When asked to explain his tacit approval of a partition he had never endorsed, the Mahatma responded by saying that 'whatever I am, I am after all a servant of the Congress. If the Congress is seized with madness, should I also go mad? Should I die in order to prove that I alone was right?'[49] Although he was unable to internalize the division of the country, he justified his reluctance to launch a movement against the Congress by reference to his commitment to an organization that he, along with colleagues, had built over decades. Reiterating his faith in the Congress, he thus argued:

> probably no one is more distressed than I am over the impending division of India. But I have no desire to launch a struggle against what promises to be an accomplished fact. I have considered such a division to be wrong and therefore I would never be party to it. But, when the Congress accepts such a division, however reluctantly, I would not carry on any agitation against that institution. Such a step is not inconceivable

under all circumstances. The Congress association with the proposed division in no circumstance [is] warranting a struggle against it of the kind you have in mind.[50]

The dilemma was sorted out and the Mahatma accepted, most reluctantly, the partition of the country despite his vehement opposition to the entire scheme, which drew on Jinnah's two-nation theory which Gandhi was never reconciled to.[51] The Congress prevailed over Gandhi who no longer remained as dominant as in the past. The Mahatma appears to have been eclipsed considerably as his colleagues in the Congress accepted partition as the most appropriate scheme to avoid further bloodshed. For Brown, Gandhi was a human being with saintly qualities who confronted a historical situation in which he had been an important actor but was unable to master.

In a refreshing manner, Brown makes a useful point in conceptualizing Gandhi's social and political ideas in the context of India's freedom struggle. According to her, there are two Gandhis: one, the activist and the other, the strategist. The activist Gandhi remained a prisoner of hope while the strategist evolved several devices to cope with the reality. As shown by the author, despite Gandhi's opposition to partition, believing it based on the wrongly construed two-nation theory, he finally agreed to accept it to avoid further disintegration of the Congress party. This strategy was probably sensible just on the eve of the 1947 transfer of power, in view of the massive bloodbaths in Bengal, Bihar and Punjab. The activist Gandhi went to quell the tension in the riot-affected areas in Noakhali, as it was strategically most significant to the Mahatma. Two Gandhis interacted dialectically, resulting in a complex web of social and political ideas evolved by Gandhi during his involvement with perhaps the most gigantic nationalist struggle of the twentieth century. This is an important contribution for it draws our attention to the processes that remained crucial in the rise of Gandhi, the public man, also famous as the Mahatma or the Great Soul, the symbol of India and the father of the nation.

J.V. Bondurant's *Conquest of violence: the Gandhian philosophy of conflict*[52] is a systematic attempt to grasp Gandhi's political ideas on non-violent resolution of conflict or *satyagraha*.[53] Unlike the conventional works on Gandhi, which usually begin with Gandhi's South African experiments, Bondurant focuses on the practice of *satyagraha* in India between 1917 and 1930. The 1918 Champaran and later Kheda *satyagrahas* were the first two experiments in political mobilization that catapulted Gandhi onto the centre-stage of Indian politics. Given the importance of *satyagraha* in Gandhi's political ideology, the author begins with its definition, underlining the principles of 'truth' and 'non-violence' that Gandhi identified with 'love'. Gandhi was so committed to these two cardinal ideas that he even suspended political action in Chauri Chaura in 1921 when the situation became violent. For Gandhi, non-violent action was the only test for truth. Bondurant makes an in-depth analysis of how these ideas were put into practice in a series of political movements, including the pan-Indian Non-Cooperation and Civil Disobedience Movements.

The theoretical importance of the book lies in its conceptualization of *satyagraha* in its most complex form. *Satyagraha* is a form of persuasion, which aims not at the conquest of the opponent but at the removal of conflict through genuine agreement. Based on truth, non-violence and self-suffering, *Satyagraha* is a force (defined as 'the exercise of power or influence to effect change') that also contains an element of coercion (defined as 'the use of force to compel action contrary to the will or reasoned judgment'). *Satyagraha* may inflict injury on the opponent – materially in such a case as boycott and through mental discomfiture in the use, for example, of fasting. In other words, although *satyagraha* is always persuasive, it also contains a positive element of coercion because policies of non-cooperation, boycott and strike involve 'an element of compulsion which may effect a change on the part of an opponent which initially was contrary to his will and he may suffer from the indirect results of these actions'.[54] Different from *duragraha* (or normal forms of coercion),[55] *satyagraha* provides strong moral strength to the *satyagrahee* who is himself willing to endure self-suffering. Furthermore, given the importance of *ahimsa* or non-violence in *satyagraha*, the *satyagrahee* does not intend to inflict injury though he may, by his act, cause injury. *Ahimsa* denotes not merely refusal to use violence, it also contains a positive psychological element seeking to eliminate ill-will. Love is an important constituent of *ahimsa* for, without love, *ahimsa* will remain a mere theoretical conceptualization. *Ahimsa* and truth, argued Gandhi, 'are so intertwined that it is practically impossible to disentangle and separate them. Nevertheless *ahimsa* is the means and truth the end.'[56] Drawing on this, Bondurant elaborates that 'testing of truth can be performed only by ... action based upon refusal to do harm or, more accurately, upon love. For truth, judged in terms of human needs, would be destroyed, on whichever side it lay, by the use of violence.'[57] As evident, the argument highlighting the importance of truth and love in non-violent protest draws on the moral strength of individuals participating in *satyagraha*. Here *satyagraha* is conceptualized as 'self-suffering' in contrast with *duragraha* (normal forms of coercion). Self-suffering is a positive course of action. The *satyagrahee*, in confronting a situation of conflict, seeks to break the deadlock by self-suffering. Hence self-suffering is not a weapon of the weak since its use demands 'unusual courage and freedom from fear'.[58] The merit of self-suffering lies in its efficiency as an instrument of social persuasion. While elaborating the concept on another occasion, Bondurant argues that the object of *satyagraha*, as viewed by Gandhi, is also

> the constructive transforming of relationships in a manner which not only effects a change of policy but also assures the restructuring of the situation which led to conflict. This calls for a modification of attitudes and requires fulfillment of the significant needs of all parties originally

in conflict. The fulfilling of needs is both an objective and a means for effecting fundamental change.[59]

As evident, Gandhi's political ideals are based on Hindu precepts. *Satyagraha* was an instant success because it drew on *satya*, *ahimsa* and *tapasya* (renunciation). To an Indian mind, not only do these ideas make sense, they also evoke a positive response for obvious reasons. What was unique in Gandhi is the fact that he used the traditional idioms to construct a novel way of articulating human relationships even when circumstances made the participants adversaries. So these precepts, though traditionally characterized as individual attributes essential for personal spiritual emancipation, gained social connotation by their applicability to those involved in Gandhian *satyagraha*.

Unlike Judith Brown, who largely dealt with the decline of Gandhi at the fag end of the nationalist struggle, Bondurant draws our attention to *satyagraha* as constituting perhaps the most significant idea in Gandhi's political philosophy. Unlike the loyal constitutionalists and revolutionary terrorists, Gandhi provides a model of direct action in which violence, in the conventional sense of the term, was peripheral. Although *satyagraha* imposes an exceptional burden on the leader and demands unusual moral and political capacity, it is nonetheless a significant intervention in political theory, underlining the importance of a moral commitment to a cause which may not always be achievable.

While Bondurant focuses on a central concept in Gandhi's political thought, the merit of Bhikhu Parekh's book[60] lies in a critical appreciation of Gandhi's political philosophy. According to Parekh, Gandhi is a profound political thinker who made a massive contribution to human civilizations. Parekh concentrates on three major areas in order to understand Gandhi's political philosophy.

First, according to Parekh, Gandhi drew on Hindu civilization when evolving his distinct political ideas. For the Mahatma, 'every tradition was a resource, a source of valuable insights into the human condition.... Every man was born into and shaped by a specific cultural tradition, which, as it were, constituted his original family.'[61] As an Indian, Gandhi was an heir to rich and diverse religious and cultural traditions. And, as a human being, he was also part of the heritage of mankind linking him with other human beings in various part of the world. This approach is theoretically significant for it allowed Gandhi to borrow from other socio-cultural traditions. Based on his belief in intercultural communication, Gandhi explained this in terms of the frequently cited metaphor of living in a house with its windows wide open. Despite having walls protecting the house, the very presence of windows allows winds from all directions to blow through to enable him to breathe fresh air uninterruptedly. So, for the Mahatma intercultural communication is just like breathing fresh air. This is crucial in his thought, for Gandhi borrowed heavily from Hindu traditions and yet he was not a traditionalist. For him, tradition was not just a resource that obviously evoked respect but also one that left room for critical evaluation. This is important simply because it allows individuals to make up their minds only in accordance with their own priorities. According to Gandhi, it is individuals, not groups, who can reason, have moral sense and exercise choice. Opposed to the holistic notion that society is ontologically prior to the individual, he argues that social choice need not necessarily depend on choices by individuals constituting the society.[62] He consistently attacked collectivist theories of state and society for he believed that 'if the individuals cease to count what is left of society?'[63]

By redefining the ways in which one needs to take into account the importance of traditions and also 'the autonomy of individuals',[64] Gandhi used completely different yardsticks for the assessment of human political action. In this way, he sought to combine 'the richest insights of different traditions to develop an ecumenical view of the world'.[65] In other words, by fusing the 'the best traditions' of the world and of Hinduism, he offered an alternative vision of universalism to the post-Enlightenment ethnocentric model of colonial rulers.

Second, Parekh dwells on the Gandhian precepts of 'non-violence' and '*satyagraha*'. According to Parekh, while conceptualizing non-violence, Gandhi had questioned the violent methods, employed by the revolutionary terrorists, as being inadequate to drive the British out of the country. The Mahatma believed that freedom remained an elusive goal unless the foundation of the British rule was effectively undermined. In order to attain freedom, Gandhi suggested three specific steps: first, to get rid of the British rule in order to gain political independence; second, to put an end to the economic exploitation of the country both by the indigenous and external vested interests; and third, to liberate the country from the cultural and moral domination of an alien civilization, thus making the Indians autonomous. These three levels were interconnected. The British came to exploit the Indian market at the outset and gradually became the rulers. So the Indian economy was completely colonized and its resources utilized by the ruler in accordance with its preferences. At the third and perhaps more serious level, it was possible for the British to establish and sustain its political hegemony largely because of the willing cooperation of the ruled, who usually believed in the superiority of the British civilization. This 'mental slavery' appears to have provided the British with perhaps the most significant device in controlling a large populace with just minimum coercive forces. Unless there was a concerted attack on these three levels of domination, freedom was simply inconceivable. For Gandhi, political freedom was necessary but not the only goal because, even after the withdrawal of the British political rule, the foreign capital would continue to function with the collaboration of the indigenous capital. Furthermore, the cessation of economic exploitation did not by itself end cultural and moral domination. For Gandhi, the solution lay in *swaraj* rather than mere political freedom.

Swaraj was a positive and cultural concept, based on a critical evaluation of what Gandhi terms as 'civilizational resources'. Since every community was autonomous, each had a specific way of conceptualizing its existence and articulation on the basis of what was defined as '*swabhava*', or the distinctive moral and spiritual characteristics underlining its deepest instincts, temperament and disposition. Communities reconstituted themselves by transforming their *swabhava* gradually in harmony with their inherent characteristics. *Swaraj* was therefore a form of collective integrity, a community's 'mode of being', consistent with what is distinctive to those constituting the collectivity. For Gandhi, the aim of the revolutionary terrorists for political freedom was thus 'partial' while *swaraj* was freedom in its totality. By according overriding importance to political freedom, those endorsing violence as appropriate did not, according to Gandhi, understand the complex and deeper roots of colonialism. Furthermore, violence provoked government to adopt stern administrative measures which, by themselves, were a deterrent and 'nervous subjects became more cowardly than before and withdrew into their private worlds'.[66] So, not only was violence inadequate, but the revolutionary terrorist aim of political freedom was highly restricted in its appeal.

In contrast, Gandhi articulated the notion of *ahimsa* or non-violence as the most appropriate organizing principle in India's freedom struggle. In his conceptualization of *ahimsa*-driven nationalist struggle, compassion, love and truth were important driving forces for his battle for *swaraj*. In this regard too, although he was deeply influenced by indigenous traditions, he radically departed from them in his articulation. His definition of *ahimsa*, 'as active and energetic love leading to dedicated service of fellow-men, represented a [significant] departure from Indian traditions'.[67] What was unique in Gandhian views was perhaps the application of *ahimsa* to mobilize people against the well-entrenched colonialism of the twentieth century. His theory was articulated in the context of a colonial power with organic roots in Indian society. The aim was not merely to conceptualize its nature, but also to overthrow the alien power. So his theory was also intended to guide political action. This places Gandhi in a completely different class altogether for, unlike the other theorists of non-violence, who were religious men primarily concerned to preserve the moral integrity of humanity in the face of evil, Gandhi led a gigantic nationalist movement for freedom. He had to therefore adjust his principles in response to the volatile political circumstances involving diverse classes with incompatible, if not conflicting, socio-economic interests. Gandhi was not static in his political views either. While he was opposed to violence in the early part of his career, as Chauri Chaura demonstrated, he appears to have endorsed violent action in the context of the 1942 Quit India Movement by expressing his preference for violence to cowardice. Probably he was aware that a theory without organic links with reality was doomed to failure. As evident, despite Gandhi's faith in non-violence, which he never compromised, there are occasions when the Mahatma privileged the context over his political ideology – which is, as Parekh suggests, a significant epistemological contribution in political philosophy.

The third important point in Parekh's study of Gandhi's political ideas relates to the conceptualization of *satyagraha*. In Gandhi's view, *satyagraha* 'involved all classes of men, brought in women, built up habits of concerted action and organizational skills, developed moral and social courage, and fitted in with what he took to be India's cultural resources'.[68] As defined, *satyagraha* was characterized by the following features: *first*, it involved a well-defined course of action including *hartal*, boycott of foreign cloths and non-cooperation with the government, entailing not only the withdrawal of essential services but also the refusal to pay taxes. *Second*, *satyagraha* stressed non-violence even under grave provocation by the opponents. This is how *satyagraha* was different from *duragraha* because, while the latter was semantically coercion-oriented, the former completely ruled out any form of coercion. *Third*, despite hardship and government repression, those involved in *satyagraha* remained committed to non-violence. This required massive moral courage, which Gandhi sought to inculcate among those fighting the British rule by drawing on India's civilizational resources supporting self-suffering and sacrifice in order to achieve a goal. *Fourth*, that Gandhi was different from typical religious leaders was evident in his articulation of *satyagraha* as a series of concerted actions of mass mobilization in which the local leadership was most significant. So, *satyagraha* was not merely theoretical, it also led to action under most adverse circumstances. In other words, articulated as a unique form of protest, *satyagraha* signified a specific type of action that revolved around local issues in the general context of colonial exploitation. This is a typical Gandhian method, where local grievances figured prominently in all the movements Gandhi organized or launched in his name, including the pan-Indian Non-Cooperation Movement (1919–21), Civil Disobedience Movement (1930–2) and Quit India Movement (1942).

Parekh's contribution is immensely useful in a) conceptualizing the foundational ideas of Gandhi's political philosophy, namely non-violence and *satyagraha*; and b) grasping their structural components. In other words, not only are these ideas indigenous, they are also articulated in Indian terms in contrast with the political discourses of both constitutional and revolutionary terrorist methods in the struggle for freedom. Unlike his erstwhile colleagues in the nationalist movement, who drew largely on Western Enlightenment, Gandhi radically altered political discourses, indianizing them by drawing on Indian vocabularies. Furthermore, what was also distinct in the Gandhian approach was the importance of local issues in mobilizing people in localities despite obvious odds. As shown, Gandhi provided an ideology to articulate issues relevant to the grassroots in essentially Indian terms. Drawing on the modes and categories of thought of a large pre-capitalist agrarian society, the Gandhian ideology was a specific reaction to the colonial economic, political and cultural domination. It was an ideology conceived as an alternative to the elite nationalist discourse of the period and was articulated and shaped by the experiences of a nationalist movement at a particular juncture of India's freedom struggle. It is only by looking at the specific historical context that one can comprehend the unique characteristics of Gandhism. So, not only was *satyagraha* a unique experiment, it also opened up the possibility for achieving perhaps the most important historical task for a successful national movement in India, namely the involvement of diverse classes, despite obvious socio-economic differences, in political campaigns against colonialism. It was Gandhism which, by effectively appropriating the local issues, led to a political ideology that lay entirely outside the constitutional opposition of the Moderates and the Extremists' militant version. Based on *satyagraha* and non-violence and drawing on local issues as well, Gandhi evolved an ideology that gradually became integral to the emerging political structure of the nationalist campaign. This was historically significant because the masses, so far peripheral, were drawn into the Gandhi-led movements since these articulated their grievances in an unprecedented manner.

As evident, Parekh's analysis revolves around the principal concepts of Gandhian political thought, namely, *satyagraha* and non-violence. The most exhaustive study of what constitutes Gandhi's moral and political thought is by Raghavan N. Iyer.[69] According to Iyer, Gandhi is a political thinker because he a) gave an account of the nature of political activity; b) presented a relationship between activity and the moral nature of man; and c) provided a set of criteria to judge the nature of political activities, undertaken at his behest by those involved in the nationalist struggle. Here Gandhi is conceptualized as a thinker and his role as a political activist appears to have receded into secondary importance. The focus is on the foundational ideas of non-violence and *satyagraha* with reference to both their ontological and epistemological roots.

Ahimsa or non-violence is an important idea in Gandhian political thought. In politics, the use of *ahimsa* is based in Gandhi's view 'upon the immutable maxim that government is possible only so long as the people consent, either consciously or unconsciously, to be governed'.[70] *Ahimsa* is a significant political resource for governance that bridges the gulf between the ruler and the ruled. As Gandhi explained,

> True democracy or the *Swaraj* of the masses can never come through untruthful and violent means, for the simple reason that the natural corollary to their use would be to remove all opposition through the suppression or extermination of the antagonists. That does not make for individual freedom. Individual freedom can have the fullest play only under a regime of unadulterated *ahimsa*.[71]

This passage is significant in two different ways: first, by saying that violence provoked violence, Gandhi made a serious political statement underlining the importance of non-violence in the true democracy of the *swaraj*. In his conceptualization, the individual was the pivot of all activities and he argued for a regime of unadulterated *ahimsa* that could only protect individual freedom. How was *ahimsa* to be articulated? Gandhi suggested four different ways: first, non-violence in its operation against legally constituted authority or government; second, the exercise of non-violence in internal disturbances, such as riots; third, the use of non-violence against external invasion; and finally, the best place for *ahimsa* was within the family for, without practising non-violence at the micro level, it could not be applied to the wider field.[72] According to Gandhi, the success of *ahimsa* could be attributed to the moral strength of those endorsing the ideal. In other words, for *ahimsa* to succeed, more and more people must be prepared to accept 'the absolute moral value of *ahimsa*, not as an elusive idea or a pious hope, but as a widely relevant principle of social and political action'.[73]

The other foundational idea in Gandhi's political thought is *satya* or truth. For Gandhi, *satya* represented the supreme value in ethics, politics and religion, the ultimate source of authority and of appeal, the *raison d'être* of human existence. According to Iyer, *satya*, derived from *sat* or being, is the source of 'eternal and universal values like truth, righteousness and justice – truth in the realm of knowledge, righteousness in the domain of conduct and justice in the sphere of social relations. [Truth, in the narrow epistemological sense] is thus only a part of the wider meaning of satya.'[74] As Gandhi himself explained,

> As I proceed in my search for truth it grows upon me that Truth comprehends everything. . . . What is perceived by a pure heart and intellect is truth for that moment. Cling to it, and it enables one to reach pure Truth . . . the wonderful implication of the great truth *Brahma Satyam Jagatmithya* (Brahma is real, all else unreal) has grown on me from day to day. It teaches us patience. This will purge us of harshness and add to our tolerance. It will make us magnify the molehills of our errors into mountains and minimize the mountains of others' errors into molehills.[75]

Gandhi appeared to have conceptualized truth at two complementary levels. At the conceptual and also philosophical level, truth was a goal that human beings sought to embody in life and action. Devotion to truth is therefore the sole reason for human existence. Whether realized or not, the goal should remain a guiding force in human activities. In other words, truth was philosophically inspiring and conceptually real in the context of human civilization. At a rather mundane level, Gandhi's formulation was a practical device to generate support for the movements he led. By defining the involvement of the masses in the nationalist movement as nothing but a search for truth, Gandhi provided a radical alternative to the prevalent political discourses seeking to attain a limited goal of political freedom. So the quest for truth was preparatory to achieving wider socio-economic and political goals including freedom from the British rule. So, for Gandhi, truth was not merely a high philosophical ideal; it was real and thus achievable. Hence there was no room for absolute truth in Gandhian thought since it had no value unless incarnated in human beings who 'represent it by proving their readiness to die for it'.[76] As he elaborated further,

> The quest for Truth involves *tapas* or self-suffering, sometimes even unto death. There can be no place in it for even a trace of self-interest. In such selfless search for Truth nobody can lose his bearings for long. Directly he takes to the wrong path he stumbles, and is thus re-directed to the right path. Therefore the pursuit of Truth is true-*Bhakti* (devotion). . . . There is no place in it for cowardice, no place for defeat.[77]

It is clear that truth was a motivating force to those involved in the freedom struggle despite all the odds. By equating truth with self-suffering, the Mahatma upheld the Indian traditions supporting self-suffering for truth. What was distinct was his ability to draw resources out of this equation for his political campaign against the alien rule. The masses were drawn to the struggle not merely for freedom but also for truth, which perhaps prepared them to continue even in adverse circumstances. Gandhi thus redefined truth by taking into account the contextual connotation and its philosophical underpinnings.

Gandhi was not merely a philosopher, he was also an activist. In his determination to achieve truth through *ahimsa*, the Mahatma evolved *satyagraha* or active resistance, with mass participation in the nationalist campaign in India. The doctrine of *satyagraha* was meant 'to show how the man of conscience could engage in heroic action in the vindication of truth and freedom against all tyranny, in his appeal to justice against every social abuse and sectional interest'.[78] For Gandhi, *satyagraha* was an endeavour to raise the deliberate suffering of a man of outraged conscience to the level of a moral sanction that evoked respect and attained results.

Satyagraha differed from passive resistance in that the former 'postulates the conquest of the adversary by suffering in one's own person'. *Satyagraha*, argued Gandhi,

> is a method of securing rights by personal suffering; it is the reverse of resistance by arms. When I refuse to do a thing that is repugnant to my conscience, I use soul force. For instance, the government of the day has passed a law which is applicable to me. I do not like it. If by using violence I force the government to repeal the law, I am employing what may be termed body-force. If I do not obey the law and accept the penalty for its breach, I use soul-force. It involves sacrifice of self.[79]

Satyagraha was not therefore physical force because a *satyagrahi* never intends to inflict pain on his adversaries. In the use of *satyagraha*, there was no ill-will whatsoever. Unlike passive resistance, where the resisters strive to cause suffering to the opponents, there is no such intention in *satyagraha*.[80] Constituted by *satya* and *ahimsa*, *satyagraha* was, Gandhi further explained on another occasion,

> a movement intended to replace methods of violence and a movement based entirely upon truth. It is, as I have conceived it, an extension of the domestic law on the political field and my experience has led me to the conclusion that that movement and that alone can rid India of the possibility of violence spreading throughout the length and breadth of the land, for the redress of the grievance.[81]

Satyagraha was also contrasted with *duragraha*, which Gandhi despised from the outset of his political campaign. While *satyagraha* nurtures no ill-feeling towards the opponents, *duragraha* approaches the conflict with a set of prejudgments. The opponent is, ipso facto, wrong. The objective is to overcome and destroy the opponent. The task, undertaken in *duragraha*, is to justify the destruction of the opponent as he is fallacious and immoral. A *duragrahee* draws strength from his preconceived righteousness and supposedly superior moral position. As shown, a *satyagrahee* sustains, in contrast with a *duragrahi*, self-suffering without holding any ill-feeling toward his opponents. This is an exercise of moral strength where individuals, imbued with truth-force, are capable of winning against the most brutal adversaries without applying physical force, as Gandhi most succinctly pointed out while defining *satyagraha* by saying that 'a satyagraha struggle is impossible without capital in the shape of character'.[82] This is the crux of the Gandhian message for those involved in *satyagraha*, the principal aim of which was to transform the opponents by truth-force.

While delineating Gandhi's political thought, Iyer also dealt with, though briefly, a relatively under-studied dimension, namely the interconnection between *swaraj* (self-rule) and *swadeshi* (self-reliance). Although the notions of *swaraj* and *swadeshi* were not typical Gandhian formulations, as they had figured in the political campaign even before the rise of the Mahatma, Gandhi reconfirmed his faith in these two concepts while evolving his social and political ideas pertaining to India. For Gandhi, *swaraj* was not merely political freedom but moral and spiritual freedom as well. Semantically, *swaraj* is different from mere political freedom, as Gandhi explained, '*swaraj* [is] rendered as disciplined rule from within. . . . [It denotes] self-rule and self-restraint, and not freedom from all restraint which "independence" often means'.[83] By underlining the widest possible connotations of *swaraj*, Gandhi conceptualized the phenomenon in contrast with his erstwhile colleagues in the nationalist movement who took *swaraj* as mere political freedom. In other words, national political freedom was necessary but not the only condition for *swaraj*, which subsumed, in Gandhi's formulation, a whole range of moral and spiritual factors for individuals to self-actualize.

If *swaraj* was the goal, *swadeshi* was the means. According to Gandhi, self-rule and self-reliance therefore remained intertwined. While the former was articulated in his social and political writings, the latter was put into practice through various constructive programmes, the most significant of which were certainly those for *khadi* (home-spun) and *charkha* (spinning wheel). For Gandhi, *khadi* was a necessary and the most important corollary of the principle of *swadeshi* in its application to society. 'What is the kind of service', argued Gandhi, 'that the teeming millions of India most need at the present time, that can be easily understood and appreciated by all, that is easy to perform and will at the same time enable the crores [several millions] of our semi-starved countrymen to live?' Gandhi had no doubt that 'the universalization of khadi or the spinning wheel alone can fulfill these conditions'.[84] Unlike the other major concepts in Gandhi's political thought, these two concepts – *swaraj* and *swadeshi* – did not receive adequate attention in Iyer's book though the author is aware of their importance in articulating Mahatma's social and political ideas. In other words, despite only a very short discussion of these twin concepts almost at the end of the book, the author is aware that they constitute a significant dimension in Gandhi's ideology, which led the nation to fight against perhaps the most brutal imperial power of the twentieth century. This serves another purpose. That Gandhism is a complex theoretical postulate is evident from the interconnectedness of multiple concepts that Gandhi evolved and elaborated through his various experiments involving the masses during India's freedom struggle.

What this book proposes to do

As evident, what is unique in Gandhian thought is its drive to combine theory with practice. During his career as a political activist, Gandhi experimented with his ideas in the context of perhaps the most well-entrenched nationalist movement of the past century. While the activist Gandhi deployed *satyagraha* to mobilize masses in adverse circumstances, the theoretical Gandhi grappled with the reality in a very rigorous manner. In other words, the activist Gandhi was, as it were, drawing on the theoretical search for appropriate models in a particular context. Unlike those who launched the anti-British campaign before his arrival on the political scene, Gandhi appears to have undertaken a thorough study of the Indian reality and also of the people who gradually became participants in the movements following Gandhian methods. So Gandhian social and political ideas involve a thorough grasping of both reality and its articulation in the writings of the Mahatma. This is where the book is unique because not only does it deal with relatively unknown dimensions of Gandhian thought it will also demonstrate the gradual but steady evolution of the man who dwelled on issues that remained relevant even after India became free.

The book is about an activist-theoretician, a role the Mahatma embodied while leading the nationalist struggle in India. By dwelling on *Harijan*, which began publication in the early 1930s, this exercise is unique not only in its focus but also in the elaboration of ideas that did not figure, for historical reasons, in his earlier writings. Gandhi was now simultaneously involved in the campaign for freedom and the preparation of a blueprint for a future India, which became all the more necessary after the Congress government assumed responsibility in the British-Indian provinces. The political scene became far more complex. Not only did the Muslim League emerge as 'the true representative' of the Indian Muslims, the *harijans* or untouchables carved an independent space in the nationalist politics. The rapid changes in India's political arithmetic in the 1930s and 1940s remained the backdrop of Gandhian socio-political formulations. His *Harijan* writings are responses to what was taking place in the changed environment when the Congress was gradually becoming a party of governance and not merely a movement.

Although Gandhi's responses in *Harijan* are issue-based, they largely followed the theoretical conceptualizations that he articulated in the *Hind Swaraj*, perhaps one of the most significant treatises that Gandhi wrote to clarify his views. *Hind Swaraj* is perhaps the most systematic exposition of Gandhi's ideas of state, society and nation. Although *Hind Swaraj* is an original tract, while writing it Gandhi was heavily influenced by some of the leading Western thinkers. As he himself admitted, 'whilst the views expressed in Hind Swaraj are held by me, I have but endeavoured humbly to follow Tolstoy, Ruskin, Thoreau, Emerson and other writers, besides the masters of Indian philosophy'.[85] It contains a statement of some of the fundamental tenets in Gandhi's politics. In other words, Gandhi stated his position quite clearly in *Hind Swaraj* and held onto it all this life. In fact, *Hind Swaraj* laid the most crucial theoretical foundation of his entire strategy for winning *swaraj* for India. As the book deals with Gandhian ideas, a brief discussion of the issues raised in the *Hind Swaraj* will be perfectly in order. Aware that this tract revealed the foundational ideas of his thought, Gandhi, in a significant comment on the *Hind Swaraj* in 1921, explained the purpose behind the book by saying

It was written ... in answer to the Indian school of violence, and its prototype in South Africa. I came in contrast with every known Indian anarchist in London. Their bravery impressed me, but I feel that their zeal was misguided. I felt that violence was no remedy for India's ills, and that her civilization required the use of a different and higher weapon for self-protection. The Satyagraha of South Africa was still an infant hardly two years old. But it had developed sufficiently to permit me to write of it with some degree of confidence.... [Hind Swaraj] teaches the gospel of love in the place of that of hate. It replaces violence with self-sacrifice. It pits soul-force against brute force.[86]

The aim of *Hind Swaraj* was 'to confront the anarchist and violence-prone Indian nationalists with an alternative to violence, derived from Gandhi's earliest experiments with *satyagraha*'.[87] As Gandhi wrote,

> Hind Swaraj [was] written in order to show that [his countrymen] are following a suicidal policy [of violence], and that, if they but revert to their own glorious civilization, either the English would adopt the latter and become Indianised or find their occupation in India gone.[88]

Even the title of the book was significant; he dealt with the version of *swaraj* that was relevant to India. This was the first and perhaps most elaborate discussion of *swaraj* or freedom from Gandhi's point of view. This was also the most authentic text of Gandhian social and political ideas dealing with *swaraj* and *satyagraha*. Furthermore, in *Hind Swaraj*, Gandhi depicted 'the dichotomies between the spiritual, moral fabric of Indian society, and the violent, politically corrupt nature of European state[s] even more dramatically than any of his predecessors'.[89] While condemning 'the brute force'[90] of Western powers, Gandhi distanced himself from the militant nationalists for their support of violence which he considered a suicidal strategy as it would provoke 'an organized violence' by the ruling authority.[91] Violence was, therefore, counter-productive. *Hind Swaraj*, as evident, served two purposes: on the one hand, it was a detailed commentary on Western civilization that thrived on naked force; it also laid down, on the other, the fundamental pillars later to become basic precepts of Gandhi's social and political ideas.

Hind Swaraj is a foundational text for understanding Gandhi and his ideology. An outcome of a cross-fertilization of ideas, both Indian and Western, *Hind Swaraj* was perhaps the most powerful exposition of Gandhian social and political ideas. A rather 'incendiary manifesto'[92] to galvanize the masses into action, *Hind Swaraj* was banned in 1910 by the government for fear of sedition. Whether it was a seditious tract is debatable; but it is certainly a significant text with refreshing ideas a) critiquing the Western civilization; and also b) seeking to build 'a vernacular model of action'[93] that the people of India understood.

Hind Swaraj provides a scathing critique of Western civilization. The three recurrent themes are (i) colonial imperialism; (ii) industrial capitalism; and (iii) rationalist materialism. According to Gandhi, colonialism triumphed in India not because of its strength but because of Indians' inherent weaknesses, which allowed 'this intimate enemy' to take root. He was probably the first to have attributed the British rule in India to a 'moral decline' affecting the entire nation. For Gandhi, the aim of his project was therefore to recover 'the self under colonialism'.[94] Attributing colonialism in India to 'our weaknesses', Gandhi thus argued,

> The English have not taken India; we have given it to them. They are not in India because of their strength, but because we keep them....

Recall the Company Bahadur. Who made it Bahadur? They had not the slightest intention at the time of establishing a kingdom. Who assisted the Company's officers? Who was tempted at the sight of their silver? Who bought their goods? History testifies that we did all this.... When our Princes fought among themselves, they sought the assistance of Company Bahadur. That corporation was versed alike in commerce and war. It was unhampered by questions of morality.... Is it not then useless to blame the English for what we did at the time?... it is truer to say that we gave India to the English than that India was lost.[95]

According to Gandhi, the British conquest of India was solely due to the Indians' moral failure. Imperialism was able to take root in India in the course of time due partly to the Indians' cooperation with the British government. There was no restraint presumably, because of a moral decadence of the race known as Indians. There is another side to the argument. Gandhi was contemptuous of the Western civilization which, under the garb of 'civilizing' the colonial 'subjects', pursued its 'selfish interests' and nothing else. Based on 'brute force', Western civilization was thus both 'narrow' and 'perverted'. So, in Gandhi's perception, by lending legitimacy to colonialism, the so-called modern civilization subverted 'the natural evolution' of societies clinging to the so-called traditional ways of life. Drawing on the civilizational resources of a traditional society like India, Gandhi produced perhaps 'the most effective trans-cultural protest against the hyper-masculine world view of colonialism'.[96]

Hind Swaraj was the most creative response to the perversion of industrial capitalism. For Gandhi, industrialization remained the driving force behind Western civilization. 'Machinery is', he characterized, 'the chief symbol of modern civilization; it represents sin. [Hence] if the machine craze grows in our country, it will become an unhappy land.'[97] Condemning the role of the machine in 'de-humanizing' the workers toiling in the factories for 'profit' in which they had no share, the Mahatma thus argued that 'it is necessary to realize that machinery is bad. We shall then be able to do away with it.... If, instead of welcoming machinery as a boon', he further mentioned, 'we would look upon it as an evil, it would ultimately go.'[98] According to Gandhi, 'a snake-bite is a lesser poison' than 'the mill industry' because, while the former merely harmed the body, the latter 'destroys body, mind and soul'.[99] Gandhi's critique of machine civilization was a creative response and thus more original than those of his erstwhile colleagues in the nationalist movement. While the earlier nationalists attributed the Western conquest of India to 'a superior military strength', Gandhi actually probed into the processes that led to such a dramatic rise of the Western powers. Unlike his colleagues, Gandhi had no doubt that 'the source of modern imperialism lies specifically in the system of social production which the countries of the Western world have adopted'. It is the limitless desire for 'ever-increased production and ever-greater consumption and the spirit of ruthless competitiveness' that not only sustained the system but also impelled these countries to establish colonies that could be exploited for economic gains.[100] Industrialism was an evil simply because the purpose of production was not to create an egalitarian but a capitalist society. For industrialism to survive and thrive, these Western industrial nations needed colonies to market their goods. Since colonialism and industrialism were complementary to each other, industrial capitalism was, as Gandhi saw, inherently harmful to human civilization.

According to Gandhi, there remained a tension between 'true civilization' and 'a civilization based on machine'. While the former is based on brute rationalist materialism, the latter draws its sustenance from *dharma*. In modern civilization, *artha* (money) and *kama* (desire) are totally divorced from *dharma* on the basis of the alleged superiority of 'rational materialism'. Critical of the unbridled march of 'reason', Gandhi was never agreeable to abdicate his 'faith' for reason. Instead, he would test his faith with his reason, but would not allow reason to destroy his faith. In other words, 'technological rationalism', defending 'crude materialism' lay at the root of the destruction of true civilization where *dharma* was a device to attain morality. 'To observe morality', argued Gandhi, 'is to attain mastery over our mind and our passions.'[101] Religion was the template for morality. He never compromised the importance of religion in our social life though he opposed religious superstitions which, according to him, were 'cruelties, practiced in the name of religion'.[102] But there was no end to this process and 'they will happen so long as there are to be found ignorant and credulous people'.[103] Although there was no space for religious superstition, for obvious reasons, Gandhi was not 'irreligious' either, for he argued that 'we will certainly fight tooth and nail, but we can never do so by disregarding religion. We can only do so by appreciating and conserving the latter.'[104] While criticizing the rationalist materialism of the West, Gandhi appears to have drawn heavily on the Hindu tradition in which *dharma* in the sense of morality and religion remained crucial. He therefore condemned the modern civilization because it

> takes note neither of morality nor of religion. Its votaries calmly state that their business is not to teach religion. Some even consider it to be a superstitious growth. Others put on the cloak of religion and prate about morality. . . . Immorality is often taught in the name of morality. This civilization seeks to increase bodily comfort by pursuing crude [rationalist materialism], and it fails miserably even in doing so.[105]

As shown, *Hind Swaraj* is Gandhi's creative response to the theoretical basis of Western civilization. Drawing on the civilizational resources of Hindu religion and its tradition, he put forward a new theoretical framework to conceptualize both colonialism and industrial capitalism.

This is one side of the exercise that he undertook in *Hind Swaraj*. The other equally important side of the story concerns the fundamental precepts of what later became Gandhism. The three important themes that recur not only in his writings but also in his deeds are *swaraj*, *swadeshi* and *satya*.[106] *Swaraj* was rule of the self by the self. It was therefore more than a political idea for to the Mahatma it meant India's spiritual liberation through a fundamental change in each individual's perception. This could hardly be achieved through political liberation. What it required was a continuous process of self-churning leading to self-actualization in its fullest possible form. Similarly, *swadeshi*, which meant self-respect, self-realization and self-reliance, was not merely glorification of traditional and indigenous methods of production but a creative application of the available means meaningful to the people in consideration. He was not critical of mechanization per se, as he argued, 'mechanization is good when the hands are too few for the work to be intended to be accomplished. It is an evil', he argued, 'when there are more hands than required for the work, as is the case in India. . . . Spinning and weaving mills have deprived the villagers of a substantial means of livelihood.'[107] So Gandhi felt that the technology appropriate to India should meet the needs of the masses. Modern technology failed to fulfil this because historically it tended to reward the skilled and the powerful and to marginalize the poor and the weak. So, his debate is not on 'whether India needs technology'; his debate is on 'the kind of technology that India needs'.[108]

Similarly, *satya* is another basic pillar in Gandhian thought. *Satya* is truth-force and only *ahimsa*, according to Gandhi, could make the quest for such truth viable. Together with *ahimsa*, *satya* constituted *satyagraha*. Although *satyagraha* appeared to be primarily a political strategy, it was 'basically a method of dialogue that would bring two disagreeing parties not just into mutual agreement, but into the realization of a deeper truth together'.[109] Based on *atmabal* (soul-force) and not *sharirbal* (physical force), *satyagraha* seeks to reach a higher mental plane where the soul is able to exercise control over the mind. And the success of 'the ethics of non violence depends on the state of the soul, the mind and the passions – in one word, on self-rule'.[110] What was distinctive about Gandhi was his ability to transform *satyagraha* into a political strategy as well. It was 'a method of securing rights by personal suffering'.[111] Clearly, Gandhi's *satyagraha* was an indigenous combination of reason, morality and politics; it appealed to the opponent's head, heart and interests.[112]

Now we are in a position to situate this book in proper perspective within the available literature. Gandhi was a political activist responding creatively to the socio-political and economic circumstances in which he was located. As evident, drawing on practice, he evolved a theory of and about practice. Hence it would be safe to argue that Gandhi was an activist-theoretician in the sense that he was a theoretician who was simultaneously a practitioner. *Swaraj* was an ideal that needed to be put into practice through human deeds. Hence self-rule without self-transformation is not Gandhian. *Swaraj* was not a utopia, as Gandhi himself argued that 'do not consider this swaraj to be a dream. There is no idea of sitting still.'[113] *Swaraj* is a complex simultaneous unfolding of a blueprint of future socio-political orders and also a method of organizing human actions in accordance with *ahimsa* and *satya*.

The above brief discussion of the issues raised in the *Hind Swaraj* provides a background to this study. Because *Hind Swaraj* was the germinating ground for most of the ideas that the Mahatma tinkled with during his activist phase, the discussion is useful in comprehending the conceptual package of what constitutes Gandhism and also to locate it within the wider theoretical discourses on state, society and politics. In this sense, his later writings, including those in *Harijan*, are either reiterations or elaborations of the ideas at the core of *Hind Swaraj*. Although *Hind Swaraj* is based on his experiments of *satyagraha* in South Africa, some of the ideas are nebulous in form or articulation, for obvious reason. Gandhi's later writings reflect the maturity of the Mahatma who, by now, not only led two pan-Indian movements – Non-Cooperation and Civil Disobedience – but had also become an undisputed leader of the Indian National Congress. The national scene was far more complex because not only were there well-defined political groups both within and outside the Congress, but the Muslim League had also emerged as a serious contender for power by the early 1930s. Gandhi confronted a dramatically changed political environment in which the British imperialism devised new strategies for exploitation. So Gandhi's interventions in the columns of *Harijan* are a good entry point in terms of grasping his social and political ideas in the changed milieu. The intellectual viability of this exercise stems from the carefully chosen themes, which are useful in grasping Gandhian thought, which was articulated and tested within the institutional processes set up and directed by the colonial state. Furthermore, these selective themes project a different Gandhi, one who constantly negotiated with the British power, in different forms, to evolve an appropriate political ideology in order to galvanize the masses into action in otherwise adverse circumstances. Surprisingly, the structure of governance that struck roots in India during the British rule continued to remain the reference point for Gandhi and the Congress even in their opposition to colonialism. So the ideas that Gandhi nurtured in his battle for freedom clearly identify a definite domain of nationalist thought, which, though different, had its root in the post-Enlightenment philosophy of nationalism. Given the public nature of *Harijan*, the views that Gandhi expressed were carefully drafted and the Mahatma therefore appeared to be less ambiguous here than anywhere else.

An extended introduction underlining the historical 'moments' that had a strong bearing on the nationalist thought in general and Gandhian thought in particular shall preface these selective pieces. Seeking to identify the underlying thread in Gandhi's articulation of the issues and problems confronting the nation, the introduction shall also draw out other formidable influences that the Mahatma was subject to while structuring the anti-

British movement in a way completely different from his predecessors. *Harijan* is a good entry point in three ways: a) it is where Gandhi usually preferred to float an issue for debate as soon as it was articulated by him; b) it was also a forum providing the ordinary reader with an opportunity to interact with Gandhi on what he wrote as well as on those issues that appeared to have gained momentum under particular circumstances; and c) for Gandhi, it was also a platform for a dialogue with other nationalist leaders opposed to him and his views. While situating Gandhi's ideas and viewpoints in a specific historical context, the introduction will also attempt to underline the theoretical/ideological foundation of what later came to be a typical Gandhian intervention in the nationalist 'discourse'.

This is a contextualized study of the Mahatma with reference to those carefully selected themes central to his social and political thoughts. And also, given the relevance of these selective themes in the contemporary world, this exercise will help articulate the civilizational Gandhi as opposed to the historical Gandhi who died in 1948. Apart from dwelling on the fundamental precepts of Gandhism, this volume is unique in two ways: a) by drawing on Gandhi's writings in *Harijan* on specific issues, the aim is to dwell on the themes that Gandhi himself dealt with extensively in this weekly. This is an exercise seeking to construct the ideas of Gandhi in his own terms. *Harijan* is perhaps the only platform from which Gandhi confronted B.R. Ambedkar and Rabindranth Tagore, among others, on issues like communal and caste identity, national reconstruction, etc. The importance of this weekly lies in the inclusion of a 'Question Box' providing Gandhi with a platform for interaction with ordinary Indians through his response to questions raised. b) The issues broached and elaborated in *Harijan* seem to be transcendental since they are topical even after more than five decades of Indian independence. Hence their historical significance can never be underestimated. What is striking is the conceptual clarity and empirical relevance of the issues that Gandhi articulated while commenting on contemporary issues and problems. Not only is *Harijan* a mirror, as it were, of the period, it has also identified a large number of socio-political issues relevant both to the Indian situation and other similar situations. So a clear articulation of these issues in this monograph will certainly bring out the hitherto unexplored dimensions of the Mahatma and his thought. Given the thrust of this work, it would not be an exaggeration to claim that this is a unique study and hence there are no competitive titles.

1 Gandhi

The idea of *swaraj*

In the context of India's freedom struggle, *swaraj* is both an ideal and a principle. As an ideal, it set the ideological tenor of a struggle against the British; as a principle, it provided the nationalists with a blueprint for an independent India. *Swaraj* was never conceptualized in its narrow meaning of 'political independence'; instead, its wider connotation was constantly hammered out to highlight that it was qualitatively different from mere political independence. Given its Indian roots, *swaraj* was always preferred presumably because of its semantic familiarity among the participants in probably the most gigantic freedom struggle in the twentieth century. It was therefore easier for the nationalists to mobilize the masses despite the adverse consequences. So the importance of *swaraj* as an ideology stems from the fact that, not only did it bring together disparate masses politically, it also contributed to a worldview with an organic link to the Indian psyche. In other words, apart from its significance in political mobilization, *swaraj* also sought to articulate a whole range of moral issues, integrally linked with India's freedom struggle, a struggle that was also unique both in its ideological character and articulation. So, it would be wrong to designate *swaraj* as a mere political mechanism that articulated the nationalist protest most effectively. Instead, it was also a device that sought to radically alter human nature by emphasizing its moral dimensions. Underlying this remains the distinctiveness of *swaraj* also instrumentalized by the nationalists during the course of the anti-British campaign in India. *Swaraj* is thus a history of the nationalist struggle with a clear impact on what the nation later became and also the language in which the nationalist protest was articulated. Politically meaningful and socially rejuvenating, *swaraj* was a unique experiment that stood out as a philosophical concept with a clear practical application. Although the role of the nationalist leadership was significant in conceptualizing *swaraj*, the context in which the idea gained ground was nonetheless important in its articulation. The aim of this chapter is therefore twofold: a) to identify the distinctive features of *swaraj*, which was never a mere political category in the historical context of India's freedom struggle; and b) to draw out the philosophical basis of the idea of *swaraj*, an idea also enmeshed in a wider search for human freedom or liberty. The Gandhian conceptualization of *swaraj* is illustrative of this, since it denotes not merely a system of governance but also epitomizes a quest for human freedom in its wider sense. While evolving *swaraj* as an integral part of the political freedom from the British rule, Gandhi drew on those nationalists who defined the concept contextually even before his arrival on the political scene. It would therefore be inappropriate to concentrate exclusively on Gandhi while dealing with this fundamental pillar of colonial nationalist thought since the Gandhian conceptualization also dwells on what was available then. This chapter has been structured accordingly. Simultaneously with focus on the context, the chapter also deals with those relevant conceptual issues organically linked with the conceptualization of *swaraj* and its articulation in an empirical context, namely, India's freedom struggle; the other significant part of this chapter relates to those implicit ideas that appear to have influenced, if not shaped, the articulation of the idea of *swaraj*, underlining its wider connotation. In other words, in order to identify the complex and varied roots of Gandhian *swaraj*, the chapter pays attention to the historical context and also to the evolution of the idea of *swaraj* during the long history of the nationalist confrontation with the British.

The perspective

First of all, the conceptualization of *swaraj* needs to be contextualized in the larger social processes of the nineteenth and twentieth centuries. The two most obvious influences are nationalism and democratization. In the context of the first, the question that deserves careful attention is why the idea of *swaraj* gained ground. Simply put, after the late nineteenth century the claim to any form of self-government was shelved so long as it was not articulated as the claim of a nation. Colonial sovereignty in part rested upon denying that India was a nation. The nationalist project was not simply something that elites dreamt up to define others in their image, it also sought to identify and highlight the distinctive features of a population to justify its claim for nationhood. And the idea of *swaraj* provided the nationalists with a clearly defined socio-political economic vocabulary, meaningful for a subject nation.

The belief in an Indian nationhood as a historical fact was based on Western models. But it 'was also an emotionally charged reply to the rulers' allegation that India never was and never could be a nation'.[1] The construction of even a vaguely defined Indian nationhood was a daunting task simply because India lacked the basic ingredients of a conventionally conceptualized notion of nation. There was therefore a selective appeal to history to recover those elements transcending the internal schism among those who were marginalized under colonialism. Hence a concerted attempt was always made to underline 'the unifying elements of the Indian religious traditions, medieval syncretism and the strand of tolerance and impartiality in the policies of Muslim rulers'.[2] So the colonial milieu was an important dimension of the processes that led to a particular way of imagining a nation in a multi-ethnic context like India, which is so different from perceptions based on Western experience. The political sensibilities of Indian nationalism 'were deeply involved in this highly atypical act of imagining'.[3]

Apart from colonialism, the major factor that contributed to *swaraj* as a conceptual vehicle for national consciousness was the freedom movement. It is therefore no exaggeration to suggest that the Indian consciousness as we understand it today 'crystallized during the national liberation movement'. So, national 'is a political and not a cultural referent in India'.[4] This perhaps led the nationalist leaders to recognize that it would be difficult to forge the multi-layered Indian society into a unified nation-state in the European sense.[5] Accepting the basic premise about the essentially 'invented' nature of national identities and the importance of such factors as 'print capitalism' in their spread and consolidation, Partha Chatterjee challenges the very idea of 'modular forms', as articulated by Benedict Anderson,[6] since this ignores the point that, if modular forms are made available, nothing is left to be imagined.[7] It is true that the non-Western leaders involved in the struggle for liberation were deeply influenced by European nationalist ideas. They were also aware of the limitations of these ideas in the non-European socio-economic context due to their alien origin. So, while mobilizing the imagined community for an essentially political cause, they began, by the beginning of the twentieth century, to speak in a 'native' vocabulary. Although they drew upon the ideas of European nationalism, they indigenized them substantially by discovering or inventing indigenous equivalents and investing these with additional meanings and nuances. This is probably the reason why Gandhi and his colleagues in the anti-British campaign in India preferred *swadeshi*[8] to nationalism. Gandhi avoided the language of nationalism primarily because he was aware that the Congress flirtations with nationalist ideas in the first quarter of the twentieth century frightened away not only the Muslims and other minorities but also some of the Hindu lower castes. Focusing on *swadeshi* seems the most pragmatic idea one could possibly conceive of in a country like India, one which was not united in terms of religion, race, culture or common historical memories of oppression and struggle. Underlying this is the reason why Gandhi and his Congress colleagues preferred 'the relaxed and chaotic plurality of the traditional Indian life to the order and homogeneity of the European nation state [because they realized] that the open, plural and relatively heterogeneous traditional Indian civilization would best unite Indians'.[9] Drawing on values meaningful to the Indian masses, the Indian freedom struggle developed its own modular forms, which are characteristically different from that of the West. Although the 1947 Great Divide of the subcontinent of India was articulated in terms of religion,[10] the nationalist language drawing upon the exclusivity of Islam appeared inadequate in sustaining Pakistan following the creation of Bangladesh in 1971.[11]

The second broader context that appears to have decisively shaped the conceptualization of *swaraj* is democratization. What sort of 'unity' does democracy require? After all, it was a staple of liberal discourse that democracy could not flourish in multi-ethnic societies. The most widely quoted theorist raising doubts about the possibility of creating a liberal democratic community in a multinational, multi-linguistic state is of course John Stuart Mill. In his opinion, '[f]ree institutions are next to impossible in a country made up of different nationalities. Among a people without fellow-feelings, especially if they read and speak different languages, the united people opinion necessary to the working of representative institutions cannot exist.'[12] Apart from Jinnah and Savarkar, who deployed precisely the liberal argument about why a unitary nationhood is necessary for a modern polity, the rest of the nationalist leadership, including Gandhi, always couched their views in terms of *swaraj*, whereby attempts were made to avoid the possible reasons for communal tension and rivalry. Second, democracy complicates the problem of 'representation'. What is being represented and on what terms? After all, the divisions between the Congress and Muslim League turned on issues of representation. *Swaraj* was an effort to articulate these complex issues, couched in both governmental and constitutional terms. This is not to suggest, however, that the state created two monolithic communities which came into being through 'the politics of representation', since the relationship between representation and democracy is far deeper and more complex than it is generally construed in contemporary discourses on South Asia. *Swaraj* is, at best, about expressing one's agency and creating new forms of collective agency. In this sense, conceptualization of *swaraj* was a significant part of the democratic ferment – where a specific type of political articulation, seeking to gloss over the divisions between the communities as far as possible, took place. This process is likely to unfold at all levels with a complicated relationship between the levels.

Furthermore, democratization is both inclusive and exclusive and *swaraj* was a serious endeavour to articulate these complementary tendencies. Inclusive because it unleashes a process to include people, at least theoretically, regardless of class, clan and creed, it is essentially a participatory project seeking to link different layers of socio-political and economic life. As a movement, democracy thus, writes Charles Taylor, 'obliges us to show much more solidarity and commitment to one another in our joint political project than was demanded by the hierarchical and authoritarian societies of yesteryears'.[13] This is also the reason why democratization tends towards exclusion that itself is a byproduct of the need for a high degree of cohesion. Excluded are those who are different in many ways. We are introduced to a situation where *swaraj* sought to protect the well-formed communal identity in the context of the freedom struggle, which failed to escape the tension as a result of created or otherwise communal rivalries,[14] though there had been attempts even by the revolutionaries, who were clearly biased against the Muslims on occasions, to appeal to the Muslim sentiments as well in their public statements. In June 1907, *Sandhya*, a powerful mouthpiece of the revolutionaries in Bengal, exhorted:

> we want *Swaraj* for all the sons of Mother India that there are. . . . And, for this reason, we cannot promote the interests of the Hindus at the cost of those of the Mussalmans, or the interest of Mussalmans at the cost of those of the Hindus. What we want is that Hindus and Muslims both should bring about this *Swaraj* in unison and concert.[15]

The merger of the 1919–21 Non-Cooperation Movement with the Khilafat Movement was perhaps a political manifestation of what was commonly characterized as an illustration of 'a composite culture'. By a single stroke, both the Hindus and Muslims were brought under a single political platform, submerging at one level their distinct separate identities. At another level, this movement is a watershed in the sense that these two communities remained separate since they collaborated as separate communities for an essentially political project.[16] So the politics of inclusion also led towards exclusion for the communities which identified different political agenda to mobilize people.

In the construction of *swaraj* as a political strategy that was relatively less controversial, both these forces of nationalism and democratization appeared to have played decisive roles. *Swaraj* was not merely unifying, it was also gradually expansive in the sense that it brought together apparently disparate socio-political groups in opposition to an imperial power.[17] The character of the anti-British political campaign gradually underwent radical changes by involving people of various strata, regions and linguistic groups. The definition of nation also changed. No longer was the nation confined to the cities and small towns, it also consisted of innumerable villages so far peripheral to the political activities, now galvanized by the freedom struggle. Whatever the manifestations, the basic point relates to the increasing awareness of those involved in nation-building both during the anti-imperial struggle and its aftermath. Tuned to India's peculiar socio-economic and philosophical identities, *swaraj* was perhaps the most appropriate strategy and a powerful nationalist vocabulary that acted decisively in political mobilization in the context of the freedom struggle.

Conceptualizing *swaraj*

As an idea and a strategy, *swaraj* gained remarkably in the context of the nationalist articulation of the freedom struggle and the growing democratization of the political processes that had already brought in hitherto socio-politically marginal sections of society. So *swaraj* was a great leveller in the sense that it helped mobilize people despite their obvious socio-economic and cultural differences. This is what lay at the success of *swaraj* as a political strategy. Underlining its role in a highly divided society like India, *swaraj* was defined[18] in the following ways: a) national independence; b) political freedom of the individual; c) economic freedom of the individual; and d) spiritual freedom of the individual or self-rule. Although these four definitions are about four different characteristics of *swaraj* they are nonetheless complementary to each other. Of these, the first three are negative in character while the fourth one is positive in its connotation. *Swaraj* as 'national independence', individual 'political' and 'economic' freedom involves discontinuity of alien rule, absence of both exploitation by individuals and poverty respectively. Spiritual freedom is positive in character in the sense that it is a state of being which everyone aspires to actualize once the first three conditions are met. In other words, there is an implicit assumption that self-rule is conditional on the absence of the clearly defined negative factors that stood in the way of realizing *swaraj* in its undiluted moral sense. Even in his conceptualization, Gandhi preferred the term *swaraj* to its English translation presumably because of the difficulty in getting the exact synonym in another language.[19] While elaborating *swaraj*, the Mahatma linked it with *swadeshi*, in which his theory of *swaraj* was articulated. In other words, if *swaraj* was a foundational theory of Gandhi's social and political thought, *swadeshi* was the empirical demonstration of those relevant social, economic and political steps towards creating a society different from the existing one. Dwelling on the nature of *swadeshi*, Gandhi thus argued,

> Swadeshi is that spirit in us which restricts us to the use and service of our immediate surroundings to the exclusion of the more remote. Thus, as for religion, in order to satisfy the requirements of the definition, I must restrict myself to my ancestral religion. That is the use of my immediate religious surroundings. If I find it defective, I should serve it by purging it of its defects. In the domain of politics, I should make use of the indigenous institutions and serve them by curing them of their proved defects. In that of economics, I should use only things that are produced by my immediate neighbours and serve those industries by making them efficient and complete where they might be found wanting.
>
> If we follow the *swadeshi* doctrine, it would be your duty and mine to find out neighbours who can supply our wants and to teach them to supply them where they do not know how to proceed, assuming that there are neighbours who are in want of healthy occupation. Then every village of India will almost be a self-supporting and self-contained unit, exchanging only such necessary commodities with other villages where they are not locally producible. This may all sound nonsensical. Well, India is a country of nonsense. It is nonsensical to parch one's throat with thirst when a kindly Mohammedan is ready to offer pure water to drink. And yet thousands of Hindus would rather die of thirst than drink water from a Mohammedan household.[20]

This is probably the most elaborate statement on *swadeshi*, which decisively influenced the conceptualization of *swaraj* that was also context-dependent. Gandhi gave no definition of *swaraj*, and this vagueness was perhaps deliberate. For the educated classes, deeply committed to the Western model of democracy and its concomitant values, it meant democratic, parliamentary government on the British model. For Gandhi, what was primary in *swaraj* was 'abandonment of the fear of death', or the ability 'to suffer' without rancour. Although he did not define the term, by identifying its characteristics, the Mahatma gave 'content to the idea [that] had clear indigenous roots'.[21]

Debates on the nature of *swaraj* among the nationalist leaders notwithstanding, there is an underlying unity among them regarding the characteristics of *swaraj*. As mentioned above, national independence seems to be the basic characteristic of *swaraj* for obvious reasons. Without freedom from alien rule, the idea of India as a separate nation is without substance. National independence means political sovereignty legitimizing the existence of a political community in the comity of nations. What is distinctive about this conceptualization is the role of non-violence in the campaign for *swaraj*, especially in the Gandhian phase of India's freedom struggle. For the Mahatma, the means by which independence was to be achieved was as important as independence itself.

However, the demand for complete freedom dawned on the nationalists gradually. The Moderate wing of the nationalist movement had, for instance, identified independence with autonomous status for India within the British Empire. The Moderates were in favour of peaceful means, articulated in the form of 'petition, prayer and protest'. In other words, they preferred absolutely constitutional means to attain *swaraj* in a context when the political base of the nationalist articulation was extremely narrowly conceived. As opposed to the Moderates, the Extremists preferred terror and violence to replace the British rule. For them, *swaraj* was the primary goal and considering the nature of means never appears to have figured prominently.[22] Gandhi held completely opposite views. For him, *swaraj* meant more than the replacement of the British rule by the Indian rule. Because he detested the coercive nature of 'a structured administration', Gandhi was never at ease with this definition of *swaraj*. The aim of *swaraj* was not just a replacement of 'one form of coercive rule by another'; it was also a device to radically alter the socio-economic circumstances in which individuals are located. Critical of a narrow definition of *swaraj*, Gandhi argued that *swaraj* for him was not 'English rule without the Englishmen. You want the tiger's nature, but not the tiger, that is to say, you would make India English and when it becomes English, it will be called not Hindustan but Englishstan. This is not the *swaraj* that I want.'[23] On another occasion in 1930, Gandhi clearly elaborated this dimension of *swaraj* by underlining the importance of national independence in its articulation. In his *The Declaration of Independence*, which he wrote for the 1930 Karachi session of the Indian National

Congress, he insisted that the legitimacy of the government depended, not only on the will of the people but also on its ability to uphold the dignity and protect the rights of the citizens. While elaborating this point, he thus argued:

> we believe that it is the inalienable right of the Indian people, as of any other people, to have freedom and to enjoy the fruits of their toil and have the necessities of life, so that they may have full opportunities for growth. We believe also that if any government deprives a people of their rights and oppresses them, the people have a further right to alter or to abolish it.[24]

This Declaration is significant in another way. According to Gandhi, *swaraj* – *à la* national independence – was the basic requirement that a nation grow in its own distinctive way that was halted due to colonialism. The British rule resulted in 'a four-fold disaster' that choked the growth of India as 'a civilization'. The four are as follows: *economically*, India was ruined because of deliberate colonial policies supporting the British economy at the cost of the Indian economy; *politically*, Indians were deprived of deciding their 'own fate'; *culturally*, the British system of education was made 'to hug the very chains' that restricted the creativity of the Indians; and *spiritually*, the compulsive disarmament made the Indians 'unmanly', with the presence of an occupation army also underlining the belief that Indians were unable to defend themselves. Yet, in the Gandhian scheme, violence or coercion never figured. Those taking part in civil disobedience should never resort to 'coercive tactics'[25] for, according to Gandhi, 'swaraj through violence will be no swaraj'.[26]

As evident, *swaraj* was not merely political liberation; it broadly meant human emancipation as well. Although the Moderates were pioneers in conceptualizing the idea in its probably most restricted sense, *swaraj* was most creatively devised by the Mahatma, who never restricted its meaning to mere political freedom from alien rule. In his words, 'mere withdrawal of the English is not independence. It means the consciousness in the average villager that he is the maker of his own destiny, [that] he is his own legislator through his own representatives.'[27]

Political freedom is the second important characteristic of *swaraj*. For the Moderates, political freedom meant autonomy within the overall control of the British administration. Even the most militant of the Moderates, like Surendranath Banerji, always supported constitutional means to secure political rights for the Indians within the constitutional framework of British India. Unlike the Moderates, the Extremists did not much care about the methods and insisted on complete independence, which meant a complete withdrawal of the British government from India. Although both these positions were qualitatively different, *swaraj* was identified simply by its narrow connotation of political freedom, glossing over its wider dimension that Gandhi always highlighted. While for the pre-Gand-hian nationalists, the idea of freedom was articulated in a negative way – *à la* absence of colonial rule – for Gandhi, freedom was a right as well. Opposed to the notion of 'received rights', the Mahatma found in *satyagraha* a device to acquire rights. In South Africa, he had no rights because he was Indian. So he argued that rights in an imperial context remained linked with what served the ruler best. In other words, the claim that rights and freedom went together was relative to the circumstances in which they were politically fashioned; and also the idea that the rights were automatically bestowed once a nation was politically free was hardly realistic given the 'hierarchical and divisive' Indian reality. Furthermore, his articulation of *satyagraha* was probably the most creative conceptualization of how to secure rights and freedom. According to him, 'passive resistance [*satyagraha*] is a method of securing rights by personal suffering. It is the reverse of resistance by arms.'[28] This is how Gandhi distanced himself from his predecessors by a) highlighting the wider connotations of *swaraj* as not merely political freedom; and b) linking the discourse of freedom with that of rights, chal-lenging the notion of 'received rights'. What separates Gandhi from those endorsing the rights discourse is his emphasis on 'duties' or *dharma* that is complementary to 'rights'. In his conceptualization, rights by themselves make no sense unless they are 'organically' connected with duties. *Dharma* is therefore a certain instinctive code of conduct, endorsed by what the Mahatma called 'soul-force'. This was further explained when he argued:

> *Dharma* does not mean any particular creed or dogma. Nor does it mean reading or learning by rote books known as *Shastras* [traditional scrip-tures] or even believing all that they say. Dharma is a quality of the soul and is present, visibly or invisibly, in every human being. Through it we know our duty in human life and our true relations with other souls. It is evident that we cannot do so till we have known the self in us. Hence dharma is the means by which we can know ourselves.[29]

According to Gandhi, *ahimsa* or non-violence was a mode of constructive political and social action just as truth-seeking was the active aspect of *satya* (truth). Taken together, truth and non-violence constituted the basis of an immutable soul-force, an essential component of *satyagraha*. *Ahimsa* was the rule for realizing the truth of *satyagraha*. 'Truth is a positive value, while non-violence is a negative value. Truth affirms [while] non violence forbids something which is real enough.'[30] *Ahimsa* is a fundamental concept in Gandhi's theory of politics and provided an ideology for the nationalist movement that he led.[31] Radically different from the prevalent ideas of poli-tics calling on violence, *ahimsa* was also a novel experiment, based on Gandhi's own assessment of the socio-political situation in India. *Satyagraha* was not mere passive resistance. It denoted 'intense activity' involving large masses of people. It was a legitimate, moral and truthful form of political activity for the people against an unjust rule. A form of mass resistance to 'free ourselves of the unjust rule of the Government by defying the unjust rule and accepting the punishment[s] that go with it',[32] *satyagraha* 'is a universal principle of which civil disobedience is one of the many applications.... [W]hat is essential is that we should not embarrass an opponent who is in difficulty and make his difficulty our opportunity.'[33]

Satyagraha is 'a science' of political struggle in the sense that a *satyagrahee*, endowed with highest moral values, is trained to fight the most ruthless state machinery in accordance with the canons of non-violence. Just like an army, '[i]t is enough if the [satyagrahee] trusts his commander and honestly follows his instructions and is ready to suffer unto death without bearing malice against the so-called enemy.... [The satyagrahee] must render heart discipline to their commander. There should be no mental reservation.'[34] The commander was Gandhi himself and he thus pronounced, '[j]ust as the General of any army insists that his soldiers should wear a particular uniform, I as your General must insist on your taking to the *charkha* which will be [your] uniform. Without full faith in truth, non-violence and the *charkha*, you cannot be my soldiers.'[35] According to the Mahatma, *khadi*, purity and the readiness to sacrifice oneself were three essential conditions for a *satyagrahee*. Of these, *khadi* was probably an instrument with both economic and political underpinnings. He thus confidently argued that '[t]he wheel is one thing that can become universal and replace the use of arms. If the millions cooperate in plying the *charkha* for the sake of their economic liberation, the mere fact will give them an invincible power to achieve political liberation.'[36]

Economic freedom of the individual is the third dimension of *swaraj*. Given the inherent exploitative nature of colonialism, the poverty of the colonized is inevitable. For the Moderates, including Gokhale and Naoroji, with the guarantee of constitutional autonomy to India, poverty was likely to disappear because Britain, the emerging industrial power, was expected to develop India's productive forces through the introduction of modern science and technology and capitalist economic organization. Soon they were disillusioned as India's economic development failed to match what they had expected under British rule. Instead, Indians were languishing in poverty despite 'a free flow of foreign capital' in India. The essence of nineteenth-century colonialism, the Moderate leaders therefore argued, 'lay in the transformation of India into a supplier of food stuff and raw materials to the metropolis, a market for the metropolitan manufacturers and a field for the investment of British capital'.[37] Underlining the most obvious contradiction between foreign and indigenous capital, the Moderate Naoroji characterized the latter as an instrument of 'exploitation of Indian resources' and unskilled Indian workers in the foreign-owned plantations and coal mines.[38] These workers, in the words of Naoroji, 'acted as mere slaves, to slave upon their own land and their own resources in [order] to give away the products to the British capitalists'.[39] This argument was reiterated forcefully by the

Extremists in their economic critique of colonialism. On this basic assumption, Bipin Chandra Pal of the Lal-Bal-Pal trio of the Extremist wing of the Congress put forward a devastating critique of colonialism by saying that

> the introduction of foreign, mostly British, capital for working out the natural resources of the country, instead [of] being a help, is, in fact, the greatest hindrance to all real improvements in the economic condition of the people. It is as much a political, as it is an economic danger. And the future of New India absolutely depends upon an early and radical remedy of this two-edged evil.[40]

What was perhaps the most original contribution to the conceptualization of economic freedom was the 'drain theory'. It was argued by the nationalists that

> a large part of India's capital and wealth was being transferred or 'drained' to Britain in the form of salaries and pensions of British civil and military officials working in India, interest on loans, taken by the Indian government, profits of British capitalism in India and Home Charges or expenses of the Indian Government in Britain.[41]

As a result, India continued to be poor while Britain flourished economically. So the economic freedom that constituted an important dimension of *swaraj* involved a complete liquidation of the alien power in India. The idea ran through what Gandhi conceptualized as economic freedom. For him, economic freedom meant 'freedom from poverty'. There are, according to the Mahatma, three criteria of judging whether a society suffered from poverty: a) the availability of the necessities of life (decent food, clothing and dwelling); b) the ability to enjoy the fruits of one's toils; and c) the opportunity for growth of the individual. Articulating his argument in a typically liberal fashion, Gandhi was qualitatively different from his predecessors in the sense that, unlike the Moderate–Extremist critique of colonialism where the individual is submerged in the collectivity, his is a serious and perhaps the most well-argued theoretical position *vis-à-vis* individuals in a collectivity. So *swaraj* operated at two levels: on the one hand, it was an individual-protecting device where individuals remained the focal point; it also operated, on the other, at the collective level as individuals participated as a nation in several political experiments conducted by Gandhi, which illustrated the possibilities of a merger of individual identity with that of the collectivity for a purpose that might not have reflected the interests of individual participants.[42]

Gandhi elaborated his idea of economic freedom while critiquing industrialism and modernity as it was imported to India in the wake of the colonial rule.[43] He attacked the very notions of modernity and progress and challenged the central claim that modern civilization was a leveller in which the productive capacities of human labour rose exponentially, creating increased wealth and prosperity for all and hence increased leisure, comfort, health and happiness. Far from attaining these objectives, modern civilization, Gandhi argued, contributed to unbridled competition among human beings and thereby the evils of poverty, disease, war and suffering. It is precisely because modern civilization 'looks at man as a limitless consumer and thus sets out to open the floodgates of industrial production that it also becomes the source of inequality, oppression and violence on a scale hitherto unknown to human history'.[44] What the Mahatma argued in *Hind Swaraj* regarding industrial civilization was further reiterated in *Harijan*. There are articles, comments and statements replete with his condemnation of industrialism and his articulation of an alternative to modern civilization.

For Gandhi, India's economic future lay in *charkha* (spinning wheel)[45] and *khadi* (home-spun cotton textile).[46] 'If India's villages are to live and prosper, the charkha must become universal.' Rural civilization, argued Gandhi, 'is impossible without the charkha and all it implies, i.e. revival of village crafts'.[47] Similarly, *khadi* 'is the only true economic proposition in terms of the millions of villagers until such time, if ever, when a better system of supplying work and adequate wages for every able-bodied person above the age of sixteen, male or female, is found for his field, cottage or even factory in every one of the villages of India'.[48] Since mechanization was 'an evil when there are more hands than required for the work, as is the case in India, [he recommended] that the way to take work to the villagers is not through mechanization but ... through revival of the industries they have hitherto followed'.[49] He therefore suggested that

> an intelligent plan will find the cottage method fit into the scheme for our country. Any planning in our country that ignores the absorption of labour wealth will be misplaced.... [T]he centralized method of production, whatever may be its capacity to produce, is incapable of finding employment for as large a number of persons as we have to provide for. Therefore it stands condemned in this country.[50]

Gandhi was thoroughly convinced that industrialization as it manifested in the West would be simply devastating in India. His alternative revolves around his concern for providing profitable employment to all those who are capable. Not only does industrialism undermine the foundation of India's village economy, it 'will also lead to passive or active exploitation of the villagers as the problems of competition and marketing come in'.[51] Critical of Jawaharlal Nehru's passion for industrialization as the most viable way of instantly improving India's economy, he reiterated his position with characteristic firmness by saying that 'no amount of socialization can eradicate ... the evils, inherent in industrialism'.[52] His target was a particular type of mind-set, seduced by the glitter of industrialism, defending at any cost industrialization of the country on a mass scale.[53] His support for traditional crafts was based not on conservative reasoning, but on solid economic grounds in the sense that, by way of critiquing the Western civilization, he had articulated an alternative model of economic development more suited to the Indian reality. In response to a question raised by Rammanohar Lohia regarding the utility of industrialism as complementary to handicrafts, Gandhi came out with a vision of a future social order and the role of industrialism. The social order of the future, argued Gandhi,

> will be based predominantly on the charkha and all it implies. It will include everything that promotes the well-being of the villagers and village life.... I do visualize electricity, ship-building, ironworks, machine-making and the like existing side by side with village handicrafts. But the order of dependence will be reversed. Hitherto the industrialization has been planned as to destroy the villages and their crafts. I do not share the socialist belief that centralization of the necessaries of life will conduce to the common welfare when the centralized industries are planned and owned by the State.[54]

Gandhi's theory of *charkha* as a counter to Western industrialization did not find easy acceptance among the nationalists. Nehru's argument was based on his appreciation of industrialization as a quick means to eradicate India's poverty. Rabindranath Tagore, while appreciating that economic freedom was basic to *swaraj*, criticized Gandhi for his obsession with *charkha* as integral to *swaraj*. As he argued,

> even if every one of our countrymen should betake himself to spinning thread, that might somewhat mitigate their poverty, but it would not be swaraj.... What a difference it would make if our cultivators, who improvidently waste their spare time, were to engage in such productive work! Let us concede for the moment that the profitable employment of the surplus time of the cultivator is of the first importance. But the thing is not so simple as it sounds. One who takes up the problem must be prepared to devote precise thinking and systematic endeavour to its solution. It is not enough to say: let them spin.[55]

Tagore's argument has two aspects: first, the poet was not comfortable with the universal application of *charkha* simply because it would adversely affect the cultivators and others who had other things to do; and second, the prescription of the Mahatma did not appear to be economically viable given the paltry contribution of *charkha* to the national wealth. Hence the Gandhian design was bound to fail. Gandhi was misunderstood by the poet, as the Mahatma claimed. In his well-argued response to the charges, Gandhi defended his views in two ways: a) he made it clear that he was not in favour of 'spinning the whole of his or her time to the exclusion of all other activity' so Tagore's views were 'far from' what he sought to convey; and b) *charkha* was not, as Gandhi firmly believed, 'calculated to bring about a deathlike sameness in the nation and thus imagining he would shun it if he could'; instead, it was 'intended to realize the essential and living oneness of interest among India's myriads'.[56] Apart from underlining the clear differences of opinion between the poet and the Mahatma on economic freedom, the debate had nonetheless brought out various shades in the contemporary conceptualization of *swaraj*, which was far more complex than mere self-determination in politics.

Fourth, self-rule is probably a unique dimension of *swaraj*, indicating its qualitative difference with political freedom. As a concept, it denotes a process of removing the internal obstacles to freedom. Unlike the first three characteristics, where *swaraj* is conceptualized in a negative way, self-rule as an important ingredient clearly indicates the importance of moral values to society. One may argue that the removal of colonial rule would automatically guarantee economic and political freedom. This is hardly applicable to the fourth dimension of *swaraj* – self-rule – presumably because it is 'a self-achieved state of affairs' rather than something 'granted' by others.

As evident, *swaraj* as self-rule was conceptualized in two contrasting ways. The Moderates viewed *swaraj* purely in its narrow political meaning, namely, limited political freedom within the British Empire.[57] In other words, self-rule was translated in political terms as demands for a share in political power and control over the purse. So it was not out of place for Dadabhai Naoroji to insist on 'self government and treatment of India like other British colonies'.[58] In other words, what Naoroji had insisted on was British rule on British principles. The Moderate opinion revolved around 'a tone of sweet reasonableness'.[59] For them, self-rule involved 'modification' of the British administrative system, but not its removal. The articulation of self-rule was historically conditioned, since the primary goal of the Moderates was to keep a low profile so as not to provoke a repression which would nip the infant nationalist effort at the bud. So, for obvious historical reasons, the Moderates were not able to transcend the limitations of their times and their aim was defined vaguely as the promotion by constitutional means of 'the interests and well being of the people of the Indian Empire'. Accordingly, they also expected those in the nationalist campaign to behave as 'responsible members' of the Empire. Naoroji therefore had no hesitation in stating that

> if we honestly expect that [the] English nation will do its duty towards us, we must prove worthy by showing that we are never unreasonable, never violent, never uncharitable. We must show that we are earnest, but temperate, cognizant of our rights, but respectful of those of others; expecting the fairest construction of our own acts and conceding these to those of others.[60]

That *swaraj* was narrowly conceptualized by the Moderate wing of the early Congress was possibly due to the constraint of the circumstances of an expanding imperial power though it was attributed by a group of contemporary nationalists to 'the fear of ruling bureaucracy'.[61] But their compromising stance *vis-à-vis* the Empire provoked those who later became the Extremists in radically altering the concept of *swaraj* in a later period. *Swaraj* in its early Extremist conceptualization refers to a particular system of governance that 'lay down a minimum standard of life, with a minimum wage rate and the taxes should be regulated by capacity to pay [because] it is extremely unjust that a man possessing one acre of land should pay the same rate as a man possessing 500 or 50,000 acres. The higher the income the higher [should] be the tax.'[62] So *swaraj* is therefore political self-rule with specific prescriptions seeking to protect the economic interests of both rich and poor. So, for Bipin Pal, one of the foremost Extremist ideologues, *swaraj* was 'autonomy absolutely free of British control' and it was for all Indians, not for any particular section or sections. India he visualized as 'democratic and federal [comprising] republican states (British Indian provinces) and constitutional monarchies (native states)'.[63] In contrast with Pal, Aurobindo equated *swaraj* with absolute political independence – 'a free national government unhampered even in the least degree by control'. In his conceptualization, *swaraj* was not 'a mere economic movement, though it openly strives for economic resurrection of the country ... not a mere political movement though [it involves] political independence. [It was] an intensely spiritual movement having for its object not simply the development of economic life or attainment of political freedom, but really the emancipation, in every sense of the term of Indian nationhood and womanhood.'[64] While Aurobindo focused on the overall nature of *swaraj*, Pal sought to identify its structural contour within the British rule.

Drawing on both these descriptions, Bal Gangadhar Tilak, perhaps the most important leader of the Extremist movement, further elaborated the conceptualization of *swaraj*. Unlike the Moderates, who argued for gradual introduction of democratic institutions in India, Tilak insisted on immediate *swaraj* or self-rule. His concept of *swaraj* was not complete independence but a government constituted by the Indians themselves that 'rules according to the wishes of the people or their representatives'. Similar to the British executive that 'decides on policies, imposes and removes taxes and determines the allocation of public expenditure', Indians should have the right 'to run their own government, to make laws, to appoint the administrators as well as to spend the tax revenue'. This is one dimension of his thought; the second dimension relates to the notion of *prajadroha* or the right of the people to resist an authority that loses legitimacy. In Tilak's conceptualization, if the government fails to fulfil their obligation to the ruled and becomes tyrannical, it loses its legitimacy to rule. What is interesting to note is that Tilak's *prajadroha* also justifies the enactment of laws to prevent unlawful activities of the people. If contextualized, this idea makes sense because he was aware that a total rejection of the government would invite atrocities on the nationalists who had neither the organizational backing nor a strong support base among the people. So his support for governmental preventive mechanisms was strategically conditioned and textured.

Tilak also added a new dimension to *swaraj* that had not only a political connotation (Home Rule) but also a moral [and] spiritual connotation (self-control and inner freedom). Keeping this in view, Tilak thus defined *swaraj* as

> a life centred in self and dependent upon self. There is *swarajya* in this world as well as in the world hereafter. The *Rishis* who laid down the law of duty betook themselves to forests, because the people were already enjoying *swarajya* or people's domination which was administered and defended in the first instance by the *Kshtriya* kings. It is my conviction, it is my thesis, that *swarajya* in the life to come cannot be the reward of a people who have not enjoyed it in the world.[65]

Tilak played a historical role in the construction of a new language of politics by being critical of 'the denationalized and westernized' Moderate leaders, who blindly clung to typical Western liberal values, disregarding their indigenous counterparts while articulating their opposition to the British rule. Tilak's political views are therefore an amalgam, argues N.R. Inamdar, 'of the Vedanta ideal of the spiritual unity of mankind and the Western notions of nationalism as propounded by Mazzini, [Edmund] Burke, [J.S.] Mill.'[66] It is possible to argue that Tilak had a wider appeal, for his campaign was couched in a language that drew upon values rooted in Indian culture and civilization, in contrast with those that the Moderates upheld, which were completely alien. So Tilak was not merely a nationalist leader with tremendous political acumen, he himself represented a new wave in the nationalist movement, which created an automatic space for it by a) providing the most powerful and persuasive critique of Moderate philosophy; and b) articulating his nationalist ideology in a language that was meaningful to those it was addressing. This is how Tilak is transcendental and his ideas of *swaraj*, boycott and strike had a significant sway on Gandhi who refined and fine-tuned some of the typical Extremist methods in a completely changed socio-economic and political context when the nationalist struggle had its tentacles not only in the district towns but also in the villages that unfortunately remained peripheral in the pre-Gandhian days of freedom struggle.

In tune with Tilak's conceptualization, Gandhi also underlined the fact that *swaraj* is also 'a self-transformative' activity. In other words, *swaraj* was about 'the constantly confirmed consciousness of being in charge of one's destiny, not just about liberty but about power'.[67] *Swaraj*, in Gandhian formulation, entails 'a disciplined rule from within'.[68] Defining *swaraj* as 'self conversion' and 'mental revolution' to experience 'inner freedom', he argued that 'Swaraj is a state of mind to be experienced by us [and it] consists in our efforts to win it.'[69] This is what runs through Gandhi's following statement:

> it is *swaraj* when we learn to rule ourselves. It is, therefore, in the palm of our hands. Do not consider this swaraj is like a dream. Here there is no idea of sitting still. The swaraj that I wish to picture before you and me is such that, after we have once realized it, we will endeavour to the end of our lifetime to persuade others to do likewise. But swaraj has to be experienced by each one for himself. One drowning man will never save another. Slaves ourselves, it would be a mere pretension to think of freeing others.[70]

The Gandhian idea of *swaraj* as self-rule seems to be based on the philosophical notion of *advaita* which is 'etymologically the kingdom or order or dispensation of "*sva*", self, myself [or] the truth that you and I are not other than one another.'[71] So the Gandhian struggle for *swaraj* and indeed the Indian struggle for *swaraj* under the leadership of thinkers and revolutionaries rooted in Indian metaphysics and spirituality such as Tilak and Aurobindo was 'always implicitly an *advaitin* struggle, a struggle for the kingdom of self or autonomy and identity as opposed to the delusion and chaos and dishonour, heteronomy and divisiveness'.[72] The British rule or modern industrial civilization were simply unacceptable because they were symbols of the power of illusion of not-self, otherness, to be precise, *Maya* hindering the effort 'to see God face to face in the truth of self-realization'.[73]

Characterizing *swaraj* in its widest possible connotations and not merely as self-determination in politics, Gandhi also sought to articulate *swaraj* in ideas. Political domination of man over man is felt in the most tangible form in the political sphere and can easily be replaced. Political subjection primarily means restraint on the outer life of a people, but the subtler domination exercised in the sphere of ideas by one culture on another, a domination with more serious consequences continues to remain relevant even after the overthrow of a political regime. So to attain self-rule in its purest sense involves a challenge to cultural subjection, perpetrated by those who are colonized as well. Gandhi's definition of *swaraj* as a self-transformative device is also an attempt to thwart this well-designed colonial endeavour of cultural subjection, which was likely to survive even after the conclusion of alien rule probably due to the uncritical acceptance of colonial modernity. Cultural subjection is different to assimilation in the sense that it leads to 'a creative process of intercommunication between separate cultures without blindly superseding one's traditional cast of ideas and sentiments'.[74] So *swaraj*, if understood in its narrow conceptualization, is reduced to a mere political programme, ignoring its wider implications whereby the very foundation of cultural subjection is challenged.

Gandhi was also aware that inner freedom cannot be realized without a conducive socio-political environment. Hence British rule needed to be removed to ensure both political and economic freedom. In other words, while a conducive environment was basic to freedom, it needed to be created and maintained by appropriate political and economic activities. The ability to act well in the socio-economic political arena is 'the test of the new meaning of self rule [that] prepares one to lead the life of an active citizen. That is why, in [Gandhi's] view spiritual freedom cannot remain ... an asocial [neither] an apolitical nor an atemporal condition.'[75] *Swaraj* in Gandhian conceptualization invariably translates into, argues Fred Dallmayr, 'the self rule of a larger community, that is, into a synonym for national democratic self government or home rule'.[76] As an empirical construct relevant to a political community, *swaraj* is also closely linked with the idea of *swadeshi* and the cultivation of indigenous (material and spiritual) resources of development. The *swaraj*-based polity comprised small, cultured, well-organized, thoroughly regenerated and self-governing village communities. They would administer justice, maintain order and take important decisions, and this would be not merely administrative but powerful economic and political units. In view of their given texture, they would have, argues Bhikhu Parekh while interpreting Gandhi's *swaraj*-based polity, 'a strong sense of solidarity, provide a sense of community, and act as nurseries of civil virtue'.[77]

The gradual unfolding of *swaraj*

The Indian freedom struggle was multi-dimensional. Though initially based on the political activity of the nationalist intelligentsia, over time the nationalist movement in India came to embody the self-activity of the Indian masses. In its later stages, especially following the 1919–21 Non-Cooperation–Khilafat Movement, it succeeded in mobilizing, regardless of religion, the youth, women, the urban middle and lower middle classes, the urban and rural poor, artisans, and large segments of workers, peasantry and small landlords. As a result, the nationalist organization, the Indian National Congress, so far confined to the large cities of India, gradually expanded its network even into remote villages. Not only were there new constituents of the nationalist movement, its ideology had undergone a metamorphosis as the hitherto peripheral sections of society participated in the anti-British offensive. The story of the freedom struggle is therefore one of radical shifts in the articulation of the nationalist aspirations. Despite 'the inclusionary' character of Indian nationalism – whether Gandhi was at the helm of affairs or otherwise – the ideas of 'freedom' and 'independence' did not dawn on those who mattered in India's recent political history all of a sudden. It was a process of intense discussion and long drawn-out debates that finally led to the acceptance of freedom as the only goal of the nationalist mobilization in which the Indian National Congress acted in a decisive manner.

There is no doubt that the 1930 Karachi Congress was a watershed in the freedom struggle simply because the famous independence resolution was unconditionally accepted as the goal of future political mobilization at the behest of the National Congress. So the idea of complete freedom – and not merely dominion status – came to be formally recognized by an organization that was crystallized by the British to accommodate the dissenters and also to create a forum for those supporting the colonial power. The role of the leadership was undoubtedly significant in shaping the political forces in accordance with the goal of complete freedom. What is also evident in the radical shift of the stance of the leadership is the changing nature of the constituencies of nationalism, especially following the participation of 'the subalterns' who had so far remained peripheral to political mobilization for independence. Seeking to galvanize the already tormented 'masses' due to the obvious adverse impact of colonialism, it was probably most appropriate for the leadership to endorse the objective of complete freedom in circumstances that witnessed a dramatic turn following the 1919–21 Non-Cooperation–Khilafat merger. The Indian freedom struggle is therefore an example of how the events at the grassroots can shape a political agenda that is both contextual and politically relevant to those spearheading the campaign for freedom.

In a nutshell, there are three major characteristics of the period that appear to have influenced, if not determined, the way in which the freedom struggle was both articulated and conducted. *First*, nationalism underwent radical changes as a result of the link between peripheral struggles with the centrally organized Congress-led freedom movement, as evident in the Non-Cooperation–Khilafat Movement. *Second*, in organizing movements, activists with political affiliations of whatever kind faced serious challenges, based sometimes on ideological differences, sometimes on communal divisions; the latter in fact became decisive in causing a permanent fissure in the nationalist political platform. Although communal divisions corresponded to a socio-economic split, as evidence from Bengal clearly suggests, both the Hindu and Muslim leadership drew on religion for political gains under circumstances when individual identity was uncritically conceptualized and strongly defended in terms of religious affiliations, disregarding other probable influences in its construction. *Third*, in the development of the nationalist ideology, several competing ideologies, not always properly articulated, had significant roles representing the views of those in the periphery. For instance, the Congress, especially in the aftermath of the Non-Cooperation Movement, formally recognized the importance of the peasantry and workers in anti-imperial movements. Although the agenda of the periphery was accommodated in the all-pervasive nationalist ideology, it was never decisive in the articulation of the nationalist response, which was largely, if not entirely, codified around the anti-British sentiments. In other words, the nationalist ideology prevailed over other alternatives which, if allowed to flourish, would have probably fashioned the struggle for freedom in a different direction. Despite various possibilities, the Indian freedom struggle continued to remain largely 'nationalist' with any goal other than resistance to a colonial power not sincerely espoused, presumably because it would dilute the campaign for independence. In India's freedom struggle, nationalism as an ideology never sought to create a nation-state but was primarily an ideology inspiring a subject nation to fight for independence. The nationalist movement was thus structured around 'freedom from British rule'. Foreign rule was unacceptable not for any conventional nationalist reasons, but because it choked and distorted India's growth as a civilization.

The freedom struggle was conducted at various levels involving different layers of society. In organizational terms, it was the Indian National Congress that was predominant in organizing the masses under various kinds of ideological commitments against the British. The Congress might have come into existence through 'a plan secretly pre-arranged with the Viceroy as an intended weapon for safeguarding British rule against the rising forces of popular unrest and anti-British feeling'.[78] In view of the historical roots of the Congress, it would however be wrong to argue that it owed its birth primarily to the government initiative. In fact, the government stepped in at the behest of the Congress to take charge of a movement which was 'in any case coming into existence and whose development it foresaw was inevitable'.[79] The arguments in favour of the oft-quoted safety valve role of the Congress[80] were gradually dispelled as it became identified with the nationalist movement in which competing ideologies flourished. Not only did the Congress articulate the views of different sections of the population, it also provided a nationalist platform with a well-defined political goal opposed to the continuity of the British rule in India.

This is not to suggest, however, that the freedom struggle was unidimensional; instead, it had nurtured various kinds of ideological possibilities within, of course, the basic political goal of freedom from foreign rule. The rise of Gandhi was a watershed in Indian politics and the 1919–21 Non-Cooperation–Khilafat merger was illustrative of this new trend. The difference between politics before and after the non-cooperation lay in the extension of the political boundaries of the nationalist movement to accommodate hitherto neglected sections of society.

The Congress, an exclusive domain of the English educated lawyers, had also undergone radical changes in terms of its ideological commitment. The publication of the 1928 Nehru Report was a significant signpost so far as the freedom struggle was concerned. The British government was given precisely one year in which to accept the Congress demand for 'dominion status'; otherwise, Gandhi would launch a nationwide *satyagraha* campaign. As the demand was not conceded, the Congress with Jawaharlal Nehru as its president adopted the famous '*purna swaraj*' resolution in the 1928 Lahore session. Nehru asserted that '[t]he brief day of European domination is already approaching its end.... The future lies with America and Asia.... India today is a part of the world movement ... we march forward unfettered to our goal ... for this Congress is to declare in favour of independence and devise sanctions to achieve it.'[81] He further stated: 'The British Government in India ... has ruined India economically, politically, culturally and spiritually. [We] believe therefore that India must sever the British connection and attain *Purna Swaraj* or Complete Independence.'[82] While launching the salt *satyagraha* in 1930, Gandhi also defended complete independence as the only option available to save the Indian masses. Reiterating his commitment to fight for the people, he thus declared:

> the British system seems to be designed to crush the very life out of the [people]. Even the salt [one] must use to live is so taxed. ... The drink and drug revenue, too, is derived from the poor. It saps the foundations both of their health and morals. It is defended under the false plea of individual freedom. ... The inequalities sampled above are maintained in order to carry on a foreign administration, demonstratively the most expensive in the world. ... A radical cutting down of the revenue, therefore, depends upon an equally radical reduction in the expenses of the administration. This means a transformation of the scheme of government ... impossible without independence.[83]

With the adoption of the goal of complete independence, not only did the Congress undergo metamorphosis in its ideological moorings, the political constituencies it represented also dramatically expanded. In fact, this resolution was indicative of a change within the Congress leadership now seeking to reach out to the masses by adopting the issues confronting their daily lives. Through the salt campaign, Gandhi involved various new social groups, hitherto peripheral, in the nationalist campaign. By selecting salt as the principal issue of the movement, he proved how effective he was as a strategist in opposition to a ruthless state. In the popular perception, the state was easily identified as a target of attack since salt was the most basic item in daily existence. The salt *satyagraha* had different kinds of manifestations at the grassroots. Yet the campaign unleashed a political process whereby the Congress activists at various levels were linked together for a common cause.

It would not be absolutely right to identify the salt *satyagraha* as an example of a mass campaign since the communal division between the Hindus and Muslims seemed to have been highlighted by characterizing the movement merely as a Congress campaign. This was also the beginning of the rise of the Muslim League as a party of mass appeal, modelled on the structure and adopting most of the populist platform of the Congress. Blaming the Congress for causing fissure between the communities by pursuing policies in support of the majority community, the League sought to articulate the voice of the Muslims who 'suffered simply because of their religion' during the 1937–9 interlude of Congress provincial rule. There were always grievances, after all, from the enforced singing of *Bande Mataram* in public schools to the unpunished 'beating' or 'killing of Muslim peasants in any number of Hindu majority villages whenever "a congress magistrate" or "minister" failed to take prompt punitive action'. 'On the very threshold of what little power and responsibility is given, the majority community have clearly shown their hand: that Hindustan is for the Hindus', Jinnah warned the League followers at Lucknow in 1937, reiterating that

> God only helps those who help themselves. . . . I want the Musalmans to believe in themselves and take their destiny in their own hands. . . . The All India Muslim League has now come to live and play its just part in the world of Indian politics. . . . The Congress attempt, under the guise of establishing mass contact with Musalmans, is calculated to divide and weaken and break the Musalmans, and is an effort to detach them for their accredited leaders. . . . it cannot mislead anyone. . . . Eighty millions of Musalmans in India have nothing to fear. They have their destiny in their hands, and as a well knit, solid, organized united force can face any danger, and withstand any opposition.[84]

This marked the birth of a new militant mass Muslim League, presaging the dawn of 'the Pakistan demand' at Lahore three years later, and of the creation of Pakistan itself in less than a decade. What had begun with the institutionalization of the Lucknow Pact in 1916 gradually became a part of the freedom struggle that was articulated differently by the Hindus and Muslims. The pre-Second World War era of provincial responsibility thus became 'an interval of increasing communal conflict and escalating political rivalry'[85] between the League and Congress, culminating in the 1947 transfer of power to two separate nations, India and Pakistan.

In order to expand the horizon of politics, the Congress sought to incorporate new actors through the merger of the Non-Cooperation and Khilafat agitations. To understand better the changed political scenario, it will be useful to distinguish between two political domains, which may be called 'the organized' and 'the unorganized' spheres.

Organized politics are conducted through the formal state machinery. Thus organized politics encompass activities articulated through the governmental institutions, political parties, and legislatures in elections. By conforming to set rules of the political game, such actors exercise political power sometimes to challenge and sometimes to defend the existing power relationships. Organized politics as an explanatory category incorporate the activities of both the opposition and those favouring the status quo. Thus a fair understanding of this type of politics requires study of the processes which surround the state. With the council entry decision in 1922, organized politics were principally centred around the Legislative Council, Municipal Corporations and various local administrative units introduced under the 1919 Montague–Chelmsford Reforms of self-rule.

The domain of unorganized politics lies outside the institutionalized state

structure. This type of politics is called unorganized because it lacks formal-
ized structure. What exist as organizational networks, although transitional
because they appear at specific junctures of history, are well rooted in the
consciousness of the participants. What is crucial is the sense of community,
maintained by activities connected with various economic, religious and cultural institutions. Thus it was not anachronistic to find that *ulemas* drawing
the attention of the Muslim masses to the wrongs of the British were more
effective as organizers than the Congress volunteers in the 1919–21 Non-
Cooperation–Khilafat Movement. This indicates the autonomous nature of
the unorganized world where political idioms are interpreted from an
altogether different perspective.

The distinction between the organized and unorganized worlds of politics
is useful in understanding the changing nature of India's freedom struggle
and its ideology because there were serious attempts by the political
activists, irrespective of ideological commitments, to link the unorganized
and the organized together.[86] By calling on the local leaders, whatever
their religion, to join the nationalist movement in the wake of the Non-
Cooperation–Khilafat Movement, the Congress leadership, C.R. Das in
particular, initiated a new trend involving a new set of actors. Contempora-
neously, the revolutionary terrorists also endeavoured to extend the bound-
ary of nationalist politics by organizing political movements on issues
relating to the agrarian and industrial economy. An Intelligence Bureau
report of 1927 made it clear that a substantial section of revolutionary
terrorists had come to the conclusion that, unless peasants and workers were
involved in the anti-British struggle, the nationalist movement would never
be strong enough to achieve India's independence. Evidence of growing
discontent, the report continued,

> was to be found in the proceedings of Political Sufferers' Conference at
> Gauhati [in Assam] and was voiced by Bhupendranath Dutta [brother
> of Vivekanada] in his presidential address. The speech was openly com-
> munistic and it [was] said to have created a profound impression on the
> minds of the youth to whom it was addressed. Dutta advocated the
> organisation of the peasants and workers and the formation of a people's
> party.[87]

In his personal recollections, Tridib Chaudhuri, an Anushilan member who
later became a leader of the Revolutionary Socialist Party, also confirmed
that, by the early 1920s, the Anushilan Party in particular had adopted definite policies and programmes along socialist lines in order to reach beyond
'the world of bhadralok politics'.[88] Side by side with the indigenous movement designed to include hitherto neglected political actors, there were also
attempts by the Communist International through its emissaries, such as
M.N. Roy, Abani Mukherjee or Gopen Chakrabarty, to spread socialist
ideas. Whatever the principal reason for this ideological change, the above

evidence indicates the awareness among the revolutionary terrorists (who increasingly became dominant politically especially in Bengal after the demise of C.R. Das) of the importance of building an organization involving the peasantry and workers. In a programme of action, published in 1931 by the Chittagong revolutionaries, the aim was clearly stated:

> The Congress platform is to be availed of. Then follow orders for the capture of trade unions, the formation of ryot associations, secret entry into social and philanthropic organizations and the formation of unity to offer resistance to troops and police. Revolutionary students should join university training corps for observation of military methods. A women's committee should be co-opted for the duty of revolutionizing the women folk and selecting from them active members for direct service.[89]

Though declaring that the Congress was dominated by 'selfish commercial interests' and 'the creed of ahimsa' was futile as a means of achieving independence, the above document appreciated Gandhism because 'it count[ed] on mass action. It [had] paved the way for the proletarian revolution by trying to harness it, however selfishly or crudely to its own political programme. The revolutionary must give the angel its due.'[90]

The awareness of linking the peasant and working-class movement with the wider anti-British struggle was manifested in Congress's decision to incorporate the peasants' and workers' demands in its policies and programmes. The Congress failure to adopt a concrete agrarian programme enabled the non-Congress and communal organizations to flourish at its expense. Among the workers, the Congress had built a support base, but its national democratic line of maintaining an amicable understanding between the workers and native industrialists prevented any consolidation of its position. In maintaining amicability, the primary concern of the Congress was not to protect the interests of groups of indigenous capitalists but to ensure India's economic future. The relationship between the Congress and native industrialists was so remarkably tilted in favour of the latter that the Congress was accused of failing to protect 'the essential economic interests of the country' when the Girni Kamgar Union caused severe disruption in the Bombay textile industry.[91] 'Strikes in the cotton and steel industries [are] highly prejudicial to the economic interests of India', argued Purushattam Thakurdas, since 'they indirectly help the foreign manufacturers in enabling them to replace the quantity which Indians could not manufacture in consequence of such strikes.'[92]

As regards the national industries, the concerns of the Congress leaders, including radicals like Subhas Chandra Bose and Jawaharlal Nehru, were substantially different from those of the workers. By according priority to the struggle for *swaraj*, the Congress obviously wanted to emphasize the need for cooperation between labour and capital in the Indian-owned industries. The argument logically flowed from its declared object to protect the native industries. The workers' experiences, however, demonstrated that national industry operated no differently from non-Indian industry in dealing with workers' demands or in its attitude toward trade unions. Thus the labourers, as an editorial in *Amrita Bazar Patrika* of May 1928 commented, 'find nothing to discriminate between the Bombay mill owners who are Indians and the proprietors of Ludlow Jute Mill, for instance, who are foreign'. In their determination to consolidate the alliance between the indigenous capitalists and the Congress-led nationalist movement, the Congress leaders eroded the possibility of a bond between the workers and the national movement in India.

Concluding observations

Swaraj is a conceptual riddle with multifarious philosophical dimensions, articulated empirically in different ways. Notwithstanding its clear political overtone, that the idea is multi-dimensional is evident from multiple intellectual discourses that emerged during the course of the freedom struggle.[93] Historically textured, the idea of *swaraj*, though emerging at the dawn of the Indian nationalist movement, had undergone radical changes in response to the changing nature of the anti-British campaign. At the outset, the Moderate nationalists defined it in a very limited manner, underlining the evident political tone of *swaraj* without seeking to explore its multifaceted nature that gradually unfolded. Nonetheless, the Moderates were pioneers in conceptualizing a nationalist movement incipient in terms of an indigenous vocabulary. Here lies the unique contribution of those who always articulated their anti-British protest in an absolutely constitutional way. Although it was politically restraining in the period that followed, *swaraj* as home rule gained salience when the nationalist movement revolved around elites with a very narrow social basis.

In its second phase, the nationalist articulation was far more complex both ideologically and also in terms of the participants, whose nature had undergone a metamorphosis probably due to the expansion of the social base of the anti-British campaign. Reflective of the ideological mood of the period, *swaraj* was redefined and reinterpreted, taking into account the ideas and discourses governing the nationalist intervention. Its limited meaning of political freedom did not remain as decisive as before in circumstances when the hitherto peripheral segments of society began to get involved in what had so far been the domain of the elites. In the Extremist phase, *swaraj* was associated with the 'inner freedom' of individuals and was translated into certain practices with roots in indigenous traditions, presumably because of their easy acceptance by the masses. Two factors seem to have been at work: a) given its Indian roots, *swaraj* had an obvious advantage as a political force and b) *swaraj* as self-government had also provided a blueprint for future governance. So it was not surprising when Tilak integrated home rule with self-control and the inner freedom of the individual in his definition of *swaraj*. As a result, not only did he accord a new salience to the nationalist campaign, he also paved the way for the Mahatma to construct *swaraj* in a way that ideologically motivated the masses even in the face of a massive retaliation by the British government.

The Gandhian intervention in *swaraj* is unique in two specific ways: first, it is neither a mere doctrine of governance nor a device to merely ensure political freedom. Hence *swaraj* in its limited sense was neither what Gandhi aspired to nor stood for. Second, by defining *swaraj* as self-rule, the Mahatma sought to capture its metaphysical basis, which, if explained in a mundane political form, would remain unrealized. Hence the departure of the British was only one of the conditions of *swaraj*. It is true that 'Swaraj does consist', thus argued Gandhi, 'in the change of government and its real control by the people, but that would be merely the form. The substance that I am hankering after is a definite acceptance of the masses and therefore a real change of heart on the part of the people.'[94] This is where Gandhi and Nehru met, in the sense that they were both convinced that *swaraj* 'must mean more than political independence, and must be seen to bring real change in the lives of the ordinary people, particularly the most disadvantaged'.[95] So this is a state of mind that needed to be experienced internally. Without such an experience, argues Anthony Parel while interpreting Gandhi's definition, '*swaraj* would remain a mere theory or doctrine; it would never become an internal principle of action in the external political sphere'.[96] In other words, *swaraj* is an interconnected theoretical terrain with a specific form and principles. This conceptualization is therefore unique in more than one way. And its significance lies in the complex unfolding of the concept as it evolved in a particular historical context with roots in the philosophical trends of what is generally conceptualized as Indian reality. In this sense, *swaraj*, both as a theory and practice, is an innovative intervention that remained meaningful in the different phases of the nationalist movement, which had undergone ideological changes for obvious reasons.

2 The Mahatma at the grassroots
The praxis of *ahimsa* or non-violence

Gandhi is an elusive figure. Although he has written extensively on various themes pertaining to India's socio-economic and political life, there are areas in his thought that often project a different Gandhi altogether. In order to deconstruct Gandhian thought in the perspective in which he was involved in a gigantic nationalist struggle of the twentieth century, it is probably incumbent to assess Gandhi in two different ways. First, Gandhian political ideas are to be related to the actual anti-British onslaught that began with the 1920–2 Non-Cooperation Movement and culminated in the 1942 Quit India campaign in which Gandhi as the leader reigned supreme. In this context, Gandhi's worldview, taking into account his role as a social reformer, aimed at changing the nature of men and women, and was thus connected with social development. Second, there were events, more significant perhaps from the point of view of 'anti-imperial' struggle which, though drawing upon Gandhian teachings, deviated from the well-established norm of non-violence. The implication of such deviations appears disastrous to Gandhi himself. But for those who participated in political movements running counter to non-violence, the means of political action seem to have been derived from Gandhi.

This chapter thus argues for the autonomy of political movements even in the context of the overarching influence of a major political ideology. In other words, a limited attempt will be made to show in what context non-violence as a means *of* struggle failed to significantly guide political action even in the absence of a parallel leadership opposed to Gandhism. This is, however, not to theoretically defend 'the spontaneity thesis', because the Gandhi-led counter-offensive between 1920 and 1942 was preceded by consistent Congress effort at mobilizing the masses both at the national and local level through either social work or direct political campaign.

The task is difficult but not insurmountable. It is difficult because, in searching for a thesis in Gandhi, the initial problem is the untidiness of the material. Gandhi wrote a partial autobiography,[1] a few pamphlets, a very large number of articles in the two weeklies that he edited, namely *Indian Opinion* and *Young India* apart from his regular contributions in *Harijan*,[2] and even a large number of letters to the viceroys, fellow politicians and disciples. Besides these, he delivered speeches at conferences, congresses, and at his regular prayer meetings. Although Gandhi never sought to develop a well-argued political thesis, he left an enormous quantity of written materials. As Pyarelal reminiscences,

> his energy was phenomenal. . . . One day I actually counted 56 letters which he had written in his own hand. [In the midst of other commitments] his remarkable faculty of switching on and off his mind to and from any thing at will and to remain unaffected by his surroundings enabled him to carry on with his usual pace and efficiency. He had a passion for precision and thoroughness in the minutest details. . . . and enforced military discipline and clock-work regularity in his own case and expected the same from those around him. . . . He insisted on his desk being clear and woe to anyone of his staff who referred to him a letter more than forty-eight hours old. . . . Any reply of more than five or ten lines was as a rule consigned to the waste paper basket. The address was no less minutely scrutinized. Not to know . . . the exact location of an out of the way place in India was regarded as a culpable failure. Vagueness about train timings or the exact time it took for the post to reach its destination by particular route was another cardinal sin.[3]

As evident, there is no dearth of materials. But Gandhi's thought is problematic for another reason, in the sense that there is neither a thesis nor consistency in his arguments as the Mahatma reacted differently at different times in response to circumstances.[4] Primarily a political activist, Gandhi was probably aware of inconsistency in his thought when he admitted:

> At times of writing I never think what I have said before. My aim is not to be consistent with my previous statements on a given question, but to be consistent with truth as it may present itself to me at a given moment. The result has been that I have grown from truth to truth. I have saved memory from an undue strain.[5]

Juxtaposed with the above, the following statement is more revealing when the Mahatma characterized his language as 'apohistoric'. In his discussion with Dharmadeva, his disciple, Gandhi is categorical by saying '[m]y language is apohistoric, it lacks precision. It is therefore open to several interpretations.'[6] Although his confession to being inconsistent on various occasions had led the analysts to accuse the Mahatma of 'displaying the inconsistency of the opportunist politicians',[7] the above quotation nonetheless shows the extent to which Gandhi, above all a man of action, was sensitive to the environment in which he articulated his political response and thus probably hints at the autonomy of political action under specific circumstances.

On another occasion, Gandhi attributed his plan of action to his 'sixth sense'. As he argued, 'my sixth sense does wake up at the right moment and afterwards goes to sleep'. He further added that 'I speak under inspiration. I cannot decide as to how I shall tackle a particular situation until I am faced with it.'[8] Hence, as he himself admitted, 'I am doing many things which are contrary to my previous practice.' As an illustration, he referred to his differing advice to the *satyagrahees*. On one occasion, he told the *satyagrahees* 'to act as model prisoners and obey every order of the officials'. In the context of the 1942 open rebellion, however, he asked the participants to respond to the situation as it demanded. The 1942 movement became violent too.[9] As evident, Mahatma's deeds were therefore generally context-dependent and what appeared to be contradictory seems actually to be strategic.

In seeking to deconstruct Gandhian thought in a constantly changing socio-economic and political milieu, one is invariably drawn to a complex process of interpenetration of ideas and the contemporary scene. Hence, the idea of a system of thought appears not to fit the Mahatma, the political leader who had intuitively responded to the demands of the day as 'it contributed to his quest for truth'.[10] In other words, since his ideas are nothing but comments on practical situations and are intended to shape men/women and events, Gandhian thought, despite apparent inconsistency on occasions, needs to be grasped both as a political guide and as a moral inspiration. Here lie some clues to understanding why the Congress-led nationalist struggle between 1920 and 1942 resorted to violence in areas where Gandhi appeared to have been accepted as the leader. What is perhaps remarkable is the efforts of the local Congress volunteers to justify violence as a means of political action perfectly in tune with Gandhian preaching. Here probably lies the defence of the argument that Gandhi, by striving to fashion and develop a new instrument or weapon of political change, introduced various other dimensions of political action which had cropped up, independent of and/or apparently contradictory with Gandhian thought, in response to a complex interplay of socio-economic and political forces involving the Congress, the British, and input from the international scene.

Moreover, the fact that Gandhi, unlike his predecessors, was able to sway the masses with the well-entrenched 'Indianness' of his lifestyle and political vocabulary, also demonstrated his ability to translate popular grievances into political action in the face of imperial oppression and atrocity. Attributing the rise of the Mahatma as an invincible leader in the nationalist struggle against the British to his physical and mental affinity with the traditions and temperament of the Indian masses, Subhas Chandra Bose, who opposed Gandhi and Gandhism almost throughout his active political career within the National Congress, thus commented that, when the Mahatma speaks,

> he does so in a language that [the people] comprehend not in the language of Herbert Spencer and Edmund Burke, as for instance, Sir Surendra Nath Banerjee would have done, but in that of the *Bhagvad Gita* and the *Ramayana*. When he talks to them about Swaraj, he does not

dilate on the virtues of provincial autonomy or federation, he reminds them of the glories of *Ramrajya* [the kingdom of the mythical king Rama] and they understand. And he talks of conquering through love and *ahimsa* (non violence), they are reminded of Buddha and Mahavira and they accept him.[11]

The basic precepts

It is crucial for our understanding of Gandhi's social and political ideas to realize the significance of the two basic precepts of Gandhism, namely, *satyagraha* and *ahimsa* or non-violence. Most authors on Gandhi seem to conflate the two. What is rather relatively less known is the fact that, during the period between his South African experiment and the agitation against the Rowlatt Act, it was *satyagraha* – in the sense of a protest without rancour – that held the key to his entire campaign. Only in the aftermath of the 1919 anti-Rowlatt *satyagraha*, *ahimsa* or non-violence was included as integral to Gandhi's *satyagraha* campaign. There is no doubt that *ahimsa* always remained a significant influence in the conceptualization of *satyagraha*; but it was not projected as crucial a component as it later became. In other words, despite its obvious importance, *ahimsa* never figured prominently in the Gandhian discourse of political action. As a method, *satyagraha* was always informed by *ahimsa*, though its role was not vividly articulated till the 1919 campaign against the Rowlatt Act. From now on, the Mahatma paid enormous attention to both conceptualizing and justifying the importance of *ahimsa* in political mobilization by referring to the ancient scriptures in his defence. That *ahimsa* acquired tremendous importance following the Rowlatt *satyagraha* is also suggestive of the nature of the movement that Gandhi was contemplating in its aftermath. Gandhi was preparing for a pan-Indian Non-Cooperation Movement in the *satyagraha* format in which *ahimsa* was to play a determining role in political mobilization. So, the micro-experiments of *satyagraha* in Champaran, Kheda and Ahmedabad where *ahimsa* was constitutive of the Gandhian model of anti-imperialism[12] were therefore decisive in Gandhi's social and political thought.

For Gandhi, *ahimsa* meant 'both passive and active love, refraining from causing harm and destruction to living beings as well as positively promoting their well-being'.[13] This suggests that *by ahimsa*, Gandhi did not mean merely 'non-injury' to others in a mere negative or passive connotation; instead, *ahimsa* had a positive or active meaning of love and charity. As Gandhi clarified by saying that

> In its negative form, [*ahimsa*] means not injuring any living being whether by body or mind. I may not, therefore, hurt the person of any wrong-doer or bear any ill-will to him and so cause him mental suffering. In its positive form, *ahimsa* means the largest love, the greatest

charity. If I am a follower of *ahimsa*, I must love my enemy or a stranger to me as I would my wrong-doing father or son. This active *ahimsa* necessarily included truth and fearlessness.[14]

As evident, Gandhi defined *ahimsa* in two contrasting ways: on the one hand, in its narrow sense, it simply meant avoidance of acts harming others; while in its positive sense, it denoted promoting their well-being, based on 'infinite love'.[15] So, to characterize *ahimsa* as merely 'non-injury' to others was not appropriate in the sense that Gandhi understood the term and artic-ulated its sense. Non-violence was certainly not a negative affair; it was not non-resistance, but non-violent resistance which was, as Jawaharlal Nehru characterized, 'a positive and dynamic method of action ... not meant for those who meekly accept the status quo'. The very purpose for which it was designed was 'to create "a ferment in society" and thus to change existing conditions. Whatever the motives of conversion behind it, in practice, it has been', Nehru argued further, 'a powerful weapon of compulsion as well, though that compulsion is exercised in the most civilized and least objec-tionable manner.'[16]

Ahimsa, in its positive connotation, was based on the highest moral values, epitomized in 'the unselfish self'. Gandhi thus wrote,

> our desires and motives may be divided into two classes – selfish and unselfish. All selfish desires are immoral, while the desire to improve ourselves for the sake of doing good to others is truly moral. ... The highest moral law is that we should unremittingly work for the good of mankind.[17]

In Gandhi's experiment of *satyagraha*, *ahimsa* was a crucial variable. Not only did it enable Gandhi to provide a new conception of anti-colonial poli-tics, it also gave him an opportunity, by completely avoiding ill-feelings towards those in opposition, to politically accommodate those who, so far, remained peripheral, in his fold. But his approach was very cautious, as he argued:

> [a]himsa with me is a creed, the breath of life. It is [however] never as a creed that I placed it before India or, for that matter, before any one. ... I placed it before the Congress as a political weapon, to be employed for the solution of practical problems.

So, *ahimsa* was complementary to Gandhi's model of conflict resolution, which was certainly the most original and creative model of social change and political action even under most adverse circumstances. This was a theory of politics that gradually became the dominant ideology of a national political movement in which Gandhi reigned supreme. What lay at the root of this theory of politics was *ahimsa*, which was 'the organizing principle for a science of politics [that] was wholly different from all the current conceptions of politics [producing] the science of violence'.[18] Not only was this theory effective in mobilizing people regardless of socio-economic differences, it also provided a moral framework for 'solving every practical problem of the organized political movement'.[19]

Satyagraha meant resistance. Not merely passive resistance, but intense activity by the people. It denoted a legitimate, moral and truthful form of political action by the people against the brutal state power. It was a movement against various forms of injustice, meted out by the state. As Gandhi argued, 'we do not desire to make armed assaults on the administrators, nor to unseat them from power, but only to get rid of injustice'.[20] What it involved was a plan of action involving large masses of people targeting the state and vested social and economic interests. In organizing people for *satyagraha*, what was needed was also a level of awareness among the people linking their 'poverty' with the exploitative alien state. Gandhi was confident that the circumstances were ready and what was required was a call for campaign. Hence he argued just on the eve of the Rowlatt *satyagraha*:

> it is said that it is a very difficult, if not an altogether impossible task to educate ignorant peasants in satyagraha and that it is full of perils, for it is a very arduous business to transform unlettered ignorant people from one condition into another. Both the arguments are silly. The people of India are perfectly fit to receive the training of satyagraha. India has knowledge of *dharma*, and where there is knowledge of *dharma*, satyagraha is a very simple matter. . . . Some have a fear that once people get involved in satyagraha, they may at a later stage take arms. This fear is illusory. From the path of satyagraha, a transition to the path of a-satyagraha is impossible. It is possible of course that some people who believe in armed activity may mislead satyagraha by infiltrating into their ranks and later making them take to arms. . . . But as compared to other activities, it is less likely to happen in satyagraha, for their motives soon get exposed and when the people are not ready to take up arms, it becomes almost impossible to lead them on to that terrible path.[21]

The Rowlatt *satyagraha* translated the Gandhian words into action. Drawing on his faith in the spontaneous resistance of the masses to injustice, Gandhi was confident of the success of the campaign against the Rowlatt Act. There is no doubt that this 1919 *satyagraha* was a watershed in Gandhi's political ideas in two specific ways: a) Gandhi now realized the potential of the growing mass discontent in the anti-British struggle; and b) this *satyagraha* was also a litmus test for the Mahatma, who now became confident in *satyagraha* as a technique for political mobilization. For Gandhi, the Rowlatt Act was an unjust order that should not be honoured. As he argued, whether you are satyagrahis or not, so long as you disapprove of the Rowlatt legislation, all can join and [he was confident] that there will be such a response throughout the length and breadth of India as would convince the Government that we are alive to what is going on in our midst.[22]

With his success in this *satyagraha*, Gandhi was now ready for a pan-Indian political movement against the ruler and the Rowlatt *satyagraha* provided the impetus. Although Gandhi underlined the importance of *ahimsa* in *satyagraha*, he did not appear to emphasize it as strongly as he later did. For him, what was crucial was an organized attack on the British interest through *satyagraha* campaigns. As he argued,

> popular imagination has pictured satyagraha as purely and simply civil disobedience, if not in some cases, criminal disobedience.... As satyagraha is being brought into play on a large scale on the political field for the first time, it is in an experimental stage. I am therefore ever making new discoveries. And my error in trying to let civil disobedience take the people by storm appears to me to be Himalayan because of the discovery, I have made, namely, that he only is able and attains the right to offer civil disobedience who has known how to offer voluntary and deliberate obedience to the laws of the State in which he is living.[23]

So Gandhi capitalized on the obvious mass discontent which he translated into *satyagraha*. Now, what are the organizational principles? In his scheme of things, a *satyagrahi* should know these principles before embarking on a campaign. As he mentioned, before they got involved in any political campaign against the ruling authority, 'they should thoroughly understand its deeper implications. That being so, before restarting civil disobedience on a mass scale, it would be necessary to create a band of well-tried, pure-hearted volunteers who thoroughly understood the strict conditions of satyagraha.'[24] Thus was conceptualized the notion of *satyagraha* as the mobilizing principle governing the behaviour of those involved in the Gandhi-led nationalist campaign. And the more 'Gandhi concerned himself with the organizational norms within which a national movement had to be conducted, the more he began to elaborate upon the concept of *ahimsa*'.[25] A leader was responsible for directing the mass discontent into a course of action. Masses were not trained and their behaviour even in resistance was always that of a mob. The leadership was crucial in transforming the mob into an organized mass capable of undertaking meaningful action. As Gandhi himself confessed, 'nothing is so easy to train [as] the mobs, for the simple reasons that they have no mind, no pre-meditation. They act in frenzy. They repent quickly.'[26] He was not hesitant to characterize demonstrations during the first phase of the Non-Cooperation Movement as 'a mob without a mind'. Hence he concluded that such demonstrations cannot ... procure swaraj for India unless disciplined and harnessed for national goal. The great task before the nation today ... is to discipline its demonstrations if they are to serve any useful purpose. ... The nation must be disciplined to handle mass movements in a sober and methodical manner. ... We can do no effective work [he further added] unless we can pass instructions to the crowd and expect implicit obedience.[27]

So, to involve the masses in meaningful political campaigns, one had to articulate *satyagraha* into specific courses of action, especially its 'modalities of resistance'. This is where *ahimsa* assumes tremendous significance. *Ahimsa* was that specific organizational principle that governed the behaviour of a *satyagrahee*. In other words, *ahimsa* was critical to the entire exercise of *satyagraha*, without which the very act of resistance would appear to be futile. *Ahimsa* was a foundational principle as well. Not only did it articulate the nature of the campaign, it would also structure the form of resistance by guiding those involved in it. This was indeed 'the science of non-violence' in the sense that it provided a grammar of Gandhian political mobilization in which 'civil resisters represent the non-violent army of the nation. And just as every citizen cannot be a soldier on the active list, every citizen cannot be a civil resister on the active list.'[28] Interestingly, the onus of strictly adhering to the science of non-violence rested with the leadership and not with the masses. Just like a soldier of an army 'who does not know the whole of the military science; so also does a *satyagrahi* not know the whole of *satyagraha*. It is enough if he trusts his commander and honestly follows his instructions and is ready to suffer unto death without bearing malice against the so-called enemy. ... [The *satyagrahees*] must render heart discipline to their commander. There should be no mental reservation.'[29] Here Gandhi was referring to mass civil disobedience, where the role of the leader was immensely important in guiding the masses whereas in individual civil resistance, 'everyone was a complete independent unit [and] every resister is his own leader'.[30]

Despite its significance in earlier *satyagrahas* in Champaran, Kheda and Ahmedabad, *ahimsa* was not clearly articulated by the Mahatma till the 1919 Rowlatt *satyagraha* when its importance was duly recognized, both in mobilizing people and also defining the goal of the campaign. *Ahimsa* came to the surface, as it were, and its political importance in Gandhian resistance was upheld beyond doubt. *Satyagraha* was thus based on the principles of *satya* (truth), *ahimsa* (non-violence) and *tapas* (self-suffering). No definition was clearer than Gandhi's own oral submission before the disorders Inquiry Committee, known as the Hunter Committee, on 9 January, 1920. Admitting that he was 'the author of the Satyagraha Movement', Gandhi defined *satyagraha* by stating that:

it is a movement intended to replace [the] method of violence and [a] movement [based] entirely upon Truth. It is, as I have conceived it, an

extension of the domestic law on the political field and my experience
has led me to the conclusion that that movement and that alone can rid
India of the possibility of violence spreading throughout the length and
breadth of the land, for the redress of grievance.[31]

According to Gandhi, *satyagraha* refers to 'holding fast to truth', and also
'adherence to truth' even under gravest provocations. Why did he choose the
expression *satyagraha* to denote the movement that he launched in South
Africa against the Asiatic Law Amendment Ordinance of 1906? Gandhi
explained that 'truth (*satya*) implies love, and firmness (*agraha*) engenders
and therefore serves as a synonym for force'. Thus he began to call the Indian
movement ' "satyagraha", that is to say, the force which is born of truth and
love or non violence.'[32] It is characterized by 'adherence to a stated truth by
means of behaviour which is not violent, but which includes self suffering'.[33]
Satyagraha was a technique of action, and yet it was entirely different from a
violent warfare because of its ingrained characteristics. *Satyagraha* was not a
technique of 'overwhelming an army corps, bombing or capturing a town
but of initiating certain psychological changes in those who offered it and in
those against whom it is directed'.[34] What was so distinct about *satyagraha*
was the self-suffering of the individuals participating in non-violent political campaigns against the ruling authority. For Gandhi, political campaigns
were not one-dimensional, namely, opposition to the unjust rule and laws of
the Empire; they also upheld the search and devotion to Truth. So, self-
suffering was elevated to a completely different level of conceptualization by
linking it with Truth, which was not merely a value, but a force inspiring
the *satyagrahi* to make even the supreme sacrifice. As Gandhi argued, 'with
the conviction that Truth is not to be renounced even unto death, they shed
the fear of death. In the cause of Truth, the prison was a palace to them and
its doors the gateway to freedom.'[35]

Satyagraha was therefore not identical with passive resistance.[36] While
identifying the features of *satyagraha* in his *Hind Swaraj*, he was of the
opinion that passive resistance 'fails to convey [what he meant]. It describes
a method, but gives no hint of the system of which it is only a part. Real
beauty, and that is my aim, is in doing good against evil.'[37] In other words,
the similarity between *satyagraha* and passive resistance was just peripheral
since both of them were clearly defined methods of political resistance,
opposed to violence. Gandhi may certainly have drawn on passive resistance
conceptually; but when he defined *satyagraha* he underlined its unique
nature and characteristics. As he elaborated in the *Hind Swaraj*,

> Passive resistance is a method of securing rights by personal suffering; it
> is reverse of resistance by arms. When I refuse to do a thing that is
> repugnant to my conscience, I use soul-force. For instance, the govern-
> ment of the day has passed a law which is applicable to me. I do not like
> it. If, by using violence, I force the government to repeal the law, I am

employing what may be termed body-force. If I do not obey the law, and accept penalty for its breach, I use soul-force. It involves sacrifice of self.[38]

As shown, passive resistance can never be equated with *satyagraha* for the simple reason, as Gandhi himself stated, that it involved application of force as well while in the latter, the application of force, of whatever variety, was completely ruled out.[39] Hence he was most categorical by saying that

> passive resistance is an all-sided sword; it can be used anyhow; it blesses him who uses it and him against whom it is used. Without drawing a drop of blood, it produced far-reaching results. It never rusts, and cannot be stolen. Competition between passive resisters does not exhaust. The sword of passive resistance does not require a scabbard. It is strange indeed that you should consider such a weapon to be a weapon merely of the weak.[40]

Satyagraha was not 'physical force' but 'soul-force' that drew on the sponta- neous sacrifice of self by the participants, which constituted, according to Gandhi, the core of his campaign.[41] Gandhi associated passive resistance with internal violence. It unleashed 'forces of prejudice and separatism rather than compassion and inclusiveness'.[42] While emphasizing this dimen- sion, he further argued:

> Everybody admits that sacrifice of self is infinitely superior to sacrifice of others. Moreover, if this kind of force is used in a course that is unjust, only the person using it suffers. He does not make others suffer for his mistakes. Men have before now done many things which were subse- quently found to have been wrong. No man can claim to be absolutely in the right, or that a particular thing is wrong, because he thinks so, but it is wrong for him so long as that is his deliberate judgment. It is, therefore, [meant] that he should not do that which he knows to be wrong, and suffer the consequences whatever it may be. This is the key to use soul-force.[43]

Unlike the participants in the Suffragette Movement, 'a satyagrahi does not inflict pain on the adversary; he does not seek his destruction'. A *satya- grahi* never 'resorts to firearms'. In the use of *satyagraha*, 'there is no ill-will whatever'. The insistence on Truth 'arms the votary with matchless power', power that constituted the core of *satyagraha*. This power/force 'can never be physical'. There was no room 'for violence'. The only force of universal appli- cation 'can be that of *ahimsa* or love', which Gandhi defined as 'soul-force'.[44] The test of love was '*tapasya*', or self-suffering. Suffering injury in one's person 'is . . . of the essence of non violence and is the chosen substitute for violence to others'.[45] Self-suffering for Truth was not 'a weapon of the weak', but a powerful device, based on a higher form of courage than that resorting to violence. And it was also an aid 'in the moral persuasion of one's opponents or oppressor'.[46]

In the Gandhian mode of conflict resolution, self-suffering was crucial but resorted to sparingly. Once reasoning with the opponent failed, the *satyagrahi* was allowed to resort to self-suffering. *Satyagraha* was therefore a device recognizing the limits of reason in resolving amicably fundamental social, religious, political and economic conflicts. So, for Gandhi, *satyagraha* was not to be immediately launched; instead, it was the last resort of action when other usual processes or reasoning with the opponents or oppressors completely failed. Gandhi was categorical in this respect, as he argued:

> since satyagraha is one of the most powerful methods of direct action, a satyagrahi exhausts all other means before he resorts to satyagraha. He will, therefore, constantly and continually approach the constituted authority, he will appeal to public opinion, educate public opinion, state his views calmly and coolly before everybody who wants to listen to him; and only after he has exhausted all these avenues will he resort to satyagraha.[47]

Two points are very clear now. *First*, Gandhi was not anarchic in his approach. While elaborating the stages of the campaign, the lawyer in Gandhi was not prepared to plunge into *satyagraha* at the outset; instead, he would exhaust all possible channels of conflict resolution before *satyagraha* was launched. *Second*, as a liberal, the Mahatma also underlined the importance of public opinion as a powerful device to persuade the authority. In his words, 'public opinion, for which one cares, is a mightier force than gunpowder'.[48] In the formation of public opinion, the role of *satyagrahi* was immensely important, for 'the satyagrahi strives to reach the reason through heart'.[49] Once reasoning failed, the *satyagrahee* was allowed to undertake *tapas* or self-suffering that was now justified as the last straw to change the 'heart' of the opponents or oppressors. When 'appeal to reason does not answer', 'self-suffering' was the only means available, Gandhi defended, to the satyagrahees because he believed that this would create the conditions in which reason could triumph. The conviction rapidly grew within him that 'things of fundamental importance to the people are not secured by reason alone, but have to be purchased with voluntary suffering'.[50] So self-suffering was integrally linked with Gandhi's theory of conflict resolution. As he argued,

> [s]uffering is the law of human beings; war is the law of the jungle. But suffering is infinitely more powerful than the law of the jungle for converting the opponent and opening his ears, which are otherwise shut, to the voice of reason. Nobody has probably drawn up more petitions or espoused more forlorn causes than I, and I have come to the fundamen-

tal conclusion that if you want something really important to be done, you must not merely satisfy the reason, you must move heart also. The appeal of reason is more to the head, but penetration of heart comes from suffering. It opens up the inner understanding of man. Suffering is the badge of [the] human race, not the sword.[51]

So self-suffering as a force to inculcate reason in the opponents constituted a significant dimension in Gandhi's social and political thought. *Satyagraha* was thus not merely a conceptual construction, but was also 'designed as an effective substitute for violence',[52] based on certain fundamental theoretical tenets in contrast with those informing Western civilization. His opposition to violence was more fundamental than assumed simply because he believed that violence distorted the Western civilization by defending the exploitation of human beings. Not only did Gandhi shape *satyagraha* as a plan of action, he also provided 'a strong institutional base for the expression of dissent' within colonialism despite the obvious adverse consequences of opposition. *Satyagraha* translated 'the voice of protest' in effective terms. It thus 'provides a means through which . . . the personal is made political', in the sense that *satyagraha* was simultaneously a device for Truth and freedom from colonial rule.[53]

Satyagraha had several forms. During the nationalist movement in India, the most frequently employed methods of campaign were 'non-cooperation' and 'civil disobedience', apart from submitting memoranda of demands to the authority. While non-cooperation (*hartal*, strikes, boycott and fasts unto death) was a mechanism for indirect pressure on the opponent, civil disobedience (picketing, non-payment of taxes and defiance of specific laws) entailed several positive steps to confront the ruling authority face-to-face. Non-cooperation appears to pave the way for civil disobedience, which was a form of non-violent rebellion.[54] Simultaneously with these two contrasting designs for political action, Gandhian *satyagraha* also entailed a constructive programme (for the promotion of communal harmony, removal of untouchability, adult education, promotion of social and economic equality, devolution of power through schemes of political and economic decentralization). *Satyagraha* was not merely a political weapon to challenge the British rule, it was also a detailed scheme to rid Indian society of the age-old social and economic prejudices. In other words, *satyagraha* was a continuous exercise with clear social and economic messages, relevant to the underprivileged and exploited, apart from the political opposition to the British rule. As Gandhi described,

the satyagraha struggle in British India had two aspects, non-violent non-cooperation with the Government and cooperation among the people themselves. Both these aspects should constantly be kept [in mind]. The constructive programme that I have set before you necessitates perfect co-operation among all section'.[55]

There is one final point. In Gandhian *satyagraha*, fasting, which was purificatory as well, was defined 'as a great weapon in the armoury of satyagraha'.[56] Gandhi also undertook fasts to put pressure on his opponents when persuasion failed to yield results. This was a device to inflict pain on himself, a process that Gandhi believed would persuade his opponents to appreciate the goals for which the fast was undertaken. Fast was to be sparingly resorted to since 'there is', according to Gandhi, 'violence behind ... fasting'.[57] He made a subtle distinction between fasting and hunger strike. While the latter is a serious political weapon with tremendous impact on opponents, the former was a soul-purifying exercise. Hunger strike was thus an innovative tool of action directed against the opponents once the usual processes of *satyagraha* aborted. As it required tremendous mental strength, hunger strike had to be used carefully Gandhi warned, because withdrawal was not possible unless its aim was fulfilled. As he stated,

> unscientific experimentation with [hunger strike] is bound to be harmful to the one who fasts, and it may even harm the cause espoused. No one who has not earned the right to do so should, therefore, use this weapon. A fast may only be undertaken by him who is associated with the person against whom he fasts. The latter must be directly connected with the purpose for which the fast is being undertaken.[58]

There were three guidelines: a) fasting was only to be undertaken as a last resort; once the usual available tools of *satyagraha* were exhausted, the *satyagrahee* was allowed to plunge into fasting; b) the individual action in this regard would be justified only when the *satyagrahees* was convinced that fasting was the only option available under the circumstances and Gandhi completely endorsed the goal; and c) fasting was allowed to be undertaken against those with whom one was connected with the ties of love. The implications are quite clear, with Gandhi setting strict limits to the way fasting could be used. Furthermore, although a crucial form of opposition, fasting was 'an adjunct to other forms of satyagraha'.[59] This was a form in which individuals articulated protests by inflicting injury on themselves. Gandhi argued that fasting was a form of love, articulated in self-suffering, and had a fourfold purpose.[60] *First*, it was his expression of a deep sense of sorrow and hurt at the way in which those, against whom this was directed, had degraded themselves and disappointed him; *second*, as their leader, he was responsible for them and his fast was his typical way of atoning for their misdeeds; *third*, it was his last desperate attempt, 'an intense spiritual effort' to activate the moribund masses and to mobilize their moral energies; *finally*, fast was his technique to defuse the communal tension between the Hindus and Muslims by deepening the sense of community and fostering mutual respect between them.

As shown, Gandhi's *satyagraha* was a well-defined plan of action with both social and political implications. The steps that constituted *satyagraha* were not only well designed, but also organically linked with his theory based on love. Hence *satyagraha* needed to be guided not by 'minds' but by 'hearts'.[61] While writing on *satyagraha*, the Mahatma always insisted on certain basic principles.[62] Before embarking on a *satyagraha*, one had to be convinced that the situation warranted such a campaign and its objectives were clear to the participants; as it was an open call, opponents were to be given an opportunity to negotiate if they wanted to avoid oppositional campaign. Hence, *satyagraha* should not be resorted to 'lightly' and, if *satyagraha* was not to be abused, it must be resorted to only by those individuals qualified to embark on it, those who have 'already acquired the habit of willing obedience to laws without fear of their sanctions' and 'those who have not learnt to obey laws for the right reasons do not have the right to obey the law'.[63] This is what Gandhi insisted when he mentioned that 'disobedience without civility, discipline [and] non violence is certain destruction'.[64] Gandhi never foreclosed the channel of communication with the adversaries, presumably because he believed that the attitudes on either side should not be allowed to be rigid. This was the grammar of *satyagraha* as a campaign in which the individual *satyagrahee* was required to take a pledge not to harm the opponents even by nurturing ill-feelings towards them. The primary duty of a *satyagrahee* was to convert the opponent by self-suffering and not by causing pain. Even while in prison, a *satyagrahee* was to behave in an exemplary manner without asking for facilities 'whose deprivation does not involve any injury to one's self-respect'.[65]

Gandhi's *satyagraha* was not only a political doctrine directed against the state,[66] it also has social and economic thrusts relevant to and drawn from human nature. In contrast with the constitutional and Extremist methods of political mobilization, *satyagraha* was a highly original and creative conceptualization of social change and political action. Opposed to violence, Gandhi's preferred way was *ahimsa*, drawing on the strength of persuasion. Once persuasion failed, Gandhi was not hesitant to adopt fasting, a slightly stronger means as it affected the opponents by moral blackmail. The principles governing *satyagraha* and its participants are illustrative of his endeavour to organize the mass protest within a strict format that clearly stipulates the duties and responsibilities of an individual *satyagrahee*. So, not only did he creatively define the nature of the struggle for freedom, he also provided a well-designed structure for political mobilization. In the narrow sense, *satyagraha* was strictly a method of political struggle, drawing on moral reasoning; in the wider sense, it was an extremely humane and creative way of dealing with disagreements and conflicts involving the ruler and the ruled as well as the socio-economically unprivileged and their *bête noire*. What is most distinct in Gandhi's conceptualization is the importance of 'rational' discussion and persuasion and also their obvious limitations in radically altering the existent moral relationships between individuals in different socio-economic locations. Hence *satyagraha* was to be a continuous process, seeking to transform the individuals involved by appealing to their humane moral values that remained captive due to colonialism and various social prejudices, justified in the name of religion.

Satyagraha was a theoretical construct of conflict resolution as well as a practical doctrine of political mobilization during the freedom struggle in India. There were competing ideologies in the anti-British campaign, but their influence did not appear to be as significant as *satyagraha*. Even for those who sought to provide a creative alternative ideology, Gandhi was a constant referent. In other words, Gandhi's concept of *satyagraha* remained critically important both as a discourse and as a practical model for organizing people for political action, especially as other possibilities for a different ideological route to freedom were always nipped in the bud, presumably because they were suicidal for the multi-class nationalist mobilization. Hence Gandhi and his colleagues always endorsed the national democratic ideology. *Satyagraha* appeared appropriate in an effort to sustain, if not strengthen, Gandhi's ideological character without radically disrupting its core. It was therefore obvious that, although peasants and workers emerged as separate constituencies in the nationalist politics by the early 1920s, they were always represented by the Congress and mobilized for the Gandhi-led political campaign for freedom. Other issues relevant to the workers and peasantry were appropriated to advance the national democratic goal of the Indian National Congress. For instance, the commitment to national democracy was so genuine and firm that the Congress involvement in the working-class movement for a better deal from the industrialists was always half-hearted.[67] As a result, the workers were as alienated as the peasantry, who never became an integral part of the nationalist platform, at least examples from Bengal clearly illustrate where the peasant response was articulated in both communal and ideologically radical terms.[68] Gandhism thus provided the conception of a national framework of politics 'in which the peasants are mobilized but do not participate, of a nation of which they are a part, but a national state from which they are for ever distanced'.[69]

There is no doubt that Gandhism was a hegemonic influence in the Indian nationalist movement. On most occasions, the Mahatma authored and scripted the anti-British political campaign in accordance with what he stood for ideologically. This is one part of the story. The other equally important part concerns the diverse nature of the movements which purportedly drew on Gandhian *satyagraha*. In other words, there was a clear hiatus between the actual articulation of the movements at the grassroots and the ideology that appeared to have inspired the participants. Suggestive of 'autonomy of politics', the Gandhian instructions were translated differently by those involved in *satyagraha*, which ran, on occasions, counter to the basic precepts of Gandhism. Although Gandhism was the most effective organizing principle for the mass movement, its texture varied from one location to another within each particular movement. What this suggests is that, in the articulation of a movement, Gandhian intervention was crucial and yet its ability to shape the movement at the grassroots was highly restricted, probably indicating the role of the local organizers in demarcating its ideological contour. Gandhi was highly significant in defusing fear from the grassroots activists who dared to defy the authority in the name of the Mahatma. But when movements were articulated they, on various occasions, flouted the core idea of *ahimsa*, for instance, thus justifying the autonomy of Gandhi's social and political ideas. Gandhi was interpreted creatively by the participants, keeping in mind the importance of the locally relevant social, political and economic issues, which easily mobilized the people for the nationalist cause. Despite undermining the basic precepts of Gandhism, Gandhi always remained a significant referent even in those movements which were hardly Gandhian either in content or spirit and yet justified as having derived from the Mahatma.

It is difficult to deal with the remarkably large number of socio-political movements in India during the nationalist struggle in which Gandhi figured prominently either as a leader or as one providing the ideology. Hence I shall be dealing selectively with three major pan-Indian nationalist campaigns – the Non-Cooperation, the Civil Disobedience and the Quit India Movements – which Gandhi launched and directed. What is theoretically innovative and intellectually refreshing is the way these movements were articulated at the grassroots by the local political activists in accordance with their priorities by redefining the core ideas of Gandhi's social and political philosophy. In other words, as in organizing movements, Gandhi also remained crucial in their sustenance, even though their nature was often at variance with what the Mahatma stood for.

Non-violence as a means of political action

Is non-violence as a means of political action a product of a particular historical conjuncture? The answer is probably 'yes'. In the midst of the 'Extremist challenge', which was confined to the noble deeds of the revolutionary terrorists, non-violence appeared to be a unique method of involving the masses regardless of religion and caste, thus extending the constituency of the nationalist politics. Hence Gandhi's arrival on the political scene was well tuned to the requirements of the day for reasons connected with the peculiar historical circumstances, which highlighted anti-British counter-offensive in the context of a mass euphoria. What is argued here is that Gandhi, with his method of non-violence, appeared invincible probably due to a peculiar combination of socio-economic and politico-cultural forces in which no method other than non-violence could gain currency.

Gandhi as a phenomenon is an offshoot of a process which began in South Africa in the late nineteenth century. Like any other political activist, nurtured in the Enlightenment tradition of knowledge,[70] Gandhi also found himself, as a colonial subject, fashioned in the loyalist discourse. Despite his strong feeling against the racist South African government, Gandhi articulated his bitterness during the 1890s in a language which appeared mild in contrast to that of the Mahatma who would effectively challenge the edifice of colonialism both as a system of thought and governance. Interestingly, the speeches and writings in which he justified his role as a colonial subject constitute what can be termed 'a classic text of collaborationist nationalism'.[71] The following excerpt seems apt in this context:

> If an unflinching devotion to duty and extreme eagerness to serve our sovereign can make us of any use in the field of battle, we trust, we would not fail. . . .
>
> The motive underlying this humble offer is to endeavour to prove that, in common with other subjects of the Queen Empress in South Africa, the Indians too, are ready to do duty for their Sovereign on the battlefield. The offer is meant to be an earnest of the Indian loyalty.[72]
>
> . . . the English-speaking Indians came to the conclusion that they would offer their services unconditionally and absolutely without payment . . . in order to show the colonists that they were worthy subjects of the Queen.[73]

Besides defining self-subjection of the colonized, these excerpts, with phrases like 'eagerness to serve' and the offer of 'their services unconditionally and absolutely without payment' are both a description and measure of the social distance between the colonizer and the colonized.[74] What is evident here is that Gandhi, who grew up in the tradition of loyalist discourse, defended his argument by reference to the duty of the subject race to the Empire in crisis. Even as a subordinated nation, Gandhi unequivocally championed the demands for the rights of South African Indians because, as British subjects, Indians were entitled to rights.[75] This is probably a watershed in Gandhi's political thinking, because he was no longer prepared to be unconditionally loyal to the British paramountcy. What can be argued here is that the South African experience appeared significant in identifying the limitations of a racist administration *vis-a-vis* the subject race. Here began the transformation of Gandhi from a loyalist whose 'loyalty to the empire drove him to the side of the British during the Boer war in the teeth of opposition from some of his countrymen'[76] to a most effective political leader, who would challenge the continuity of the Raj in the subcontinent of India by organizing non-violent mass campaigns in opposition to the mighty imperial power. By asserting the rights of the subject people, Gandhi therefore moved from loyalism to opposition to the British rule. Hence what began as a stray reference became an important feature of Gandhian political thought that was to unfold later. Similarly non-violence as a means of political action acquired new dimensions in the light of changes in Gandhi himself, who asserted, though within the constraints of bargaining and pressure politics, subjects' right to rebel.

Non-violence: definition

Semantically, non-violence means refraining from causing harm and destruction to others and is thus a negative concept. For Gandhi, however, non-violence connotes positive resistance – probably an appropriate method to politically mobilize Indians against the British at a particular juncture of history. Not only is the method well tuned to the Indian situation, it is also a means to build character in conformity with the well-entrenched Indian tradition. So, despite its apparent negative content, non-violence, in its positive and active sense, results in organization for political action which is grounded in compassion and love. Drawing on the Hindu, Buddhist and Jainist traditions, Gandhi seems to have arrived at an all-encompassing definition of non-violence by means of three crucial steps:[77] (i) non-violence, in Gandhi's explanation, is compassion which is equated with love; (ii) like all other emotions, love constitutes a formidable force; and (iii) love is thus an alternative to the prevalent ideology for political mobilization. While endorsing these basic characteristics, Gandhi thus elaborated:

> [b]efore you aspire to drive the British from this country, you must drive every vestige of violence from your system. Remember that it is not going to be a fight with sticks and knives or guns, but only with love. Until you are sure you have an overpowering love at heart for your enemy, don't think of driving him out. You must generally forget the term 'Enemy'. You must think of him as a friend who must leave you. You must train yourself to become a hundred per cent *ahimsa* soldier. You must become so sensitive that it is not possible for you to wear sandals of the hide of slaughtered animals; you should prefer to go barefoot rather than wear the hide of an animal killed for your sake, that is if you are unable to secure the skin of an animal that had died a natural death.[78]

What is significant here is Gandhi's ability to translate natural human emotions and feelings into an all-pervasive and powerful ideology which broadened the base of Indian nationalism by incorporating new social groups into nationalist politics.

Although non-violence is derived from the traditional Indian *ahimsa* (non-violence), in Gandhi's view it is separate from the age-old connotation. He was categorical on a number of occasions by arguing that 'complete non-violence means complete cessation of all activity. Not such, however, is my definition of nonviolence'.[79] On another occasion, the Mahatma emphatically defended the view that non-violence is not merely an individual value but could also be a rule of conduct for the collectivity. In his words, 'nonviolence is not cloistered virtue to be practised by the individual for his peace and final salvation, but a rule of conduct for society if it is to live consistently with human dignity'.[80] He carried the argument further by making non-violence obligatory on all. He observed that 'the religion of nonviolence is not meant merely for the *rishis* and saints. It is meant for the common people as well.'[81] Gandhi had no doubt that 'the power of unarmed non-violence is any day far superior to that of armed force. Its superior strength [he realized] in South Africa where [he] had to pit it against organized violence and racial prejudice' of the South African government.[82]

Gandhi was not merely arguing for non-violence as an ideal to be prac-tised. As an activist who challenged the mighty imperial power, he defined non-violence as a political ideology, designed to inspire and mobilize the masses irrespective of caste, class and religion, for the counter-offensive against the British. Insisting on the active participation of the people in the Congress-led nationalist struggle, he exhorted: 'Yours should not be a passive spirituality that spends itself in ideal meditation, but it should be an active thing which will carry war into the enemy's camp.'[83] Non-violence, Gandhi thus argued, 'does not mean meek submission to the will of the evil-doer, but it means the pitting of one's whole soul against the will of the tyrant'.[84] As he further elaborated in his response in *Harijan*,

> non-violence is not mere disarmament. Nor is it the weapon of the weak and impotent. A child who has no strength to wield the lathi [stick] does not practise non-violence. More powerful than all the armaments, non-violence is a unique force that has come into the world. He who has not learnt to feel it to be a weapon infinitely more than brute force has not understood its true nature. This non-violence cannot be 'taught' through word of mouth. But it can be kindled in our hearts through the grace of God, in answer to earnest prayer.[85]

Non-violence was therefore the weapon of those with tremendous mental strength. Adoption of non-violence was not a strategic consideration contin-gent on the circumstances because Gandhi never allowed space for violence in his conceptualization of *satyagraha*. Hence those 'who harbour violence in their breasts and simply await opportunity for its display' had no place in his political campaign. It was necessary, therefore, for Congressmen individ-ually and collectively, Gandhi insisted, 'to examine the quality of their non-violence. If it does not come out of real strength, it would be best and honest for the Congress to make such a declaration and make the necessary changes in its behaviour.'[86] Central to his civil disobedience campaign was non-violence and Gandhi never compromised because, for him, 'the acid test of non-violence is that one thinks, speaks and acts non-violently, even when there is the gravest provocation to be violent'.[87]

Gandhi's defence of non-violence seems a derivative one in the sense that he drew upon the Hindu, Buddhist and Jainist traditions, besides the Euro-pean influence, while developing his ideology. By consistently arguing for non-violence, the Mahatma developed a political discourse in which non-violence is always championed against violence. His preference for *ahimsa* is a conscious choice because, according to him, the use of violence is futile because it does not secure a genuine change at all. In his words, 'violence may destroy one or more bad rulers, but like *Ravana's* head, others will pop up in their places for the root lies elsewhere. It lies in us. If we reform ourselves, the rulers will automatically do so.'[88] Gandhi's undiluted faith in changing the attitude of the rulers may not sound plausible in the context of the British atrocities unleashed in the wake of a nationalist struggle which had discarded violence altogether. What Gandhi probably hinted at was its limitation in transforming social relations simply because hatred and enmity, instead of containing animosity, create and sustain a situation where violence alone can flourish.

Although Gandhi was a true apostle of non-violence, he on occasions upheld violence in preference to cowardice. He observed: '[w]here there is only a choice between cowardice and violence, I would advise violence'.[89] Non-violence, he asserted, 'is not a cover for cowardice ... [it] requires far greater bravery than swordsmanship'.[90] For a coward, bravery is incomprehensible because 'he is less than [a] man' and he therefore 'does not deserve to be [a] member of a society of men and women'.[91] Having distinguished cowardice from non-violence, Gandhi justified the application of violence if an individual 'cannot protect himself or his nearest and dearest or their honour by nonviolently facing death, [he] may and ought to do so by violently dealing with the oppressor. He who can do neither of the two is a burden.'[92] Explicit in Gandhi's statement is his unequivocal support for violence as a means under specific circumstances. Here probably lies the root of Gandhi sometimes being evoked to justify happenings where violence had triumphed despite constant vigil by the Congress high command which, true to the spirit of non-violence, never approved political campaigns opposing the Gandhian creed. These perhaps illustrated either the limitation of non-violence as an effective ideology at the all-India level or the autonomy of politics at various levels of the nationalist movement where *ahimsa*, in contrast to other prevalent ideologies, failed significantly so far as political mobilization was concerned. There were occasions, as the discussion below shows, when the Congress nationalists consciously resorted to violence with the understanding that Gandhi would have approved of violence under those circumstances. A remarkable twist in the shape of an irony of history is thus evident. Gandhi the leader was readily acceptable and political action defying non-violence was also justified in his name. Gandhism, the ideology, however, was being questioned and even jettisoned in several cases where *ahimsa* was eclipsed and other ideologies blossomed.

Notwithstanding arguments and counter-arguments, non-violence remained integrally connected with Gandhi's value system despite heavy odds. Able to justify convincingly that non-violence meant active involvement in India's freedom struggle, Gandhi had thus introduced a new dimension to Indian nationalism, which had hitherto failed to provide a united resistance due to infighting among the nationalists on ideological grounds.

So Gandhi's appearance on the political scene transformed the nature of the anti-British campaign. Not only did he put forward a new ideology in otherwise adverse circumstances, he also personified the qualities of a political leader who transcended the limitations of the day by virtue of his charisma. What seems significant here is Gandhi's capacity to absorb the traditional Indian value system in order to construct an ideology in which Indians, regardless of religion and other primordial schisms, believed themselves well represented. Politically, it appears, no other ideology was likely to reinvigorate the freedom struggle against British repression as *ahimsa* did in the context of the feud among the nationalists due to ideological cross-currents.

Non-violence as a method

For Gandhi, the adoption of non-violence as a method of political action was probably most expedient because, as he himself admitted: 'We do not know how to handle arms. It is not our fault, it is perhaps our misfortune that we cannot.'[93] In the course of his direct involvement in the Congress-led nationalist movement, he both tested and consequently perfected the method, which became a singularly important yardstick to the Mahatma in judging the nature of the movement. A deviation from *ahimsa*, as was evident in the later part of the Non-Cooperation Movement of 1920–2, was enough to suspend an otherwise successful anti-British political campaign. With hindsight, his apparent obsession with non-violence was justified in the light of the failures of both the Moderates and the revolutionary terrorists who, despite their dedication and sincerity to the cause of national emancipation, failed to emerge as a formidable political force. Moreover, in the context of the British repression neither the terrorist nor the Moderate method appeared effective.

Between 1920 and 1942, Gandhi was at his most powerful and probably the only acceptable leader in the faction-ridden Congress party. Although his first interaction with the Indian political scene was through the Non-Cooperation Movement, he had begun effective political activity in 1906 in South Africa, where he organized non-violent resistance against the white settlers' racist policies. Mobilizing Indians for a direct but non-violent confrontation with authority, he launched bonfires of registration documents and an Indian march into the prohibited territory. The campaign saw a remarkable unity among the variety of Indians in South Africa, ranging from Muslim traders to low-caste indentured labourers. The South African experience between 1907 and 1914 had thus shown Gandhi how effective a tool non-violence could be in achieving mass mobilization in adverse circumstances.[94]

Before launching the 1920–2 Non-Cooperation Movement, Gandhi had undertaken non-violent campaigns against injustice in three different localities. In the Champaran district of Bihar, he launched non-violent confrontation to redress the grievances of the peasant tenants being forced to grow indigo at disadvantageous terms by white planters. By mobilizing peasants in the Kheda district of Gujarat against the enhancement of land revenue, the South African rebel gave a new twist to the nationalist movement, which soon expanded its constituency by upholding the Ahmedabad Cotton Mill workers' demand for a wage increase in 1918. Despite failure in Kheda, his success in Champaran and Ahmedabad highlighted the effectiveness of non-violent campaigns in the face of large-scale atrocities.[95]

Non-violence attained all-India publicity in the wake of Gandhi's campaign against the Rowlatt Bills.[96] He offered non-violent civil disobedience in the form of *satyagraha* and sought the cooperation of the Moderates on the grounds that 'the growing generation will not be satisfied with petition etc. We must give them something effective. *Satyagraha* is the only way, it seems to me, to stop terrorism. From this point of view, I am justified in seeking your help.'[97] The Rowlatt *satyagraha* failed because the objective of repealing the Rowlatt Bills was not realized. Gandhi suspended the action because it ceased to be non-violent in Gujarat and Punjab. That Gandhi was a true apostle of non-violence was evident with this revocation of the movement once it erupted into violence. Notwithstanding Gandhi's disappointment, the Rowlatt campaign was a breakthrough for him who was so far a stranger in Indian politics. Besides putting him on the centre-stage of nationalist politics, dominated by revolutionary terrorism and Moderates, the 1919 *satyagraha* projected the extent to which *ahimsa* as a means of political action could be effective.

The 1919 Rowlatt *satyagraha* seems to have set the tone of the anti-British campaign. Between 1920 and 1942, not only did Gandhi consolidate his position in the Congress, non-violence also appeared invincible both as an ideology and as a method of political struggle. The 1920–2 Non-Cooperation was Gandhi's answer to those who clung to violence and the Western style of politics. Non-violence was not merely a novel form of direct political action but also an effective alternative to the prevalent Western mode of politics, which appeared stagnant and powerless against the iron rule of British administration. Although Gandhi's overzealous ambition to attain *swaraj* within a year[98] did not materialize, his new form of politics using non-violence as an instrument for mobilization threatened the very foundation of the Empire.[99] Like the Rowlatt *Satyagraha*, Gandhi called off the Non-Cooperation Movement because of a vicious attack on a police station in Uttar Pradesh (UP). However, during the period between August 1920 and February 1922, Gandhi rose as the most powerful leader in the struggle for freedom who, through non-violent non-cooperation, infused new zeal into an otherwise stagnant nationalist politics.[100] In the official correspondence, it was thus noted:

The outstanding feature of the 1920 Nagpur Congress has been the personal domination of Gandhi over all political leaders and followers alike.

He has carried through the policy that he had decided for this Congress without any material modification. All opposition to his views has been overcome without difficulty owing to his strong hold over the bulk of the delegates and visitors with whom his word is law.[101]

Gandhi's remarkable success in the 1920 political offensive can partly be attributed to the Hindu–Muslim consolidation which was possible due to the merger of the Non-Cooperation Movement with the Khilafat cause.[102] The decision to incorporate the Khilafat demands in the Congress-launched Non-Cooperation Movement was an offshoot of the practical consideration of eliciting Muslim support, which would have been impossible otherwise. Although the 1920–2 merger was the last instance of a combined Hindu–Muslim challenge to the British, it nonetheless draws our attention to the consolidation of Muslims as a separate political identity in the nationalist politics. The 'two-nation theory', so far a mental construct, became a reality with the organization of Muslims following the Khilafat ideal, which percolated down to the villages, though the Khaliph was a distant object to the Indian Muslims. Both the Hindus and Muslims therefore agreed to the merger for completely different political considerations. For the Hindus, the Non-Cooperation Movement was a direct nationalist challenge, whereas for the Muslims, it meant an assault on the British who had undermined the institution of the Khaliph elsewhere.

After the collapse of the Non-Cooperation Movement, India seemed to lapse into 'political torpor'; the Hindu–Muslim unity went to pieces; the *Raj* seemed firmly in the saddle; and 'the heady goal of *Swaraj* in a year lay in ruins'.[103] Gandhi's decision to stay away from the nationalist politics in the aftermath of the Non-Cooperation campaign was probably determined by his awareness that 'with the present temper of many Congressmen, with our internal dissensions, with the communal tension ... it may be impossible to offer civil disobedience at this stage in the name of the Congress'. Referring to the situation which culminated in the suspension of the Non-Cooperation Movement because of the Chauri Chaura incident, he insisted in January 1930 that 'a time must come when there may be a fight to the finish with one's back to the wall'.[104] Within two months, in March 1930, however, Gandhi, was prepared to launch the Civil Disobedience Movement, which lasted from 1930 to 1934 with an intermission for most of the year 1931, 'when the Congress negotiated with the *Raj*'.[105]

During the Civil Disobedience campaign, non-violence manifested itself in attacks on the government's salt monopoly and the boycott of foreign cloth. The salt *satyagraha* was all-pervasive, affecting almost all the provinces though, for geographical reasons, there was little opportunity for making salt in some areas except as token gestures. Bombay presidency witnessed the most successful salt campaign, where salt was produced under the protection of a human chain, formed by the Congress volunteers, thereby making it virtually impossible for the police to intervene without resorting to force – thus creating the moral outrage towards the alien administration which the Congress had long been striving to engender. In contrast, the boycott of foreign cloth appeared a more forceful campaign, in that not only did it put moral pressure on those selling foreign cloth in India, it also helped cultivate a constituency among the indigenous manufacturers. In fact, the boycott caused economic hardship as far as the British interest was concerned. Anticipating the adverse consequences of the Congress campaign in this regard, the government expressed concern and accordingly suggested steps to nip the movement in the bud.[106]

Ahimsa had triumphed as a means of political action, though its impact varied in style and intensity from region to region. Bombay and Gujarat were hit the hardest compared with other provinces for reasons connected with their physical location. Unlike the Non-Cooperation Movement, the Civil Disobedience one posed a serious threat to the Raj on a continental scale in terms of numbers, areas and the types of people involved. Despite being a successful anti-British campaign, the 1930–4 movement failed in the sense that the Hindu–Muslim unity, evident during the Non-Cooperation days, was almost absent, except on the frontier where, under Badshah Khan's stewardship, Gandhi's non-violence received a favourable response. In the Muslim-majority provinces like Bengal and Punjab, the campaign lost its vigour largely due to the absence of Muslims. The imperial divide-and-rule policy thus paid off in these two politically vibrant provinces. Alarmed by the consolidation of the Hindu–Muslim schism, the Congress adopted measures which were neutralized, if not defeated, by the internecine feud among the Congressmen in Bengal[107] and the lack of organization in Punjab.[108]

Non-violence, so far a guiding force in the Congress-led freedom struggle, seems to have been largely undermined in the wake of the 1942 Quit India Movement[109] due to circumstances which went beyond Gandhi's control. Although the movement had shown symptoms of a mass upheaval, it collapsed under a fierce imperial retaliation, possible due to the military preparedness of the British in the context of the Second World War. In the absence of the major Congress leaders, including Gandhi, the movement, though shortlived, took a violent turn which *inter alia* provoked ruthless military intervention by the British.[110]

Whatever the attainments of the Congress in the Quit India Movement, it projected a different Gandhi who, in a rather belligerent mood, seemed to have justified any means for fighting the British, especially in his passionate 'do or die' speech. Although reiterating the need for non-violence, the famous 8 August resolution espoused the call for 'mass struggle on nonviolent lines on the widest possible scale' under Gandhi's leadership, with the instruction that, if the Congress leadership was removed by arrest, 'every man and woman who is participating in this movement must function for himself or herself'.[111] Apart from this resolution, Gandhi's statements urging people to fight till death inspired them to resort to means other than *ahimsa* in this last battle against the *Raj*. In his public statements, the Mahatma appears to have appreciated the value of violence when circumstances so demanded. For instance, in a press interview, he urged that 'this orderly disciplined anarchy (in the shape of the British administration) should be removed at any cost and if as a result, there is a complete lawlessness, I would risk it'.[112] In another interview in August 1942, he defended a general strike by exhorting 'if a general strike becomes a dire necessity, I shall not flinch',[113] thus undermining his well-argued justification for trusteeship.

The Quit India campaign, though assuming massive proportions, waned rather quickly at the all-India level. It, continued unabated, however, for at least two years in Midnapur (Bengal), Talcher (Orissa) and Satara (Maharashtra)[114] where both violence and non-violence were resorted to in the name of Gandhi. In the case of Midnapur, as I have shown elsewhere, the Congress volunteers drew upon Gandhi to justify violence as it meant a contribution to the cause of freedom.[115] *Biplabi*, the Congress journal, published in Midnapur, exhorted that the Mahatma would have approved violence in the name of serving the motherland.[116] There are instances when the death penalty was inflicted on those who committed a heinous crime, like raping the village women in order to terrorize. Though the Congress decision ran counter to Gandhi's *ahimsa*, it was nonetheless justified by drawing attention to his writings in which he was reported to have defended violence for protecting women's honour.[117]

The events during the Quit India Movement show that on occasions, Gandhi the person appears insignificant in comparison with the Mahatma, the idea which was thought out and reworked in the popular vision in a completely different way, a way which Gandhi and the Congress high command would never have approved. In an in-depth study of the events in Gorakhpur subsequent to Gandhi's visit in February 1921, it has been demonstrated that 'Gandhi's *Swaraj* . . . appears to have taken shape quite independently of the district leadership of the Congress Party'.[118] Similarly, in Champaran, where the Mahatma launched a successful non-violent resistance against the illegal exaction by the planters, he was reported to have been

> sent into Champaran by the Viceroy, or even the King to redress all the grievances of the *raiyats*. He was said to be about to abolish all the unpopular obligations which the planters imposed on their *raiyats*, so that there was no need to obey the word of any planter any more. A rumour was also in the air that the administration of Champaran was going to be handed over to the Indians themselves and that the British would be cleared out of the district within a few months.[119]

The British administration, taking note of the tremendous influence of Gandhi in shaping the popular psyche, seemed perplexed by the rather rapid

dissemination of Gandhian ideas in the remote areas. That Gandhi was identified as a saviour of the poverty-stricken masses was evident in a police
report mentioning that 'the real power of his name is perhaps to be traced
back to the ideal that [it was] he who got *bedakhli* [illegal exaction] stopped
in Pratapgrah in UP'.[120] Accordingly, the UP peasants were reported to have
believed that Gandhi would 'provide holdings for them through ahimsa'.[121]
These illustrations indicate and probably justify the role of rumour in
underscoring the institutionalized form of politics in the context of a transitional society like India. Underlying this is probably the explanation as to
why the Gandhi-type leadership, exemplified, for instance, in Swami Prajnananda in Bengal, Swami Darshanananda in Bihar or Baba Ramchandra in
Pratapgarh, had strong religious overtones. Besides arguing that these out-
siders established the crucial link between the upper and lower courses of
the nationalist struggle which had its manifestation in both the organized
and unorganized worlds of politics,[122] their involvement brought out
another interesting dimension of the Gandhi-led freedom movement, that
is, the peasants still needed an outsider to organize themselves in a society
going through a period of acute strain and tension due to peculiar circumstances. This argument, if pursued with vigour, is likely to identify significant lapses in the analysis of some of the early writings of the subaltern school
which, while challenging the so-called elitist historiography, tended to
somewhat romanticize the revolutionary potential of the rural masses.[123]

Concluding observations

There was no doubt that Gandhi was able to galvanize the people into action
because he articulated the voice of protest in a much more comprehensible
language than anyone else in the past. He was also able to involve more
people in the nationalist intervention because of an easy acceptance of his
model of conflict resolution by the Indian masses. Gandhism remained
politically relevant simply because of its organic roots in India's social, economic and political circumstances.[124] This was evident time and again.
Whatever the ramifications in leadership, non-violence was easily accepted
by the Indian populace at large probably because *ahimsa* articulated the anti-
British feeling, in the form of *satyagraha*, better than the prevalent ideologies. Furthermore, Gandhi's strategic sense made *satyagraha* a viable mode
of protest. As Ravinder Kumar argued, Gandhi pursued 'class politics' in the
struggles he led in Champaran, Kheda and Ahmedabad, but shifted to 'com-
munitarian politics' in the larger national movement which he launched
against colonialism.[125] The explanation lies in the logic of national democracy that Gandhi and Congress religiously pursued during the freedom
struggle. Class issues were divisive while moral issues appeared to be inte-
grating. Thus from the 1919 Rowlatt *satyagraha* onwards, Gandhi mobilized people on moral issues rather than class issues 'to cement a grand
alliance of Hindus and Muslims, rich and poor . . . the working class and the

industrial magnates ... the zamindars and peasants, in a great struggle against the British Government'.[126]

Moreover, the fact that Gandhi, unlike his predecessors, swayed the masses with well-entrenched Indianness in his lifestyle and political vocabulary, demonstrated his ability to translate the popular grievances into political action in the face of imperial oppression and atrocities. This is part of the story narrating the rise of Gandhi in the context of the freedom struggle. In order to grasp the quintessence of the Mahatma as an organic leader of the nationalist movement, attention should be drawn to the process projecting Gandhism as an ideology which developed through a dialogue with rapidly changing socio-economic and political arrangements. What is noticeable in such a construct is the absence of familiar Gandhian ideas which are justified, in turn, as being in tune with non-violence and its concomitant value system. So what had happened in Chauri Chaura in 1922 and during the Quit India Movement, which defied the fundamental precepts of Gandhism, seemed to be an offshoot of a peculiar interpenetration between ideology and reality. That Gandhism had a firm grip over the mass psyche despite tendencies otherwise was evident with the unconditional submission of those, believing in violence, to the Mahatma in both the above cases. Therefore the eclipse of non-violence and its subsequent triumph merely identify the relative weakness of the contesting ideologies which, though they posed a serious threat to non-violence in Punjab, Maharashtra and Bengal, appeared peripheral at the national level. Hence the historical impact of Gandhism on the evolution of nationalism was immensely significant.

There were innumerable occasions when the Congress-led anti-British campaign largely deviated from non-violence and yet the participants justified their action as being inspired by the Mahatma. So there are several Gandhis – each being interpreted differently according to the priorities of the participants. Translating Gandhism in such a way as to gain maximum mileage, the grassroots leaders articulated the political agenda by attributing the popular grievances to imperialism. Furthermore, the interpretation of Gandhi's ideas also varied in accordance with the preference of the leadership involved in the mobilization for the anti-British offensive. Thus, for instance, one type of leadership, exemplified in Swami Prajnananda in Bengal, Swami Darshanananda in Bihar or Baba Ramchandra in Pratapgarh, invested the Gandhian system of thought with particularly strong religious overtones.

The science of non-violence[127] was the form in which Gandhism addressed itself to the question of nationalism. By sincerely championing *ahimsa*, the Mahatma provided a format for articulating the anti-British sentiments in the form of *satyagraha*, which was probably the most appropriate strategic method of struggle at a particular juncture of India's nation-building.[128] Unlike other prevalent ideologies, Gandhism thus succeeded in providing for the first time in nationalist politics an ideological basis for including the whole people, irrespective of caste, class and creed, in an imaginary construct called 'political nation'. In other words, not only did Gandhian non-violence put up an effective challenge to the British domination, it also created conditions for the inclusion of the largest segment of the nation, namely the peasantry, into the Indian state that was to emerge with the eclipse of imperialism. Gandhism, with its concomitant value system, however, appropriated the peasantry only in so far as it contributed to the nationalist struggle, conceived and directed by the Indian National Congress. Although Gandhi introduced new constituencies in the anti-British political campaign by including both the peasantry and the workers, his endeavour in an otherwise elite-dominated freedom struggle aimed not to train the masses in self-consciousness and the attainment of power by themselves, but to solicit their cooperation in the Congress-led struggle for *swaraj*. That Gandhi succeeded in reinvigorating the 'otherwise sterile' nationalist movement despite the ideological limitations of what he offered through non-violence indicated the extent to which 'national democracy' triumphed and other ideologies were marginalized. Notwithstanding the anti-Gandhi wave in independent India, Gandhi appeared invincible in whatever he undertook between 1920 and 1942, primarily because of his physical and mental affinity with the traditions and temperament of the Indian masses, which yielded results in the context of a volatile socio-economic and political order.

3 Politics and ideology
Critique of Gandhi

There are three Gandhis that appear to have emerged in India during the freedom struggle. *First*, the Gandhi of South Africa, who rose to prominence after his successful *satyagraha* campaign in Natal and Transvaal against the racist Asiatic Registration Act. Not only did he articulate *satyagraha*, his personality took shape in South Africa. There is no doubt that Indian freedom struggle was conducted on a much larger scale and on much bigger issues, but his South African experiment contributed immensely to his ideas that gradually evolved in the context of his struggle against colonialism in India. *The second Gandhi* was crystallized during and after the 1919–21 Non-Cooperation Movement in India. What he learnt in South Africa was applied on a wider scale, involving Hindus and Muslims in his *satyagraha* campaign. Although what brought the Muslims to the nationalist campaign was largely the Khilafat cause, there is no doubt that this was perhaps the most significant mass movement where the centre of gravity shifted to the villages, unlike in the past when the anti-British movements were confined mostly to the urban centres of Calcutta and Bombay. For whatever reasons, the strength of the Non-Cooperation lay in the Hindu–Muslim amity. *The third Gandhi*, perhaps the most complex and thus theoretically innovative, was shaped by the events and socio-economic and political processes of the period following the withdrawal of the Non-Cooperation Movement in the wake of the Chauri Chaura incident. Muslims rose as a distinct political group demanding their share by virtue of their demographic preponderance in Bengal and Punjab. The *Harijans* or the untouchables had found in B.R. Ambedkar an able leader who could confront the leading nationalist forces, including the Congress and the British, demanding a legitimate place in society and politics. The Congress was not as united as it was before; it was fractured due to ideological incompatibility among those who remained loyal to Gandhi in the past. The 1939 Tripuri Congress in which Subhas Chandra Bose, a *bête noire* of Gandhi, defeated the official Congress candidate for presidency, brought out the rivalry between the left and right wings in the Congress. Gandhi was placed in peculiar circumstances where he appeared to have lost control of the organization. Despite the temporary hiccups that undoubtedly affected the Congress adversely, Gandhi regained control with the support of the right-wingers, who gradually shifted their loyalty away from the Mahatma as India's freedom struggle drew to a close. This is a phase when Gandhi, so far the supreme leader of India's freedom struggle, spoke in a vocabulary that redefined some of his basic precepts concerning, for example, non-violence. Furthermore, he upheld views that ran counter to those he had espoused in the past, especially before the 1930–4 Civil Disobedience Movement.[1] Apart from the transformed nature of the imperial power, one possible explanation for the changes in Gandhi's social and political ideas may have been his interaction with colleagues who held views contrary to his own. Not only did he negotiate with the ruling authority with his reformed political agenda, he engaged in regular dialogues with those who, while appreciating Gandhi's contribution to the nationalist struggle, critiqued his conceptual framework to analyze India's complex socio-economic reality. It would be difficult, if not impossible, to study all those who expressed views on Gandhi. Hence the aim of this chapter is to identify and critically evaluate the major trends in critiques of Gandhi by those leading personalities with different perspectives on nationalism and other relevant socio-economic and political issues with a strong bearing on the former.

The chapter draws on the critiques by M.N. Roy, Rabindranath Tagore and B.R. Ambedkar simply because not only are they refreshing theoretical interventions, but they also helped Gandhi reformulate some of the ideas that he had held so dear in his earlier writings. While Roy provides a Marxist critique of Gandhi, Ambedkar evaluates Gandhi on the basis of his conceptualization of distributive justice that privileged 'the untouchables' or *dalits* over others. Tagore's critique of Gandhi is perhaps the most creative response, which is both indigenous and Western-influenced. These varied critiques influenced Gandhi dialectically and on occasions transformed his ideas. So the blueprint for a future India that the Mahatma sought to articulate was reflective of various different but authentic influences. Here lies the significance of the dialogue that Gandhi had with his colleagues on issues of socio-economic and political importance. Notwithstanding the significant contribution of M.A. Jinnah in articulating the idea of a sovereign state for the Muslims, this chapter does not deal with his critique of Gandhi for two reasons: a) the critical literature on this theme is plentiful and hence the discussion will be merely repetitive; and b) since both Jinnah and Gandhi were primarily political activists it would be improper to deal with the dialogue without contextualizing the issues that figured in their discussion. Just like Gandhi, Jinnah too carved out an independent place in the Indian freedom struggle that culminated in the bifurcation of British India following his two-nation theory.[2]

Ideas do not emerge in a vacuum. The context seems to play a significant, if not determining role in the dialogue that unfolded in pursuance of the freedom struggle in India. In other words, the political ideas of Gandhi, Roy, Tagore and Ambedkar were rooted in the larger socio-economic and political processes in the nineteenth and twentieth centuries. The socio-historical and cultural perspective of British India remained, for obvious reasons, a constant reference to M.N. Roy, Rabindranath Tagore and B.R. Ambedkar. Gandhi conceptualized a model that, for a variety of reasons, gained currency both as a nationalist strategy for political mobilization and a blueprint for India's future. Drawing on their respective beliefs and ideas, Roy, Tagore and Ambedkar put forward their views both in contrast and juxtaposition with that of Gandhi and in that sense, the Mahatma appears to have broadly set the discourse and its articulation. Although the ideologically inspired critiques of Gandhi by Roy, Tagore and Ambedkar articulated different voices, they were nonetheless largely theoretical because none had been involved in the nationalist movement as organically as Gandhi. What was unique about Gandhi was his ability to guide the nation towards a goal following a model which the Mahatma articulated on the basis of his experience as a practitioner of different kinds of politics.

The aim of the following discussion is therefore twofold: a) to underline the distinctive issues that figured in the dialogue; and b) to identify, if possible, the conceptual basis of the arguments which they made either in their defence or to counter the Mahatma.

M.N. Roy and Gandhi

M.N. Roy (1887–1954)[3] provides perhaps the best and well-argued Marxist critique of Gandhi's social and political ideas. What was evident in the Congress in the 1920s, especially following the appearance of the Mahatma, is clearly articulated by Roy while commenting on the socio-economic circumstances of India under colonialism. In expressing his views, Roy stands apart because of his attempt at conceptualizing nationalism from the Marxist point of view. Apart from his ideological conviction, the larger colonial context seemed to have cast obvious significant influences on Roy's radicalism, which sought to redefine the ideological goal of the national bourgeoisie in India. So Roy was significantly different from other radicals due to his attempt to mix nationalism with what he drew from Marxism. This also gave a peculiar theoretical twist to Roy's conceptualization of radicalism, underlining the impact of both nationalist and Marxist ideas. In other words, this conceptualization, drawing on nationalism and Marxism, brings out its innovative nature, identifying 'both the astonishing daring of Roy's radicalism, and a tragic heteronomy within its historical consciousness'.[4]

Inspired by revolutionary terrorism, Roy was politically baptized when he was entrusted with the task of receiving a German steamer carrying arms for the terrorists. This 1914 attempt to smuggle arms in ships failed and the plan for an armed insurrection against the British was aborted. An attempt to procure arms from China also failed. Inducted into the revolutionary terrorist movement in Bengal, Roy appears to have endorsed the 'terrorist' methods in the nationalist campaign for freedom. This allegiance was, however, shortlived. As he himself realized, these revolutionary organizations could be easily crushed and prevented 'from constituting any serious danger because they relied more upon conspiracies than upon revolutionary social forces'.[5] Roy escaped to America where he was introduced to socialist ideas and went on to participate in the formation of the Mexico Communist Party. It was his involvement in the Mexico Communist Party which gave him an opportunity to take part in the Second Congress of the Communist International. In 1927, he redefined Lenin's draft thesis on the national and colonial question, which immediately made him a celebrity in the political circle. While elaborating his views on national and colonial question, he argued:

> it will be necessary to examine which social class is the most revolutionary in the respective country so as to make the contact with this social class and in this manner to rally the entire people and to support it in its struggle against Imperialism. If we do not consider the problem from this viewpoint, we will make no headway at all.... The only way to fulfill the great task of [revolution] is through the organization of the exploited classes to become the revolutionary parties of the people.[6]

As a representative of the (Communist) International, he led, in 1926, a delegation to China. Soon he fell out with the International Communist leadership and was expelled from the Comintern in 1929. Roy returned to India in 1930 with the sole goal of participating in the nationalist struggle. During the 1930–40 period, he was involved in the nationalist movement. The honeymoon was over by 1940, when Roy founded his own party, known as the Radical Democratic Party, seeking to provide a combined platform involving peasants, workers and petty bourgeoisie. By 1948, he dismantled his party and founded a new movement for a radical or new humanism.

As evident from this small biographical account, Roy's political journey, from revolutionary terrorism to radical humanism, allowed him to conceptualize radicalism in different perspectives. His critical alternative to Lenin's draft thesis on nationalism and colonialism is based on his attempt to understand Marxism in the context of colonialism. Opposed to the ideology of the Indian National Congress, he suggested that the future of the Indian liberation movement depended on the participation of the neglected sections of society. While commenting on the new basis of the national struggle, Roy thus exhorted:

> the future of Indian politics [of national liberation] will ... be determined by the social forces which still remain and will always remain antagonistic to Imperialism even in the new era dominated by the 'higher ideals of Swaraj within the Empire'.[7]

He was convinced, as his draft thesis on nationalism and the colonial question demonstrates, that 'the mass movements in the colonies are

growing independently of the nationalist movements [and] the masses distrust the political leaders who always lead them astray and prevent them
from revolutionary action'.[8] While pursuing this argument further, he also
underlined the growing importance of the proletariat in political movements against imperialism. Critical of 'the bourgeois national democrats in
the colonies', Roy was in favour of supporting

> revolutionary mass action through the medium of a communist party of
> the proletarians [that] will bring the real revolutionary forces to action
> which will not only overthrow the foreign imperialism but lead progres-
> sively to the development of Soviet power, thus preventing the rise of
> native capitalism in place of the vanquished foreign capitalism, to
> further oppress the people.[9]

This overall assessment of the national and colonial question appears to have
provided the basic theoretical framework Roy used in assessing Gandhi and
his political ideology. Gandhism was, according to him, the most important
of all the ideologies of class collaborations within the nationalist movement.
Since it 'will fall victim to its own contradictions',[10] the Indian national
movement actuated by the spirit of non-violence was bound to fail. The
inability of the Mahatma to comprehend the changing nature of the social
and political forces opposed to the prevalent nationalist movement remained
at the root of its failure. Sharing Gandhi's criticism of capitalist civilization,
Roy was also, however, critical of the alternative that Gandhi offered, simply
because it was neither 'realistic' nor 'practicable'. He further argued that
'one need not be a sentimental humanitarian, nor a religious fanatic in order
to denounce the present order of society in the countries where capitalism
rules'. Capitalism was unavoidable and 'will not collapse because sentimental humanitarians find it full of cruelty and injustice, [but because] of its
own contradictions'.[11] Illustrative of 'the satanic western civilization', the
British rule in India provided the most obvious missing link in India's
growth as a national economy. Gandhi's role was significant in conceptualizing the adverse economic impact on India of capitalism, which was fever-
ishly introduced into the sub continent in the form of large capitalist
industries at the cost of handicrafts and other indigenous efforts. Not only
did he articulate the devastating nature of Western capitalism, he also radically altered the nature of the anti-British political campaign of the Moderate
and Extremist varieties. While analyzing the success of Gandhi in mobilizing people in the 1919 anti-Rowlatt *satyagraha*, Roy pointed out:

> by inaugurating the campaign of Satyagraha (passive resistance to evil),
> an active vent was given to the Opposition, which could thus transcend
> the limits of mere indignation-meetings and passing resolutions of
> protest. Devoid of any other weapons to fight the British government,
> the Indian people were provided with a way of making their energy felt

by the opponent. Gandhi postulated that the Indian people would 'refuse to obey these ... and other such laws', but at the same time 'faithfully follow the truth and refrain from violence to life, person and property'.... For the first time in its history, the Indian national movement entered into the period of active struggle, and in doing so it had to call upon the masses of the people.[12]

So Gandhi represented a clear departure from the past. Despite the limited goals of *satyagraha* due to its inherent weaknesses, it had 'penetrated the villages, it had rudely shaken the resignation of the masses'. There was no doubt of Gandhi's contribution to the articulation of this mass movement, characterized by Roy as 'a huge popular upheaval', caused essentially by 'economic exploitation not alone by imperial capital, but by native agencies as well'. Roy therefore concluded that 'the imminent popular upheaval', inspired by Gandhi and organized on the principles, he devised, was 'a social outburst, the rise of a socially revolutionary force uncompromising, unrelenting, implacable, which would mark the commencement of the inevitable class war'.[13] As evident, Roy was critical of the ideology of non-violence and *satyagraha* for being politically restrictive; and yet he found in Gandhi the most effective political leadership in extending the constituencies of nationalist politics by involving the peripheral sections of society.

For him, non-violence was a cloak 'to serve the interests of those who have built castles of social privilege and economic exploitation. If the end of nationalism is to glorify the privileged few, then non violence is certainly useful; but to nationalism of a broader kind, which is the expression of the desire of the entire Indian people, it is a positive hindrance.'[14] The cult of non-violence was a convenient tool for both the Gandhi-led nationalist political forces as well as those supporting imperialism. Hence Roy predicted that both these forces 'will bury their hatchet [in due course] in order to carry on the crusade against those forces of revolution which menace the security of vested interests'.[15] The idea of non-cooperation that drew on non-violence was just a cloak to pursue the narrow vested interests at the cost of the majority. Quoting an editorial in the *Amrita Bazar Patrika*, Roy argued that Gandhi did not invent the strategy of non-cooperation. What he did was simply

> to find organized and outer expression to the latent discontent in the country. Gandhi saw the danger of this latent discontent. He did not want that this discontent should be left to itself and burst out in fatal physical revolt or revolution.... This was the true inwardness of his campaign.[16]

It was clear to Roy that the non-violence was tuned to protecting the vested interests and non-cooperation was the best strategy to contain the revolutionary fervour of the masses. In other words, this strategy was ideologically governed and dictated in order to 'thwart the development of dynamic revolutionary forces which threaten to push Indian nationalism dangerously farther than the so-called politically-minded middle class desired it to go'.[17] By drawing attention to the sudden withdrawal of the Non-Cooperation Movement, Roy sought to prove his point. According to him, Gandhi called off the movement because he apprehended a revolutionary outburst challenging the ideological basis of the Non-Cooperation Movement. In his words, 'with one single breath, the Mahatma thus blows up the beautiful castle built so laboriously during all these years of storm and stress'.[18] Not only did he stall a revolutionary upsurge, he also became an instrument in the hands of the colonial power to contain those movements threatening its very foundation. As Roy put it, Gandhi was immediately released as soon as the movement was withdrawn simply because the government understood that 'he will be a very valuable asset in the coming game of "change of heart"'.[19] Furthermore, in releasing Gandhi, the government was not generous but calculating because 'none will appreciate this act of generosity more than the Mahatmaji who will pay it back [in some form or another] when required'.[20]

Critical of Gandhi's *swaraj*, which he considered doomed to fail because 'the time is gone when the people could be inspired by a vague promise of Swaraj', Roy further outlined the programme of a revolutionary nationalist party in the following way:

a   nationalist independence: complete break from the empire; a democratic republic based on universal suffrage;
b   abolition of feudalism and landlordism;
c   nationalization of land; none but the cultivator will have the right of landholding;
d   modernization of agriculture by state aid;
e   nationalization of mines and public utilities;
f   development of modern industries;
g   protection of workers; minimum wages; eight-hour day; abolition of child labour; insurance; and other advanced social legislation;
h   free and compulsory primary education;
i   freedom of religion and worship;
j   rights of minorities.

As the programme suggests, Roy provided a critical alternative to the Congress-led nationalist movement that was more 'reconciliatory' and less 'revolutionary'. These programmes are mere reiteration of what he had written in his *India in Transition* in 1922 while outlining the meaning of *swaraj*. In the aftermath of the Non-Cooperation Movement, the Congress, as Roy believed, appeared to have lost its revolutionary potential for two reasons: a) the Congress lacked a revolutionary leadership; and b) it had lost the support of the masses. Roy recommended that, in order to regain its strength, the Congress should go to the trade unions and the peasant Sabhas; listen to the grievances there discussed; and incorporate them into a truly constructive programme to draw the masses once more into the folds of the Congress Party, to fight under its command for Swaraj.[21] Critical of Gandhian *swaraj* as it evolved in the aftermath of the 1919–21 Non-Cooperation Movement, Roy was convinced that this Congress-led movement was bound to fail since it aimed at protecting the exploiting classes, ignoring 'the political rights of the workers and peasants'. As a Marxist, he also felt the need to join hands with 'the proletariats' elsewhere, otherwise these movements remained just ripples. He suggested that 'the revolutionary nationalists should, therefore, not only join hands with the Indian workers and peasants, but should establish close relations with the advanced proletariat of the world'.[22] By attributing the abject poverty in India to the British policy of 'forcibly making India an agricultural adjunct to industrial Britain', Roy was, for obvious reasons, critical of the dominion status within the Empire. Hence he argued that 'neither Self-government realized progressively by Non Cooperation will change the economic condition of the toiling [masses] . . . Therefore, the interests of the majority demand *complete separation from all imperial connection and the establishment of a Republican State* based on the democratic principles of *Universal Suffrage*' (emphasis original).[23]

Roy made a thorough analysis of Gandhi's constructive programme which, he felt, was totally inadequate for India's 'economic salvation'. The constructive programme was announced by the Congress Working Committee on 12 February, 1922 at Bardoli[24] immediately after the events at Chauri Chaura where violence broke out in the wake of the Non-Cooperation Movement. Gandhi had a significant role in articulating the constructive programme since the Bardoli resolution vested in him the full powers of the All-India Congress Committee. In order to ensure the economic well-being of the masses, the constructive programme included a) *charkha*; b) *khaddar*; c) removal of untouchability; and d) fight against alcohol consumption. While the first two programmes were essentially economic in nature, the others addressed social problems with economic implications. There was no doubt that the campaign against the removal of untouchability and drinking alcohol made people aware of the adverse implications of these social evils. But the *charkha–khaddar* programme was, as M.N. Roy was convinced, doomed to fail due to its obvious adverse economic consequences on the consumers. Two basic requirements for its success were a) *charkha* must be introduced into every house; and b) *khaddar* must be worn by all. These conditions could never be met since *charkha* was not as popular as was conceived and *khaddar* cost more than mill-made cloth. Given the cost of *khaddar* being beyond the capacity of Indian workers and peasants, this campaign was bound to fail. Taking into account the average income of the Indian workers and peasants, argued Roy, *khaddar* could never become an attractive proposition in the nationalist campaign. Their paltry income never got them 'the minimum quantity of clothing' they needed; they also 'cannot be expected to go naked rather than wearing "the unholy" foreign stuff'. Roy also reminded Gandhi that the forcible application of home-spun during the *swadeshi* campaign had been responsible for the movement's decline. 'Sentiment can keep a movement going for a certain length of time', Roy further underlined, 'but it cannot last forever unless fed with more substantial factors.'[25] Similarly, Gandhi's insistence on *charkha* was based on hollow economic logic. In other words, as not economically viable, the fate of *charkha* was equally sealed. As he explained, since its high price was daily restricting the sale of *khaddar* and also the market for home-spun yarn, its manufacture thus gradually became economically unviable. So, the future of *charkha* was uncertain since *khaddar* never became an automatic choice for the masses due to its inherent limitations. Unless *charkha–khaddar* was made economically viable, 'propaganda for the revival of cottage industry does not prepare the people for a purely political movement'.[26]

The other two items, namely, the removal of untouchability and the campaign against alcohol consumption, might have had propaganda value, but were hardly effective, as Roy underlined, for two reasons: first, given the historically well-entrenched prejudices against those identified as untouchables, 'no amount of ethical propagandizing' struck at the foundation of such an age-old practice. What was required was a constant campaign, coupled with changes in the mode and relations of production to redefine interpersonal relationships by challenging 'the prejudices' as harmful for India's evolution as 'a healthy polity'. Likewise, it was difficult, if not impossible, to counter effectively, simply by sermon, the drinking habit that provided the poor with a handy device 'to drown their sorrows in unconsciousness'.[27]

Roy's analysis of Gandhi's constructive programmes clearly suggests his view of them as basically verbal and couched in sentiment, rather than as effective programmes involving the masses. In view of these serious weaknesses, the programmes thus failed to achieve the goals that the Mahatma had so assiduously set for the masses. According to Roy, these programmes 'should be such as to appeal to the immediate interests of the masses of the people'.[28] For him, the non-payment of taxes that already had galvanized the peasants in UP, Bengal and Punjab into action should be pursued with zeal. Advising the Congress to adopt the agenda of the masses, Roy recommended that 'the preparatory work consists of demonstrating practically and not by sentimental humanitarian cant, that the Congress is the leader of the worker and peasant population. [Only then] Civil Disobedience can be inaugurated with all the possibilities of a revolutionary development.'[29] As demonstrated, Roy carved a space for himself by providing a critique of Gandhi's social and economic ideas. Despite his admiration for Gandhi, who he believed had infused India's struggle for independence with a new zeal, Roy was perhaps one of those few never swayed by the charisma of the Mahatma when it involved social, economic and political issues affecting the masses. Hence, his critique remains a significant intervention underlining both the weaknesses and the natural strength of the ideology that the Mahatma sought to articulated as an activist-theoretician.

What is clear in Roy's thought is his attempt to conceptualize a response drawing upon Marxism and his specific experiences in the context of the Indian nationalist movement. Gandhi was a constant referent for obvious reasons. In fact, political radicalism acquired a completely different connotation with the growing participation of the so-called 'peripheral' sections of society. As shown, it was during the Non-Cooperation Movement that the constituencies of the Indian National Congress went beyond the cities and educated middle class. M.N. Roy seems to have captured this moment of colonialism in India and provided a theoretical framework that largely drew on Marxism. In other words, by seeking to capture the 'neglected voice' of the people, Roy performed a historical task along with those radicals striving to involve the subalterns in the nationalist movement. Whether his radicalism was politically viable in that particular context is debatable though there is no doubt that his ideas were ideologically refreshing simply because they took into account the growing revolutionary ferment among the masses. Like his radical counterparts in the nationalist movement, Roy put forward a well-argued theoretical model that explained the predicament of the Gandhi-led nationalist leadership due to its failure to comprehend the mass fervour confronting both the colonial power and also the indigenous vested interests. Yet Roy's analysis of Gandhi from a strictly Marxist point of view, though creative, failed to understand 'the cultural power of Gandhi', and the Mahatma's ability to fashion weapons of political struggle out of unorthodox material. This led him to misconstrue what, in retrospect, was the strength of Gandhi's politics as 'an impotent mysticism'.[30]

Rabindranath Tagore and Gandhi

While M.N. Roy evaluated Gandhi's social and political ideas from a specific point of view, partly Marxist and partly eclectic, Rabindranath Tagore, the poet, built his critique on India's cultural heritage and plural ways of life. His critique was based on a certain reading of Indian civilization and the actual political processes that unfolded in the context of the struggle against imperialism. There was another difference: while Gandhi hardly responded to Roy's comments on the Mahatma's views based on his own interpretation, Tagore was in a constant dialogue with the Mahatma. Not only did they interact regularly on various philosophical issues pertaining to India as a civilization – either through personal correspondence or through the media – they also exchanged views on the mundane political agenda of the Indian National Congress. So Tagore's critique was, unlike Roy's, an offshoot of a dialogue, rooted in the contemporary milieu. As a poet not directly involved in the nationalist agitation, Tagore sought to voice the unarticulated concerns of Indian public consciousness. And, obviously, his perspective was different from that of M.N. Roy, who took part in the struggle for freedom in various forms. Perhaps this is the reason why Roy couched his critique in largely politico-economic terms, seeking to identify the weaknesses of Gandhism within the Gandhian parameters, while Tagore was transcendental in his conceptualization, presumably because he drew more on civilizational values about human society and less on worldly socio-political and economic ideas.[31]

Rabindranath Tagore was perhaps the first to emphatically argue against the view that identity in the subcontinent was unidimensional. Challenging the concept of 'nation' as undermining the multi-layered Indian identity, Tagore reminds us of the combined role of the 'little' and 'great' traditions in shaping what he loosely defined as the Indian nation.[32] India's diversity, Tagore felt, was her 'nature [and] you can never coerce nature into your narrow limits of convenience without paying one day very dearly for it'.[33] Not only 'have religious beliefs cut up society into warring sections ... social antagonisms [between the Hindus and Muslims] have set up impassable barriers – barriers which are guarded night and day by forces wearing the badge of religion'.[34] For Tagore, the gulf between the communities was largely due to 'the cultural forces', released by British colonialism, which 'fractured the personality of every sensitive exposed Indian and set up the West as a crucial vector within the Indian self'.[35] As India's social system got distorted, '[l]ife departed', argued Tagore, 'from her social system and in its place she is worshipping with all ceremony the magnificent cage of countless compartments that she has manufactured'.[36] While Tagore was critical of artificial division among the communities, created and consolidated by forces supporting colonialism, he was equally alarmed by the drive to gloss over India's diversity for the sake of creating a nation-state like Europe since this would strike at the very foundation of the civilizational society, which had flourished in India for centuries.[37] Interrogating the 'totalizing' dimension of the nationalist project – where a single entity, called nation, always prevails over other forms of identity – Tagore sought to provide an alternative to an 'essentialistic' invocation of identity in the shape of a nation. According to him, in articulating the civilizational identity of India, the importance of underlying cognitive and ethical claims, which are invariably lodged in and emanate from contradictory social locations, could never be undermined. So the European modular form of nation was conceptually futile and politically inapplicable, presumably because India's civilizational identity was not singular but multiple and thus difficult to capture on a single axis.

Gandhi held identical views. Like Tagore, he rarely used the term 'nation', in the sense that Jinnah referred to it. Yet Gandhi failed to halt the historical processes leading to Indian Muslims becoming a nation and bargaining successfully for a separate Muslim state. Jinnah's role was equally significant. In the penultimate year of the transfer of power, the Jinnah-led Muslim League secured parity with the Congress and, in the 1946 Shimla conference, the League and Congress representation were equated.[38] The

1940 Lahore resolution became feasible. And Jinnah's appeal to 'unsettle the settled notions ... of Muslims being a minority [that] had been around for so long'[39] was finally translated into reality. So, not only did the *Quaid-i-Azam* succeed in dramatically altering the role of the Muslims in the overall constitutional settlement on the eve of the Great Divide, he also transformed the Muslim community into a nation[40] by ascertaining 'territorial sovereignty to a heterogeneous community turned homogeneous nation'.[41] The Muslim community for Jinnah was, therefore, not 'an abstract historical-political entity ... but a separate nation with distinct interests [which] could not be treated only as a minority'.[42]

Gandhi's opposition to the concept of nation was based on two specific arguments: first, his contextual argument insisted that the logic of creating a religion-based nation-state was faulty because religion could be neither 'a stabilizing nor a unifying factor in humanity', but 'divisive'. So, by seeking to gloss over the obvious diversities among the Indian Muslims for a sovereign state, Jinnah ignored the long drawn-out historical processes in the community formations. For Gandhi, nation was hardly a criterion to conceptualize the complex and deeply heterogeneous communities in the subcontinent regardless of religion. Couched in a humanitarian fashion, the second argument dwells on the devastating consequences of conceptualizing Hindus and Muslims as separate nations. Holding politics responsible for the Hindu–Muslim schism, Gandhi pledged to 'rescue people from this quagmire and make them work on solid ground where people are people. [Therefore his] appeal [was] not to the Muslims as Muslims nor to the Hindus as Hindus, but to ordinary human beings who [had] to keep their villages clean, build schools for their children and take many other steps so that they [could] make life better'.[43] To Gandhi, as the above passage demonstrates, nation, as a categorizing device, was perhaps the narrowest in its manifestation as it ignored the inherent diversities of the communities. Nation is a project of homogenizing people regardless of historical space and time.[44] Conceptually unviable and practically inappropriate, the application of nation as a category weakened the anti-British struggle due to the clash of interests between the Hindus and Muslims once they were characterized as separate nations.

What Tagore and Gandhi had in common was the idea that nation was totally inapplicable to Indian people.[45] Both of them regarded nationalism as a byproduct of the Western nation-state system and of the forces of homogenization let loose by the Western worldview. To them, 'a homogenized universalism', itself a product of the uprootedness and deculturation brought about by British colonialism in India, struck at the heart of Indian civilization. In contrast with an imported category like nationalism, their alternative was 'a distinctive civilizational concept of universalism embedded in the tolerance encoded in various traditional ways of life in a highly diverse, plural society'.[46] This conceptualization within an absolutely non-nationalist philosophical framework defused the arguments in favour of

Hindu nationalism in the context of the freedom movement in India. So, not only was this critique of nation and nationalism morally acceptable and politically effective, it also laid the foundation of a community-based society drawing on the resources of a civilization of which it was a part.

The honeymoon was shortlived and differences between the poet and the Mahatma loomed large in the course of time. Gandhi launched the Non-Cooperation Movement in 1920. It was based on the idea that, since the continuity of the British government depended on the cooperation of the Indian subjects, it would collapse once the Indians withdrew their support. The programmes involved resignation from government jobs, refusal to participate in government institutions and schools and later to pay taxes as well as the burning of foreign clothes.[47] His idea of burning foreign cloths provoked much unease in Tagore, who wondered if Gandhi was not fanning the flames of narrow nationalism and xenophobia. As he argued,

> the clothes to be burnt are not mine, but belong to those who most sorely need them. If those who are going naked should have given us the mandate to burn, it would, at least, have been a case of self-immolation and the crime of incendiarism would not lie at our door. But how can we expiate the sin of the forcible destruction of clothes which might have gone to women whose nakedness is actually keeping them prisoners unable to stir out of the privacy of their homes?[48]

Similarly, withdrawal from the schools and colleges never appeared to be a wise call. Tagore refused to endorse the campaign because 'the great injury and injustice which had been done to those boys who were tempted away from their career before any real provision was made, could never be made good to them'.[49] He was not persuaded to believe that Western education 'injured' the young minds and should be altogether rejected. The root of the misconception lies elsewhere. As Tagore pointed out:

> what has caused the mischief is the fact that for a long time we have been out of touch with our own culture and therefore the Western culture has not found its perspective in our life; very often [it has] found a wrong perspective, giving our mental eye a squint.[50]

Tagore adopted a nuanced argument *vis-à-vis* the Non-Cooperation Movement, which was a relatively successful political campaign involving a wide section of the population across the length and breadth of India.

While Tagore was convinced, like MN Roy, that this programme would alienate the masses since mill products were cheaper and hence more affordable, Gandhi defended the agenda by saying that it would not only harm the British commercial interests but also foster the cultural self-confidence of the masses. In his words,

Non cooperation is the nation's notice that it is no longer satisfied to be in tutelage. The nation had taken to the harmless, natural and religious doctrine of Non-Cooperation in the place of the unnatural and irreligious doctrine of violence.... Non Cooperation is intended to give the very meaning that the Poet is yearning after. An India prostrate at the feet of Europe can give no hope to humanity. An India awakened and free has a message of peace and goodwill to a groaning world. Non Cooperation is designed to supply her with a platform from which she will preach the message.[51]

On another occasion, he further added:

Our Non Cooperation is neither with the English nor with the West. Our Non Cooperation is with the system the English have established, with the material civilization and its attendant greed and exploitation of the weak. Our Non Cooperation is a retirement within ourselves. Our Non Cooperation is a refusal to cooperate with the English administrators in their own terms.[52]

Similarly, Gandhi did not endorse Tagore's criticism of the boycott of English education. While appreciating English learning, the Mahatma was critical of the pernicious effect of English education on Indian minds. According to him,

English is being studied because of its commercial and political value.... English is being made mother tongue in families. Hundreds of youth believe that without a knowledge of English freedom of India is practically impossible.... The only meaning of Education is a knowledge of English.... All these are for me signs of our slavery and degradation. It is unbearable to me that the vernaculars should be crushed and starved as they have been.[53]

As will be shown, Tagore's critique of the aim of the Non-Cooperation Movement drew on his own perception of the 'constructive work' that he experimented with during the 1905–8 *swadeshi* movement in Bengal.[54] He was opposed to coercion because his experience of the *swadeshi* mobilization had shown him its adverse consequences. When the movement was at its zenith, Tagore denounced its reliance on coercion and the alienating impact it had on the masses it claimed to enthuse and activate. His critique of the Non-cooperation techniques followed the same logic. The pervasive use of social boycott and other forms of coercion was therefore 'regarded by him as evidence of the Swadeshi activist's failure to persuade people to their cause'.[55] He thus argued that 'we have not been patient enough to work our way gradually towards winning popular consent'.[56] That was at the root of the nationalist failure to unite all Indians in 'a grand patriotic mobilization'.

The debate between Gandhi and Tagore brought out their contrasting perspectives on this subject that had, as shown, their roots in the *swadeshi* movement as well. While Gandhi was confident that the non-cooperation agenda was the most appropriate socio-politically, Tagore expressed his doubts on the grounds that the 'narrow political aim' of the movement was likely to jeopardize its wider goal and objectives. The debate remained inconclusive, but raised certain major questions about Gandhi's social and political ideas that appear to have decisively influenced Indian minds.[57]

Just like the debate over the strategy of non-cooperation, the exchange of views between Gandhi and the poet on *charkha* and *khaddar* reflected the different perspectives in which they were conceptualized. Tagore was not persuaded, let alone impressed, by the campaign for *charkha*. As he admitted,

> the depths of my mind have not been moved by the charkha agitation
> ... for its inherent weaknesses [and he therefore apprehended] that all
> intense pressure of persuasion brought upon the crowd psychology is
> unhealthy for it will create blind faith on a very large scale in the
> charkha ... which is liable to succumb to the lure of short cuts when
> pointed out by a personality about whose moral earnestness they can
> have no doubt.[58]

In two articles, published in the *Modern Review*, Tagore summarized his arguments questioning the applicability of *charkha* in the context of colonial India. First, he was confident that *charkha* was not a competitive substitute for the machine especially, given the complex problems that the masses confronted both due to colonialism and other obvious social and political constraints. For Tagore, 'no wealth is greater than lightening man's material burdens'. In a figurative way, he further argued that the 'wheel in the shape of the spinning wheel, or the potter's wheel or the wheel of a vehicle, the wheel has rescued innumerable men from [poverty] and [reduced] their burden'. Seeing the wheel as a symbol for the growth of science, Tagore thus concluded by underlining the importance of the wheel in augmenting resources for human civilization. As he articulated, 'man gradually realized that his wealth has gone on compounding itself in the ever-increasing rotation, refusing to be confined to the limited advantage of the original charkha'.[59] As an archaic tool that had been useful at a particular historical juncture, *charkha* appeared to have exhausted its potential to contain poverty effectively. His second argument against *charkha* was built on this. He was unambiguous in stating that 'the charkha is not competent to bring us the swaraj, or remove the whole of our poverty because it is based on the false expectation that people will automatically be drawn to spinning'. Seeking to delink *swaraj* from *charkha*, Tagore further argued that:

> to give the charkha the first place in our striving for the country's
> welfare is only a way to make our insulted intelligence recoil in despair-

ing inaction. A great and vivid picture of the country's well-being in its universal aspect, held before our eyes, can alone enable our countrymen to apply the best of head and heart to carve out the best way along which their varied activities may progress towards their end.[60]

Swaraj represented people's self-fulfillment regardless of their differences in ethno-religious terms. It was not simply an act of 'spinning thread, weaving khaddar or holding discourses'; it was a plan of action involving the masses with a vision of society, free from exploitation of all kinds. So Tagore, not persuaded by the narrow conceptualization of *swaraj* merely in terms of *charkha*, highlighted both the depth of *swaraj* as a socio-economic blueprint for the future India and also its significance in inculcating mass interest in certain specific meaningful programmes relevant to the people of British India. The third argument that Tagore made against *charkha* relates to the realistic feasibility of this device when imposed on the people without their consent. Gandhi felt that the success of *charkha* lay in utilizing the surplus time of the cultivator; the more the cultivators involved themselves, the more effective the *charkha* would become. Tagore was not in agreement simply because the basic assumption behind the argument concerning the profitable employment of the surplus time of the cultivator was flawed unless the cultivators themselves spontaneously accepted *charkha*. This he believed unlikely for two reasons: first, the cultivator acquired a special skill with his hands, and a special bent of mind by dint of consistent application to his particular work. Hence 'to ask the cultivator to spin is to derail his mind; he may drag on with it for a while, but at the cost of disproportionate effort and therefore waste of energy'.[61] Second, if *charkha* was imposed on the cultivators with no inclination for it, it would lose its significance and effectiveness. In other words, the acceptance of *charkha* could not be spontaneous and hence its consequences could be devastating because, as Tagore most eloquently put it,

> it would be wrong to make the cultivator either happier or richer by thrusting aside, all of a sudden, the habits of body and mind which have grown upon him through his life.... To tell the cultivator turn the charkha instead of trying to get him to employ his whole energy in his own line of work is only a sign of weakness. We cast the blame for being lazy on the cultivator, but the advice we give him amounts rather to a confession of the laziness of our mind.[62]

According to Tagore, spinning was not creative for, 'by turning its wheel man merely becomes an appendage of the charkha; that is to say, he but does himself what a machine might have done; he converts his living energy into a dead turning movement. [In the process] he becomes a machine, isolated, companionless'.[63] Critical of this mechanical involvement in spinning that was of no consequence for *swaraj*, Tagore suggested concrete steps which were organically linked with the way of life. For instance, as he perceived, the village that was self-sustained economically and able to support each of its inhabitants in distress could lay the foundation of *swaraj* in the true sense of the term. As he most unambiguously put it, 'the village of which people come together to earn for themselves their food, their health, their education, to gain themselves the joy of so doing, shall have lighted a lamp on the way to swaraj'.[64]

Gandhi responded to the poet's critique in his rejoinders in the *Young India*. Instead of countering the arguments made by Tagore, the Mahatma, in a very cryptic way, stated his viewpoint in defending *charkha* as indispensable for India's economic well-being. In response to the charge that he insisted on spinning to the exclusion of all other activities, Gandhi argued that this was far from the truth because he never wanted 'the Poet to forsake his muse, the farmer his plough, the lawyer his brief and the doctor his lancet. [Instead], he asked the famishing to spin for a living and the half-starved farmer to spin during his leisure hours to supplement his slender resources'.[65] The idea based on sound logic articulated a device for supplementary incomes for the starving peasants and their families. Juxtaposed with this idea was his unequivocal condemnation for the machine. He was not opposed to the machine *per se*; what he apprehended was the consequence of a machine civilization making human labour redundant, a consequence most devastating where human labour was in abundance. As Gandhi argued, the

> machine must not be allowed to displace the necessary human labour. An improved plough is a good thing. But if by some chance one man could plough up by some mechanical invention of his the whole of the land of India and control all the agricultural produce and the millions had no other occupation, they would starve, and being idle, they would become dunces, as many have already become. . . . [i]t is therefore criminal to displace hand labour by the introduction of power-driven spindles unless one is at the same time ready to give millions of farmers some other occupation in their homes.[66]

The other part of the argument is equally significant with *charkha* seen as a symbol of involvement with the day-to-day life of the poor and thus as a powerful device to conceptualize reality. He suggested to the poet that, 'if [he] spun half an hour daily his poetry would gain in richness [for] it would then represent the poor man's wants and woes in a more forcible manner than now'.[67] Furthermore, Gandhi replied to the charge that the *charkha* was calculated to bring about a deathlike sameness in the nation. To Gandhi *charkha* was a powerful symbol to unite the disparate Indian masses and hence 'intended to realize the essential and living oneness of interest among India's myriads'. *Charkha* was not simply an economic activity. Instead, it brought people together by involving them in an activity that was a) a source of supplementary income; and b) a device to link them automatically with the rest of India politically.[68] In other words, although articulated as an economic activity, it was an organizing device with a clear political message to those involved in Gandhian *satyagraha*.[69] Spinning for Gandhi was therefore a symbolic form of identification with the masses while Tagore, as shown, was suspicious of any such appeal that tended to gloss over the inherent diversity among the Indian people.

Apart from these major issues, an interesting debate took place following Gandhi's characterization of the Bihar earthquake in February, 1934 as 'divine chastisement' for the great sin committed against those known as *harijans*.[70] Tagore took a serious view of this by saying that 'it has caused me painful surprise to find Mahatma Gandhi accusing those who blindly follow their own social custom of untouchability of having brought down gods' vengeance upon certain parts of Bihar'.[71] Coming from the most revered political leader of the country, the statement, he felt, was most devastating for its obvious impact on the interpersonal relationships between *harijans* and others. So it should not go 'unchallenged'.[72] Tagore prefaced his critique of this superstitious view of Gandhi's by saying that 'it is all the more unfortunate, because this kind of unscientific view of things is too readily accepted by a large section of our countrymen'. Emphasizing that 'physical catastrophes [like earthquake etc.] have their inevitable and exclusive origin in certain combinations of physical facts', he further argued that:

> if we associate ethical principles with cosmic phenomena, we shall have to admit that human nature is morally superior to Providence that preaches its lessons in good behaviour in orgies of the worst behaviour possible. . . . What is truly tragic about it is the fact that the kind of argument that Mahatmaji uses by exploiting an event of cosmic disturbance far better suits the psychology of his opponents. . . . [He thus felt] profoundly hurt when any words from [Gandhi's] mouth may emphasise the elements of unreason . . . which is a fundamental source of all the blind powers that drive us against freedom and self-respect.[73]

Gandhi reacted against Tagore's views equally strongly. Reiterating his views on the Bihar earthquake, the Mahatma argued:

> to me, the earthquake was no caprice of God nor a result of a meeting of mere blind forces. . . . Visitations like droughts, flood, earthquakes and the like, though they seem to have only physical origins, are, for me, somehow connected with man's morals. Therefore, I instinctively felt that the earthquake was visitation for the sin of untouchability. [He firmly believed] that our sins have more force to ruin the structure than any mere physical phenomenon.[74]

On this occasion, they held diametrically opposite views. A scientific Tagore upheld reason[75] while a moralist Gandhi privileged faith over reason. The point here is not to ascertain the validity of their respective arguments objectively, but to dig out their appropriateness in the context of India's struggle for a *swaraj* that was more than mere political freedom from imperialism. Tagore's was a reasoned argument with a limited application while Gandhi's had a wider application, given his influence over the masses. It was, as it were, a Gandhian preemptive measure, based on his wider acceptability as a political leader. What motivated Gandhi was perhaps his confidence in dissuading those practising untouchability because of the impending god's wrath. For Gandhi, the linking of the Bihar calamity with the sin of untouchability, though unscientific logically, was a significant step in his battle against untouchability. In other words, the statement on the Bihar earthquake acquired completely different connotations which one may not comprehend without gauging Mahatma's popularity among the masses. So, given the typical Gandhian methodology of mass mobilization for freedom, it was just another method of launching an effective and meaningful campaign against untouchability.

As evident, the differences between Tagore and Gandhi were fundamental on specific political strategies for mass mobilization. Unlike Gandhi, Tagore never appreciated the non-cooperation strategy, for instance, due to its inbuilt weaknesses. Similarly, on *charkha* and *khaddar*, the poet was critical of the Mahatma since these neither provided an appropriate alternative to the masses nor adequately addressed the problem of poverty. It was largely 'a hollow political slogan', as Tagore believed, given the obvious adverse political and economic consequences on the masses if forced on them. Despite the validity of Tagore's argument in a wider perspective, there is no doubt that *charkha* and *khaddar* instrumentalized the Gandhi-led mass movement; they, in other words, became symbols of mass involvement in the anti-imperial struggle. While they differed in regard to politico-economic strategies, they held uniform views on nationalism. Given the nature of disparate Indian masses, nation, to both of them, never appeared to be a viable organizing principle. Tagore was perhaps first to confront the devastating consequences of the application of the principle of nationalism in the context of the *swadeshi* movement of 1903–8 in Bengal, when the schism between the Hindus and Muslims was articulated in a nationalist language. The growing strength of the Muslims, defined later as a separate nation by Jinnah, the architect of Pakistan, caused a permanent fissure between these two major religious communities that ultimately led to the 1947 partition of the subcontinent. Expressing their views in a non-nationalist language, Gandhi and Tagore, perhaps the finest product of the Indo-British cultural encounter, provided the most creative and also challenging response to the nationalist 'oneness' of the Western world.

Ambedkar and Gandhi

The complexities of Gandhi's social and political thought owe a lot to various different ideological discourses, articulated by his colleagues in the Indian freedom struggle. M.N. Roy drew on a creative interpretation of Marxism to critique Gandhian ideas while Tagore privileged his faith in humanism to assess what constituted the core of Gandhi's social and political philosophy. Bhimrao Ramji Ambedkar (1891–1956), popularly known as Babasaheb Ambedkar, introduced a new critique by drawing on 'the *dalit*' perspective. Critical of the nationalist movement that upheld caste and untouchability at the behest of Gandhi, Ambedkar sought to articulate an alternative political ideology by challenging the very foundation of the 'Hinduized' nationalist movement. One of the most significant arguments that Ambedkar made against Hinduism was that caste and untouchability struck at its foundation and rendered it inherently divisive. Gandhi, by clinging to the basic philosophy of caste never seriously challenged, as Ambedkar accused, untouchability in Hinduism. According to him, Gandhism was 'a paradox' because 'it stands for freedom from foreign domination [and] at the same time it seeks to maintain intact a social structure which permits the domination of one class by another on a hereditary basis which means a perpetual domination of one class by another'.[76] To Ambedkar, Gandhi's loyalty to Hinduism amounted to supporting 'untouchability' because that had also evolved as integrally linked with Hinduism and was thus justified. This assumption however contradicts what the Mahatma sincerely believed. According to him, 'untouchability is not a sanction of religion; it is a device of Satan. . . . There is neither nobility nor bravery in treating the great and uncomplaining scavengers of the nation as worse than dogs to be despised and spat upon.'[77]

Ambedkar criticized Gandhi further for eulogizing the Indian villages as illustrative of unique units of social, economic and political equilibrium. Instead, Ambedkar argued, Indian villages

> represent a kind of colonialism of the Hindus designed to exploit the Untouchables. The Untouchables have no rights. They are there only to wait, serve and submit. They are there to do or to die. They have no rights because they are outside the village republic and because they are outside the so-called republic, they are outside the Hindu fold. This is a vicious circle. But this is a fact which cannot be gainsaid.[78]

For Gandhi, the village was the basis for building a republican society,[79] unpolluted by colonialism while for Ambedkar it was 'the black hole' of Indian civilization. The village, for Gandhi, was not merely a geographical location where people lived in a small settlement on the land. For him, it reflected the essence of Indian civilization. The Indian village had a design, a way of life with the potential to become 'an alternative to the city-based and technology-driven capitalist West'.[80] His conception of the village was not anchored 'on the modern notion of development but on the post-modern perspective of quality of life'.[81] And, yet for the *dalits*, 'the village . . . could never be an embodiment of justice [since] to remain in village meant remaining tied to the same humiliating occupation that had so far been their fate'.[82] So, for Ambedkar, the structure of village settlements reflected the basic tenets of Hinduism, which never recognized *dalits* as an integral part. In other words, the village contributed and simultaneously sustained the divisive nature of Hindu society, where the untouchables always remained 'outside the fold'. As he most eloquently put it,

> the Hindu society insists on segregation of the untouchables. The Hindu will not live in the quarters of the untouchables and will not allow the untouchables to live inside the Hindu quarters. . . . It is not a case of social separation, a mere stoppage of social intercourse for a temporary period. It is a case of territorial segregation and of a cordon sanitaire putting the impure people inside the barbed wire into a sort of a cage. Every Hindu village has a ghetto. The Hindus live in the village and the untouchables live in the ghetto.[83]

In contrast with Gandhi, Ambedkar conceptualized the village as a model of the oppressive Hindu social organization, a microcosm of the overall demeaning circumstance in which *dalits* were located. It was 'the working plant of the Hindu social order' where one could see the atrocious nature of Hinduism. Given the obvious role of the villages in sustaining the atrocious social circumstances of the *dalits*, Ambedkar could never endorse Gandhi's eulogy of Indian villages because they represented an exclusive domain for the touchables at the cost of the untouchables who were invariably pushed into the ghetto.

The conflict between Gandhi and Ambedkar on the issue of the separate electorates for the untouchables and the depressed classes illustrated the two contrasting perspectives which fundamentally altered the nature of political participation by the Scheduled Castes and tribes in British India and its aftermath. Once the separate electorate for the Muslims was conceded by the Congress while accepting the 1935 Government of India Act, Ambedkar argued, on behalf of the *dalits*, that they must be allowed to constitute a separate electorate and elect their own representatives to the central and provincial legislatures. He further defended the claim by saying that, since voting was severely restricted by property and educational qualifications, the geographically highly disparate depressed classes were unlikely to have any influence in the decision-making process. So the solution lay in a separate electorate for them. Ambedkar held the view that untouchables were absolutely separate from Hinduism and hence he tried 'to find a solution to their problem through political separatism'.[84] In order to substantiate, he further argued that the Hindus 'had much to lose by the abolition of untouchability, though they had nothing to fear from political reservation leading to this abolition'.[85] The matter was 'economic' rather than 'religious'. In an unambiguous way, Ambedkar brought out the economic dimension of untouchability by stating that:

> the system of untouchability is a gold mine to the Hindus. In it the 240 millions of Hindus have 60 millions of Untouchables to serve as their retinue to enable the Hindus to maintain pomp and ceremony and to cultivate a feeling of pride and dignity befitting a master class, which cannot be fostered and sustained unless there is beneath it a servile class to look down upon. In it the 240 millions of Hindus have 60 millions of Untouchables to be used as forced labourers . . . in it the 240 millions of Hindus have 60 millions of Untouchables to do the dirty work of scavengers and sweepers which the Hindu is debarred by his religion to do and which must be done by non-Hindus who could be no other than Untouchables. In it the 240 millions of Hindus have 60 millions of Untouchables who can be kept to lower jobs. . . . In it the 240 millions of Hindus have the 60 millions of Untouchables who can be used as shock-absorbers in slumps and dead-weights in booms, for in slumps, it is the Untouchables who is fired first and the Hindu is fired last and in booms the Hindu is employed first and the Untouchables is employed last. [So, untouchability is not a religious] but an economic system which is worse than slavery.[86]

Unable to appreciate Ambedkar's demand, Gandhi declined to accept that the untouchables were a community separate from the Hindus and was instead prepared to offer reserved seats for them in general constituencies. For him, the matter was highly 'religious', as he stated: 'for me the question of these classes is predominantly moral and religious. The political aspect, important though it is', he further added, 'dwindles into insignificance compared to the moral and religious issue'.[87] He reacted strongly when a charge was labelled that the upper-caste Congress leaders could never properly represent the untouchables. When his attention was drawn to the Congress acceptance of the 1932 Communal Award, Gandhi insisted that, unlike the question of religious minorities, the issue of untouchability was a matter internal to Hinduism and had to be resolved within it. Underlining the adverse consequences of such division on the Hindus, the Mahatma thus emphatically argued that:

> I cannot possibly tolerate what is in store for Hinduism if there are two divisions set forth in the villages. Those who speak of the political rights of Untouchables do not know their India, do not know how Indian society is today constructed, and therefore I want to say with all the emphasis that I can command that if I was the only person to resist this thing I would resist it with my life.[88]

Gandhi's protest against the extension of the separate electorate to the *dalits* was double-edged: on the one hand, Gandhi sincerely believed that the separate electorate would also split them from Hindu society and absolve the latter of its moral responsibility to fight against the practice of untouchability. There were also clear political calculations that, as Bhikhu Parekh argues, governed Gandhi's mind, for 'the separate electorate would have reduced the numerical strength of the Hindu majority, encouraged minority alliance against it, and fragmented the country yet further'.[89] So the Gandhian intervention was the result of skilful political strategy as well as of his passionate concern for Indian unity. Ambedkar was equally assertive and insisted on a separate electorate as the best device to protect the social, economic and political interests of the *dalits*. As he stated, 'I trust [that] the Mahatma would not drive me to the necessity of making a choice between his life and the rights of my people. For I can never consent to deliver my people bound hand and foot to the caste Hindus for generations to come.'[90] No solution was visible. For Gandhi, the separate electorate for the untouchables would divide Hindu society further, perpetuating their inferiority. Ambedkar denounced this as a strategic argument for using the untouchables as 'weightage for the Hindus against the Muslims'.[91] When the British government endorsed the separate electorate in the Communal Award of August 1932, Ambedkar had an edge over his rival. Now, the only course of action open to Gandhi was to embark on a fast. He went on a fast rather than approve the demand for a separate electorate for the depressed classes. Gandhi, who was in Yervada prison in Poona, began the fast on 20 September and ended it on 24 September only once Ambedkar agreed to accept the reservation of seats for *dalits* within the caste-Hindu constituencies.[92] An agreement between Gandhi and Ambedkar, known as the Poona Pact, was signed in 1932[93] and the depressed classes were given a substantial number of reserved seats but within the Hindu electorate.[94]

The Poona Pact represented a victory for the Mahatma in two ways: a) it was accepted that untouchability was 'a social' and not 'a political problem'; and b) it was a problem of Hindu religion and not of the Hindu economy. Nonetheless, what was unique about the Pact was that it, for the first time, placed the backward classes, later classified as the Scheduled Castes, in the 1935 Government of India Act on the centre-stage of Indian politics with an identity of their own.[95] From now on, the Scheduled Castes invariably figured in any discussion on national identity. Although in Ambedkar, the Scheduled Castes found a powerful leader, they continued to remain a politically significant 'minority' with narrow social, economic and political goals. As a dissenter bent on dismantling an oppressive caste system, Ambedkar therefore 'fulfilled the historical role of dissent not only to question hateful religious dogma but also unbuckle the consolidating ambitions of the secular state within which former religious orthodoxies are subsumed'.[96] What is striking is that, despite having opposed Hindu orthodoxy, manifested in caste rigidity of which he was a victim, Babasaheb attempted to steer a steady course between a separatist, sectarian stance and an unconditional citizenship function in which the identity of untouchables would be subsumed within Hinduism.[97] It would be wrong, however, to suggest that Ambedkar believed that the problem of untouchability would be solved not through legislative feats but through institutionalized social measures. As he argued,

> any electoral arrangement, I believe, cannot be a solution of the larger social problems. It requires more than any political arrangement and I hope that it would be possible for you to go beyond this political arrangement that we are making today [of joint electorate] and devise ways and means whereby it would be possible for the Depressed Classes not only to be part and parcel of the Hindu community but also to occupy an honourable position, a position of equality of status in the community.[98]

Despite Ambedkar's reservations, the 1932 Poona Pact is the first well-articulated arrangement in which the Scheduled Castes were identified as a separate group within Hinduism;[99] their emergence with a distinct political identity significantly influenced the provincial elections that followed the 1935 Government of India Act. Apart from the Muslims who had already asserted their existence as a significant community, the ascendancy of the Scheduled Castes clearly indicated the complexity of the future course of Indian history, which had so far glossed over the well-entrenched fragmented identities within both the Hindu and Muslim groups. In fact, the Pakistan demand that drew upon Jinnah's 'two-nation theory' hinges on the exclusive identities of both the principal communities, Hindus and Muslims, despite sharing the same socio-economic and politico-cultural milieu. For the nationalists, the idea of separate Hindu and Muslim identities had no natural basis and also the two communities were politically separated through the manoeuvres of communal forces and imperial *divide-et-impera*.[100] For Jinnah and the Muslim League, the demand for a sovereign and independent Muslim state was logical, since Muslims constituted a separate nation with a different religious philosophy, social customs and literature. Hindus and Muslims belong to two completely different civilizations with conflicting ideas and conceptions.[101] The Hindu counterpart of this logic was voiced by V.D. Savarkar, who argued strongly for a separate Hindu identity, due to the distinctive features separating Hindus from Muslims, though the root of this logic can be traced back to the eighteenth century, when the English writing on India clearly afforded the Hindus with a distinct identity 'in racial, religious and linguistic terms'.[102]

That Muslims constituted a self-determining political community was always emphasized to completely dissociate them from the Hindus seeking to establish 'a Hindu Raj'.[103] The Hindu–Muslim schism was not merely based on religious differences but also on certain fundamental principles guiding their respective lives. As Muslims drew upon completely different socio-cultural values, it was unthinkable that they could live as 'a mere minority in a Hindu-dominated India'. While explaining the Hindu–Muslim chasm in colonial India, Ambedkar thus argued that the Hindu–Muslim 'antagonism . . . is formed by causes which take their origin in historical, religious, cultural and social antipathy of which political antipathy is only a reflection'. These form, he further elaborated, 'one deep river of discontent which, being regularly fed by these sources, keeps on mounting to a head and overflowing its ordinary channels'.[104] So Ambedkar held the Hindus equally responsible for the rise of the Muslim separatism that was finally resolved in the emergence of Pakistan as a nation.[105]

B.R. Ambedkar, in his *Pakistan or the Partition of India*,[106] endorsed the claim for Pakistan in terms of realist politics. According to him, partition was possibly the best solution to the constitutional impasse in India for two reasons. First, given the hostility of the Muslims to the idea of a single central government, inevitably dominated by the Hindu majority, it was certain that if there was no partition, the animosities and suspicion between the communities would remain: 'burying Pakistan is not the same thing as burying the ghost of Pakistan'.[107] Furthermore, given the demographic composition of what was proposed as Pakistan, there was no doubt that it would be a homogeneous state and hence free from communal bickering and mutual distrust. Second, Ambedkar felt that in united India, where more than a third of the population was Muslim, 'Hindu dominance' could pose 'a serious threat to the very existence of the polity'. In such a state, Muslims apprehending the tyranny of the Hindu majority were likely to organize themselves into 'a theocratic party' provoking in turn the rise of Hindu fundamentalist forces seeking to establish 'a Hindu raj'. Partition would radically alter the situation where Muslims in Hindustan would be 'a small and widely scattered minority' joining whichever political parties they judged 'as most protective' of their socio-economic and political interests. As a result, a party like Hindu Mahasabha, based on the principle of 'a Hindu raj', would gradually disappear. Persuaded by the logic of his argument, Ambedkar suggested that the lower castes of Hindu society should join hands with the Muslim minority to fight the Hindu high castes for their rights of citizenship and social dignity.[108]

The Poona Pact was a political response, authored by Gandhi and Ambedkar. This also triggered debates on the relevance of caste in Indian society. While Gandhi's faith in caste was unquestionable, Ambedkar attributed untouchability to caste and other obnoxious and archaic practices, justified in the name of Hinduism.[109] According to Ambedkar, the caste system 'is a hierarchy in which the divisions of labour are graded one above the other. . . . This division of labour is not spontaneous, it is not based on natural aptitudes . . . in so far as it involves an attempt to appoint tasks to individuals in advance, selected not on the basis of trained original capacities, but on that of the social status of the parents.'[110] Since the caste system was based on ascription of status by birth, it was inherently exclusive, losing its public-ness. As Ambedkar argued, 'caste has killed public spirit. Caste has destroyed the sense of public charity. Caste has made opinion impossible. [To the Hindus], virtue has become caste-ridden and morality has become caste-bound.'[111] By attacking *Chaturvarnya*, the basic institution holding the caste system *in tact*, Ambedkar countered Gandhi's defence of the former as an innocent typology of human beings on *guna* (worth). By dividing the Hindu society into four different categories – *Brahmins, Kshtriya, Vaishya* and *Sudra* – on the basis of birth, *Chaturvarnya*, argued Babasaheb,

> sanctions not only a differentiation of persons but also their gradation. [The labels, *Brahmin, Kshtriya, Vaishya* and *Sudra*] are names which are associated with a definite and fixed notion in the mind of every Hindu. The notion is that of a hierarchy based on birth. So long as these names continue, Hindus will continue to think of the *Brahmin, Kshtriya, Vaishya* and *Sudra* as hierarchical divisions of high and low, based on birth, and act accordingly. The Hindu must be made to unlearn all this. But how can this happen if the old labels remain and continue to recall to his mind old notions. . . . To continue the old name is to make reform futile. To allow this *Chaturvarnya*, based on worth to be designated by such stinking labels of *Brahmin, Kshtriya, Vaishya, Sudra*, indicative of social divisions based on birth, is a snare. . . . To, this *Chaturvarnya* with its old labels is utterly repellent and my whole being rebels against it.

As demonstrated, Ambedkar advocated a total rejection of *Chaturvarnya* simply because of its justification of division within the Hindu society on the basis of birth. Gandhi made his defence in the columns of *Harijan*. Appreciating Ambedkar for his critique of caste,[112] the Mahatma reiterated his faith in Hinduism and its institutions, including the *Chaturvarnya*, presumably to avoid further divisions within the Hindu society. Instead of confronting Ambedkar head-on, Gandhi simply provided an interpretation of caste and *varnashrama* to defend his point of view in contrast with that of Ambedkar. He believed in *varnashrama* of the *Vedas*, which in his opinion was based on absolute equality of status, notwithstanding passages to the contrary in the *smrits* and elsewhere.[113] Defending *varnashrama* as a mere social arrangement of universally applicable divisions of occupation, he thus argued:

> [The four] *Varnas* . . . have been sanctioned by the *Shastras* [holy books]. Whether or not people are conscious of them, they do exist all over the world as we see. There are everywhere these four classes: one to impart knowledge of god for the welfare of the world, another to protect the people against manifold dangers, a third one to carry on the work of farming, etc., to sustain the community and one class to work for these three classes. There is no feeling of high and low to this division.[114]

Integrally linked with Hinduism, *Chaturvarnya*, he believed, was

> based on absolute equality of status, notwithstanding passages to the
> contrary in the *smritis* [the holy scriptures] and elsewhere. . . . There was
> no prohibition of intermarriage and inter-dining. Prohibition there is of
> change of one's hereditary occupation for purposes of gain. The existing
> practice is, therefore, doubly wrong in that it has set up cruel restric-
> tions about inter-dining and intermarriage and tolerates about choice of
> occupation . . . it must be left to the unfettered choice of the individual
> as to where he or she will marry or dine.[115]

On another occasion, he was critical of the ways caste evolved as a social
system governing interpersonal relations by saying 'restrictions as regards
inter-marriage and inter-dining which defy reason . . . are very harmful and
stand in the ways of the community's progress. It has nothing to do with religion.'[116] He thus made a distinction between caste and *varnashrama*; while
the former, by endorsing various kinds of social restrictions was distorted, the
latter was 'a cooperative society with its members divided into occupational
groups, each fulfilling their own functions, but all of equal status';[117] and it
was this ideal of caste to which Gandhi adhered throughout his life.[118]

For Ambedkar, this was an attempt to scuttle the contentious issue. Furthermore, his critique of the caste system was misleading if it was juxtaposed with his defence for the *Chaturvarnya*, the core of the caste system.
This conformed to the endeavours of other Hindu leaders who criticized the
practice of caste discrimination to fulfil their own narrow political agenda at
the cost of the *dalits*. As he argued,

> Hindu leaders became filled with an illicit passion for their belief when
> any one proposes to rob them of their companionship. The Mahatma is no
> exception. [He] appears not to believe in thinking. He prefers to follow
> his saints. . . . One must sympathise with him. . . . But . . . dependence on
> saints cannot lead us to know the truth. . . . In so far as he does think, to
> me he really appears to be prostituting his intelligence to find the reasons
> for supporting this archaic social structure of the Hindus. He is the most
> influential apologist of it and therefore the worst enemy of the Hindus.[119]

Why was Gandhi in favour of the caste system despite its divisive nature?
Ambedkar attributed this to the Mahatma's narrow political calculations.
He thus bluntly placed, on record, his views by saying that:

> the reason why the Mahatma is always supporting Caste and *Varna* is
> because he is afraid that if he opposed them he will lose his place in
> politics. Whatever the source of his confusion the Mahatma must be
> told that he is deceiving himself and also deceiving the people by
> preaching Caste under the name of *Varna*.[120]

His diatribe against Gandhi and Hindu society continues in his lecture entitled Ranade,[121] Gandhi and Jinnah. The lecture has two clearly defined
parts. On the one hand, Ambedkar evolved his critique of Hinduism by
drawing extensively on Ranade's view of Hinduism. The second part dwells
on his criticism of the role of Gandhi and Jinnah as political leaders of 'the
respective groups of Hindus and Muslims' in India. While appreciating
Ranade for his critique of Hinduism, Ambedkar stated that Ranade was the
first Indian politician who argued that 'there were no rights in the Hindu
society,.... there were privileges and disabilities, privileges for a few and
disabilities for a vast majority'. Linking this argument with his criticism of
Gandhi, Babasaheb felt that there was no alternative for the Mahatma but to
support Hinduism and the caste system simply because 'Mr Gandhi wants
the untouchables to remain as Hindus ... [n]ot as partners but as poor relations of Hindus.'[122] Characterizing Gandhi as 'a Tory by birth as well as
faith'[123] because of his rigid views on social and religious issues, he accused
the Mahatma of 'demoralizing' his followers and also 'politics'. Like Jinnah,
he made 'half of his followers fools and the other half hypocrites'. He attributed the rise of Gandhi rather simplistically to 'the aid of big business and
money magnates'. As a result, Indian politics,

> at any rate the Hindu part of it, instead of being spiritualized has
> become grossly commercialized, so much so that it becomes a byword of
> corruption. . . . Politics has become a kind of sewage system: intolerably
> unsavoury and insanitary. To become a politician is like going to work
> in the drain.[124]

The debate between Gandhi and Ambedkar is significant for two important
reasons. *First*, Ambedkar's sharp critique has not only problematized
the twin concepts of justice and freedom by taking into account the *dalit*
point of view, it has also posed new social, economic and political
issues involving the peripheral sections of Indian society. Ambedkar's intervention captured a serious gap in the nationalist socio-political thought.
Gandhi, despite being universal in his approach, failed to incorporate the
specific dalit issues while organizing the campaign for freedom. That
Gandhi represented all regardless of class, caste and creed was based on
assumptions inflating the claim of the Mahatma to amicably settle the conflicting socio-political and economic interests of the diverse Indian
population. Not until the 1932 Poona Pact did Gandhi effectively negotiate
with the *dalits* as an emerging and socially formidable constituency of
the nationalist politics. Only after this Pact, the Congress leadership formally accorded a legitimate space to the *dalits* who had so far remained
peripheral to the struggle for freedom. The role of the British government
was not insignificant either. By accepting Ambedkar as a representative
of the *dalits* in the 1932 Round Table Conference, the ruling authority
deflated Gandhi's claim to epitomize India as a whole. Gandhi was pushed

to the periphery and Ambedkar was brought in, presumably due to his success in articulating the issues concerning *dalits* which, though important, had never been adequately addressed either by the nationalist political leadership or by the colonial government. So justice and freedom acquired new connotations in the changed milieu when *dalits* had already emerged as a politically significant constituency under the stewardship of B.R. Ambedkar. By providing a new conception of emancipatory politics, Babasaheb went beyond a comprehensive 'de-legitimation' of slavery, which was but another name for untouchability. It entailed, as shown, a wide-ranging programme of equality and equity measures seeking to fulfil a wide variety of the material and non-material needs of those identified as untouchables. It is this programme of total societal transformation that constituted his conception of *swaraj* as being not just freedom from colonialism; it was a just freedom.[125] *Swaraj*, thus defined, was not merely political and economic freedom from colonialism, as conceptualized by Gandhi, but a significant socio-political package striving to ameliorate the conditions of those 'outside the Hindu fold'. It would not be wrong to argue therefore that the Gandhi–Ambedkar debate is theoretically innovative and politically crucial in grasping the most volatile phase of Indian nationalism when the Mahatma no longer remained the undisputed leader of the nationalist articulation of freedom struggle.

Second, it is alleged that Ambedkar manipulated the *dalit* agenda in order to undermine the efforts of the Indian National Congress to achieve freedom. His 'separatist ideology' caused a fissure in the nationalist campaign, for obvious reasons. Ambedkar was not persuaded because he regarded 'with great suspicion all attempts, [including that by Gandhi], to portray democratization as a process independent of caste manipulation'.[126] His sustained criticism of Gandhi for supporting the *Chaturvarnya*-based *Brahminical* social order has wider theoretical implications. According to him, the collusion between *Brahminism* and colonialism was possible because of the support accorded by Gandhi. His analogy between a colonial government that drained resources from the colony and a caste ideology that lived off the labour of outcaste groups is 'consistent with his rhetorical strategy of conflating disparate historical moments within a single frame, in order not only to illuminate the interchangeability of British colonialism and *Brahminism*, but also to expose the claims of an ideology negated by its own practices'.[127] The debate between Gandhi and Ambedkar is therefore most instructive in both grasping relatively non-visible dimensions of Indian reality and also in conceptualizing the *dalit* intervention in the nationalist discourse that had so far failed to address the *dalit* issues.

Concluding observations

There is no doubt that Gandhi remained a constant referent to those seeking to articulate an ideological alternative to what constituted Gandhism. The Mahatma had an edge over his colleagues and compatriots for two important reasons: *first*, Gandhi was undoubtedly the organic leader of the nationalist movement, which acquired completely different characteristics once its constituencies went beyond the metropolis and other urban centres of political activities. Whatever the immediate response to Gandhi's arrival on the Indian political scene, it was he who galvanized the masses into action despite the obvious adverse consequences of challenging a well-entrenched colonial power. The Mahatma was perhaps the first to have realized the political inadequacies of the urban-centric national movement in a diverse society like India. Indian nationalism became mass-based and geographically widespread in contrast with its earlier phases when the national movement had a very narrow base. The territorial expansion of nationalism was directly linked with the gradual, but steady expansion of the Indian National Congress which was no longer a platform for mere constitutional opposition to the British rule, but a forum for well-organized campaigns for freedom. By involving the so-called peripheral sections of India, he also let lose another significant process, empowering people to endorse and also challenge the nationalist articulation of freedom struggle by Gandhi and his colleagues in the Indian National Congress. So the Gandhian hegemony in conceptualizing even his critique can never be undermined.

Second, despite their roots in Gandhism, these critiques also provide alternatives to what the Mahatma stood for. It is true that neither M.N. Roy, Rabindranath Tagore nor B.R. Ambedkar was involved in the nationalist struggle as organically as the Mahatma. Hence they missed the wider story which Gandhi both authored and scripted. There is no doubt that the Mahatma paid less attention to some of the major social evils, including the caste system, presumably because the political goal took priority over any other. Furthermore, the issues that figured in critiques of Gandhi were contingent on the contemporary socio-economic and political circumstances. For instance, Tagore's critical response to nation and nationalism owed largely to his own experience of the 1903–8 *swadeshi* movement when the flirtations with the idea of nation had completely alienated the Muslims. Hence, he was not appreciative of a conception that was likely to be divisive in the context of multicultural India. Similarly, M.N. Roy failed to conceptualize Gandhi presumably because of his inability to comprehend the Indian reality which the Mahatma grasped so comprehensively. Despite the creative nature of his well-articulated response, the class model that Roy sought to apply to Indian reality was inadequate to explain the caste-ridden, complex Indian society. Here Gandhi was unique and politically appropriate. By drawing on civilizational resources, not only did he create a stable constituency for the nationalist cause, he also sustained it by providing a proper organizational backing involving people irrespective of class, clan and religion. Despite the success of the Muslim League in carving out an independent space for the Muslims, the Indian National Congress under Gandhi's stewardship maintained its secular character even in circumstances where exclusive ideologies seems to have flourished. In other words, Gandhi's strength lay in his ability to sustain a multi-class nationalist platform seeking primarily to attain political freedom from the British rule, a platform which would allow the nationalists to properly address the relevant social and economic issues crippling the nation. This is where the intervention by Ambedkar was very important. Insisting on 'a just swaraj' for all, Babasaheb was the first to have identified a major flaw in Gandhi's conceptualization of *dalit* and the issues, relevant to their social, political and economic existence. Whereas Gandhi was, in a typical *Brahminical* way, accommodative of the *dalit* issues in the nationalist agenda, Ambedkar endeavoured to carve out an independent space for the *dalits* while negotiating with the British government as well as the dominant nationalist groups, including the Gandhi-led Indian National Congress. More specifically, through a serious contestation of Gandhi's social and political ideas, Ambedkar drew out a new mental map, based on a redefinition of 'freedom' and 'justice' that remained ideologically constrained if conceptualized in caste terms.

There is one final point. Drawing on different, if not contrasting perspectives, these critiques are illustrative of creative nationalist responses to imperialism suggesting the theoretical inadequacies of the so-called modular forms that tend to homogenize the nationalist discourses. In other words, because the modular forms gloss over the peculiar socio-economic and political milieu in which the nationalist response is articulated, they fail to grasp, let alone conceptualize, the ideological basis of most of the nations involved in anti-imperial struggles. As evident in the discussion, instead of approximating to the Western modular forms of nation and nationalism, the Afro-Asian nationalist responses always remain innovative presumably because of the dialectics of anti-imperial movements, the nature of which vary, for obvious reasons, from one location to another. Moreover, the nationalist discourse is neither uniformly structured nor evenly poised. Gandhi was certainly a dominant strand, but not the only one. Hence the importance of the critiques which provide an alternative, based on different ideological perspectives and also differently articulated. So the modular forms appear to be inappropriate within a particular nationalist discourse. In that sense, the alternative points of view of Roy, Tagore and Ambedkar are theoretically innovative and practically useful to understanding the inner tension within the nationalist discourses, in which Gandhism was certainly dominant. They provided critiques within a critique since the Indian response was a critique of the larger nationalist discourses defending the modular forms. Therefore the argument that the nationalist discourses are nothing but 'derivative' does not seem to be plausible by any stretch of the imagination. Furthermore, even Gandhism, which remained one of the major forms of nationalist articulation, had varied manifestations at different levels of the anti-British struggle in India. The major nationalist discourse was, as evident, not only differently textured due perhaps to diverse participants, but also articulated differently, underlining the importance of context. So both Gandhism, and the critiques of those who critically evaluated Gandhi and Gandhism, constitute an important pillar of the nationalist discourse that was neither derivative nor imitative but creative and innovative.

4 Gandhi's writings in *Harijan*

Discussion and interpretation

Gandhi's social and political ideas remain a significant milestone in India's freedom struggle and its aftermath. Although these ideas were constructed during Gandhi's encounter with colonialism, they appear to be transcendental both in connotation and application. What this suggests is the civilizational relevance of Gandhi's ideas in post-colonial societies where political power shifted from the colonial ruler without radically altering the social context in which colonialism flourished. While confronting the British government politically, Gandhi also launched crusades against socially crippling practices, which had been justified in the name of religion. Gandhism was not merely a political ideology, but one with social and political aims. The basic model that Gandhi provided in *Hind Swaraj*[1] remained a constant referent to his later writings in *Harijan*. There is a difference, however, because *Hind Swaraj* was written after the South African experiment of *satyagraha*, whereas many of his articles on pertinent themes in *Harijan* were written after he had become the supreme leader of the Indian national movement. These articles in *Harijan* were less philosophical and tended to be commentaries on the contemporary issues relating to the national movement and the evolution of India as an independent political entity after independence. The aim of this chapter is twofold: first, it deals with five different issues of contemporary relevance that Gandhi dealt with in *Harijan*; and second, it contains a selective number of excerpts from Gandhi's own writings in *Harijan* on these themes to lend the entire text an original flavour. Not only will this section acquaint the readers with Gandhi's prose and style, it will also bring in 'the thematic' focus of Gandhism in conjunction with its 'problematic'.[2] These selective texts are very useful in understanding Gandhi's social and political ideas in the context of an incipient but independent nationalist thought confronting colonialism. This will also enable us to undertake a critical analysis of the nationalist thought, which was hardly derivative and yet had its roots in the discourse of colonialism.

Why *Harijan?*

Harijan, the mouthpiece of the *Servants of Untouchables Society*, was a weekly, usually published on Saturdays. It made its appearance in 1933 and continued publication almost uninterruptedly even after 1947. R.V. Shastri,[3] the founder-editor, held this responsibility while it was published from Poona. One of the reasons contributing to its emergence was as a defence of the 1932 Poona Pact in which Gandhi forced the Congress to accept the reservation of seats for the 'untouchables' even within the quota of caste Hindus,[4] as suggested by the 1932 Communal Award. Gandhi began writing in *Harijan* with arguments in favour of the arrangement as the only solution to avoid 'a caste war' at 'a historical juncture'[5] when he believed that the nationalist movement should not lose sight of its principal goal. As a regular contributor – except when he was incarcerated – Gandhi commented on the major socio-economic and political issues in lucid language. Unlike the *Hind Swaraj*, which had articulated his vision of a good society, his contributions in *Harijan* are varied and dwell on themes which he might not have dealt with in detail elsewhere. Since the weekly was popular and read by millions of Indians, the Mahatma, on occasions, preferred to be polemical to establish an argument defending the Harijan cause. After one year of its publication, Gandhi stated its purpose very unambiguously by saying:

> [i]t devotes itself solely to [the] Harijan cause. Even so it eschews all matters which may be calculated to bring it in conflict with the Government. It eschews politics altogether. These limitations were [obvious] because of the [context] in which it is working. [Given its focus, it will] draw only those men and women who are interested in the campaign against untouchability and who would help the cause even if it is only to the extent of subscribing to the paper and thus helping the only paper that is solely devoted to the cause of anti-untouchability and is the mouthpiece of the Harijan Sevak Sangh.[6]

So *Harijan* provided a forum where Gandhi interacted with his colleagues and contemporaries over issues affecting the anti-British political movement in particular and the nation in general.

Apart from long pieces by Gandhi, a regular section in *Harijan* was the 'Question Box', where Gandhi responded to questions on various issues of contemporary relevance. Questions were generally structured around what Gandhi had written in the weekly and elsewhere. Since the Question Box ensured a dialogue with those seeking to grapple with his views, the Mahatma was always favourably disposed towards the section.[7] *Harijan* was significant in another respect, as the forum where Gandhi generally dealt with the criticism of his published views. While defending his arguments concerning 'the untouchables' and the reservation scheme, as enunciated in the 1932 Poona Pact,[8] Gandhi, for instance, confronted Ambedkar, who declined to publish his views in *Harijan* simply because it was tilted in favour of caste Hindus.[9] Not only was Ambedkar critical of the inherent castist tendencies of the weekly, he was unhappy with the term *harijan* being used to identify the untouchables. By designating the untouchables as *harijans*, Gandhi sought, as Ambedkar argued, to shift our attention from the curse of untouchability. The new name, he added:

> has not elevated them in the eyes of the Hindus. The new name has become completely identified with the subject matter of the old. Everybody knows that Harijans are simply no other than the old untouchables. The new name [therefore] provides no escape to the Untouchables from the curse of untouchability.[10]

A believer in the caste system, Gandhi attributed the articulation of untouchability to 'the distinction between high and low that has crept into Hinduism and is corroding it'.[11] Despite being critical of untouchability as it was practised in Hinduism, he was in favour of 'untouchability of a healthy kind [since] it is a rule of sanitation'.[12] He therefore emphatically declared,

> the moment untouchability [in its present form] goes, [the] caste system itself will be purified, that is to say, according to my dream, it will resolve into the true *varnadharma*, the four divisions of society, each complementary of the other and none inferior or superior to the other, each is necessary for the whole body of Hinduism as any other.[13]

Apart from the Gandhi–Ambedkar debate on this issue, *Harijan* also published the views of Rabindranath Tagore, which ran counter to those of Gandhi, especially after the 1932 Poona Pact. Reducing the seats of the caste Hindus both in the central and provincial legislatures in order to accommodate the 'Depressed Classes', the Pact, Tagore lamented, 'will be a source of perpetual communal jealousy leading to a constant disturbance of peace and fatal break in the spirit of mutual cooperation in [Bengal]'.[14] Gandhi addressed the points raised by Tagore regarding the alleged injustice to Bengal since no representatives from Bengal participated in the deliberations. Articulating the difference with Tagore as an outcome of the difference in their viewpoints, Gandhi did not seem to be persuaded, though this exchange of views adds hitherto unknown dimensions to the debate on untouchability in which Ambedkar has so far been identified as the only nationalist figure opposing Gandhi in this regard.

This chapter seeks to organize Gandhi's views, as published in *Harijan*, in terms of a number of themes, which are as important today as they were then in unravelling the dynamics of a transitional society like India. *Harijan* is a reconfirmation of a particular point of view that the Mahatma began espousing in a systematic manner in the *Hind Swaraj*. These themes also laid the foundation of a political theory which informed what later came to be identified as 'Gandhism'. As a practitioner of what he preached, Gandhi's comments on these themes are very helpful in grasping the context, which underwent dramatic changes in the wake of colonial rule. Gandhi's intervention is useful in another respect. His views on these key themes contributed to a substantial text, one which lends itself to the study of comparative political thought. Seeking to integrate what was worth salvaging in modern civilization within the framework of Indian civilization, Gandhi went beyond the conventional approach to 'nationalist' thought, where the so-called Indian vision was always uncritically glorified, to champion 'a sectarian' political thought.

Nation, nationalism and national identity

Harijan is also very useful in grasping Gandhi's views on nation, nationalism and national identity. Gandhi elaborated his views on these in two different ways: on occasion, he made statements explaining these concepts in the context of India. However, he preferred to deal with them via responses in the Question Box. Unlike Jinnah, Gandhi conceptualized the Indian struggle for independence in a non-nationalist and non-national language. He rarely used the term nation except when forced to do so under circumstances in which Jinnah defended the two-nation theory. In opposition to Jinnah, Gandhi argued that the language of nationalism was both incompatible with the Indian situation and inherently absurd. India was not a nation but a civilization which had benefited from the contributions of different races and religions over the centuries. Indians were, therefore, not 'a motley collection of groups but shared common aspirations and interests and a vague but nonetheless deeply felt commitment to the historical civilization'.[15] Challenging the basis of two-nation theory, Gandhi therefore asked:

> [I]s India composed of two nations? If it is, why only two? Are not Christians a third, Parsis a fourth, and so on? . . . How are the Muslims of Punjab different from the Hindus and Sikhs? Are they not all Punjabis, drinking the same water, breathing the same air and deriving the sustenance from the same soil?[16]

On another occasion, he emphatically argued:

> I have never heard it said that there are as many nations as there are religions on earth. If there are, it would follow that a man changes his nationality when he changes his faith. Thus [according to this logic], the English, Egyptians, Americans, Japanese, etc., are not nations, but Muslims, Parsis, Sikhs, Hindus, Christians, Jews, Buddhists are

different nations no matter where born. I am afraid, the logic [on which the argument is being defended] is very weak in maintaining that nations are or should be divided according to their religions.[17]

As regards the texture of a composite nation like India, Tagore seems to be in agreement with Gandhi. A champion of composite culture, Tagore lamented that

> [T]he Hindu–Moslem disunity is . . . alarming because nothing is more difficult to bridge than the gulf created by religious differences. [T]he disunity between [the two principal] communities is owing to a lack of proper mutual understanding due to differences of habits and customs. Thus Religion and Custom have between them usurped the throne of Reason, thereby destroying all clarity of minds.[18]

Unlike Tagore, Ambedkar found the processes favouring the rise of Pakistan as a separate nation-state perfectly in tune with logic and reason. Since 'Pakistan is [a] manifestation of a cultural unit demanding freedom for the growth of its own distinctive culture', Jinnah's campaign, argued Ambedkar, was both logical and reasonable. He added: 'the Muslims have developed "a will to live as a nation". For them, nature has found a territory which they can occupy and make it a state as well as a cultural home for the new-born Muslim nation'.[19]

The communal question

Harijan was a forum where Gandhi dealt with the Hindu–Muslim question at some length by publishing his views at regular intervals. There seem to be two definite ways in which the Mahatma sought to conceptualize the inter-communal relationship. On the one hand, Gandhi was disturbed by the rapid deterioration of Hindu–Muslim relations primarily because without Hindu–Muslim unity, there could be no *swaraj*. He thus argued: 'I must be impatient for Hindu–Muslim unity because I am impatient for swaraj. [And] the present bickering and petty recriminations between communities are an unnatural aberration.'[20] Attributing the continuity of the British power in India to 'the Hindu–Muslim division',[21] Gandhi, on the other hand, argued that 'the British established themselves by taking advantage of our mutual quarrels and have remained by keeping them alive'.[22] What is striking and clear is that Gandhi appears to have over-emphasized the divisive nature of the British rule and undermined the socio-economic dimension of the Hindu–Muslim schism largely due to the catholicism of Hinduism. It seems that Gandhi strove to analyze the issue on the basis of a surface reading of the problem. This is reflected in his statements seeking to show the apparent unanimity between Hindus and Muslims despite their different faiths. On one occasion, he, for instance, referred to Sir Ali Imam whose 'dress, manners, food were the same as the majority of the Hindus'. Even the name Jinnah, Gandhi argued, 'could be that of any Hindu'. He also mentioned 'Sir Mahommed Iqbal [who] used to speak with pride [of] his brahminical descent. Iqbal and Kitchlew are names common to Hindus and Muslims.' Hence, Gandhi concluded, 'Hindus and Muslims of India are not two nations'.[23] What puzzled Gandhi was the radical transformation of his colleagues who became members of the League later, since 'they were wholeheartedly with the Congress during the memorable Khilafat days. [He therefore] refused to think that these erstwhile comrades can be bitter in their heart towards their fellow-workers as [indicated by] their speeches and writings of today.'[24] So emphatic was his faith in the underlying fraternity among the Hindus and Muslims that he declared:

> I have no doubt that if the British rule which divides us by favouring one or the other as it suits the Britishers were withdrawn today, Hindus and Muslims would forget their quarrels and live like brothers which they are. But supposing the worst happened and we had a civil war, it would last for a few days or months and we would settle down to business. In status, we are equal. Immediately, the British rule is really ended, we shall grow as never before. You don't know how the [British] rule has stunted the nation.[25]

Critique of industrialism/Western civilization

Gandhi was an ardent critic of modern civilization as it emerged in the West and as it was imported to India in the wake of colonial rule. He attacked the very notions of modernity and progress and challenged the central claim that modern civilization was a leveller in which the productive capacities of human labour rose exponentially, creating increased wealth and prosperity for all and hence increased leisure, comfort, health and happiness. Far from attaining these objectives, modern civilization, Gandhi argued, contributed to unbridled competition among human beings and thereby the evils of poverty, disease, war and suffering. It is precisely because modern civilization 'looks at man as a limitless consumer and thus sets out to open the floodgates of industrial production that it also becomes the source of inequality, oppression and violence on a scale hitherto unknown to human history'.[26] What the Mahatma argued in the *Hind Swaraj* regarding industrial civilization was reiterated in *Harijan*. There are articles, comments and statements replete with his condemnation for industrialism and the articulation of an alternative to modern civilization.

For Gandhi, India's economic future lay in *charkha* (spinning wheel)[27] and *khadi* (home-spun cotton textile).[28] 'If India's villages are to live and prosper, the charkha must become universal.' Rural civilization, argued Gandhi, 'is impossible without the charkha and all it implies, i.e. revival of village crafts'.[29] Similarly, *khadi* 'is the only true economic proposition in terms of the millions of villagers until such time, if ever, when a better system of supplying work and adequate wages for every able-bodied person above the age of sixteen, male or female, is found for his field, cottage or even factory in every one of the villages of India'.[30] Since mechanization was 'an evil when there [are] more hands than required for the work, as is the case in India, [he recommended] that the way to take work to the villagers is not through mechanization but it lied [sic] through revival of the industries they have hitherto followed'.[31] He therefore suggested that

> an intelligent plan will find the cottage method fit into the scheme for our country. Any planning in our country that ignores the absorption of labour wealth will be misplaced.... [T]he centralized method of production, whatever may be its capacity to produce, is incapable of finding employment for as large a number of persons as we have to provide for. Therefore it stands condemned in this country.[32]

Gandhi was thoroughly convinced that industrialization as it manifested in the West would have a devastating effect in India. His alternative revolves around his concern for providing profitable employment to all those who are capable. Not only would industrialism undermine the foundation of India's village economy, it 'will also lead to passive or active exploitation of the villagers as the problems of competition and marketing come in'.[33] Critical of Jawaharlal Nehru's passion for industrialization as the most viable way of instantly improving India's economy, he reiterated his position with characteristic firmness by saying that 'no amount of socialization can eradicate ... the evils, inherent in industrialism'.[34] His target was a particular type of mind-set, seduced by the glitter of industrialism, defending at any cost industrialization of the country on a mass scale.[35] His support for traditional crafts was based not on conservative reasoning, but on solid economic grounds in the sense that, by way of critiquing Western civilization, he had articulated an alternative model of economic development that was more suited to the Indian reality. He was critical of the machine-dependent civilization of the West because he believed that 'machinery makes you its slave [and since] we want to be independent and self-supporting ... we should not take the help of machinery when we can do without it'. As his mission was to make Indian villages self-sufficient, he thus reiterated that 'If I can produce my things myself, I become my master and so need no machinery'.[36] In response to a question raised by Rammonohar Lohia regarding the utility of industrialism as complementary to handicrafts, Gandhi came out with a vision of a future social order and the role of industrialism. The social order of the future, argued Gandhi,

> will be based predominantly on the charkha and all it implies. It will include everything that promotes the well-being of the villagers and village life.... I do visualize electricity, ship-building, ironworks,

machine-making and the like existing side by side with village handi-crafts. But the order of dependence will be reversed. Hitherto the indus-trialization has been planned as to destroy the villages and their crafts. I do not share the socialist belief that centralization of the necessaries of life will conduce to the common welfare when the centralized industries are planned and owned by the State.[37]

Non-violence, *khadi* and *satyagraha*

According to Gandhi, *ahimsa* or non-violence was a mode of constructive political and social action just as truth-seeking was the active aspect of *satya* (Truth). Taken together, truth and non-violence constituted the basis of an immutable soul-force, an essential component of *satyagraha*. *Ahimsa* was the rule for realizing the truth of *satyagraha*. 'Truth is a positive value, while non-violence is a negative value. Truth affirms [while] non violence forbids something which is real enough.'[38] *Ahimsa* is a fundamental concept in Gandhi's theory of politics which provided an ideology for the nationalist movement that he led.[39] Radically different from the prevalent ideas of poli-tics that drew on violence, *ahimsa* was also a novel experiment, based on Gandhi's own assessment of the socio-political situation in India. *Satyagraha* was not mere passive resistance. It denoted 'intense activity' involving large masses of people. It was a legitimate, moral and truthful form of political activity of the people against an unjust rule. A form of mass resistance to 'free ourselves of the unjust rule of the Government by defying the unjust rule and accepting the punishment[s] that go with it',[40] *satyagraha* 'is a uni-versal principle of which civil disobedience is one of the many applica-tions. . . . [W]hat is essential is that we should not embarrass an opponent who is in difficulty and make his difficulty our opportunity.'[41]

Satyagraha is 'a science' of political struggle in the sense that a *satyagrahee*, endowed with the highest moral values, is trained to fight the most ruthless state machinery in accordance with the canons of non-violence. Just like an army, '[i]t is enough if the [satyagrahee] trusts his commander and honestly follows his instructions and is ready to suffer unto death without bearing malice against the so-called enemy. . . . [The satyagrahee] must render heart discipline to their commander. There should be no mental reservation.'[42] The commander was Gandhi himself and he thus pronounced, '[j]ust as the General of any army insists that his soldiers should wear a particular uniform, I as your General must insist on your taking to the charkha which will be [your] uniform. Without full faith in truth, non-violence and the charkha, you cannot be my soldiers.'[43] According to the Mahatma, *khadi*, purity and the readiness to sacrifice oneself were three essential conditions for being a *satyagrahee*. Of these, *khadi* was probably an instrument with both economic and political underpinnings. He thus confidently argued that '[t]he wheel is one thing that can become universal and replace the use of arms. If the millions cooperate in plying the charkha for the sake of their economic

liberation, the mere fact will give them an invincible power to achieve political liberation.'[44] It was not surprising therefore when Gandhi argued that the
identity of India was to be sought not in its history or culture, as the mainstream nationalists felt, but in *khadi* or home-spun and home-woven cloth.
Indeed, he insisted that without *khadi* there could be no *swaraj*. In the
ashram, for instance, it was compulsory for all to spin for at least one hour 'in
the name of God, incarnated as the Poor (*daridranarayan*)'.[45] So important was
khadi in his political ideology that he also insisted that all members of the
Congress should weave a certain amount of *khadi* annually to qualify and
maintain membership in the party. *Khadi* was therefore all-pervasive and was
constitutive of the nation that Gandhi conceptualized.

The future state

Harijan is a tract in which Gandhi documented his views on the future state
of India. Although Gandhi declined to comment on the nature of government in a society based deliberately on non-violence, he nonetheless mentioned that the structure of a state, 'constructed in accordance with the law
of non-violence . . . will be different in material particulars from what it is
today'.[46] Holding the federal structure, as conceived by the 1935 Government of India Act, as 'an utter impossibility [since] it contemplates a
partnership, however loose, among dissimilars',[47] he argued that

> [i]mposed federation is likely to divide India more than it is today. It
> would be a great step if the British Government were to declare that
> they would not impose their federal structure on India. The Viceroy
> seems to be acting in that fashion if he is not saying so. . . . [A] clear
> declaration will . . . probably pave the way for real federation and there-
> fore unity. That federation can naturally never be of the Government of
> India Act brand. Whatever it is, it must be a product of the free choice
> of all India.[48]

Once a declaration to free India from bondage was made, the Mahatma
was confident that it would not be difficult to defuse the minorities' fear of
being submerged by the majority since 'No charter of freedom will be worth
looking at which does not ensure the same measure of freedom for the
minorities as for the majority'.[49] He seemed to have applied the same logic
while conceptualizing an alternative world order. Just like a 'nation'-state
where the distinction between the majority and minority appears redundant,
in 'an International League of nations [in which] all nations, big or small . . .
are fully independent', Gandhi argued, 'the smallest nation will feel as tall as
the tallest. The idea of superiority and inferiority will be wholly
obliterated.'[50]

Aware of the difficulties of bringing together disparate units under one
central authority, Gandhi therefore suggested 'cooperative federalism' as

probably the most appropriate scheme for a multicultural, multi-lingual and multi-religious state like India. Confronting a famine in Kathiawar (part of present-day Gujarat) Gandhi realized the importance of what he described as 'voluntary federation'. By simply controlling the movement and prices of grain and fodder during famine and scarcity, the government of India also prevented hoarding by speculators or disposal to the extent of starving the places where they were grown and stored. Furthermore, the government decision to collect grain and fodder from outside the province and distribute them in the famine areas also demonstrated the utility of a federal authority in grave circumstances. So, federation in Gandhi's conceptualization is nothing but another way of attaining his 'humanitarian' goal. Seeking to substantiate his contention, Gandhi further elaborated:

> If the Kathiawar States would voluntarily federate, say, for water, forests and roads, purely for saving life there would be no danger of a water famine such as threatens that cluster of States. There are States rich enough who can provide water for the whole of Kathiawar. I know it cannot be done in a day.... Kathiawar has fairly good rivers and hills. There is no limit to the possibility of artesian wells. If all the States combine and the rich ones use their riches for the common good, they will be saved the awful prospect of people and cattle having to die of thirst.... This cannot be done unless States and the people regard the whole of Kathiawar as their joint and common land and have wisdom enough to desire to live on their land without perpetual dread of having to die of thirst when the God of rain stops supplies.[51]

A voluntary federation draws its sustenance from a constitutional arrangement dispelling the fear of majoritarianism. Gandhi's suggestion regarding the proposed constituent assembly was therefore tuned to protect the multicultural character of the country. As the assembly would be elected on the widest possible franchise, it would possibly be the most appropriate forum to sort out the majority–minority conundrum through discussion. Given the composition of the assembly

> The Muslims, the Scheduled Classes and every other class will be fully represented in the constituent assembly and they will have to decide their own special rights. Even the princes and the zamindars have nothing to fear if they become, and appear, as representatives of the ryots. Independent India will not tolerate any interests in conflict with the true interests of the masses, whether the latter are known as Muslims, Scheduled Classes, Parsis, Jews, Sikhs, Brahmins and non-Brahmins or any other.[52]

In his comment on the Congress resolution of 14 September, 1939 regarding the constituent assembly,[53] he upheld that 'the Constituent Assembly alone can produce a constitution indigenous to the country and truly and fully representing the will of the people. Undoubtedly such a constitution will not be ideal, but it will be real, however imperfect it may be in the estimation of the theorists or legal luminaries.'[54] Not only was the constituent assembly desirable because of its representative character, it was also a platform to 'obviate all clash of communal and class interest'.[55] Gandhi was thus candid when he stated that

> My hope in desiring a Constituent Assembly is that whether the Muslims are represented by the Muslim League mentality or any other, the representatives when they [are] face to face with the reality will not think of cutting up India according to religions but will regard India as an indivisible whole and discover a national, i.e. Indian solution of even specially Muslim questions.[56]

A careful study of his arguments in favour of the constituent assembly clearly shows a shift in his perception of the Muslim League. His confession that the Congress 'does not represent every single interest irrespective of class, caste, colour or creed ... [and also] it has not on its register as many Muslims as it would like'[57] is illustrative here. *Harijan* is thus a unique document because nowhere else had the Mahatma articulated his views on the constituent assembly as clearly as he had done in this weekly.

Primary education was another area that Gandhi pondered over with the utmost seriousness since it was one of the basic ingredients of a non-violent state. While emphasizing the normative meaning and function of education, Gandhi sought to tune education to national goals. He contributed to those institutional and pedagogic practices which revolved around needs rather than abstract ideals, and around experience rather than information. Critical of the British system of primary education, since it was 'devised without any thought of the economic advancement of the country', Gandhi's alternative was based on sound economics for all education was to be through the medium of a craft. It was not education plus training in a craft, 'but it is education', he underlined, 'by means of a craft'.[58] On another occasion, he therefore emphasized that:

> Primary education shall be given only through some craft or the other. Real education and an all-round development of the child is not possible without it. And such education must be self-supporting. This does not mean that each class will be self-supporting. However, boys or girls who will go through the seven-year curriculum in a craft-based school will be able to pay all these years' expenses through their earnings from the crafts.[59]

As regards the script for the Indian languages, Gandhi's comments are more indicative than substantial. Although the issue was regarded 'as an impertinence' in view of 'aggressive provincialism', Gandhi nonetheless argued that 'every nationalist [is] duty-bound to master the two major scripts of *Devnagari* and *Urdu*'.[60]

As one who was critical of institutionalized coercive forces like the police and military, Gandhi never appreciated them even when his attention was drawn to their role in the maintenance of law and order. While commenting on the character of the Russian police and military, he condemned their anti-people mentality since they opposed the 1917 revolution so long as the balance was tilted in favour of the ruling Czar. They joined the revolutionaries only when the defeat of the Czar was imminent. Like their Russian counterparts, the police in a colonial state were 'insensitive'.[61] Gandhi's comments on the British police are illustrative of what he perceived as an ideal form of bureaucracy that was to emerge in the aftermath of colonialism. Drawing on and inspired by *ahimsa*, Gandhi perceived the police as conducive to a radically different socio-economic and political order in which 'the spirit of violence will have all but vanished and internal disorder will have come under control'. Characteristically different from the present-day force, its ranks

> will be composed of believers in non-violence. They will be servants, not masters, of the people. The people will instinctively render them every help, and through mutual cooperation they will easily deal with ever-decreasing disturbances. The police force will have some kind of arms, but they will be rarely used, if at all. In fact the policemen will be reformers. Their police work will be confined to primarily robbers and dacoits. Quarrels between labour and capital and strikes will be few and far between in a non-violent state, because the influence of the non-violent majority will be so great as to command the respect of the principal elements in society.[62]

Gandhi's views on women and their role in the nationalist movement are rather cryptic.[63] His ideology relating to women was contingent on his involvement in contemporary political events and his response to them. Gandhi was an important figure of that historical moment and his ideas on gender were governed accordingly.[64] The epic heroines, Sita and Draupadi, have thus been discussed as examples of women's capacity to suffer in situations underlining the struggle between 'absolute' and 'relative' dharma.[65] The Congress leadership effectively mediated women discontents so that they remained targeted against imperialism.[66] Gandhi too recognized the power of women and contained it for the cause of independence, uniting the nation behind the freedom struggle at the cost of injustice within caste, class and gender relations. Women therefore appear in the history of nationalism only 'in a contributive role'.[67] In this perspective, Gandhi viewed the role of women as complementary to that of men. According to him,

Men and women are of equal rank, but they are not identical. They are a peerless pair, being supplementary to one another; each helps the other so that without the one, the essence of the other cannot be conceived. . . . Man is the supreme in the outward activities of a married pair and therefore, it is in the fitness of things that he should have a greater knowledge thereof. On the other hand, home life is entirely in the sphere of women, and therefore, in domestic affairs, in the upbringing and education of children, women ought to have more knowledge.[68]

Like other nationalists, he also believed that since women were 'naturally' constrained, their 'vocations' must be different. Because '[s]he is passive, he is active. She is essentially mistress of the house, . . . [h]e is the bread-winner.' Compartmentalizing their role on the basis of 'biological attributes' Gandhi thus argued:

they become good householders only by dividing their labour and a wise mother only finds her time fully occupied in looking after her household and children. But when both husband and wife have to labour for mere maintenance, the nation becomes degraded. It is like a bankrupt living on his capital.[69]

Hence it is degrading that women should be called upon or induced

to forsake the hearth and shoulder the rifle for the protection of that hearth. It is a reversion to barbarity and the beginning of the end. In trying to ride the horse that man rides, she brings herself and him down. The sin will be on man's head for tempting or compelling his companion to desert her special calling. There is as much bravery in keeping one's home in good order and condition as there is in defending it against attack from without.[70]

Gandhi's image of women is governed by his perception of what a woman should be. He thus created for her a distinct role in society, as a mother and wife and gave her a primary role in the household. Given his clearly stipulated position, the contribution of women was articulated in such a way as to accommodate them in the well-defined nationalist agenda. Hence Gandhi specified 'spinning' as the exclusive domain of women. Spinning, he argued, 'will remain woman's specialty . . . [since it] is essentially a slow and comparatively silent process'.[71] Since they suffer silently for the betterment of humanity, they 'are the incarnation of *ahimsa* [that means] infinite love and infinite capacity for suffering. Who but woman, the mother of man, shows this capacity in the largest measure?'[72]

As evident, Gandhi provided a nuanced approach to the gender question that was contingent on his role in the nationalist movement as well.[73] However, he made woman an integral part of the freedom struggle, making her realize that she had freedom, qualities and attributes which were crucial both to political independence and social equilibrium. In a path-breaking intervention, the Mahatma therefore made possible not only the involvement of women in politics, but made them indispensable for the national movement against colonialism.

Concluding observations

Harijan is both a plan of action and an articulation of a philosophical stance on the basis of what Gandhi sincerely believed. Unlike *Hind Swaraj*, which the Mahatma wrote while travelling, *Harijan* is a well-argued response to those issues confronting the nationalist movement and its supreme leader. There is no doubt that the issues that had figured prominently in his earlier writings appeared in sharper relief, presumably because the Mahatma was also engaged in the social reconstruction which had probably been peripheral in the period before the 1930s. While in *Hind Swaraj* Gandhi sought to present a coherent argument on society, history and politics, *Harijan* is a compilation of a series of arguments on those contemporary issues which, according to him, required immediate attention. What is clear now is that, in the aftermath of the 1921–2 Non-Cooperation–Khilafat Movement, Gandhi had fashioned his role more as a social reformer and less as a political leader. The most important task Gandhi appears to have undertaken was to build an India that was not tormented by divisions due to 'prejudices, which are essentially artificial'.[74] Accordingly, Gandhi challenged religious, gender-based, national, racial and other divisions. It is altogether a different story that the Congress finally accepted partition as the best available formula to avoid a further bloodbath and Gandhi was rendered totally peripheral in the last days of negotiations for the transfer of power.

Gandhi continues to remain as relevant as before. The historical Gandhi was killed in 1948, but the civilizational Gandhi[75] continues to flourish even in the twenty-first century, through his 'dreams and aspirations for a great evolutionary leap in human civilization'.[76] His greatest contribution as a thinker comes with his invitation to think freshly about the future, and he does so 'by reaching for both the past and the present'.[77] By questioning the inevitability and intractability of modernity, he wants to expose it as a construction that can be resisted. Although it is impossible to return to an earlier cosmos, the Gandhian experiments are powerful endeavours to fill in some of the blank spaces left by modernity. And the Mahatma was aware that the experiment that he had undertaken was neither novel nor unique because 'truth and non violence are as old as the hills'. All he had done was 'to try experiments in both on as vast a scale as [he] could do'.[78]

5   Introducing the text

The following representative excerpts from *Harijan* are useful in articulating Gandhi's social and political thoughts during the period of the Indian nationalist movement when he spearheaded the campaign against colonialism. The philosophical foundation of these ideas was not different from that of his earlier conceptualization. The *Hind Swaraj* continued to remain the primary reference point in the sense that these ideas had their theoretical roots in this seminal text. The ideas in *Harijan* seem to be different in three ways: *first*, while the *Hind Swaraj* was based on his limited experience of *satyagraha* in South Africa, his responses in *Harijan* were shaped by the gigantic nationalist struggle that he conceptualized and led in collaboration with those in the Congress holding more or less identical social and political views. *Second*, the Gandhian ideas in the *Harijan* were dialectically constituted since they had their roots in constant dialogues with other leading personalities of the era who held views contrary to Gandhi. Although his faith in non-violence remained undiluted, he appears to have adapted his political strategies to accommodate others in the nationalist movement. As shown in Chapter 3, the Mahatma, despite his serious differences with Rabindranath Tagore, M.N. Roy and B.R. Ambedkar, never alienated them by simply dismissing the alternatives they suggested. The 1932 Poona Pact, which was nothing but 'a trade-off' between Gandhi and Ambedkar, confirms his unambiguous belief in the national democratic ideology that cemented a bond among classes with contradictory social and economic interests. Similarly, Gandhi's success in articulating the working-class grievances within the nationalist ideological framework also demonstrates his astute sense of strategy in a context when freedom from colonialism was probably prior to other socio-economic agendas. *Third*, his writings in *Harijan* provide explanations for his actions which, to him, were not always goal-oriented, but illustrative of a specific way of life. His life was a series of 'experiments' and hence could not be planned in advance. He therefore wrote about his experiments to gain further out of the responses that his experiments usually evoked. It was a dialectical exercise, for the Mahatma always responded to the reactions to his views, published in *Harijan*. These excerpts are therefore useful in conceptualizing Gandhi, who was not merely a political activist but a theoretician who evolved his plan of action on the basis of a specific understanding of India as a distinct social, economic and political entity.

Gandhi's writings in *Harijan* are copious. The following excerpts are therefore chosen selectively to highlight the distinctive features of Gandhi's social and political thoughts, which, though articulated in the aftermath of the first Civil Disobedience Movement (1931–2), had its ideological roots in his earlier writings, particularly the *Hind Swaraj*. Apart from highlighting the fundamental precepts of Gandhi's social and political ideas, one of the primary aims here is also to define Gandhism by drawing on what the Mahatma wrote in the columns of *Harijan*. Gandhi interpreted and re-interpreted his ideas sometimes in response to the critiques and sometimes in response to the circumstances, although he never compromised his faith in non-violence. There are innumerable passages in *Harijan* to demonstrate this remarkable aspect of Gandhi's social and political thought. In this way, Gandhi was perhaps the most consistent nationalist leader, one who never relinquished his faith nor withdrew from the political scene despite serious challenges from within the Congress. *Harijan* is replete with articles by Gandhi defending non-violence as probably the most appropriate means to launch and sustain a successful *satyagraha* campaign in opposition to social and political oppression. Not only did he deal with civil disobedience against the alien government in *Harijan*, he also paid adequate attention to the age-old social and cultural exploitation in the name of religion and caste. His arguments on certain social issues may not have been persuasive, as the critiques by Tagore and Ambedkar illustrate. What is unique, however, is his concern for issues that were either absent or only peripherally figured in the earlier nationalist articulation. The Gandhian ideology is a peculiar admixture of dialectically linked socio-political and economic issues. Illustrative here are articles in *Harijan*, where Gandhi's emphasis on *khadi* and *charkha* did not merely mean economic regeneration but also provided a clearly defined political ideology, based on the indigenous system of production. This was also Gandhi's critique of the machine civilization of the West which was simply inappropriate to eradicate poverty in India. By drawing on the traditional roots of *khadi* and *charkha*, the Mahatma provided a moral justification for his economic thought; by underlining the obvious inadequacies of industrialism in the context of India's mass poverty, he also articulated a realistic argument in defence of his theory of self-sufficient village republics. Based on this theoretical assumption, he evolved the 'constructive programmes', containing not only specific economic strategies to tackle poverty but also to strengthen social harmony by redefining caste and *varnashrama* in a creative way. Similarly, his *nayeei talim* (alternative education) was a clear departure from the prevalent methods. By characterizing education as a device to bring about an all-round development of the human being (in body, mind and spirit), Gandhi was in fact forging a new path by dissociating himself as much from those clinging to the spiritually oriented

Hindu educational system as from those colonialists who uncritically accepted the English system.

Given the vast nature and complex character of Gandhi's writings in *Harijan*, the excerpts are structured thematically. As the space is limited, it is not possible to incorporate a large number of articles which are equally relevant. I have selected those Gandhi-written *Harijan* pieces that have either been quoted in the text of this book or are too significant to be ignored. Apart from three excerpts from *Harijansevak* (*Harijansevak*, 26 February, 1938, p. 142) and *Harijanbandhu* (*Harijanbandhu*, 19 January, 1936, pp. 155–6, *Harijanbandhu*, 17 October, 1937, pp. 161–2), this exercise is limited to selected articles, published by the Mahatma in *Harijan*, to accord an authentic flavour to Gandhi's social and political thought. In other words, since *Harijan* was the Mahatma's contextualized response to contemporary social, economic and political issues, it is a unique literary commentary on nationalism in India that, given its peculiar characteristics, was not derivative of the modular European form. So, notwithstanding its stated objective of dwelling only on social issues, *Harijan* virtually becomes an authentic text of Gandhi's social and political thought in the context of perhaps the most gigantic nationalist struggle of the twentieth century.

GANDHI'S WRITINGS IN *HARIJAN*

Satyagraha

What is satyagraha?

Satyagraha is a universal principle of which civil disobedience is one of the many applications. Satyagraha goes on no matter whether the opponent is in difficulty or not, for offered in the proper spirit it is service of the opponent. What is essential is that we should not embarrass an opponent who is in difficulty and make his difficulty our opportunity. That is why civil disobedience, which can be applied only under certain conditions and circumstances, may not be applied against an opponent in difficulty. Civil disobedience is not the law of life: satyagraha is. Satyagraha, therefore, never ceases; civil disobedience can cease and ought to when there is no occasion for it. Then there are two kinds of civil disobedience – aggressive and defensive. Defensive civil disobedience becomes a duty when insult or humiliation is imposed upon us by an opponent. That duty would have to be done whether the opponent is in difficulty or not. An opponent in difficulty may not expect people to obey unjust or humiliating laws or orders. Aggressive civil disobedience embarrasses the opponent, whether we mean to embarrass him or not. Traveling in a railway train without a ticket – assuming for a moment that it is civil disobedience, which it is not – would be taboo, for it would be merely to embarrass the opponent. In brief, there is nothing which being normally justifiable and conducive to swaraj would be taboo even if it seems to embarrass the opponent. To do what is morally necessary and beneficial is a duty and quite a different thing from that which may not be morally indefensible but calculated to vex and embarrass an opponent in difficulty. To make his difficulty one's opportunity is in no case justifiable.

(*Harijan*, 6 January, 1940, *CWMG*, Vol. 71, pp. 62–3)

Non-violence

(a) *Non violence* is the law of the human race and is infinitely greater than and superior to brute force. (b) In the last resort it does not avail to those who do not possess a living faith in the God of Love. (c) Non-violence affords the fullest protection to one's self respect and sense of honour, but not always to possession of land or movable property, though its habitual practice does prove a better bulwark than the possession of armed men to defend them. Non violence in the very nature of things is of no assistance in the defence of ill-gotten gains and immoral acts. (d) Individuals or nations who would practise non-violence must be prepared to sacrifice (nations to the last man) their all except honour. It is therefore inconsistent with the possession of other people's countries, i.e., modern imperialism which is frankly based on force for its defence. (e) Non-violence is a power which can be wielded equally by all – children, young men and women or grown-up people – provided they have a living faith in the god of love and have therefore equal love for all mankind. When non-violence is accepted as the law of life it must pervade the whole being and not [be] applied to isolated acts. (f) It is a profound error to suppose that whilst the law is good enough for individuals it is not for [the] masses of mankind.

(*Harijan*, 5 September, 1936, *CWMG*, Vol. 63, p. 262)

Non-violence cannot be taught to a person who fears to die and has not power of resistance. A helpless mouse is not non-violent because he is always eaten by pussy. He would gladly eat the murderess if he could, but he ever tries to flee from her. We do not call him a coward, because he is made by nature to behave no better than he does. But a man who, when faced by danger, behaves like a mouse, is rightly called a coward. He harbours violence and hatred in his heart and would kill his enemy if he could without being hurt himself. He is a stranger to non-violence. All sermonizing on it will be lost on him. Bravery is foreign to his nature. Before he can understand non-violence he has to be taught to stand his ground and even suffer death in the attempt to defend himself against the aggressor who bids fair to overwhelm him. To do otherwise would be to confirm his cowardice and take him further away from non-violence. Whilst I may not actually help anyone to retaliate, I must not let a coward seek shelter behind non-violence so called. Not knowing the stuff of which non-violence is made many have honestly believed that running away from danger every time was a virtue compared to offering resistance especially if it is fraught with danger to one's life. As a teacher of non-violence, I must, so far as it is possible for me, guard against such an unmanly belief.

Non-violence is the greatest force at the disposal of mankind. It is mightier than the mightiest weapon of destruction devised by ingenuity of man. Destruction is not the law of the humans. Man lives freely only by his readiness to die, if need be, at the hands of his brother, never by killing him. Every murder or other injury, no matter for what cause, committed or inflicted on another is a crime against humanity.

(*Harijan*, 20 July, 1935, *CWMG*, Vol. 61, pp. 265–6)

How non-violence works

My faith in *non-violence* remains as strong as ever. I am quite sure that not only should it answer all our requirements in our country, but that it should, if properly applied, prevent the bloodshed that is going on outside India and is threatening to overwhelm the Western world.

My aspiration is limited. God has not given me the power to guide the world on the path of non-violence. But I have imagined that he has chosen me as His instrument for presenting non-violence to India for dealing with her many ills. The progress already made is great. But much more remains to be done. And yet I seem to have lost the power to evoke the needed response from Congressmen in general. It is a bad carpenter who quarrels with his tools. It is a bad general who blames his men for faulty workmanship. I know I am not a bad general. I have wisdom enough to know my limitations. God will give me strength enough to declare my bankruptcy if such is to [be] my lot. He will perhaps take me away when I am no longer wanted for the work which I have been permitted to do for nearly half [a] century. But I do entertain the hope that there is yet work for me to do, that the darkness that seems to have enveloped me will disappear, and that, whether with another battle more brilliant than the Dandi March or without, India will come to her own demonstrably through non-violent means. I am praying for the light that will dispel the darkness. Let those who have a living faith in non-violence join me in the prayer.

(*Harijan*, 23 July, 1938, *CWMG*, Vol. 67, pp. 197–8)

I hold that *non-violence* is not merely a personal virtue. It is also a social virtue to be cultivated like the other virtues. Surely society is largely regulated by the expression of non-violence in its mutual dealings. What I ask for is an extension of it on a larger, national and international scale.

(*Harijan*, 7 January, 1939, *CWMG*, Vol. 68, p. 278)

In theory, if there is sufficient *non-violence* developed in any single person, he should be able to discover the means of combating violence, no matter how widespread or severe, within his jurisdiction. I have repeatedly admitted my imperfections. I am not an example of perfect ahimsa. I am evolving. Such ahimsa as has been developed in me has been found enough to cope with situations that have hitherto arisen. But today I feel helpless in the face of the surrounding violence. There was a penetrating article in the *The Statesman* on my Rajkot statement. The editor had therein contended that the English had never taken our movement to be true satyagraha, but being practical people they had allowed the myth to continue though they had known it to be a violent revolt. I was none the less so because the rebels had no arms. I have quoted the substance from memory. When I read the article, I felt the force of the argument. Though I had intended the movement to be pure non-violent resistance, as I look back upon the happening of those days, there was undoubtedly violence among the resisters. I must own that had I been perfectly tuned to the music of ahimsa, I would have sensed the slightest departure from it and my sensitiveness would have rebelled against any discord in it.

It seems to me that the united action of the Hindus and the Muslims blinded me to the violence that was lurking in the breasts of many. The English who are trained diplomats and administrators are accustomed to the line of least resistance, and when they found that it was more profitable to conciliate a big organization than to crush it by extensive frightfulness, they yielded to the extent that they thought was necessary. It is, however, my conviction that our resistance was predominantly non-violent in action and will be accepted as such by the future historian. As a seeker of truth and non-violence, however, I must not be satisfied with mere action if it is not from the heart. I must declare from the house-tops that the non-violence of those days fell far short of the non-violence as I have so often defined.

Non-violent action without the co-operation of the heart and the head cannot produce the intended result. The failure of our imperfect ahimsa is visible to the naked eye. Look at the feud that is going on between Hindus and Muslims. Each is arming for the fight with the other. The violence that we had harboured in our breasts during the non-co-operation days is now recoiling upon ourselves. The violent energy that was generated among the masses, but was kept under check in the pursuit of a common objective, has now been let loose and is being used among and against ourselves.

(*Harijan*, 8 July, 1939, *CWMG*, Vol. 69, pp. 389–90)

I believe that a State can be administered on a non-violent basis if the vast majority of the people are non-violent. So far as I know, India is the only country which has a possibility of being such a State. I am conducting my experiment in that faith. Supposing, therefore, that India attained independence through pure non-violence, India could retain it too by the same means. A non-violent man or society does not anticipate or provide for attacks from without. On the contrary such a person or society firmly believes that nobody is going to disturb them. If the worst happens, there are two ways open to non-violence. To yield possession but non-co-operate with the aggressor. Thus, supposing that a modern edition of Nero descended upon India, the representatives of the State will let him in but tell him that he will get no assistance from the people. They will prefer death to submission. The second way would be non-violent resistance by the people who have been trained in the non-violent way. They would offer themselves unarmed as fodder for the aggressor's cannons. The underlying belief in either case is that even a Nero is not devoid of a heart. The unexpected spectacle of endless rows upon rows of men and women simply dying rather than surrender to the will of an aggressor must ultimately melt him and his soldiery. Practically speaking, there will be probably no greater loss in men than if forcible resistance was offered; there will be no expenditure in armaments and fortifications. The non-violent training received by the people will add inconceivably to their moral height. Such men and women will have shown personal bravery of a type far superior to that shown in armed warfare. In each case the bravery consists in dying, not in killing. Lastly, there is no such thing as defeat in non-violent resistance. That such a thing has not happened before is no answer to my speculation. I have drawn no impossible picture. History is replete with instances of individual non-violence of the type I have mentioned. There is no warrant for saying or thinking that a group of men and women cannot by sufficient training act non-violently as a group or nation. Indeed, the sum total of the experience of mankind is that men somehow or other live on. From which fact I infer that it is the law of love that rules mankind. Had violence, i.e., hate, ruled us, we should have become extinct long ago. And yet the tragedy of it is that the so-called civilized men and nations conduct themselves as if the basis of society was violence. It gives me ineffable joy to make experiments proving that love is the supreme and only law of life. Much evidence to the contrary cannot shake my faith. Even the mixed non-violence of India has supported it. But if it is not enough to convince an unbeliever, it is enough to incline a friendly critic to view it with favour.

(*Harijan*, 13 April, 1940, *CWMG*, Vol. 71, pp. 407–8)

Ahimsa cannot be dismissed so lightly as [one seems to think]. Ahimsa is the strongest force known. But if all can use the strongest force with equal ease, it would lose its importance. We have not been able yet to discover the true measure of the innumerable properties of an article of daily use like water. Some of its properties fill us with wonder. Let us not, therefore, make light of a force of the subtlest kind like ahimsa, and let us try to discover its hidden power with patience and faith. Within a brief space of time we have carried to a fairly successful conclusion a great experiment in the use of this force. As you know I have not set much store by it. Indeed I have hesitated even to call it an experiment in ahimsa. But according to the legend, as Rama's name was enough to float stones, even so the movement carried on in the name of ahimsa brought about a great awakening in the country and carried us ahead. It is difficult to forecast the possibilities when men with unflinching faith carry this experiment further forward. To say that those who use violence are all insensible is an exaggeration. Some do seem to lose their senses, but we are bound to be mistaken if we try to base a moral law on those exceptions. The safest course is to lay down laws on the strength of our usual experience, and our usual experience is that in most cases non-violence is the real antidote to violence, and it is safe to infer from it that the highest violence can be met by the highest non-violence.

But let us consider for a moment inanimate objects. He will surely break his head who strikes it against a stone. But supposing a stone comes against us through space, we can escape it by stepping aside, or if there is nowhere to step aside, we can bravely stay where we are and receive the stone. That will mean minimum injury and, in case it proves fatal, the death will not be as painful as it would be if we made an effort to ward it off.

Extend the thought a little further, and it is easy to see that, if a senseless man is left alone and no one tries to resist him, he is sure to exhaust himself. Indeed it is not quite inconceivable that the loving sacrifice of many may bring an insane man to his senses. Instances are not wanting of absolutely insane people having come back to their senses.

(*Harijan*, 28 July, 1940, *CWMG*, Vol. 72, p. 307)

Let us confine ourselves to *ahimsa*. We have all along regarded the spinning-wheel, village crafts, etc. as the pillars of ahimsa, and so indeed they are. They must stand. But have now to go a step further. A votary of ahimsa will of course base upon non-violence, if he has not already done so, all his relations with his parents, his children, his wife, his servants, his dependants, etc. But the real test will come at the time of political or communal disturbances or under the menace of thieves and dacoits. Mere resolve to lay down one's life under the circumstances is not enough. There must be the necessary qualification for making the sacrifice. If I am a Hindu, I must fraternize with the Mussalmans and the rest. In my dealings with them I may not make any distinction between my co-religionists and those who might belong to a different faith. I would seek opportunities to serve them without any feeling of fear or unnaturalness. The word 'fear' can have no place in the dictionary of ahimsa. Having thus qualified himself by his selfless service, a votary of pure ahimsa will be in a position to make a fit offering of himself in a communal conflagration. Similarly, to meet the menace of thieves and dacoits, he will need to go among, and cultivate friendly relations with, the communities from which thieves and dacoits generally come.

(*Harijan*, 21 July, 1940, *CWMG*, Vol. 72, pp. 281–2)

How will (one) run administration non-violently?

If you assume that we would have won independence by non-violent means, it means that the bulk of the country had been organized non-violently. Without the vast majority of people having become non-violent, we could not attain non-violent swaraj. If, therefore, we attain swaraj by purely non-violent means, it should not be difficult for us to carry on the administration without the military. The *goondas* [outlawed] too will then have come under our control. If, for instance in Sevagram we have five or seven goondas in a population of seven hundred who are non-violently organized, the five or seven will either live under the discipline of the rest or leave the village.

But you will see that I am answering the question with the utmost caution, and my truth makes me admit that we might have to maintain a police force. But the police will be after our pattern, and not the British pattern. As we shall have adult suffrage, the voice of even the youngest of us will count. That is why I have said that the ideally non-violent State will be an ordered anarchy. That State will be the best governed which is governed the least. The pity is that no one trusts me with the reins of government! Otherwise I would show how to govern non-violently. If I maintain a police force, it will be a body of reformers.

[. . .]

So long as we are not saturated with pure ahimsa we cannot possibly win swaraj through non-violence. We can come into power only when we are in a majority or, in other words, when the large majority of people are willing to abide by the law of ahimsa. When this happy state prevails, the spirit of violence will have all but vanished and internal disorder will have come under control.

(*Harijan*, 1 September, 1940, *CWMG*, Vol. 72, p. 403)

The nature of the police force

Nevertheless I have conceded that even in a non-violent State a police force may be necessary. This, I admit, is a sign of my imperfect ahimsa. I have not the courage to declare that we can carry on without a police force as I have in respect of any army. Of course I can and do envisage a state where the police will not be necessary; but whether we shall succeed in realizing it, the future alone will show.

The police of my conception will, however, be of a wholly different pattern from the present-day force. Its ranks will be composed of believers in non-violence. They will be servants, not masters, of people. The people will instinctively render them every help, and through mutual co-operation they will easily deal with the ever-decreasing disturbances. The police force will have some kind of arms, but they will be rarely used, if at all. In fact the policemen will be reformers. Their police work will be confined primarily to robbers and dacoits. Quarrels between labour and capital and strikes will be few and far between in a non-violent state, because the influence of the non-violent majority will be so great as to command the respect of the principal elements in society. Similarly there will be no room for communal disturbances. Then we must remember that when such a Congress government comes into power the large majority of men and women of 21 years and over will have been enfranchised. The rigid and cramped Constitution of today has of course no place in this picture.

(*Harijan*, 1 September, 1940, *CWMG*, Vol. 72, pp. 403–4)

Role of women

I had flattered myself that my contribution to the woman's cause definitely began with the discovery of satyagraha. But the writer of the letter is of [the] opinion that the fair sex requires treatment different from men. If it is so, I do not think any man will find the correct solution. No matter how much he tries, he must fail because nature has made him different from woman. Only the toad under the harrow knows where it pinches him. Therefore ultimately woman will have to determine with authority what she needs. My own opinion is that, just as fundamentally man and woman are one, their problem must be one in essence. The soul in both is the same. The two live the same life, have the same feelings. Each is a complement of the other. The one cannot live without the other's active help.

But somehow or other man has dominated woman from ages [in the] past, and so woman has developed an inferiority complex. She has believed in the truth of man's interested teaching that she is inferior to him. But the seers among men have recognized her equal status.

Nevertheless there is no doubt that at some point there is bifurcation. Whilst both are fundamentally one, it is also equally true that in the form there is a vital difference between the two. Hence the vocations of the two must also be different. The duty of motherhood, which the vast majority of women will always undertake, requires qualities which man need not possess. She is passive, he is active. She is essentially mistress of the house. He is the bread-winner, she is the keeper and distributor of the bread. She is the caretaker in every sense of the term. The art of bringing up the infants of the race is her special and sole prerogative. Without her care the race must become extinct.

In my opinion it is degrading both for man and woman that women should be called upon or induced to forsake the hearth and shoulder the rifle for the protection of that hearth. It is a reversion to barbarity and the beginning of the end. In trying to ride the horse that man rides, she brings herself and him down. The sin will be on man's head for tempting or compelling his companion to desert her special calling. There is as much bravery in keeping one's home in good order and condition as there is in defending it against attack from without.

[. . .]

[W]oman is the incarnation of ahimsa. Ahimsa means infinite love, which again means infinite capacity for suffering. Who but woman, the mother of man, shows this capacity in the largest measure? She shows it as she carries the infant and feeds it during nine months and derives joy in the suffering involved. What can beat the suffering caused by the pangs of labour? But she forgets them in the joy of creation. Who again suffers daily so that her babe may wax from day to day? Let her transfer that love to the whole of humanity, let her forget she ever was or can be the object of man's lust. And she will occupy her proud position by the side of man as his mother, maker and silent leader. It is given to her to teach the art of peace to the warring world thirsting for that nectar. She can become the leader in satyagraha which does not require the learning that books give but does require the stout heart that comes from suffering and faith.

(*Harijan*, 24 February, 1940, *CWMG*, Vol. 71, pp. 206–9)

The *charkha* and *khadi* vs the machine

Charkha-swaraj-ahimsa

The spinning-wheel represents to me the hope of the masses. The masses lost their freedom, such as it was, with the loss of the charkha. The charkha supplemented the agriculture of the villagers and gave it dignity. It was the friend and solace of the widow. It kept the villagers from idleness. For the charkha included all the anterior and posterior industries – ginning, carding, warping, sizing, dyeing and weaving. These in their turn kept the village carpenter and the blacksmith busy. The charkha enabled the seven hundred thousand villages to become self-contained. With the exit of the charkha went the other village industries, such as the oil-press. Nothing took the place of these industries. Therefore the villages were drained of their varied occupations and their creative talent and what little wealth these brought them.

[. . .]

Twenty years' experience of charkha work has convinced me of the correctness of the argument here advanced by me. The charkha has served the poor Muslims and Hindus in almost an equal measure. Nearly five crores of rupees have been put into the pockets of these lakhs of village artisans without fuss and tom-tomming [*sic*].

Hence I say without hesitation that the charkha must lead us to swaraj in terms of the masses belonging to all faiths. The charkha restores the villages to their rightful place and abolishes distinctions between high and low.

But the charkha cannot bring swaraj, in fact it will not move, unless the nation has faith in non-violence. It is not exciting enough. Patriots yearning for freedom are apt to look down upon the charkha. They will look in vain to find it in history books. Lovers of liberty are fired with the zeal to fight and banish the foreign ruler. They impute all the vices to him and see none in themselves. They cite instances of countries having gained their freedom through seas of blood. The charkha devoid of violence seems an utterly tame affair.

(Harijan, 13 April, 1940, CWMG, Vol. 71, pp. 410–11)

Is khadi *economically sound?*

If by the question is meant whether khadi can compete with Japanese 'fent' or even with the cloth manufactured by the Indian Mills in price, the answer must be emphatically 'no'. But the negative answer would have to be given about almost everything turned out by man-power as against labour-saving power. It would have to be so even with regard to goods manufactured in Indian factories. Both iron and sugar made in factories require State aid in some from or other to withstand foreign competition. It is wrong to put the question in that way at all. In the open market a more organized industry will always be able to drive out a less organized one, much more so when the former is assisted by bounties and can command unlimited capital and can therefore afford to sell its manufactures at a temporary loss. Such has been the tragic fate of many enterprises in this country.

Any country that exposes itself to unlimited foreign competition can be reduced to starvation and therefore subjection if the foreigners desire it. This is known as peaceful penetration. One has to go only a step further to understand that the result would be the same as between hand-made goods and those made by power-driven machinery. We are seeing the process going on before our eyes. Little flour mills are ousting the chakkis, oil mills the village *ghani*, rice mills the village *dhenki*, sugar mills the village *gur*-pans, etc. This displacement of village labour is impoverishing the villagers and enriching the monied men. If the process continues sufficiently long the villages will be destroyed without any further effort. No Chengis Khan could devise a more ingenious or more profitable method of destroying these villages. And the tragedy of it all is that the villagers are unconsciously but none the less surely contributing to their own destruction. To complete the tale of their woe let the reader know that even cultivation has ceased to be profitable. For some crops the villager does not cover even the cost of seed.

With all these deadly admissions, what do I mean by saying that khadi is the only true economic proposition? Let me then state the proposition fully: 'Khadi is the only true economic proposition in terms of the millions of villagers until such time, if ever, when a better system of supplying work and adequate wages for every able-bodied person above the age of sixteen, male or female, is found for his field, cottage or even factory in every one of the villages of India: or till sufficient cities are built up to displace the villages so as to give the villagers the necessary comforts and amenities that a well-regulated life demands and is entitled to.' I have only to state the proposition thus fully to show that khadi must hold the field for any length of time that we can think of.

The present pressing problem is how to find work and wages for the millions of villagers who are becoming increasingly pauperized, as anyone who will take the trouble of going to the villages can testify for himself and as is amply proved by contemporary expert evidence that people are becoming poorer economically, mentally and morally. They are fast losing the will to work, to think and even to live. It is a living death that they are living.

Khadi supplies them with work, tools and a ready market for their manufactures. It gives them hope where but yesterday there was blank despair.

(*Harijan*, 20 June, 1936, *CWMG*, Vol. 63, pp. 77–9)

{K}*hadi* is pure swadeshi. I have also been claiming that swaraj hangs by the handspun yarn; the latter is also the foundation of our independence. Some say that this is an exaggerated statement and that I speak of khadi in hyperboles like a bard who makes much of some petty thing. But I have never resorted to exaggeration. I claim to be a satyagrahi. Such a one does not tell a lie. Whether one describes a single thing as two or a hundred thousand, both involve falsehood. How then did I, a satyagrahi, make such a statement? After so many years I have again started repeating the same thing. Khadi can bring swaraj only if we are convinced of the principle underlying it. Swaraj cannot be won just by donning khadi without any understanding. What do the wealthy people of Ahmedabad know of business dealings? They just fill their own bellies, bring up their own children, and throw money to a few labourers. I claim to be a [real] businessman. I propose to bring dal, rice, roti and ghee to every Indian. I wish no one to remain unclothed. So long as this is not accomplished, my business is not worth its name. I shall be able to carry on true business if you carry out my suggestions.

(*Harijansevak*, 26 February, 1938, *CWMG*, Vol. 66, pp. 372–3)

How to popularize khadi?

There is no doubt that khadi cannot compete with mill-cloth, it was never meant to. If the people will not understand or appreciate the law governing khadi, it will never be universal. It must then remain the fad of moneyed people and cranks.

But khadi has a big mission. Khadi provides dignified labour to the millions who are otherwise idle for nearly four months in the year. Even apart from the remuneration the work brings, it is its own reward. For if millions live in compulsory idleness, they must die spiritually, mentally and physically. The spinning-wheel automatically raises the status of millions of poor women. Even though, therefore, mill-cloth were to be given gratis to the people, their true welfare demands that they should refuse to have it in preference to khadi, the product of their labours.

Life is more than money. It is cheaper to kill our aged parents who can do no work and who are a drag on our slender resources. It is also cheaper to kill our children whom we do not need for our material comfort and whom we have to maintain without getting anything in return. But we kill neither our parents nor our children, but consider it a privilege to maintain without getting anything in return. But we kill neither our parents nor our children, but consider it a privilege to maintain them no matter what their maintenance costs us. Even so must we maintain khadi to the exclusion of all other cloth. It is the force of habit which makes us think of khadi in terms of prices. We must revise our notion of khadi economics. And when we have studied them from the point of view of the national well-being, we shall find that khadi is never dear. We must suffer dislocation of domestic economy during the transition stage. At present we are labouring under a heavy handicap. Cotton production has been centralized for the sake of Lancashire and, if you will, for the sake of Indian mills. Prices of cotton are determined by the prices in foreign lands, when the production of cotton is distributed in accordance with the demands of khadi economics, cotton prices would not fluctuate and, in any case, will be, in effect, lower than today. When the people, either through state protection or through voluntary effort, have cultivated the habit of using only khadi, they will never think of it in terms of money, even as millions of vegetarians do not compare the prices of flesh foods with those of non-flesh foods. They will starve rather than take flesh foods even though they may be offered free.

[. . .]

Khadi was an integral part of the original swaraj programme of 1920. In 1921–2 thousands of Congressmen repeated from hundreds of platforms that swaraj for the millions depended upon the spinning-wheel humming in every village. The late Ali Brothers used to say, at the numerous meetings they addressed, that without the charkhas in every cottage and the loom in every village there was no freedom. Maulana Mahomed Ali used to say in his picturesque language that our *charkhas* were our instruments of war and the cones of yarn turned out by them were our ammunition. He said this with a conviction that went home to his audiences. But the faith of those early days was not sustained. Congressmen in general have ceased to connect khadi with swaraj. Shri Jawaharlal Nehru has called khadi the livery of our freedom. For how many does it bear that meaning? If congressmen could have that belief, khadi itself would be current coin. Freedom is never dear at any price. It is the breath of life. What would a man not pay for living? The Congress flag was designed to represent not civil disobedience which is but a phase, but it was designed to represent the essentials of freedom. Its background is khadi. The spinning-wheel covers and sustains it. Its colours show how necessary communal unity is for the attainment of freedom. Given the fulfillment of these conditions, civil disobedience and the suffering it implies may not be at all necessary. To wear khadi is for me to wear freedom.

(*Harijan*, 10 December, 1938, *CWMG*, Vol. 68, pp. 173–4, 175)

Khadi *and spinning*

From the economic point of view it is enough to take to khadi. But if khadi is to be our weapon for winning swaraj, spinning is of equal necessity. Khadi gives us economic self-sufficiency, whereas spinning links us with the lowest paid labour. In militarized countries everyone gives a certain time for military purposes. Ours being a non-violent basis, everyone should do sacrificial spinning for a minimum period from year to year. Maulana Mohomed Ali used to call the *takli* (spinning wheel) and the yarn our arms and ammunition for winning swaraj. The analogy is telling. Is it too much for us to give half an hour or one hour per day to spinning as a measure of voluntary conscription? I remember, at the beginning of the last war when I was in England I was given pajama suits to stitch for the soldiers. Many others from the most aristocratic families including some venerable old ladies and gentlemen were doing such work. We all finished our quota of work as we were required to. No one considered it beneath his or her dignity to do so. Towards the end of the war far more work was given by the whole nation. Yet no one complained. I warn you that, although today I am asking you only to give half an hour or one hour per day to spinning, I may have to be more exacting as the situation develops.

(*Harijan*, 6 April, 1940, *CWMG*, Vol. 71, pp. 381–2)

Spinning wheels vs. mills

Congressmen should not weary of my filling these columns with everything about the charkha and khadi. Heart peace among communities and reinstatement of the wheel in every home are my politics, for I expect to gain the freedom of the country from political and economic bondage through these means in the place of red rebellion.

The problem before every Congressman is how to displace mill-cloth, whether foreign or indigenous. It is often believed in Congress circles that indigenous mill-cloth is as good as khadi and superior because of its cheapness. The cheapness theory in terms of the crores of artisans has been exploded. Mill-spun for these millions is dearer than hand-spun. The former means deprivation of their wages. Imagine what would happen if, on the score of foreign wheat being cheaper, the wheat-grower was displaced!

If the village spinners and weavers are to come into their own, and that quickly, every Congressman has to become a master spinner and master weaver. He should be able to teach and guide the poor villagers. He has to be a khadi technician. He has to spin for the sake of the country. I have shown that khadi cannot be made cheap enough for the middle class unless there is enough sacrificial yarn or unless the spinner is put upon the old *begar* [forced labour] wage of one paisa to one anna for eight hours' strenuous spinning.

No Congressman would put in the required labour and skill unless he believed that the indigenous factory mills had to be and could be replaced by the charkha and the handloom.

If Congressmen have this faith, all Congress organizations will become efficient spinning and weaving schools. I remember how in 1921 Congress offices used to collect indifferently spun yarn and expect it to be woven somehow. It was all a huge waste. Nobody knew how to deal with it nor what to do to ensure good spinning. Things are different now. . . . Every Congress office should become a model laboratory and spinning and weaving institute for the organization of villages. And, as I have suggested, khadi is the centre round which other village industries should revolve and be organized. Congressmen will discover the tremendous possibilities of this kind of service. It is chiefly mental lethargy that is in the way of quick and successful organization of villages. I suggest that, if India is to evolve along nonviolent lines, it will have to decentralize many things. Centralization cannot be sustained and defended without adequate force. Simple homes from which there is nothing to take away require no policing; the palaces of the rich must have strong guards to protect them against dacoity. So must huge factories. Rurally organized India will run less risk of foreign invasion than urbanized India, well equipped with military, naval and air forces.

Assuming then that Congressmen have understood the meaning and implications of the charkha, they would, without a moment's delay, set about qualifying themselves for the service. Assume further that they are novices. Then they will procure some cotton, preferably grown in their villages, *taluks* or districts. They should gin it with the hand or at the most on a board with the help of a rod. They will keep the seed and, when they have enough, either sell it or use it for their cattle if they have any. They will card the cotton with a hand-bow, costing next to nothing. They can improvise one themselves. This carded cotton should be turned into slivers. These will be spun on the *takli* (spinning wheel). When they have fairly mastered these processes, they can proceed to speedier ones. They will also put themselves and the members of their families right regarding the use of khadi. They will keep an accurate record of their daily progress and will learn the arithmetic of yarn.

The economics of khadi require that from cultivation of cotton to the manufacture of khadi and its disposal all the processes should, as far as possible, be gone through in the same village or centre. Thus, it is wrong to spin yarn in the Punjab, weave it in Bombay, and sell in Malabar the khadi thus manufactured. If Congressmen and committees attend to this simple rule when beginning khadi work, they will not find themselves appalled by the difficulty of the task. If they succeed in their own district, there is no reason why the other 249 districts [in Malabar] should not be successfully organized. The reasoning is valid even if villages were treated as units. It must be confessed that we have not as yet one single village organized in that fashion.

(*Harijan*, 30 December, 1939, *CWMG*, Vol. 71, pp. 55–6)

Critique of machine civilization

We should not use machinery for producing things which we can produce without its aid and have got the capacity to do so. As machinery makes you its slave, we want to be independent and self-supporting; so we should not take the help of machinery when we can do without it. We want to make our villages free and self-sufficient and through them achieve our goal – liberty – and also protect it. I have no interest in the machine nor [do] I oppose it. If I can produce my things myself, I become my master and so need no machinery.

(Harijan, 6 April, 1940, CWMG, Vol. 71, p. 383)

Motor vs. cart

Gram Udyog Patrika for August examines the respective merits of motor-vans and carts for village propaganda. Those who will read the whole argument should send for the Patrika. I give below the most important part of the argument.[1]

We have been asked whether District Boards and such other local bodies, who wish to set apart a certain amount of money for village work, will do well to invest in motor-vans for propaganda work of various kinds in villages.... The question is whether speeding up matters by the use of motor-vans which can visit more than one village in a night will suit the purpose.

In all our expenditure, especially when that expenditure is under-taken expressly for the benefit of the village people, it is necessary to see that the money spent goes back to the villager. District and local Boards obtain their money from the people, and their purchases must be such as will help to circulate money among the people...

What the villager needs above all is profitable employment. We steadily deprive him of employment by buying imported articles, and by way of compensation give him lectures, magic-lantern shows and tinned music all at his expense, and pat ourselves on the back that we are working for his welfare. Can anything be more absurd?

Compare with this what happens if in the place of the motor-van the much despised bullock-cart were used. It can reach the most remote villages which a motor-lorry cannot do. It costs only a fraction of the money required for a van, so that many bullock-carts can be bought, if necessary, to serve groups of villages in the district. The money spent on them goes to the village carpenter, blacksmith and cart-driver. Not a pie of it need go out of the district.

Rural work and motor-vans appear, therefore, to go ill together. What is required is steady, constructive effort, not lightning speed and empty show. We would commend to local Boards and public institutions genuinely interested in village welfare to start by using only village-made goods, to study the conditions which are steadily producing poverty in the villages, and concentrate on removing them one by one. When every side of village life needs intensive, well-considered effort, it seems a waste of public money to throw it away on methods which attempt to bring about village uplift overnight.

It is to be hoped that those who interest themselves in village welfare will take to heart the obvious argument advanced in favour of the cart. It will be cruel to destroy the village economy through the very agency designed for village welfare.

(*Harijan*, 16 September, 1939, *CWMG*, Vol. 70, pp. 118–19)

Religion and self-rule

Religion and politics

I cannot conceive [of] politics as divorced from religion. Indeed, religion should pervade every one of our actions. Here religion does not mean sectarianism. It means a belief in ordered moral government of the universe. It is not less real because it is unseen. This religion transcends Hinduism, Islam, Christianity, etc. It does not supersede them. It harmonizes them and gives them reality.

(*Harijan*, 10 February, 1940, *CWMG*, Vol. 71, p. 177)

[T]he British Government can . . . retain their hold on India only by a policy of divide and rule. A living unity between Muslims and Hindus is fraught with danger to their rule. It would mean an end of it. Therefore it seems to me that a true solution will come with the end of the rule, potentially if not in fact.

What can be done under the threat of Pakistan? If it is not a threat but a desirable goal, why should it be prevented? If it is undesirable and meant only for the Muslims to get more under its shadow, any solution would be an unjust solution. It would be worse than no solution. Therefore I am entirely for waiting till the menace is gone. India's independence is a living thing. No make-believe will suit. The whole world is in the throes of a new birth. Anything done for a temporary gain would be tantamount to an abortion.

I cannot think in terms of narrow Hinduism or narrow Islam. I am wholly uninterested in a patch-work solution. India is a big country, a big nation composed of different cultures, which are tending to blend with one another, each complementing the rest. If I must wait for the completion of the process, I must wait . . . it may not be completed in my day. I shall love to die in the faith that it must come in the fullness of time. I should be happy to think that I had done nothing to hamper the process. Subject to the condition, I would do anything to bring about harmony. My life is made up of compromises, but they have been compromises that have brought me nearer the goal. Pakistan cannot be worse than foreign domination. I have lived under the latter though not willingly. If God so desires it, I may have to become a helpless witness to the undoing of my dream. But I do not believe that the Muslims really want to dismember India.

(*Harijan*, 4 May 1940, *CWMG*, Vol. 72, pp. 26–7)

But I do not believe that Muslims, when it comes to a matter of actual decision, will ever want vivisection. Their good sense will prevent them. Their self-interest will deter them. Their religion will forbid the obvious suicide which the partition would mean. The 'two nations' theory is an untruth. The vast majority of Muslims of India are converts to Islam or are descendants of converts. They did not become a separate nation as soon as they became converts. A Bengali Muslim speaks the same tongue that a Bengali Hindu does, eats the same food, has the same amusements as his Hindu neighbour. They dress alike. I have often found it difficult to distinguish by outward sign between a Bengali Hindu and a Bengali Muslim. The same phenomenon is observable more or less in the south among the poor who constitute the masses of India. When I first met the late Sir Ali Imam I did not know that he was not a Hindu. His speech, his dress, his manners, his food were the same as of the majority of the Hindus in whose midst I found him. His name alone betrayed him. Not even that with Quaid-e-Azam Jinnah. For his name could be that of any Hindu. When I first met him, I did not know that he was a Muslim. I came to know his religion when I had his full name given to me. His nationality was written in his face and manner. The reader will be surprised to know that for days, if not months, I used to think of the late Vithalbhai Patel as a Muslim as he used to sport a beard and a Turkish cap. The Hindu law of inheritance governs many Muslim groups. Sir Mahommed Iqbal used to speak with pride of his Brahmanical descent. Iqbal and Kitchlew are names common to Hindus and Muslims. Hindus and Muslims of India are not two nations. Those whom God has made one, man will never be able to divide.

And is Islam such an exclusive religion as Quaid-e-Azam would have it? Is there nothing in common between Islam and Hinduism or any other religion? Or is Islam merely an enemy of Hinduism? Were the Ali Brothers and their associates wrong when they hugged Hindus as blood brothers and saw so much in common between the two? I am not now thinking of individual Hindus who may have disillusioned the Muslim friends. Quaid-e-Azam has, however, raised a fundamental issue. This is his thesis.[2]

(*Harijan*, 6 April, 1940, *CWMG*, Vol. 71, pp. 388–9)

As a man of non-violence I cannot forcibly resist the proposed partition if the Muslims of India really insist upon it. But I can never be a willing party to the vivisection. I would employ every non-violent means to prevent it. For it means the undoing of centuries of work done by numberless Hindus and Muslims to live together as one nation. Partition means a patent untruth. My whole soul rebels against the idea that Hinduism and Islam represent two antagonistic cultures and doctrines. To assent to such a doctrine is for me denial of God. For I believe with my whole soul that the God of the Koran is also the God of the Gita, and that we are all, no matter by what name designated, children of the same God. I must rebel against the idea that millions of Indians who were Hindus the other day changed their nationality on adopting Islam as their religion.

But that is my belief. I cannot thrust it down the throats of the Muslims who think that they are a different nation. I refuse, however, to believe that the eight crores of Muslims will say that they have nothing in common with their Hindu and other brethren. Their mind can only be known by a referendum duly made to them on that clear issue. The contemplated Constituent Assembly can easily decide the question. Naturally on an issue such as this there can be no arbitration. It is purely and simply a matter of self-determination. I know of no other conclusive method of ascertaining the mind of the eight crores of Muslims.

(*Harijan*, 13 April, 1940, *CWMG*, Vol. 71, pp. 412–13)

Hindu–Muslim tangle

The partition proposal[3] has altered the face of the Hindu–Muslim problem. I have called it an untruth. There can be no compromise with it. At the same time I have said that, if the eight crores of Muslims desire it no power on earth can prevent it, notwithstanding opposition, violent or non-violent. It cannot come by honorable agreement.

That is the political aspect of it. But what about the religious and the moral which are greater than the political? For at the bottom of the cry for partition is the belief that Islam is an exclusive brotherhood, and anti-Hindus as practically untouchables. Nothing good can come out of Hindus or Hinduism. To live under Hindu rule is a sin. Even joint Hindu–Muslim rule is not to be thought of. The cuttings show the Hindus and Muslims are already at war with one another and that they just prepare for the final tussle.

Time was when Hindus thought that Muslims were the natural enemies of Hindus. But as is the case with Hinduism, ultimately it comes to terms with the enemy and makes friends with him. The process has not been completed. As if nemesis had overtaken Hinduism, the Muslim league started the same game and taught that there could be no blending of the two cultures. In this connection I have just read a booklet by Shri Atulanand Chakrabarti which shows that ever since the contact of Islam with Hinduism there has been an attempt on the part of the best minds of both to see the good points of each other, and to emphasize inherent similarities rather than seeming dissimilarities. The author has shown Islamic history in India in a favorable light. If he has stated the truth and nothing but the truth, it is a revealing booklet which all Hindus and Muslims may read with profit. He has secured a very favorable and reasoned preface from Sir Shafaat Ahmed Khan and several other Muslim testimonials. If the evidence collected there reflects the true evolution of Islam in India, then the partition propaganda is anti-Islamic.

Religion binds man to God and man to man. Does Islam bind Muslim only to Muslim and antagonize the Hindu? Was the message of the Prophet peace only for and between Muslims and war against Hindus or non-Muslims? Are eight crores of Muslims to be fed with this which I can only describe as poison? Those who are instilling this poison into the Muslim mind are rendering the greatest disservice to Islam. I know that it is not Islam. I have lived with and among Muslims not for one day but closely and almost uninterruptedly for twenty years. Not one Muslim taught me that Islam was an anti-Hindu religion.

(*Harijan*, 1 June, 1940, *CWMG*, Vol. 72, pp. 27–8)

Pakistan and Constituent Assembly

[One] speak[s] of the Constituent Assembly side by side with Pakistan. The latter is wrong, as I conceive it, in every way. There is nothing wrong in the idea of a Constituent Assembly. At its worst, dangers surround its formation. Every big experiment is beset with dangers. These risks must be taken. Every effort should be made to minimize them. But there seems to me to be nothing like a Constituent Assembly for achieving the common purpose. I admit the difficulty of illiteracy. Indeed adult suffrage was introduced at the instance of Muslim nationalists including the late Ali Brothers. The danger of corruption is also there. The greater the organization the less felt is the effect of corruption because it is so widely distributed. Thus in the Congress there are much corruption and jealousy, but they are confined to those few who run the machinery. But the vast body of Congressmen are untouched by these defects, though they profit by the good the Congress does. The danger you mention about safeguards will be reduced to the vanishing point if they come through a Constituent Assembly. For safeguards laid down by the representatives elected by the adult Muslim population will depend for their safety not on the goodwill or honesty of the majority but on the strength of the awakened Muslim masses. Fatality really attaches to your wrong conception of the majority, not to a Constituent Assembly. There is a majority of Hindus undoubtedly, but we observe that in popular political assemblies parties are not rigidly divided according to religious opinions, but they are according to political and other opinions. The curse of communalism became intensified by the introduction of separate electorates. The cry for partition is the logical outcome, but it is also the strongest condemnation, of separate electorates. When we have learnt wisdom we shall cease to think in terms of separate electorates and two nations. I believe in the innate goodness of human nature. I therefore swear by the Constituent Assembly. The

Muslim vote will surely decide the issue so far as their special interest is concerned. Arguing communally, therefore, the fear, if there is any, about a Constituent Assembly should surely be on the part of the Hindus. For if the Muslim vote goes in favour of partition, they have either to submit not to one but many partitions or to a civil war. As things are, all satisfy themselves by passing resolutions and seeing their names in print. In practice all of us remain where we are in a state of subjection. A Constituent Assembly is a reality. It will not be a debating or legislative irresponsible body. By registering its final decision it will decide the fate of millions of human beings. You may oppose it. If you are successful in your opposition, there is the dread prospect of anarchy, not an orderly civil war. There seems to me to be no solution of the painful deadlock except through a Constituent Assembly.

(Harijan, 29 June 1940, CWMG, Vol. 72, pp. 200–2)

On the nature of governance

I had thought that Dominion Status according to the Statute of Westminster was equivalent to independence. The expression Dominion Status has a special connotation. It refers to a commonwealth of whites who are themselves pillars of imperialism engaged in exploiting the non-European races whom they regard as uncivilized. India free will be no party to such exploitation. But there is nothing to prevent free India from entering into an alliance with Britain for the protection of the freedom of all, whether black, brown or white. Therefore, if Dominion Status is less than independence, India cannot be satisfied with less. If it is synonymous with independence, then India has to choose how she would describe her status.

The critic then condemns the Congress for not coming to terms with the Muslim League. It is a pity that even responsible Englishmen will not take the trouble to study questions which they judge freely. The Congress has never given up the effort to solve the communal question. It is even now engaged in the difficult task. But it is wrong to use Congress inability to reach a solution for keeping India from her destined goal. British officials including viceroys [have] admitted that they have ruled by following the policy of 'divide and rule'. The British established themselves by taking advantage of our internal quarrels and have remained by keeping them alive. It is unnecessary for my argument to prove that the policy is being followed deliberately.

The British have made themselves believe that they are ruling because of our quarrels, and that they will gladly retire when we have ceased to quarrel. Thus they are moving in a vicious circle. The British rule must be permanent if the adjustment of the communal quarrel is a condition precedent to India becoming independent. It is a purely domestic problem which we are bound to solve if we are to live at peace with one another. May I remind the critic and those who argue like him that only a short while ago it was said that if the British withdrew, Hindus would be left to the mercy of the virile races from the north, that not a virgin would be safe or a monied man retain his wealth? Now Princes and Muslims, who are able enough to protect themselves against the unarmed millions whom the Congress claims specially to represent, are sought to be protected by the British bayonet against the latter! Be that as it may, the congress must pursue its even course. It must work for communal unity in spite of odds against it. It is a plank in its programme. It is part of the non-violent technique.

(Harijan, 2 December, 1939, CWMG, Vol. 70, pp. 387–8)

Implications of constructive programme

The constructive programme is a big undertaking including a number of items: (1) Hindu–Muslim or communal unity; (2) Removal of untouchability; (3) Prohibition; (4) Khadi; (5) Other village industries; (6) Village sanitation; (7) New or basic education; (8) Adult education; (9) Uplift of women; (10) Education in hygiene and health; (11) Propagation of Rashtrabhasha; (12) Cultivating love of one's own language; (13) Working for economic equality. This list can be supplemented if necessary but it is so comprehensive that I think it can be proved to include items appearing to have been omitted.

The reader will see that it is the want of all these things that is responsible for our bondage. He will also see that the constructive programme of the Congress is not supposed to include all the items. That is understood to include only four items, or rather six, now that the Congress has created the All-India Village Industries Association and the Basic Education Board. But we have to go further forward, we have to stabilize and perfect ahimsa, and so we have to make the constructive programme as comprehensive as possible. There should be no room for doubt that, if we can win swaraj purely through non-violence, we can also retain it through the same means. In the fulfillment of the constructive programme lies the non-violent attainment of swaraj.

The items I have mentioned are not in order of importance. I have put them down just as they came to my pen. Generally I talk of khadi only nowadays, because millions of people can take their share in this work, and progress can be arithmetically measured. Communal unity and the removal of untouchability cannot be thus assessed. Once they become part of our daily life, nothing need be done by us as individuals.

Let us now glance at the various items. Without Hindu–Muslim, i.e., communal unity, we shall always remain crippled. And how can a crippled India win swaraj? Communal unity means unity between Hindus, Sikhs, Mussalmans, Christians, Parsis, Jews. All these go to make Hindustan. He who neglects any of these communities does not know constructive work.

As long as the curse of untouchability pollutes the mind of the Hindu, so long is he himself an untouchable in the eyes of the world, and an untouchable cannot win non-violent swaraj. The removal of untouchability means treating the so-called untouchables as one's own kith and kin. He who does treat them so must be free from the sense of high and low, in fact free from all wrong class-sense. He will regard the whole world as one family. Under non-violent swaraj it will be impossible to conceive of any country as an enemy country.

Pure swaraj is impossible of attainment by people who have been or who are slaves of intoxicating drinks and drugs. It must never be forgotten that a man in the grip of intoxicants is generally bereft of the moral sense.

Everyone now may be said to believe that without khadi there is no just and immediate solution of the problem of the starvation of our millions. I need not therefore dilate upon it. I would only add that in the resuscitation of khadi lies the resuscitation of the ruined village artisans. Khadi requisites (wheels, looms, etc.) have to be made by the village carpenter and black-smith. For unless these requisites are made in the village it cannot be self-contained and prosperous.

The revival of khadi presupposes the revival of all other village industries. Because we have not laid proper stress on this, khadi-wearers see nothing wrong in using other articles which are foreign or mill-made. Such people may be said to have failed to grasp the inner meaning of khadi. They forget that by establishing the Village Industries Association the Congress has placed all other village industries on the same level as khadi. As the solar system will be dark without the sun, even so will the sun be lusterless without the planets. All things in the universe are interdependent. The salvation of India is impossible without the salvation of villages.

If rural reconstruction were not to include rural sanitation, our villages would remain the muck-heaps that they are today. Village sanitation is a vital part of village life and is as difficult as it is important. It needs a heroic effort to eradicate age-long insanitation. The village worker who is ignorant of the science of village sanitation, who is not a successful scavenger, cannot fit himself for village service.

It seems to be generally admitted that without the new or basic education the education of millions of children in India is well-nigh impossible. The village worker has, therefore, to master it, and become a basic education teacher himself.

Adult education will follow in the wake of basic education as a matter of course. Where this new education has taken root, the children themselves become their parents' teachers. Be that as it may, the village worker has to undertake adult education also.

Woman is described as man's better half. As long as she has not the same rights in law as man, as long as the birth of a girl does not receive the same welcome as that of a boy, so long we should know that India is suffering from partial paralysis. Suppression of woman is a denial of ahimsa. Every village worker will, therefore, regard every woman as his mother, sister or daughter as the case may be, and look upon her with respect. Only such a worker will command the confidence of the village people.

It is impossible for an unhealthy people to win swaraj. Therefore we should no longer be guilty of the neglect of the health of our people. Every village worker must have a knowledge of the general principles of health.

Without a common language no nation can come into being. Instead of worrying himself with the controversy about the Hindi-Hindustani and Urdu, the village worker will acquire a knowledge of the Rashtrabhasha, which should be such as can be understood by both Hindus and Muslims.

Our infatuation about English has made us unfaithful to provincial languages. If only as penance for this unfaithfulness the village worker should cultivate in the villagers a love of their own speech. He will have equal regard for all the other languages of India, and will learn the language of the part where he may be working, and thus be able to inspire the villagers there with a regard for their speech.

The whole of this programme will, however, be a structure on sand if it is not built on the solid foundation of economic equality. Economic equality must never be supposed to mean possession of an equal amount of worldly goods by everyone. It does mean, however, that everyone will have a proper house to live in, sufficient and balanced food to eat, and sufficient khadi with which to cover himself. It also means that the cruel inequality that obtains today will be removed by purely non-violent means. This question, however, requires to be separately dealt with.

(*Harijan*, 18 August, 1940, *CWMG*, Vol. 72, pp. 378–81)

Caste

Caste has to go

1 I believe in varnashrama of the Vedas which in my opinion is based on absolute equality of status, notwithstanding passages to the contrary in the smrits and elsewhere.

2 Every word of the printed works passing muster as Shastras is not, in my opinion, a revelation.

3 The interpretation of accepted texts has undergone evolution, and is capable of indefinite evolution, even as the human intellect and heart are.

4 Nothing in the Shastras which is manifestly contrary to universal truths and morals can stand.

5 Nothing in the Shastras which is capable of being reasoned can stand if it is in conflict with reason.

6 Varnashrama of the Shastras is today non-existent in practice.

7 The present caste system is the very antithesis of varnashrama. The sooner public opinion abolishes it the better.

8 In varnashrama there was and should be no prohibition of intermarriage or inter-dining. Prohibition there is of change of one's hereditary occupation for purposes of gain. The existing practice is, therefore, doubly

wrong in that it has set up cruel restrictions about inter-dining and intermarriage and tolerates anarchy about choice and occupation.

9 Though there is in *varnashrama* no prohibition against intermarriage and inter-dining, there can be no compulsion. It must be left to the unfettered choice of the individual as to where he or she will marry or dine. If the law of *varnashrama* was observed there would naturally be a tendency, so far as marriage is concerned, for people to restrict the marital relations to their own *varna*.

10 As I have repeatedly said there is no such thing as untouchability by birth in the *Shastras*. I hold the present practice to be a sin and the greatest blot on Hinduism. I feel more than ever that if untouchability lives, Hinduism dies.

11 The most effective, quickest and the most unobtrusive way to destroy caste is for reformers to begin the practice themselves and where necessary take the consequences of social boycott. The reform will not come by reviling the orthodox. The change will be gradual and imperceptible. The so-called higher classes will have to descend from their pedestal before they can make any impression upon the so-called lower classes. Day-to-day experience of village work shows how difficult the task is in bridging the gulf that exists between the city-dwellers and the villagers, the higher classes and the lower classes. The two are not synonymous terms. For the class distinction exists both in the cities and the villages.

(*Harijan*, 11 November, 1935, *CWMG*, Vol. 62, pp. 121–2)

Caste and varna

Castes are numerous. They are man-made. They undergo constant change. The older ones die and new ones spring up. Castes based on occupation are to be found all over the world. It is only in India that there are restrictions, as regards intermarriage and inter-dining, which defy reason. This is very harmful. It stands in the way of the community's progress. It has nothing to do with religion.

Varnas are just four and not numerous. They have been sanctioned by the Shastras [holy books]. Whether or not people are conscious of them, they do exist all over the world as we see. There are everywhere these four classes: one to impart knowledge of god for the welfare of the world, another to protect the people against manifold dangers, a third one to carry on the work of farming, etc., to sustain the community and one class to work for these three classes. There is no feeling of high and low to this division. But since this is not understood as a great law of nature, there has been confusion in it, that is, these four functions are no more confined to the respective varnas. Instead men have been taking up occupation[s] they choose with a view to achieving their selfish ends. At one time in India people used to consciously follow this law and thus lived in peace. One accepted the calling of one's varna and was satisfied in its pursuit for general welfare. There was unhealthy competition among people to jump from one varna to another for the sake of money or fame. At present this significance of the varna system seems to have disappeared even in India. Destructive competition is on the increase, everyone takes [the] liberty of following any profession and the meaning of varna has been restricted to unnatural and meaningless restrictions on intermarriage and inter-dining. And that is why the country has stopped progressing. Hinduism will once again shine forth if such senseless restrictions are abolished, the pristine varna system is resurrected and the distinctions of high and low are banished. This would be to the good of India as well as the whole world.

(*Harijanbandhu*, 19 January, 1936, *CWMG*, Vol. 62, pp. 142–3)

Untouchability

Untouchability is a curse, a blot and a powerful poison that will destroy Hinduism. It is repugnant to our sense of humanity to consider a single human being as untouchable by birth. If you were to examine the scriptures of the world and the conduct of peoples other than Hindus, you would not find any parallel to the untouchability I have brought to your attention just now. I can well understand a person being untouchable whilst he is performing a task which he himself would feel makes him untouchable. For instance a nurse, who is nursing a patient who is helpless and bleeding . . . soiling his clothes and suffering from a disease giving out from his body a foul smell, such a nurse whilst she is nursing such a patient is untouchable. But when she has washed herself, she becomes as touchable as ourselves not only that. She is not only just as fit to move in society as any of us, but she is also adorable for the profession which she follows. She is worthy of our respect and, so long as we have ranks in our society, she must occupy a very high place amongst us.

Now look at the other side of the picture. Take, for instance, Dr. Ambedkar. He is pronounced as belonging to the Depressed Classes and as being untouchable. Intellectually he is superior to thousands of intelligent and educated caste Hindus. His personal cleanliness is as high as that of any of us. Today he is as eminent lecturer in Law. Tomorrow you may find him a Judge of the High Court. In other words, there is no position in the Government of this country to which he may not aspire and rise, and to which an orthodox Brahmin can rise. But that orthodox Brahmin will be defiled by the touch of Dr. Ambedkar and that because of his unpardonable sin that he was born a Mahar (Untouchable)!

If we had not been habituated to think that untouchability by birth is an integral part of Hinduism, we would not conduct ourselves towards fellow human beings as many of us conduct ourselves even today.

I know that I have told you nothing new in my talk to you today. I know I have said this same thing in a much more burning language than I have done today. Yet what I say is not, and will not be, superfluous so long as this simple fact of the need for the removal of untouchability does not affect your understanding or conduct.

Untouchability is a phenomenon which is peculiar to Hinduism only and it has got no warrant either in reason or in the Shastras, and what little I have studies of the Shastras and what I have been told by people who have made a deeper study of them shows that there is no warrant for untouchability by birth in Hinduism. I have not the time now to go into the Shastric precepts. Nor is it necessary at this time of the day to give you Shastric proofs for my statement. But what is necessary is that if you are satisfied that untouchability is a blot on Hinduism and that there is a danger of its destroying Hinduism, you must set about removing it.

What will you do to remove it? If all of you will say that you have done your duty by declaring that untouchability is a blot on Hinduism, it will be a mockery. It will not be enough even if you in a flush of enthusiasm go to a Harijan and touch him and embrace him, and then forget all about him. It will not do even if you go to the Harijan quarters every day and make it a point to touch a number of Harijans as a token of your conviction.

What is required of you is that you should regulate your day-to-day conduct in such a manner that you make it absolutely evident to the Harijans whom you come across that a better day has dawned for them all.

You will begin by taking the Harijans along with you to the temple if you are in the habit of going to a temple. But if you discover that you will not be allowed into the temple along with your Harijan companions, then if you have the living belief that I have that untouchability is wrong, you will shun that temple as you shun a scorpion of fire. You will then believe with me that such a temple is not inhabited by God.

(*Harijan*, 20 June, 1936, *CWMG*, Vol. 63, pp. 34–5)

Education

Education (nayee talim)

My [aim] is to change the very system of education. The new system will fulfil the needs of the country as well as the individual and bring about self-reliance. Self-reliance is also a true test of the fulfillment of education. Hence it makes no difference to my scheme of education even if someone gives a donation for running a primary school. And here is the scheme in a nutshell:

Primary education shall be given only through some craft or the other. Real education and an all-round development of the child is not possible without it. And such education must be self-supporting. This does not mean that each class will be self-supporting. However, boys or girls who will go through the seven-year curriculum in a craft-based school will be able to pay all these years' expenses through their earnings from the crafts.

(From a copy of the Hindi: *Pyarelal Papers*, *CWMG*, Vol. 70, p. 277)

Education and handicraft

If we want to impart education best suited to the needs of the villagers, we should take the *Vidyapith* [school] to the villages. We should convert it into a training school in order that we might be able to give practical training to teachers in terms of the needs of villagers. You cannot instruct the teachers in the needs of villagers through a training school in a city. Nor can you so interest them in the condition of villagers. To interest city-dwellers in villages and make them live in them is no easy task. I am finding daily confirmation of this in Segaon [name of a village]. I cannot give the assurance that our year's stay in Segaon has made of us villagers or that we have become one with them for common good.

Then as to primary education my confirmed opinion is that the commencement of training by teaching the alphabet and reading and writing hampers their intellectual growth. I would not teach them the alphabet till they have had an elementary knowledge of history, geography, mental arithmetic and the art (say) of spinning. Through these three I should develop their intelligence. Question may be asked how intelligence can be developed thorough the *Takli* or the spinning-wheel. It can be, to a marvelous degree, if it is not taught merely mechanically. When you tell a child the reason for each process, when you explain the mechanism of the *takli* or the wheel, when you give him the history of cotton and its connection with civilization itself and take him to the village field where it is grown, and teach him to count the rounds he spins and the method of finding the evenness and strength of his yarn, you hold his interest and simultaneously train his hands, his eyes and his mind. I should give six months to this preliminary training. The child is probably now ready for learning how to read the alphabet, and when he is able to do so rapidly, he is ready to learn simple drawing, and when he has learnt to draw geometrical figures and the figures of birds, etc., he will draw, not scrawl, the figures of the alphabet. I can recall the days of my childhood when I was being taught the alphabet. I know what a drag it was. Nobody cared why my intellect was rusting. I consider writing as a fine art. We kill it by imposing the alphabet on little children and making it the beginning of learning. Thus we do violence of the art of writing and stunt the growth of the child when we seek to teach him the alphabet before its time.

Indeed in my opinion what we have reason to deplore and be ashamed of is not so much illiteracy as ignorance. Therefore adult education, too, should have an intensive programme of driving out ignorance through carefully select[ed] teachers with an equally carefully selected syllabus according to which they would educate the adult villagers' mind[s]. This is not to say that I would not give them knowledge of the alphabet. I value it too much to despise or even belittle its merit as a vehicle of education. I appreciate Prof. Laubach's immense labours in the way of making the alphabet easy and Prof. Bhagwat's great and practical contribution in the same direction. Indeed I have invited the latter to come to Segaon whenever he chooses and try his art on the men, women and even children of Segaon.

As to the necessity and value of regarding the teaching of village handicraft as the pivot and centre of education I have no manner of doubt. The method adopted in the institutions in India, I do not call education, i.e, drawing out the best in man, but a debauchery of the mind. It informs the mind anyhow, whereas the method of training the mind through village handicrafts from the very beginning as the central fact would promote the real, disciplined development of the mind resulting in conservation of the intellectual energy and indirectly also the spiritual. Here, too, I must not be understood to belittle fine arts. But I would not misplace them. Matter misplaced has been rightly described as dirt. In proof [of] what I am saying, I can only cite the tons of worthless and even indecent literature that in pouring in upon us with the result which he who runs may see.

(*Harijan*, 5 June, 1937, *CWMG*, Vol. 65, pp. 233–5)

Talks on vocational education

I had long been impressed with the necessity for a new departure as I knew the failure modern education had been through the numerous students who came to see me on my return from South Africa. So I started with the introduction of training in handicrafts in the Ashram school. In fact an extra emphasis was placed on manual training, with the result that the children soon got tired of the manual training and thought that they had been deprived of literary training. There they were wrong, for even the little that they gained was more than children ordinarily get in the orthodox schools. But that set me thinking, and I came to the conclusion that not vocation cum literary training, but literary training through vocational training was the thing. Then vocational training would cease to be a drudgery and literary training would have a new content and new usefulness.

Now you might well ask me why I picked up the *takli* out of the many other existing handicrafts. Because *takli* was one of the first crafts that we found out and which has subsisted through the ages. In the earliest ages all our cloth used to be made of *takli* yarn. The spinning-wheel came later, and [as] the finest counts could not be produced on the spinning-wheel, one had to go back to the *takli*. In devising the *takli* man's inventive genius reached a height that had not been reached before. The cunning of the fingers were put to the best possible use. But as the *takli* was confined to the artisans who were never educated, it fell into disuse, if we want to revive it today in all its glory, if we are to revive and reconstruct the village life, we must begin the education of children with the *takli*. My next lesson would therefore be to teach the boys the place the *takli* used to occupy in our daily life. Next I would take them into a little history and teach them how it declined. Then would follow a brief course in Indian history, starting from the East India Company, or even earlier from the Muslim period, giving them a detailed account of the exploitation that was the stock in trade of the East India Company, how by a systematic process our main handicraft was strangled and ultimately killed. Next would follow a brief course in mechanics – construction of the *takli*. It must have originally consisted of a small ball of clay or even wet flour dried on to a bamboo splinter running through its centre. This has still survived in some parts of Bihar and Bengal. Then a brick disc took the place of the clay ball and then in our times iron or steel and brass have taken the place of the brick disc and a steel wire the place of the splinter. Even here one might expatiate with profit on the size of the disc and the wire, why it is of a particular size and why not more or less. Next would follow a few lectures on cotton, its habitat, its varieties, the countries and the provinces of India where it is at present grown and so on. Again some knowledge about its cultivation, the soil best suited for it, and so on. That would make us launch into a little agriculture.

You will see that this takes a fund of assimilated knowledge on the part of the teacher before he can impart it to his pupils. The whole of elementary arithmetic can be taught through the counting of yards of spinning finding out the count of yarn, making up of hanks, getting it ready for the weaver, the number of cross-threads in the warp to be put in for particular textures of cloth and so on. Every process from the growing of cotton to the manufacture of the finished product – cotton picking, ginning, carding, spinning, sizing, weaving – all would have their mechanics and history and mathematics correlated to them.

The principal idea is to impart the whole education of the body and the mind and the soul through the handicraft that is taught to the children. You have to draw out all that is in the child through teaching all the processes of the handicraft, and all your lessons in history, geography, arithmetic will be related to the craft.

If such education is given, the direct result will be that it will be self-supporting. But the test of success is not its self-supporting character, but that the whole man has been drawn out through the teaching of the handicraft in a scientific manner. In fact I would reject a teacher who would promise to make it self-supporting under any circumstances. The self-supporting part will be the logical corollary of the fact that the pupil has learnt the use of every one of his faculties. If a boy who works at a handicraft for three hours a day will surely earn his keep, how much more a boy who adds to the work a development of his mind and soul!

(*Harijan*, 11 June, 1938, *CWMG*, Vol. 67, pp. 113–15)

Education – the future state

(Gandhi commented on the nature of the education in British India in the following manner.)

1   The present system of education does not meet the requirements of the country in any shape or form. English, having been made the medium of instruction in all the higher branches of learning, has created a permanent bar between the highly educated few and the uneducated many. It has prevented knowledge from percolating to the masses. This excessive importance given to English has cast upon the educated class a burden which has maimed them mentally for life and made them strangers in their own land. Absence of vocational training has made the educated class almost unfit for productive work and harmed them physically. Money spent on primary education is a waste of expenditure inasmuch as what little is taught is soon forgotten and has little or no value in terms of the villages or cities. Such advantage as is gained by the existing system of education is not gained by the chief taxpayer, his children getting the least.

2   The course of primary education should be extended at least to seven years and should include the general knowledge gained up to the matriculation standard less English plus a substantial vocation.

3   For the all-round development of boys and girls all training should so far as possible be given through a profit-yielding vocation. In other words vocations should serve a double purpose – to enable the pupil to pay for his tuition through the products of his labour and at the same time to develop the whole man or woman in him or her through the vocation learnt at school.

    Land, building and equipment are not intended to be covered by the proceeds of the pupil's labour.

All the processes of cotton, wool and silk, commencing from gathering, cleaning, ginning (in the case of cotton), carding, spinning, dyeing, sizing, warp-making, double-twisting, designing and weaving, embroidery, tailoring, paper-making, cutting, book-binding, cabinet-making, toy-making, *gur*-making are undoubtedly occupations that can easily be learnt and handled without much capital outlay.

This primary education should equip boys and girls to earn their bread, by the State guaranteeing employment in the vocations learnt or by buying their manufactures at prices fixed by the State.

(*Harijan*, 2 October, 1937, *CWMG*, Vol. 66, pp. 194–5)

Now, if primary education is to be imparted through a craft, that task can be carried out for the present only by the people who have faith in the spinning-wheel and other village industries. For, on the subject of the charkha, which occupies a central position in cottage industries, the Spinners' Association has collected considerable information and on other industries the Village Industries Association has been collecting it. Hence, in my view, whatever immediate provisions we can make can only be through the charkha and allied crafts. But all those who have faith in the charkha are not teachers. Every carpenter is no authority on carpentry. One who has no knowledge of the science of the craft cannot impart general education through the craft. And so, only those who are interested in the science of education and have faith in the charkha, etc., can introduce the scheme of primary education which I have suggested. I am reproducing the letter[4] from Shri Dilkhush Diwanji with the idea that it would be useful to such persons.

(*Harijanbandhu*, 17 October 1937, *CWMG*, Vol. 66, p. 249)

I am a firm believer in the principle of free and compulsory primary education for India. I also hold that we shall realize this only by teaching the children a useful vocation and utilizing it as a means for cultivating their mental, physical and spiritual faculties. Let no one consider these economic calculations in connection with education as sordid, or out of place. There is nothing essentially sordid about economic calculations. True economics never militates against the highest ethical standard just as all true ethics to be worth its name must at the same time be also good economics, an economics that inculcates mammon worship and enables the strong to amass wealth at the expense of the weak, is a false and dismal science. It spells death. True economics, on the other hand, stands for social justice, it promotes the good of all equally, including the weakest, and is indispensable for decent life. I therefore make bold to suggest that Bombay would be setting a noble example for the whole country to follow if, by teaching its children a useful industry, it can make primary education pay its way. Supposing a student works at a vocation for four hours a day, then taking the number of working days in a month to be 25 and the rate of remuneration two paisa [monetary denomination] per hours, he or she would be earning Rs. 3–2–0 per month for the school. The vocational exercises will keep the mind of the student fresh and alert while providing at the same time a means for drawing out his or her intellect. This does not mean that the child would begin to pay 2 paisa per hour from the commencement, but he will pay during the whole period of seven years at the rate of 2 paisa per hour.

It is a gross superstition to think that this sort of vocational exercise will make education dull, or cramp the child's mind. Some of my happiest recollections are of the bright and joyful faces of children while they were receiving vocational instruction under competent teachers. As against this, I have also known the most fascinating of subjects [be] boring [to] children, when taught in the wrong way by an incompetent instructor. But it may be asked wherefrom are we going to get capable instructors of the kind that we require? My reply is that necessity is the mother of invention. Once we realize the necessity for reorientation of our education policy, the means for giving effect to it will be found without much difficulty. I am sure that, for a fraction of the time and expense incurred on the present educational system and the staff to man it, we could easily train all the manual instructors that we should require for our work. It ought to be possible for a committee of educational experts of Bombay, if they are in earnest, to draw up a scheme of primary education on the lines suggested by me and to put it into operation without loss of time. Only they must have a living faith in it as I have. Such faith can only grow from within; it cannot be acquired vicariously. Nothing great in this world was ever accomplished without living faith.

What kinds of vocations are the fittest for being taught to children in urban schools? There is no hard and fast rule about it. But my reply is clear. I want to resuscitate the village of India. Today our villages have become a mere appendage to the cities. They exist, as it were, to be exploited by the latter and depend on the latter's sufferance. This is unnatural. It is only when the cities realize the duty of making an adequate return to the villages for the strength and sustenance which they derive from them, instead of selfishly exploiting them, that a healthy and moral relationship between the two will spring up, and if the city children are to play their part in this great and noble work of social reconstruction, the vocations through which they are to receive their education ought to be directly related to the requirements of the villages. So far as I can see, the various processes of cotton manufacture from ginning and cleaning of cotton to the spinning of yarn answer this test as nothing else does. Even today cotton is grown in the villages and is ginned and spun and converted into cloth in the cities. But the chain of processes which cotton undergoes in the mills from the beginning to the end constitutes a huge tragedy of waste in men, materials and mechanical power.

My plan to impart primary education through the medium of village handicrafts like spinning and carding, etc., is thus conceived as the spearhead of a silent social revolution fraught with the most far-reaching consequence. It will provide a healthy and moral basis of relationship between the city and the village and thus go a long way towards eradicating some of the worst evils of the present social insecurity and poisoned relationship between the classes. It will check the progressive decay of our villages and lay the foundation of a juster (*sic*) social order in which there is no unnatural division between the 'haves' and 'have-nots' and everybody is assured of living wage and the right to freedom. And all this would be accomplished without the horrors of a bloody class war or a colossal capital expenditure such as would be involved in the mechanization of a vast continent like India. Nor would it entail a helpless dependence on foreign imported machinery or technical skill. Lastly, by obviating the necessity for highly specialized talent, it would place the destiny of the masses, as it were, in their own hands. But who will bell the cat? Will the city folk listen to me at all? Or, will mine remain a mere cry in the wilderness? Replies to these and similar questions will depend more on lovers of education like my correspondent living in cities than on me.

(*Harijan*, 9 October, 1937, *CWMG*, Vol. 66, pp. 168–70)

Language

Hindustani, Hindi and Urdu

It is great pity that bitter controversy has taken place and still continues regarding the Hindi–Urdu question. So far as the Congress is concerned Hindustani is its recognized official language designed as an all-India language for inter-provincial contact. It is not to supplant but to supplement the provincial languages. The recent resolution of the working Committee should set all doubt at rest. If the Congressmen who have to do all-India work will only take the trouble of learning Hindustani in both the scripts, we shall have taken many strides in the direction of our common language goal. The real competition is not between Hindi and Urdu but between Hindustani and English. It is a tough fight. I am certainly watching it with grave concern.

Hindi–Urdu controversy has no bottom. Hindustani of the Congress conception has yet to be crystallized into shape. It will not be so long as Congress proceedings are not conducted exclusively in Hindustani. The Congress will have to prescribe the dictionaries for use by Congressmen and a department will have to supply new words outside the dictionaries. It is great work, it is work worth doing, if we are really to have a living, growing all India speech. The department will have to determine which of the existing literature shall be considered as Hindustani, books, magazines, weeklies, dailies, whether written in Urdu script or Devanagari. It is serious work needing a vast amount of plodding if it is to achieve success.

For the purpose of crystallizing Hindustani, Hindi and Urdu may be regarded as feeders. A Congressman must therefore wish well to both and keep in touch with both so far as he can.

This Hindustani will have many synonyms to supply the varied requirements of a growing nation rich in provincial languages. Hindustani spoken to Bengali or Southern audiences will naturally have a large stock of words of Sanskrit origin. The same speech delivered in the Punjab will have a large admixture of words of Arabic or Persian origin. Similar will be the case with audiences composed predominantly of Muslims who cannot understand many words of Sanskrit origin. All-India speakers will have therefore to command a Hindustani vocabulary which will enable them to feel at home with audiences drawn from all parts of India. Pandit Malaviyaji's name comes uppermost in this connection. I have known him handle Hindi-speaking and Urdu-speaking audiences with equal ease. I have never found him in want of the correct word. The same is true of Babu Bhagwandas who uses synonymous words in the same speech, and he sees to it that it does not lose in grace. Among the Muslims at the time of writing I can think of only Maulana Mahomed Ali whose vocabulary was varied enough to suit both audiences. His knowledge of Gujarati acquired in Baroda service stood him in good stead.

Independently of the Congress, Hindi and Urdu will continue to flourish. Hindi will be mostly confined to Hindus and Urdu to Muslims. As a matter of fact, comparatively speaking, there are very few Muslims who know Hindi well enough to be called scholars, though, I expect, in Hindi-speaking parts, to Muslims born there, Hindi is the mother tongue. There are thousands of Hindus whose mother tongue is Urdu and there are hundreds who can be aptly described as Urdu scholars. Pandit Motilalji was one such. Dr. Tej Bahadur Sapru is another. Illustrations can be easily multiplied. There is therefore no reason for any quarrel or unhealthy competition between the two sisters. Healthy competition there always must be.

(*Harijan*, 29 October, 1938, *CWMG*, Vol. 68, pp. 23–4)

Conclusion

I

The historical Gandhi is dead, but the civilizational Gandhi survives in his country of origin and elsewhere where similar kind of socio-economic and political circumstances prevail. Gandhi was 'the consummate problematizer' of conventional ideas about human society. His creative intervention sparked off new debates on relevant issues involving other leading personalities holding similar/dissimilar views. For instance, instead of insisting only on political independence from colonial rule, he devoted a great deal of attention to purging Indian society of indigenous patterns of domination. Although he continuously drew upon the tradition while conceptualizing his ideas, he nonetheless challenged what he took to be its defects in order to reform it. So the importance of Gandhi's creative work lay precisely in seizing upon 'the fugitive and supplementary' forms of everyday life and in infusing them with a rigorous 'anti-disciplinary discipline' which allowed them to no longer be 'fugitive'. It is this extraordinary 'ordinariness' that makes Gandhi's socio-political ideas so astonishingly salient today.

Gandhi's social and political thought is multi-dimensional.[1] If its kernel is derived from India's civilizational resources, its actual evolution was shaped by his experiences in South Africa and India. His political ideology was a radical departure from the past in the sense that it was neither the constitutional loyalism of the Moderates nor the Extremism of the revolutionary terrorists. In his articulation of Indian nationalism, he sought to incorporate the emerging constituencies of nationalist politics that had remained peripheral in the bygone era. Gandhi brought about an era of mass politics, though he dismissed the role of the masses in the early part of the Non-Cooperation Movement as nothing but 'mobocracy'. Gandhi knew India, and especially the Indian masses. He could merge, argued Jawaharlal Nehru, 'with the masses and feel with them, and because they were conscious of this they gave him their devotion and loyalty'.[2] So, an analysis of the role of the Mahatma in India's freedom struggle clearly indicates the changing nature of the movement in response to the zealous participation of various sections of India's multicultural society. It was possible because

Gandhi was perhaps the only effective nationalist leader who 'truly attempted to transcend the class conflicts [by] devising a method which, for the first time, brought about the national aggregation of an all-India character'.[3] This is where Gandhi was unique. Not only did he articulate the peripheral voices, he also translated them into action by linking with the obvious adverse consequences of colonialism.[4] His social and political ideas are therefore dialectically constituted in the context of foreign rule. Gandhi simultaneously launched movements not only against the British rule but also against the atrocious social structures, customs, norms and values, justified in the name of India's age-old traditions. While defining the character of the Gandhi-led nationalist movement, Nehru thus stated that Gandhi had a twofold aim. Apart from challenging and resisting foreign rule, Gandhi launched a serious campaign against, to quote Nehru, 'our social evils'. Besides the freedom of India, the principal planks of the Gandhian non-violent struggle were 'national unity, which involved', he argued further, 'the solution of the minority problems and the raising of the depressed classes and the ending of the curse of untouchability'.[5] Hence, Gandhian thought is neither purely political nor absolutely social, but a complex mix of the two, which accords conceptual peculiarities to what the Mahatma stood for.

Gandhi was primarily a political activist whose writings emerged mainly during the process of social, economic and political actions. He never claimed 'to have originated any new principle or doctrine. [He] simply tried to apply the eternal truths to our daily life and problems'[6] although he wrote on every subject of human life in an attractive and easily comprehensible prose style. Most of his writings were situational and they constituted only a fraction of his activities. Hence, as Bondurant argues,

> one cannot . . . turn to the writings of Gandhi for definite statement in political theory. Gandhi was a political actionist and a practical philosopher as he was not a theorist. His writings abound with inconsistencies . . . one result of his persistent habit of thinking in public. Whatever philosophical formulations he made were inspired by and directed towards the solving of immediate problems. The unsophisticated explanations, which Gandhi offered for his methods, his objectives, his policy, and creed, were part of a programme of action. They should not be interpreted in terms either of theory or of practical master-planning.[7]

Gandhi produced only four book-length works. The most important of these was his autobiography, which first appeared in a serialized form in one of his journals.[8] Gandhi was conscious of the inadequacies of his writings at the theoretical and scholarly levels. He insisted that his life was his message and that he should not be judged either on the basis of particular actions or writings.

As a matter of fact, my writings should be cremated with my body. What I have done will endure, not what I have said and written. I have often said that even if all our scriptures perish one mantra of *Ishopan-ishad* [Hindu religious scripture] was enough to declare the essence of Hinduism – but even that one verse will be of no avail if there is no one to live it.[9]

Unlike his erstwhile colleagues in the nationalist movement, Gandhi was probably the only one who clearly understood the mass psyche in a situation that was highly volatile due to colonial rule and a society justifying exploitation of the masses as inevitable to sustain social stability. His ideology of non-violence seemed to offer a way out of the *impasses* created by two contrasting strands of Indian nationalism: the violence of revolutionary terrorists and the insipid constitutionalism of the Moderate Congress. Gandhi struck a responsive chord in Hindu culture, and struck in such a way as to galvanize the country into 'opposition against the British without threatening vested interests in Indian society'.[10] Although his campaign was never directed against the caste system per se, he nonetheless initiated movements to rid the system of distortions that were defended as civilizational values. The most important feature of Gandhism seems to be located in the growing importance of the masses as a crucial constituency in movements for social reform and political rights. To put across the emerging role of the masses, he, in an unambiguous manner, wrote:

the fact is that the formation of opinion today is by no means confined to the educated classes, but the masses have taken it upon themselves not only to formulate opinion but to enforce it. It would be a mistake to belittle or ignore this opinion, or to ascribe it to a temporary upheaval. . . . The masses are by no means so foolish or unintelligent as we sometimes imagine. They often perceive things with their intuition, which we ourselves fail to see with our intellect. But whilst the masses know what they want, they often do not know how to express their wants and, less often, how to get what they want. Herein comes the use of leadership.[11]

This passage is very significant in understanding the foundational ideas of Gandhi's social and political thought. *First*, Gandhi was aware that the masses became an integral part of the freedom struggle and hence they could be ignored only at the peril of the nationalist movement. *Second*, under the changed circumstances, the role of the leadership in articulating the oppositional voices of the masses was immensely important. Mass actions were 'intuitive' and they needed to be guided properly to address their grievance. So the leadership of the 'educated classes' continued to remain as significant as before. The implication is that the leadership was to contain the mass discontent within the parameters set by the nationalists, in accordance with the goal which they deemed fit for the nation. Gandhi's theory of leadership thus amounted, argues Ranajit Guha, 'to a formula to dissolve the immediacy of mobilization in the subaltern domain, and open up a space for the nationalist elite to step in with its own will, initiative, and organization in order to pilot the political activity of the masses towards [specific goals]'. Gandhism was therefore a mediating force between the spontaneous mass response and the calculated political leadership of the nationalist movement. Despite the fact that Gandhi had a class role, his doctrines, in stark contrast with prevalent theories of mass mobilization, had also brought the masses into the movement for independence, giving it power and effectiveness, while at the same time 'they helped to keep the movement safe for those with property'.[12]

Gandhi was most strategic in articulating his ideas. He kept, for instance, his vision of civil disobedience rather vague, which disheartened the Congress radicals like Subhas Chandra Bose, who was critical of Gandhi's failure to provide a blueprint for the future course of action. He thus argued: 'what his real expectation was, I was unable to understand. Either he did not want to give out all his secrets prematurely or he did not have a clear conception of the tactics whereby the hands of the Government could be forced.'[13] His colleague Jawaharlal Nehru was not critical but underlined the 'vagueness' in Gandhi's ideas of *swaraj*, for instance, by saying the 'it was obvious that to most of our leaders Swaraj meant something much less than independence. Gandhiji was delightfully vague on the subject, and he did not encourage clear thinking about it either.'[14] Gandhi did not seem to bother as he believed in the natural blossoming of mass civil disobedience and hence remained vague for obvious reasons. As it was described in the official history of the Indian National Congress,

> mass civil disobedience was the thing that was luring the people. What was it, what would it be? Gandhi himself never defined it, never elaborated it, never visualised it even to himself. It must unfold itself to discerning vision, to a pure heart, from step to step, much as the path-way in a dense forest would reveal itself to the wayfarer's feet as he wends his weary way until a ray of light brightens the hopes of an all but despairing wanderer.[15]

Despite the vagueness, there was no doubt that Gandhi's presence radically altered the nature of the freedom struggle and also the Indian National Congress which had so far remained merely a platform for ventilating political grievances and not a forum for political action. Even the communist critics admitted that Gandhi breathed new life into the Congress. While criticizing Gandhi's social and political programmes for being ideologically conservative and operationally restrictive, R. Palme Dutt argued:

> the new programme and policy inaugurated by Gandhi marked a giant's advance for the National Congress. The Congress now stood out as a

political party leading the masses in struggle against the Government for the realization of national freedom. From this point the National Congress won its position (a position at which the militant nationalists of the earlier years would have rubbed their eyes) as the central focus of the united national movement, a position which, through good and evil repute, through whatever changes of tactics and fortunes, it has maintained and carried forward up to this day.[16]

The Congress gained ground and Gandhi appeared to have infused new life into it. The growing strength of the nationalist movement is attributed to Gandhi's role in mediating between various groups and forces. Even before he became a Congress member, he had become the acknowledged leader and symbol of the anti-British movements in India. As such, he held together 'a group of political leaders, mediating between their diverse ideologies and aims'.[17] This was certainly a major factor that contributed to his increasing importance in the Congress even when it was terribly faction-ridden. What was also remarkable was the easy acceptance of his ideas by the rank and file of the political activists who participated in the freedom struggle in response to the call by Gandhi. While admitting that 'the innocent-seeming term, non violence'[18] was most effective in political mobilization by Gandhi, R. Palme Dutt also underlined the ideological vacuum that it created in the mass struggle, of which freedom from the British rule was just one objective. Hence in his critique of the 'non violent struggle' of Gandhi, Dutt argued that

> the subsequent experience of events and the ever-developing interpretation of [this form of struggle] were to demonstrate, that seemingly innocent humanitarian or expedient [form] contained concealed within it, not only the refusal of the final struggle, but the thwarting also of the immediate struggle by the attempt to conciliate the interests of the masses with the big bourgeois and landlord interests which were inevitably opposed to any decisive mass struggle. Herein lay the contradiction which was to lead to the collapse of the movement . . . and the failure to win that speedy victory of *Swaraj* which was freely promised as the certain and rapid outcome of the new policy'.[19]

Similarly, his vehement opposition to separate electorate for the dalits in 1932 did not reflect his sincere concern for the untouchables but a desperate effort to initiate further negotiations with the British following the breakdown of the first Round Table Conference in 1934. His interest in the *harijan* cause and the activities flowing thereupon, argued a veteran Marxist,

> should be considered as nothing but an effort on his part to disengage the Congress from the situation in which it had been placed following its break with the government. It was an effort to find points of contact

with the British, pursue the negotiations on constitutional reform started and temporarily broken at the second Round Table Conference, and to reorganise the Congress with a view to enabling it to meet the new situation.[20]

Similarly, by conceding to a separate electorate for the untouchables within the general constituencies through a protracted negotiation with Ambedkar in 1932, Gandhi carved a space where the nationalist logic could take root. There is a paradox however. The Congress argument that the nation was indivisible appeared to have lost its validity with the acceptance of a separate electorate for the Muslims. Gandhi was not ready to extend this constitutional guarantee to the untouchables because they, he insisted, represented a problem internal to Hinduism. So 'the homogeneity of India slides into the homogeneity of Hinduism'.[21] Because untouchability was internal to Hinduism, its removal was therefore to be accomplished by social reform, if necessary by law. And, no colonial intervention was thus permissible because it would amount to allowing the colonial ruler to intervene in an exclusive domain of Hindu society. This is a significant political articulation in conceptualizing anti-colonial nationalism which created, argues Partha Chatterjee, 'its domain of sovereignty within colonial society well before it [began] its political battle with the imperial power'.[22] According to Chatterjee, there were two domains – material and spiritual – which significantly influenced the nationalist articulation. The material domain constituted in the economy, science, technology and statecraft in which the West had proved its superiority and the East had 'succumbed'. There was however an inner domain, a domain of spiritual and cultural identity that remained the source of strength for the subject people. Although the West was politically dominant, its role was marginal in the inner domain, presumably due to its failure to comprehend the complexity of the spiritual and cultural world of the East. This had a significant consequence. With the growing influence of the West in the public sphere, the nationalist project need to be strengthened by looking more and more at the inner domain. By drawing upon the spiritual and cultural strength of the imagined nation, those seeking to identify its 'distinctiveness' *vis-à-vis* the West initiated a process that, though it began with the Extremist phase of Indian nationalism, loomed large particularly in the twentieth century when Gandhi organized a mass campaign by underlining the role of the colonial power in undermining India's age-old 'civilization'.[23] The Mahatma thus remained the most decisive leader who intervened in the nationalist movement without compromising what he believed. He was more instrumental than anyone else in bringing about the mass mobilization which finally led to decolonization in India. So decisive was the role of Gandhi in India's freedom struggle that he easily charted the course of political action in accordance with what he thought appropriate. Gandhi's words and actions therefore articulated 'the parallel themes of unleashing popular initiative and controlling it at the same time'.[24]

II

It is true that Gandhi's social and political ideas were class-governed and thus ideologically restrictive. Yet these were the ideas that brought into the nationalist effort against the British an element beyond that of making only constitutional demands. Essentially a liberal strand, the non-violent politics was a creative response to the situation when both the 'mendicant' political constitutionalism of the Moderates and the 'violent' revolutionary action of the Extremists had become futile. So Gandhi's strategy of civil disobedience, at once a non-violent and yet a non- or extra-constitutional strategy, fashioned India's freedom struggle in a manner which was neither purely constitutional nor revolutionary terrorist but a unique strategy containing the spirit of both. Hence it is argued that

> non violence, ahimsa and satyagraha to Gandhi personally constituted a deeply-felt and worked-out philosophy owing something to Emerson, Thoreau and Tolstoy but also revealing considerable originality. The search for truth was the goal of human life, and as no one could ever be sure of having attained the truth, use of violence to enforce one's own view of it was sinful.[25]

In this sense, Gandhi's view is similar to one of the most celebrated liberal arguments for tolerance – the meta inductive argument of J.S. Mill's *On Liberty* underlining that truth is never something we are sure that we have attained. We must not therefore impose our own conceptions of the truth on others. To do so would be a form of violence, especially if it was imposed by the apparatus of the state.[26] Whatever the similarities or dissimilarities between Gandhi and Mill, the fact remains that non-violent mass politics fitted in with the interests and sentiments of socially decisive sections of the Indian people. The Gandhian model was widely acceptable presumably because of its accommodative nature despite the obvious contradictions of interests among those involved in the nationalist movement against the British. The doctrine of *ahimsa* therefore 'lay at the heart of the essentially unifying, "umbrella-type" role assumed by Gandhi and the Gandhian Congress, mediating internal social conflicts, contributing greatly to joint national struggle against foreign rule, but also leading to periodic retreats and some major reverses'.[27] Gandhi's social and political ideas were revolutionary, but at the same time ideologically conciliatory. There were, as Chatterjee identifies, two contradictory yet integrated/reconciled aspects: a) a traditional peasant-communal moral critique of the political, economic and techno-scientific features of modernity or 'civil society'; and b) a set of procedural or organizational norms for the formation and operation of the political and legal structures of bourgeois modernity. While the former, he argued, served to politically mobilize the peasantry for the national bourgeoisie against the foreign and comprador bourgeoisie without modernizing

or revolutionizing them culturally, the latter gave the indigenous bourgeoisie dominance over the state structure, from which the peasantry was
kept away. Gandhi was probably the only nationalist who successfully combined these two contradictory ideological strands into an effective 'moment
of manoeuvre' in the passive national democratic revolution in India.[28]
Satyagraha was a tool of political action of which *ahimsa* was a cementing
factor. Although *satyagraha* triggered off mass movements, it was also most
undemocratic in the sense that it meant an imposition of the absolute moral-
ism of Truth by the *satayagrahi* leaders. *Ahimsa* was, therefore, not merely a
non-violent political action; it also denoted a well-crafted ideologically
meaningful strategy to ensure conflict accommodation rather than conflict
resolution through class struggles. Whatever the political consequences, this
Gandhian strategy provided for the first time in Indian politics 'an ideological basis for including the whole people within the imagined nation'.[29]
Hence the monumental significance of the Mahatma, who not only devised
an effective political strategy to combat colonialism, but also contributed to
the formation of a nation that was hardly derivative of the Western models.

III

Gandhi fell to an assassin's bullet. Presumably because of his policy of
appeasement towards the Muslims,[30] the killer of Gandhi justified this
extreme step.[31] The historical Gandhi died leaving behind a rich legacy of
his social and political thoughts which is as relevant today as in the past.
Unlike his colleagues in the constitutional mode of protest or revolution-
ary-terrorist means, Gandhi was perhaps the only nationalist leader who
devised a creative course of socio-political action on the basis of what he
sincerely believed. Not only did he provide a theory of social change and
political action, he also charted a definite course of action involving the
masses. 'A practical leader with his pulse on the Indian masses,'[32] he was
both a man of action and thought. As a man of action, his major contribution consisted in leading perhaps the most gigantic nationalist movement
of the twentieth century. His role in decolonizing India in 1947 is undeni-
able.[33] In *satyagraha*, he devised a unique method of political change which
was an effective alternative to violence, drawing on *satya* (truth) and *ahimsa*.
His language of politics and course of action were clearly in the tradition of
liberal political theory and thus the British rule, despite being oppressive,
continued to remain a constant referent in his social and political ideas.
Gandhism was translated into a national political movement within the
institutional processes set up and directed by the colonial state. While
articulating his response, he 'had perforce to reckon with the practical real-
ities of a bourgeois legal and political structure as indeed of the organizational issues affecting [a national democratic movement]'.[34] The
significance of Gandhi lies in reconciling these two contradictory aspects
which formed the core of his social and political ideas. In contrast with the

'mendicant' or revolutionary politics of the past, Gandhism was articulated in a theory of nationalism with roots in bourgeois modernity, supported by a movement which rejected the idea of 'progress' and the ideology of a political organization fighting for the creation of 'a modern national state'. His language was 'traditional' and yet he articulated his oppositional 'voice' within the structural forms of a bourgeois organizational order. It would be wrong to dismiss Gandhi as 'a traditionalist' since he always spoke in 'traditional idioms'. What drove him to cling to these idioms was their effectiveness in mobilizing the masses even under the most adverse circumstances. For him, they were simply an effective 'means' of communicating with the vast masses of the people which immediately struck a chord with them. So Gandhism became an ideology of mass politics regardless of region and strata whereby the demands of the people were easily articulated into 'the message of the Mahatma'.[35] There is therefore no single Gandhian thought or politics. It would be theoretically inappropriate to historicize Gandhi, characterizing him essentially as a figure in the history of the Indian nationalist movement.[36] It is true that Gandhian social and political thought was rooted in a particular context. This is not to defend the historical Gandhi but to underline the appropriateness of his ideas in addressing socio-politically disparate audiences, each operating within differing temporalities.

Seeking to provide an alternative vision, Gandhi's critique of modernity combined 'the best insights of both the pre-modern and modern worldviews while avoiding the naïve individualism and moral vacuum of the currently fashionable post-modernism'.[37] By engaging in such outmoded historical practices as fasts and silences or weaving his own cloth, Gandhi discovered 'a powerful resource to infuse symbolic meanings into the world of high politics'.[38] This also enabled Gandhi to strike an emotional chord with the masses, who were automatically drawn to the public sphere, which remained an exclusive elite-domain before the onset of the Mahatma. He aimed to give political significance to the everyday pictures of the world used by his fellow countrymen. While articulating his political response, Gandhi therefore preferred to show ways in which the past seeped into the present, thus dissolving what were thought to be 'historical inevitabilities'. It was possible for him 'to tear through historical fixities', presumably because he understood so well 'the role of belief and consciousness in politics [which, for him] was a struggle to make and unmake selves, individuals and collective character'.[39]

IV

Gandhi was not a theorist, but he had theories. His comments on contemporary social, economic and political issues were couched in liberal terms whereby individuals were privileged over the collectivity. Rejecting 'the collectivist' theory of both state and society, Gandhi argued that only an

individual could exercise 'conscience' and therefore 'morality'. His critique
of modernity drew on this assumption. By challenging the inevitability and
intractability of modernity, he upheld the idea that 'this mindless modernity' can be non-violently resisted. He tempered his criticism by contextualizing modernity 'within a cosmological framework that guards individual
autonomy'.[40] The Gandhian formulation thus underlined the inescapably
unique *swabhava* (instinct behaviour) and different ways in which individuals defined and led the good life. Each individual had a distinct identity
and was rooted in a specific cultural tradition. Hence not only was the past
important in his construction, he also defended the local traditions whereby
individuals lived and worked with purpose and dignity. Unlike the Enlightenment conceptions of individualism, which separate individuals from their
tradition and *vice versa*, Gandhi provided a theory of the autonomy of individuals, designed to empower individuals within their traditions and
community.[41] By homogenizing individuals, Western rationalism, defined
as part of modernity, tended to gloss over the diverse nature of human
beings due to their socio-economic and cultural roots. Rationalism was
inherently hierarchical and missionary with 'a deep imperialist orienta-
tion',[42] which was articulated in South Africa and India, where the rulers
justified their 'atrocious rule' in the name of rationality. What was creative
in Gandhi's response was the idea that, although Western modernity was
unavoidable in a colonial context,[43] it needed to be reinvented by taking into
account the specificities of the immediate context of the Indian reality. In
this sense, Gandhi sought to fill in some gaps in our conceptualization of
modernity. He did so by continually applying ethical standards to
contemporary practices and institutions. For him, the modern tendency to
define and judge human beings in terms of economic criteria 'reduces
[them] to means and with such an outlook, talk about their dignity is
futile'.[44] What was most refreshing in Gandhism was a seriously argued case
against modernity believed to have unleashed processes embodying progress,
reason and liberation. While being critical of appreciating modernity
without qualification, Gandhi also carved a space for the alternative practices, distinctly local or relevant to specific contexts that could never be
ignored without costly consequences. For instance, his idea of *panchayati raj*
may not be appropriate in 'the crowded polity of late modern India', but his
argument in favour of people's participation in governance remains at the
heart of the democratic project. His critique therefore laid the foundation of
a theoretically meaningful concept of democracy in a large polity and, at the
same time, he had also demonstrated the dangers of concentration of power
and the need for its devolution through a process of mass participation.[45]

Issues raised and dealt with in *Harijan* were not new, but a re-articulation
in a changed political context when the Mahatma no longer remained the
supreme leader of the nationalist movement because of the Hindu–Muslim
fissure and the growing importance of social divisions among the Hindus in
political terms. Unlike the *Hind Swaraj*, which was a consistently argued

text with clear social and political relevance, Gandhi's responses in *Harijan* lacked the same intellectual rigour presumably because they were articulated in response to the immediate demands of the circumstances. And yet they remained within the ideological parameters of non-violence. In other words, by problematizing the issues in a context when the nationalist movement had a wider social reach, especially in the aftermath of the 1931–2 Civil Disobedience Movement, Gandhi was constantly negotiating with a reality that became far more complex with the involvement of peripheral sections of society in the political processes. There was also the changed imperial government, which already reaped the benefit of divide-and-rule strategy when Hindus and Muslims were politically alienated to the satisfaction of the ruler. And Gandhi had also to take into account the changing international scenario with the rising importance of fascism in Europe. Hence the issues which the Mahatma dwelled on in *Harijan* were varied and multidimensional. Their significance lay, however, in constructing a blueprint for the future India, organically linked with the Indian socio-economic and cultural circumstances. For Gandhi, the primary aim of the freedom struggle was not merely to wrest political power from the British, but also to evolve a suitable socio-economic and political system, capable of successfully addressing the myriad problems confronting India. His version of non-violent civil disobedience was an ideological alternative to the constitutional means of the bygone era. The purpose here was to evolve an alternative means that was not dependent or derivative of the ideas and institutions of the British rule. Otherwise, even if the British left, the Indian population would remain a subject people. This went deep in Gandhi and his responses in *Harijan* were full of a detailed anxiety about the cognitive enslavement even of the nationalist and anti-colonial Indian mind, which might, even in the aftermath of independence, never recover from that enslavement.[46]

Furthermore, the Gandhian social utopia as outlined in the *Hind Swaraj* and *Harijan* may appear to be 'unrealistic' or 'obscurantist' as a model for social and economic reconstruction.[47] But it was undoubtedly a firm response to the 'alienating effects of modernization' under colonialism. Modernity was an evil and not a panacea for human ills. Socially divisive, economically disruptive and culturally alienating, modernity became a symbol of Western domination. Critical of 'the madness of modernity', Gandhi articulated his alternative vision through the programmes of *khadi* and *charkha*, village reconstruction and *harijan* welfare. These ideas were not adequately radical in the sense that they altered the ingrained atrocious social and economic relations among individuals; their significance lay in constructing a utopia that was readily acceptable by the people, presumably due to the obviously devastating nature of colonialism. His message of self-reliance and self-help of the *swadeshi* period thus acquired wider acceptance.[48] For Gandhi, the *charkha* represented not a mere hand-spinning device that could provide employment and income to the poor, but an ideology with wider implications for the entire human life. 'The message of the spinning-wheel', he thus argued, 'is much wider than its circumstance. Its message is one of simplicity, service to mankind, living so as not to hurt others, creating an indissoluble bond between the rich and poor, capital and labour, the prince and the peasant.'[49] *Charkha* was thus a way of life, integrally linked with Gandhi's social and political thought. Meaningful in the Indian colonial context, the symbols that defined Gandhism contributed immensely to an articulation of nationalism that was not at all derivative. The nationalism imported from the West suffered from an inadequacy because the symbols which had evolved historically in Western civilization did not, for obvious reasons, produce 'any resonance in Indian mind[s]'.[50] Indian nationalist leaders had to create them and to redefine them in such a way as to make them meaningful in the Indian context. By articulating a transformative vision and a programme of action with indigenous roots, Gandhi had a significant role in the entire process. No other leader in history in his own lifetime had done so much 'to make a people into a nation'.[51] While evaluating the Mahatma as a nationalist leader, Nehru thus commented that '[w]ith all his greatness and his contradictions and power of moving the masses, he is above the usual standards. One cannot measure him or judge him as we would others'.[52]

Apart from its wider ideological connotations, the Gandhian model also worked in two complementary ways in so far as political mobilization was concerned: on the one hand, it provided a feasible alternative with roots in Indian socio-economic reality and hence people were drawn to it; it was also, on the other hand, a mobilizing device in the sense that those participating in *khadi/charkha*, for instance, were automatically linked with their counterparts in various parts of the country. This served dual purposes. *First*, it infused a new meaning to *khadi* and *charkha* that was integral to peasant cosmology and hence not an invention, but a reiteration of familiar ideas; *second*, by linking *swadeshi* with political freedom, the Mahatma also redefined 'politics' making it more than something confined to 'a defined sphere', but something that invades everyday life instead. Gandhi's social and political thought acquired immediate salience presumably because it was supplemented by his pastoral style in daily life: travelling in third-class compartments, speaking in simple *Hindustani*, wearing self-spun *khadi*, using the imagery of Tulshidas' *Ramayana*, so deep-rooted in the popular religion of the north Indian Hindu rural masses.[53]

Glossary

Adhikar a right, a right that is earned or deserved
Advaita non-dualism, monism
Ahimsa non-violence, absence of a desire to harm a living being
Anashakti non-attachment
Ashram a commune of spiritual aspirants organized around a guru
Atman soul or spirit
Bania of the class of traders and moneylender
Brahmacharya celibacy, chastity
Buddhi intelligence
Charkha spinning wheel
Chetana consciousness
Crore ten million
Dalits those previously described as untouchables. The untouchables were
    people considered so low as to be placed outside the pale of normal
    physical contact with those who are considered ritually superior.
Dharma duty, moral law, characteristic activity of a class of objects or
    beings
Dharna a form of sit-down strike
Duragraha stubborn persistence
Ekpraja a sense of belonging to a single community
Fakir Muslim ascetic or mendicant
Goonda ruffian/hooligan
Harijan untouchables; literally, people of God
Hartal cessation of work as an expression of protest
Himsa violence, injury
Karma action, law of moral retribution
Khaddar, Khadi hand-spun cloth
Lakh one hundred thousand
Lathi stick
Lokshakti people's power, power generated by people's collective action
Mahatma great soul. An honorific title conferred on Gandhi by
    Rabindranath Tagore
Maitri friendliness

Manas   mind

Moksha   liberation, release from the cycle of rebirth

Nishkam dharma   disinterested action

Panchayat   originally a committee or council of five members, now a small local council

Quran   Koran, the holy book of Islam

Sabha   assembly, society

Sadbhava   goodwill, a wish to see someone flourish

Sanatiani   a strict follower of ancient Vedic religion, orthodox

Sarvodaya   welfare for all

Satya   truth

Satyagraha   non-violent resistance

Satyagrahi   one who engages in non-violent resistance

Shakti   energy or power

swabliava   nature

Swadeshi   belonging to or made in one's country

Swaraj   self-rule, individual or collective autonomy

Tapasya, Tapas   religious penance, austerity, sacrifice

Ulema   Muslim theologian

Untouchables   see dalits

Varna   caste

Varnashrama   fourfold division of Hindu society

Yajna   any activity undertaken in the spirit of sacrifice to a deity

Yantravad   mechanization as an end in itself or for its own sake

Yoga   Hindu system of contemplation for effecting union of the human soul with the Supreme Being

Yogi   one who practises yoga

Zamindar   landlord

Notes

By way of introduction

1 Gandhi wrote a partial autobiography (*My Experiments with Truth*), a political treatise (*Hind Swaraj*), a few pamphlets, a very large number of articles in the two weeklies that he edited, namely *Indian Opinion* (South Africa) and *Young India* (India) and an even larger number of letters to viceroys, fellow politicians and disciples. Besides these, he delivered speeches at conferences, congresses and at his regular prayer meetings.

2 Ronald J. Terchek, *Gandhi: struggling for autonomy*, Vistaar Publications, New Delhi, 1998, pp. 3–4.

3 Ainslie T. Embree, *Imagining India: essays on Indian history*, Oxford University Press, Delhi, 1989, p. 165.

4 Lloyd I. Rudolph and Susanne Hoeber Rudolph, *The Modernity of Tradition: political development in India*, University of Chicago Press, Chicago and London, 1967, p. 159.

5 According to Morris-Jones, Gandhi represented saintly politics in which his image as a renouncer mattered a lot. W.H. Morris-Jones, 'India's political idioms', in C.H. Philips (ed.), *Politics and Society in India*, George Allen & Unwin, London, 1963, p. 140.

6 Oriental and India Office Collections, London, Mss Eur. F238/3, Reading Papers, Reading, the Viceroy to Montague, the Secretary of State, 19 May, 1921.

7 Claude Markovits, *The Un-Gandhian Gandhi: the life and afterlife of the Mahatma*, Permanent Black, New Delhi, 2003, p. 32.

8 For a quick summary of Gandhi's role in Indian freedom struggle and the ideas he stood for, see Judith Brown, 'The Mahatma and modern India', *Modern Asian Studies*, 3 (4), 1969, pp. 321–42.

9 R.K. Narayan, the novelist, then in his early twenties, provided a firsthand account of Gandhi's arrival in a small town in Tamil Nadu. He was amazed by the electrifying presence of the Mahatma, who was impressive neither in terms of his 'attire' nor 'speech' he delivered. What perplexed the young Narayan was how the Mahatma struck an emotional chord almost instantaneously with those who had waited long hours for him. Narayan was drawn to him, appreciating Mahatma's charisma and the ideology of non-violence. R.K. Narayan, *Waiting for the Mahatma*, Indian Thought Publications, Chennai, 2003 (reprint).

10 Dhanki Joginder Singh (ed.), *Perspectives on Indian National Movement (selected correspondence of Lala Lajpat Rai)*, New Delhi, National Book Organizations, 1998.

11 Markovits, op. cit., p. 34.

12 Judith M. Brown, *Gandhi's Rise to Power: Indian politics, 1915–22*, Cambridge University Press, Cambridge, 1972, p. 356.

13 Shahid Amin, 'Gandhi as Mahatma: Gorakhpur district, eastern UP, 1921–2' in Ranajit Guha (ed.), *Subaltern Studies: writings on South Asian history and society*, Vol. III, Oxford University Press, Delhi, 1984.

14 Sekhar Bandyopadhyay, *From Plassey to Partition: a history of modern India*, Orient Longman, New Delhi, 2004, pp. 292–3. This point is elaborated in Chapter 2.

15 Bhikhu Parekh, *Gandhi*, Oxford University Press, Oxford, 1997, p. 92.

16 Rudolph and Rudolph, op. cit., p. 183.

17 Douglas Allen, 'Discovering Gandhi', *The Times of India*, New Delhi, 4 July, 2004.

18 J.B. Kripalani, *Gandhi: his life and thought*, New Delhi, 1970, p. 61. This was not surprising because the earlier generation of the nationalist leaders appeared to be less concerned with those at the grassroots. For instance, this was also the feeling when young Jawaharlal Nehru visited Pratapgarh for the first time. 'The visit was', Nehru confessed,

> a revelation to me. . . . [Though] I had often passed through villages, stopped there and talked to the peasants, . . . I had not fully realized what they were and what they meant to India. Like most of us, I took them for granted. This realization came to me during these Pratapgarh visits and ever since then my mental picture of India always contains this naked, hungry mass. Perhaps there was some kind of electricity in the air, perhaps I was in a receptive frame of mind and the pictures I saw and the impressions I gathered were indelibly impressed on my mind.
> (Jawaharlal Nehru, *An Autobiography*, John Lane The Bodley Head, London, 1941, p. 57)

19 Rajendra Prasad, *At the Feet of Mahatma Gandhi*, Bombay, 1961, p. 7.

20 A report of the sub-divisional officer, Bettiah on 23 September, 1917, quoted in Jacques Pouchepadass, *Champaran and Gandhi: planters, peasants and Gandhian politics*, Oxford University Press, New Delhi, 1999, pp. 217–18.

21 In his historical novel, Kanthapura, Raja Rao depicted how Gandhi became 'a symbol of hope' to the people despite police atrocities. Mahatma was not there in Kanthapura, and yet he galvanized the masses into action against the British police. On one occasion,

> Rachanna, [a sincere Gandhi supporter], cries out, '*Mahatma Gandhi ki jai*' [victory to Mahatma Gandhi], the policeman rushes at the crowd and bangs them with his *lathi* [cane] and Rachanna quavers out the louder, '*Gandhi Mahatma ki jai*' and other policemen come and bang them too, and the women raise such a clamour and cry that the crows and bats set up an obsequial wail, and the sparrows join them from the roofs and eaves and the cattle rise up in the byre and the creaking of their bones is heard. . . . There is again such a clamour – Mahatma Gandhi ki jai – the police inspector shouts 'disperse the crowd' . . . policemen beat the crowd this side that side, and groans and moans and cries and coughs and oaths and bangs and kicks are heard, and more shouts of '*Mahatma Gandhi ki jai! Mahatma Gandhi ki jai!*'.
> (Raja Rao, *Kanthapura*, New Directions, New York, 1967, pp. 83–5)

22 Pouchepadass, op. cit., p. 234.

23 For a detailed account of the Kheda *satyagraha*, see David Hardiman, *Peasant Nationalists of Gujarat: Kheda district, 1917–1934*, Oxford University Press, New Delhi, 1981.

24 David Hardiman, op. cit., pp. 85–113.
25 The only comprehensive account of this strike is available in M.V. Kamath and V.B. Kher, *The Story of Militant but Non-violent Trade Unionism: a biographical and historical study*, Navajivan Trust, Ahmedabad, 1993 (reprint).
26 B.R. Nanda, *In Search of Gandhi: essays and reflections*, Oxford University Press, New Delhi, 2004, p. 199.
27 *Bombay Chronicle*, 20 March, 1918.
28 *The Times*, 8 April, 1918.
29 Bandyopadhyay, op. cit., p. 295.
30 Partha Chatterjee, *Nationalist Thought and the Colonial World: a derivative discourse*, Oxford University Press, Delhi, 1986, pp. 124–5.
31 David Hardiman, *Gandhi In His Time and Ours*, Permanent Black, New Delhi, 2003, p. 51.
32 Jawaharlal Nehru, *An Autobiography*, John Lane The Bodley Head, London, 1941, pp. 254–5.
33 The most comprehensive discussion of the Non-Cooperation Movement is Judith Brown's *Gandhi's rise to power*, op. cit.
34 There is no doubt that the merger of the Khilafat cause with the political agenda of the Non-Cooperation Movement strengthened the anti-British campaign simply because Hindus and Muslims came together to fight the British who, according to the Muslims, had disrupted the religious sanctity of the Khaliph. For details, see Gail Minault, *The Khilafat Movement: religious symbolism and political mobilization in India*, Oxford University Press, Delhi, 1999 (reprint).
35 For a detailed description of the movement and the role of Gandhi, see Judith Brown, *Gandhi and Civil Disobedience: the Mahatma in Indian politics, 1928–1934*, Cambridge University Press, Cambridge, 1977.
36 For a discussion of the Quit India Movement as a pan-Indian campaign, see F.G. Hutchins, *Spontaneous Revolution: the Quit India Movement*, Manohar, New Delhi, 1971; also by the same author, *India's Revolution: Gandhi and the Quit India Movement*, Harvard University Press, Cambridge, 1973.
37 The most interesting discussion of how the message of the Mahatma was decoded differently by those who participated in the Gandhi-led Non-Cooperation Movement, for instance, is pursued in Shahid Amin, *Event, Metaphor, Memory: Chauri Chaura, 1922–1992*, Oxford University Press, New Delhi, 1995.
38 I have elaborated the nature of the Quit India Movement in the district of Midnapur, which ran counter to what the Mahatma preached. Bidyut Chakrabarty, *Local Politics and Indian Nationalism: Midnapur, 1919–1944*, Manohar, New Delhi, 1997.
39 This is not an exhaustive, but a selective, review of literature. The aim here is to identify the trends in literature on Gandhi. Since the book dwells on the issues, raised in the *Harijan*, this brief review is highly relevant to understand the growing importance of those issues which, though peripheral in Gandhi's earlier writings, assumed tremendous significance especially in the 1930s and 1940s.
40 Brown, *Gandhi's Rise to Power*, op. cit. Brown, *Gandhi and Civil Disobedience*, op. cit.
41 Judith Brown, *Gandhi: prisoner of hope*, Oxford University Press, Delhi, 1990, p. 359.
42 Gandhi had immense resilience and abounding faith in whatever he undertook. Although he was very upset after the partition riots in Bengal, Bihar and Punjab, he never lost hope, as evident in his reply to the Chinese Ambassador, Lo Chia Luen. He responded:

I am an irrepressible optimist. We have not lived and toiled all these years that we should become barbarians as we appear to be becoming at all the senseless bloodshed in Bengal, Bihar and the Punjab. But I feel that it is just an indication that, as we are throwing off the foreign yoke, all the dirt and froth is coming to the surface. When the Ganges is in flood, the water is turbid, the dirt comes to the surface. When the flood subsides, you see the clear, blue water which soothes the eye. That is what I hope for and live for. I do not wish to see Indian humanity becoming barbarian.

(Quoted in Louis Fischer, *The Life of Mahatma Gandhi*, Harper and Row, New York, 1981 p. 470)

43 Judith Brown, *Gandhi: prisoner of hope*, op. cit., p. 311.
44 Ibid., pp. 312–13.
45 Undated note to GD Birla which *The Collected Works of Mahatma Gandhi*, Publication Division, Ministry of Information and Broadcasting, Government of India, New Delhi, 1958–84 (hereafter *CWMG*) places at the 1946, *CWMG*, Vol. 86, p. 295.
46 Nehru to Gandhi, 25 March, 1947, *CWMG*, Vol. 87, p. 125, fn. 1.
47 Patel to Gandhi, *CWMG*, Vol. 87, p. 138, fn. 2.
48 Speech at prayer meeting in Delhi, 1 April, 1947, *CWMG*, Vol. 87, p. 187.
49 Speech at prayer meeting, 2 June, 1947, *CWMG*, Vol. 88, p. 84.
50 Prayer meeting, 2 June, 1947, *CWMG*, Vol. 88, p. 63.
51 Sucheta Mahajan elaborated the dilemma that Gandhi confronted as soon as the Congress accepted the partition plan for freedom. For details, see Sucheta Mahajan, *Independence and Partition: the erosion of colonial power*, Sage, New Delhi, 2000, pp. 360–81.
52 J.V. Bondurant, *Conquest of Violence: the Gandhian philosophy of conflict*, University of California Press, Berkeley, 1969 (revised edition). The most detailed review underlining the theoretical contribution of this book is available in W.H. Morris-Jones' postscript to his article entitled 'Mahatma Gandhi – political philosopher?', *Political Studies*, Vol. VIII (1), February, 1960, pp. 31–6. I have borrowed heavily from this review in writing this section.
53 The term '*satyagraha*' had its root in a slogan contest that Gandhi conducted in South Africa in 1906 when he wanted an Indian word to describe his programme. The winning term was *sadagraha*, denoting firmness in a good cause. Gandhi coined *satyagraha* because 'truth' or *satya* was to be the guiding force in his search for a good society. M.K. Gandhi, *Satyagraha in South Africa*, Navajivan Publishing House, Ahmedabad, 1950, p. 109. While explaining his preference for *satyagraha* to *sadagraha*, Gandhi wrote in *Harijan* that

I liked the word, but it did not fully represent the whole idea I wished to connote. I therefore corrected it to 'satyagraha'. Truth (*satya*) implies love, and firmness (*agraha*) engenders and therefore serves as a synonym for force. I thus began to call the Indian movement 'satyagraha' that is to say, the force which is born to Truth and Love or non violence, and gave up the use of the phrase 'passive resistance'.

(*Harijan*, June, 1939)

54 Bondurant, op. cit., p. 11. *Satyagraha*, argues Bondurant further,

allows for several stages of winning over an opponent. The first stage is characterized by persuasion through reason. The subsequent stages enter the realm of persuasion through suffering wherein the satyagraha attempts to dramatize the issues at stake and to get through to the opponent's unprejudiced judgment so that he may willingly come again into a level where he may be persuaded through rational argument. Finally if persuasion by reason or by suffering does not succeed, the satyagraha may resort to non-violent coercion characterized by such tools as non-cooperation or civil disobedience.

55   The *duragraha* may avoid open violence yet still use wrong means. As Gandhi stated,

> [t]he man who follows the path of *duragraha* becomes impatient and wants to kill the so-called enemy. There can be but one result of this. Hatred increases. The defeated party vows vengeance and simply bides its time. The spirit of revenge thus descends from father to son. It is much to be wished that Indians never give predominance to this spirit of *duragraha*. If the members of this [Congress] assembly deliberately accept *satyagraha* and chalk out its programme accordingly, they will reach their goal all the more easily for doing so. They may have to face disappointment in the initial stages. They may not see results for a time. But *satyagraha* will triumph in the end.
>
> (*The CWMG*, Vol. 55, p. 427)

56   *CWMG*, Vol. 55, p. 426.
57   Bondurant, op. cit.
58   W.H. Morris-Jones, 'Mahatma Gandhi – political philosopher?', *Political Studies*, Vol. VIII (1), February, 1960 p. 33.
59   J.V. Bondurant, 'Satyagraha versus duragraha' in Subrata Mukherjee and Sushila Ramaswamy (eds), *Facets of Mahatma Gandhi: non violence and satyagraha*, Deep & Deep, New Delhi, 1996, p. 96.
60   Bhikhu Parekh, *Colonialism, Tradition and Reform: an analysis of Gandhi's political discourse*, Sage, New Delhi, 1999 (revised edition).
61   Ibid., p. 25.
62   In his study of Gandhi's economic thought, Ajit Dasgupta extended this argument further. For details, see Ajit Dasgupta, *Gandhi's Economic Thought*, Routledge, London, 1996, pp. 181–2.
63   *Harijan*, 1 February, 1942, *CWMG*, Vol. 73, p. 93.
64   Ronald Terchek deals with this extensively – see Terchek, op. cit.
65   Parekh, *Colonialism, Tradition and Reform*, op. cit., p. 26.
66   Gandhi's prayer meeting, 15 October, 1942, reproduced in Sushila Nayar, *Mahatma Gandhi's Last Imprisonment: the inside story*, Har-Anand, New Delhi, 1996, p. 136.
67   Parekh, *Colonialism, tradition and reform*, op. cit., p. 129.
68   Ibid., p. 307.
69   Raghavan N. Iyer, *The Moral and Political Thought of Mahatma Gandhi*, Oxford University Press, Delhi, 1973.
70   Ibid., p. 184.
71   *Harijan*, May, 1939.
72   As Gandhi argued, 'for the love we have to practice towards our relatives or colleague in our family or institution, we have to practice towards our foes, dacoits etc.' *Harijan*, July, 1940.
73   Iyer, op. cit., p. 189.
74   Ibid., p. 151.
75   *To a Gandhian capitalist*, Hind Kitabs, 1951, pp. 49–51 – quoted in Iyer, op. cit., p. 157.
76   *Young India*, December, 1921.
77   *Young India*, July, 1931.
78   Iyer, op. cit., p. 252.

79 Parel, op. cit., p. 90.
80 See M.K. Gandhi, 'Satyagraha in South Africa' (1928), where he writes:

> passive resistance conveyed the idea of Suffragette Movement in England. Burning of houses by these women was called passive resistance and so also their fasting in prison. All such acts might very well be passive resistance but they were no satyagraha. . . . Satyagraha is pure soul force. Truth is the very substance of the soul. That is why this force is called satyagraha. The soul is informed with knowledge. In it burns the flame of love. If someone gives us pain through ignorance, we shall win him through love. [That] Non violence is the supreme dharma is the proof of this power of love. Non violence is a dormant state. In the waking state, it is love.
>
> (quoted in Rudrangshu Mukherjee (ed.), *The Penguin Gandhi Reader*, Penguin, New Delhi, 1993, pp. 125–6)

81 Gandhi's oral submission before the Hunter Committee in Ahmedabad on 9 January, 1920, *CWMG*, Vol. 16, p. 391.
82 *Harijan*, March, 1946. On an earlier occasion, Gandhi wrote the following about *satyagraha*:

> It is a test of our sincerity. It requires solid and silent self-sacrifice. It challenges our honesty and our capacity for national work. It is a movement that aims at translating ideas into action. And the more we do, the more we find that much more must be done than we had expected. And this thought of our imperfection must make us humble.
>
> (*Young India*, January, 1921)

83 *Young India*, March, 1931.
84 Gandhi, 'The law of swadeshi', *Young India*, June, 1931, quoted in Mukherjee, op. cit., pp. 77–8.
85 Gandhi's preface to the English edition of the *Hind Swaraj* in Parel, *Hind Swaraj and Other Writings*, Cambridge University Press, Cambridge, 1997, p. 6.
86 *CWMG*, Vol. 19, p. 277.
87 Dennis Dalton, *Non-violence in Action: Gandhi's power*, Oxford University Press, Delhi, 1998 (reprint), pp. 16–17.
88 Gandhi's preface to the English edition of the *Hind Swaraj* in Parel, op. cit., p. 7.
89 Dennis Dalton, 'The ideology of sarvodaya: concepts of politics and power in Indian political thought' in Thomas Pantham and Kenneth L. Deutsch, *Political Thought in Modern India*, Sage, New Delhi, 1986, p. 283.
90 In his *Hind Swaraj*, Gandhi extensively commented on 'Brute Force'. Parel, op. cit., Chapter 16 (pp. 79–87).
91 While comparing the Western brute force with his conceptualization of 'soul-force or truth-force', Gandhi charged the Extremist political leaders with nurturing 'narrow ends, infected by British methods'. M.K. Gandhi, 'The doctrine of the sword', *CWMG*, Vol. 10, pp. 42–4. He further argued, 'Violence is the law of the brute. The spirit lies dormant in the brute and he knows no law but that of physical might. The dignity of man requires obedience to a higher law – to the strength of spirit.'
92 Erik H. Erikson, *Gandhi's Truth: on the origins of militant non-violence*, Norton, New York, 1966, p. 217.
93 Bhikhu Parekh, *Gandhi's Political Philosophy: a critical appreciation*, Ajanta, Delhi, 1995, p. 211.
94 These expressions are borrowed from Ashis Nandy's *The Intimate Enemy: loss and recovery of self under colonialism*, Oxford University Press, Delhi, 1983.

95 Parel, op. cit., Chapter 7 (pp. 39–41).
96 Nandy, op. cit., p. 48.
97 Parel, op. cit., Chapter XIX, p. 107.
98 Ibid., p. 111.
99 Ibid., p. 108.
100 Partha Chatterjee, *Nationalist Thought and the Colonial World*, op. cit., p. 87.
101 Parel, op. cit., p. 67.
102 Ibid., p. 43.
103 Ibid., p. 43.
104 Ibid., pp. 43–4.
105 Ibid., p. 37. He further noted

> the tendency of Indian civilization is to elevate the moral being; that of
> Western civilization is to propagate immorality. The latter is godless, the
> former is based on a belief in god. So understanding, so believing, it
> behoves every lover of India to cling to old Indian civilization even as a
> child clings to its mother's breast.
>
> (Parel, op. cit., p. 71)

106 A detailed exposition of these concepts is available in the section on major
     trends in Gandhian social and political thought. Hence to deal with them
     again is redundant. These concepts – *swaraj, swadeshi* and *satya* – remain the
     fundamental tenets of Gandhism though Gandhi redefined them in response to
     circumstances keeping their basic thrust and spirit intact.
107 M.K. Gandhi, 'Village industries', *CWMG*, Vol. 59, p. 356.
108 Parel, op. cit., Introduction to the *Hind Swaraj*, p. lvii.
109 Rudolph C. Heredia, 'Interpreting Gandhi's Hind Swaraj', *Economic and Polit-
     ical Weekly*, Vol. 34 (24), 12 June, 1999, p. 1499.
110 Parel, op. cit., Introduction to the *Hind Swaraj*, p. lvi.
111 Parel, op. cit., p. 90.
112 Parekh, *Gandhi's Political Philosophy*, op. cit., p. 156.
113 Parel, op. cit., p. 73. 'Swaraj is', Gandhi further argued, 'when we learn to rule
     ourselves'.

1 Gandhi: the idea of *swaraj*

1 Tapan Raychaudhiri, *Perceptions, Emotions, Sensibilities: essays on India's colonial and
   post-colonial experiences*, Oxford University Press, Delhi, 1999, p. 18.
2 Ibid., p. 19.
3 Ibid., p. 19.
4 T.K. Oommen, *State and Society in India: studies in nation-building*, Sage, New
   Delhi, 1990, p. 39.
5 Ravinder Kumar thus argues, 'Any nationalist transformation of Indian civilization, which rested upon a dozen and more well articulated regional and linguistic cultures, could not be easily compared to the emergence of the
   European Nation-States, which grew out of the consolidation of disaggregated
   polities, or a breakdown of composite empires'. Ravinder Kumar, 'India: a
   "Nation-State" or a "Civilization-State"?', *Occasional paper on perspectives in
   Indian development*, Nehru Memorial Museum and Library, No. VIII, New
   Delhi, 1989, p. 22.
6 For Benedict Anderson, historical experience of nationalism in Western Europe,
   America and Russia had supplied for all subsequent nationalisms a set of
   modular forms from which nationalist elites of Afro-Asian countries had chosen
   the ones they liked. Benedict Anderson, *Imagined Communities: reflections on the
   origin and spread of nationalism*, Verso, London, 1983.

7 Partha Chatterjee, *The Nation and Its Fragments: colonial and post-colonial histories*, Oxford University Press, Delhi, 1994, p. 5.

8 *Swadeshi* is an Indian expression, popularized with loaded meanings in the course of the freedom struggle, including a) collective pride; b) ancestral loyalty; and c) communal integrity or amity.

9 Bhikhu Parekh, 'Ethnocentricity of the nationalist discourse', *Nations and Nationalism*, Vol. 1, 1, p. 39.

10 This is particularly true of the Muslims engaged in redefining their religiously informed cultural identity in the face of a modernity underwritten by the fact of British sovereignty. Ayesha Jalal thus argues: '[C]ontinued recourse to the colonial privileging of religious distinctions thwarted many well-meaning attempts at accommodating differences within a broad framework of Indian nationalism'. Ayesha Jalal, 'Nation, reason and religion: Punjab's role in the partition of India', *Economic and Political Weekly*, 8 August, 1998, p. 2183.

11 The critique of nationalism does not undermine, however, the outstanding role the nationalist movement had in liberating India from the clutches of colonialism – political, economic and intellectual. Instead, what it seeks to suggest is that nationalism, as articulated by Gandhi and his colleagues in the nationalist struggle, was the expression of a particular historical conjuncture in which the role of colonialism was no less insignificant. Gyanendra Pandey pursues this argument at length in his *Remembering Partition: violence, nationalism and history in India*, Cambridge University Press, Cambridge, 2001, pp. 18–19.

12 John Stuart Mill, *Consideration on Representative Government* (1861) from Geriant Williams (ed.), *Utilitarianism, On Liberty, Consideration on Representative Government*, Everyman, London, 1993, p. 396. Variants of Mill's argument are still extremely influential among major thinkers in the nationalism, democratization and rational choice literatures.

13 Charles Taylor, 'The dynamics of democratic exclusion', *Journal of Democracy*, Vol. 9 (4), October, 1998, p. 144.

14 While conceptualizing social recognition, Charles Taylor paid special attention to the inbuilt tension, usually reflected in a process of 'othering' the so-called marginal communities because he recognised that the socio-political identity of a community can be formed or malformed by contact with significant 'others', generally projected with 'an inferior or demeaning image'. For Charles Taylor, the politics of exclusion is an absolutely modern phenomenon since in the past

> social recognition was built in to the socially derived identity from the very fact that it was based on social categories everyone took for granted. The thing about inwardly derived, personal, original identity is that it doesn't enjoy this recognition a priori. It has to win it through exchange. What has come about with the modern age is not the need for recognition but the conditions in which this can fail. And that is why the need is now *acknowledged* for the first time. In pre-modern times, people didn't speak of 'identity' and 'recognition' not because people didn't have (what we call) identities or because these didn't depend on recognition, but rather because these were too unproblematic to be thematized as such.

15 *Sandhya*, 19 July, 1907 in A.K. Samanta (ed.), *Terrorism in Bengal: a collection of documents on terrorist activities, 1905–1939*, Vol. 11, Government of West Bengal, Calcutta, 1995, p. 622.

16 Gail Minault argues that, although the 1919–21 Non-Cooperation–Khilafat Movement did not succeed in forging a permanent Hindu–Muslim nationalist alliance, it certainly created 'a self-conscious and unified Indian Muslim political constituency'. Gail Minault, *The Khilafat Movement: religious symbolism and political mobilization in India*, Oxford University Press, Delhi, 1999 (reprint).

17 One of the major constraints of the Gandhi-led freedom struggle, writes M.N. Roy, is the fact that 'it rests on the reaction against a common oppression. This negative basis, however, renders the national liberation movement inherently weak [because it failed to combat] the dividing forces, generated and nurtured by nationalism itself'. M.N. Roy, *India in Transition*, Nachiketa Publications, Bombay, 1971, p. 150.

18 Rabindranath Tagore was critical of the nationalist leaders for not defining the concept of *swaraj* in a meaningful way. In his words, 'our political leaders have refrained from giving us a clear explanation of what is *swaraj*'. Rabindranath Tagore, 'Striving for swaraj', *Modern Review*, September, 1925, reproduced in Sabyasachi Bhattacharya (compiled and edited), *The Mahatma and the Poet: letter and debates between Gandhi and Tagore, 1915–1941*, National Book Trust, New Delhi, 1997, p. 114.

19 Gandhi defined *swaraj* as separate from 'freedom' and 'independence' which he claimed 'were English words lacking such connotations and which could be taken to mean a licence to do whatever one wished'. His *swaraj* 'allowed no such irresponsible freedom and demanded rather a rigorous moulding of the self and a heavy sense of responsibility'. David Hardiman, *Gandhi in His Times and Ours*, Permanent Black, New Delhi, 2003, p. 26.

20 *Speeches and Writings of Mahatma Gandhi*, fourth edition, Madras, 1933, pp. 336–7 and 341–2, cited in Barrington Moore, Jr. *Social Origins of Dictatorship and Democracy: lord and peasant in the making of the modern world*, Beacon Press, Boston, 1966, pp. 373–4.

21 B.R. Nanda, *Mahatma Gandhi*, Oxford University Press, Delhi, 1996 (reprint), p. 205.

22 A detailed discussion follows later.

23 Gandhi in Anthony Parel (ed.), *Hind Swaraj and Other Writings*, Cambridge University Press, Cambridge, 1997, p. 28.

24 *CWMG*, Vol. 42, p. 384.

25 Placing Gandhian civil disobedience within the theoretical discourse of the Rawls-Singer non-coercive position and the coercive kind of civil disobedience advocated by others, Vinit Haksar thus argues that 'Gandhi seems to present an alternative that is not mentioned by other theorists'. Vinit Haksar, *Rights, Communities and Disobedience: liberalism and Gandhi*, Oxford University Press, New Delhi, 2001, p. 113.

26 Gandhi's speech at Gandhi Seva Sangh meeting, Hudli, 20 April, 193, *CWMG*, Vol. 65, p. 121. Gandhi further stated that 'I have given the sovereign place to non-violence. To Jawaharlal [Nehru], violence may well not be dispensable, but if swaraj could be gained through non-violence he would be happy. He, therefore, cooperates with me in my experiments.'

27 *CWMG*, Vol. 42, p. 469.

28 Parel, op. cit., p. 90.

29 Ibid., p. 82.

30 'Meaning of the Gita', *CWMG*, Vol. 28, p. 317.

31 Gandhi was persuaded because, as he himself argued, '[W]e have also discovered through our progress that in the application of non-violence we have been able to reach the mass mind far more quickly and far more extensively than before'. *Harijan*, 24 February, 1946.

32 Gandhi wrote this piece entitled 'Satyagraha – not passive resistance' on 2 September, 1917, *CWMG*, Vol. 13, p. 523.

33 *Harijan*, 6 January, 1940, *CWMG*, Vol. 71, p. 62.

34 'What are the basic assumptions?', *Harijan*, 22 October, 1938, *CWMG*, Vol. 67, p. 437.

35 *Harijan*, 30 March, 1940, *CWMG*, Vol. 71, p. 360. The analogy of an army and

its functioning is striking given Gandhi's well-defined opposition to the Western military. He was probably inspired by the organized strength of an army which he sought to instil in the *satyagrahees*.

36 *Harijan*, 6 April, 1940, *CWMG*, Vol. 71, p. 378.

37 Bipan Chandra, Aditya Mukherjee and Mridula Mukherjee, *India's Struggle for Independence*, Viking, New Delhi, 1988, p. 92.

38 Dadhbhai Naoroji, *Poverty and Un-British Rule in India*, London, 1901, p. 34, quoted in Chandra *et al.*, op. cit., p. 96.

39 Speech of Dadabhai Naoroji, 20 March, 1903, quoted in Bipan Chandra, *Nationalism and Colonialism in Modern India*, Orient Longman, New Delhi, 1979, p. 110.

40 *New India*, 12 August, 1901, quoted in Chandra *et al.*, op. cit., p. 94.

41 For an elaboration of this nationalist argument, see Chandra *et al.*, op. cit., pp. 96–8.

42 Philosophically, Gandhi drew on 'methodological individualism' where the individual is the relevant unit of account because it is individuals who reason, have moral sense and exercise choice. As Gandhi believed that 'if the individual ceases to count what is left of society?', he had little sympathy with the holistic notion 'that society is ontologically prior to the individual'. Ajit Dasgupta, *Gandhi's Economic Thought*, Routledge, London and New York, 1996, pp. 182–3.

43 Gandhi rejected industrialization as a solution for mass poverty and in doing so dissented from the mainstream of Indian economic thought. Gandhi argued both that machinery was by nature labour-displacing anywhere and at all times; and that the widespread use of mechanized techniques of production would have disastrous social and economic consequences for countries such as India which had meagre capital resources but a large labour force and which were already suffering from rural underemployment. For an elaboration of this argument, which gradually unfolded in Gandhi's writings, see ibid., pp. 64–80.

44 Partha Chatterjee elaborates this argument with reference to his analysis of Gandhi on the basis of what he wrote in the *Hind Swaraj*. See his 'Gandhi and the critique of civil society' in Ranajit Guha (ed.), *Subaltern Studies: writing on South Asian history and society*, Oxford University Press, Delhi, 1984, p. 158.

45 *Charkha*, Gandhi described, 'Is our ammunition – guns and artillery – and so we cannot afford to forsake it'. *Harijan*, 6 April, 1940, *CWMG*, Vol. 71, p. 383.

46 *Khadi*, as Gandhi characterized, 'is the chief village handicraft' and 'is a symbol of identification with the poorest in the land'. *Harijan*, 20 January, 1940, *CWMG*, Vol. 71, p. 103; *Harijan*, 30 December, 1939, *CWMG*, Vol. 71, p. 52.

47 *Harijan*, 4 November, 1939, *CWMG*, Vol. 70, p. 316.

48 'Is khadi economically sound?', *Harijan*, 20 June, 1936, *CWMG*, Vol. 63, pp. 77–8.

49 'Village industries', *Harijan*, 16 November, 1934, *CWMG*, Vol. 59, p. 356. The opposition to machine stems from his genuine concern for providing 'profitable employment' to all. He thus argued on another occasion,

> We should not use machinery for producing things which we can produce without its aid and have got the capacity to do so. As machinery makes you slave, we want to be independent and self-supporting; so we should not take the help of machinery when we can do without it. We want to make our villages free and self-sufficient and through them achieve our goal – liberty – and also protect it. I have no interest in the machine nor [do] I oppose it. If I can produce my things myself, I become my master and so need no machinery.
>
> (*Harijan*, 6 April, 1940, *CWMG*, Vol. 71, p. 383)

50 'Mills vs. Charkha', *Harijan*, 12 August, 1939, *CWMG*, Vol. 70, p. 74.

51 *Harijan*, 29 August, 1936, discussion with Maurice Frydman on 25 August, 1936, *CWMG*, Vol. 63, p. 241. Maurice Frydman, a Polish engineer interested in the village reconstruction movement, had met Gandhi earlier and was given the name Bharatanand.

52 *Harijan*, 29 September, 1940, interview to Francis G. Hickman, 17 September, 1940, *CWMG*, Vol. 73, pp. 29–30. The differences between Nehru and Gandhi may have had their roots in the former's insistence on the creation of a planning commission in the Soviet style as a mechanism to bring about radical changes in the economy. See my 'Jawaharlal Nehru and planning, 1937–40', *Modern Asian Studies*, Vol. 26 (2), 1922.

53 Condemning the blind supporters of industrialism, Gandhi thus sarcastically stated:

> instead of giving [the villagers] employment, by way of compensation, [we] give them lectures, magic-lantern shows and tinned music all at their expense, and pat ourselves on the back that we are working for their welfare. Can anything be more absurd?
> (Motor vs. Cart', *Harijan*, 16 September, 1939, *CWMG*, Vol. 70, p. 118)

54 *Harijan*, 27 January, 1940, *CWMG*, Vol. 71, p. 130.

55 Rabindranath Tagore, 'Striving for swaraj', *Modern Review*, September 1925, reproduced in Bhattacharya, op. cit., pp. 114–15.

56 Gandhi, 'The poet and the charkha', *Young India*, 5 November, 1925, reproduced in Bhattacharya, ibid., p. 122.

57 Chandra *et al.*, op cit., p. 100.

58 Dadabhai Naoroji's statement, published in *India*, 2 September, 1904, Chandra *et al.*, op. cit., p. 547.

59 B.R. Nanda, *The Moderate era in Indian Politics*, Oxford University Press, Delhi, 1983, p. 14.

60 *Report of the Second National Congress, 1886*, p. 112, quoted in ibid., pp. 14–15.

61 Lajpat Rai to Josiah C. Wedgwood, 3 February, 1919, in Joginder Singh Dhanki (ed.), *Perspectives on Indian National Movement: selected correspondence of Lala Lajpat Rai*, National Book Organization, New Delhi, 1998, p. 119.

62 Ibid., pp. 120–1.

63 Bipin Chandra Pal, *Swadeshi and Swaraj*, Dasgupta & Company, Calcutta, 1954, pp. 117–18. This volume contains Pal's 1907 Madras speeches entitled 'The new movement, "The gospel of swaraj", and "Swaraj".'

64 Aurobindo Ghose, *Bande Mataram*, 11 May, 1907.

65 Tilak's statement in *Kesari*, 18 November, 1897 – quoted in N.R. Inamdar, 'The political ideas of Lokmanya Tilak', in Thomas Pantham and Kenneth L. Deutsch (eds), *Political Thought in Modern India*, Sage, New Delhi, 1986, p. 114.

66 Ibid., p. 116.

67 Raghavan Iyer (ed.), *The Moral and Political Writings of Mahatma Gandhi*, Clarendon Press, Oxford, 1986, Vol. III, p. 275.

68 Gandhi's interview with journalist, 6 March, 1931, *CWMG*, Vol. 51, p. 220.

69 *CWMG*, Vol. 23, pp. 71–2.

70 Parel, op. cit., p. 73.

71 Ramchandra Gandhi, 'The *svaraj* of India', *Indian Philosophical Quarterly*, Vol. XI (4), October, 1984, p. 461.

72 Ibid.

73 Ibid., p. 462.

74 Krishna Chandra Bhattacharya, 'Svaraj in ideas', *Indian Philosophical Quarterly*, Vol. XI (4), October, 1984, p. 383. While explaining the implication of the slavery of ideas, Bhattacharya further argues that:

We are beginning to realize that we have for long wrongly counted on principles that have application only to countries that are already free and already established and have not had sufficient perception of the dark thing they call 'power' which is more real than any logic of political scholarship. In the field of social reform, we have never cared to understand the inwardness of our traditional social structure and to examine how far the social principles of the west are universal in their application. We have contented ourselves either with an unthinking conservatism or with an imaginary progressiveness merely imitative of the west.

(Ibid., pp. 385–6)

75 Anthony J. Parel (ed.), *Gandhi, Freedom and Self-Rule*, Vistaar, New Delhi, 2000, p. 17.
76 Fred Dallmayr, 'What is Swaraj? Two conflicting visions' in Parel, *Gandhi, Freedom and Self-Rule*, op. cit., p. 111.
77 Bhikhu Parekh, *Gandhi*, Oxford University Press, Oxford, 1997, p. 81.
78 R. Palme Dutt, *India Today*, Victor Gollancz Ltd, London, 1940, p. 277.
79 Ibid., p. 279.
80 It was Lajpat Rai who put forward the safety valve theory to attack the Moderates in the Congress in his *Young India*, published in 1916. While elaborating the theory, he argued that 'the Congress was started with the object of saving the British Empire from danger [rather] than with that of winning political liberty for India. The interests of the British Empire were primary and those of India only secondary'. For a detailed discussion on this theory, see Chandra *et al.*, op. cit., pp. 61–70.
81 S. Gopal (ed.), *Selected Works of Jawaharlal Nehru*, Vol. IV, Orient Longman, New Delhi, 1978, pp. 185–8.
82 Ibid., p. 188.
83 Gandhi to Irwin, 2 March, 1930 in B. Pattabhi Sitaramayya, *The History of the Indian National Congress*, S. Chand & Co., Delhi, pp. 633–4.
84 S.S. Pirzada (ed.), *Foundations of Pakistan: All India Muslim League documents*, Vol. II (1924–7), National Publishing House, Karachi, no date, pp. 265–73.
85 Stanley Wolpert, 'The Indian National Congress in nationalist perspective' in Richard Sission and Stanley Wolpert (eds), *Congress and Indian Nationalism: the pre-independence phase*, Oxford University Press, Delhi, 1988, p. 37.
86 There was a growing awareness among those involved in the freedom struggle of the importance of linking these two complementary worlds of politics. Where the peripheral struggles were strong enough, the nationalist leadership conveniently appropriated those issues to sustain the momentum at the grassroots. If, however, the movements at the subaltern level challenged the nationalist campaign, they were either bypassed or sought to be controlled by emphasizing the importance of national freedom at that particular juncture of the anti-colonial struggle. Since the exploration of this dimension of the freedom struggle is beyond the scope of the present exercise, this aspect shall not be dealt with extensively except by referring the reader to the published volumes of *Subaltern Studies*, which have brought out this dimension of India's freedom struggle, namely the linking of the mainstream struggle with its peripheral counterparts, by focusing on the issues militating the 'unorganized' masses against the stereotypical nationalist campaign and its *bête noire*, the colonial power.
87 India Office Records (IOR hereafter), L/PO/3, extract from a daily report of the Director of Intelligence Bureau, Home Department, Government of India, New Delhi, 10 February, 1927.
88 Foreword by Tridib Chaudhuri in B. Bhattacharya, *Origins of the RSP: from national revolutionary politics to non-conformist communism*, Calcutta, 1982, pp. 5–8.

89 *Our Aims*, published in *The Statesman*, 23 December, 1931.
90 Ibid.
91 Nehru Memorial Museum and Library, Purushattam Thakurdas Papers, PT 42 (2), G.D. Birla to Purushattamdas Thakurdas, 22 May, 1929.
92 Ibid. Purushattamdas Thakurdas to G.D. Birla, 16 July, 1929.
93 For instance, M.N. Roy conceptualized *swaraj* in a completely different way. Critical of Gandhi's notion, Roy argued that

> neither self-government realized progressively by constitutional means, nor 'swaraj' conquered by Non Cooperation will change the economic condition of the [masses]. Even full Dominion Status, conceded overnight, would not give political rights to the workers and peasants. A Dominion Parliament controlling the entire policy of the government would not protect the toiling masses from the exploitation of the capitalist and land-owning classes. Such a parliament would defend the interests of the property-owners and act at the beck and call of the Money-bag. The national would still remain in the bonds of slavery. Therefore, the interests of the majority demand *complete separation from all imperial connection and the establishment of a Republican State* based on the democratic principles of *Universal suffrage.*
>
> (M.N. Roy, 'Definition of swaraj', *The Vanguard*, Vol. II (2), 1 March, 1923, reproduced in Sibnarayan Ray, *Selected Works of M.N. Roy*, Vol. II, 1923–7, Oxford University Press, New Delhi, 2000, p. 101)

94 *CWMG*, Vol. 21, p. 458.
95 Judith Brown, *Nehru: a political life*, Oxford University Press, New Delhi, 2004, p. 223. Gandhi, argues Brown,

> came to this conclusion as a result of his religious conviction that for the individual, service to the poorest was the way to discover the divine and that true self rule depended on a new sense of moral community rather than on political arrangements. Nehru's approach [on the other hand] was secular and political. He argued that freedom would only be genuine if people were released from bondage of poverty and of ascribed social status, and given new life chances and choices. He also recognized that the nation had to go on being forged, that is created in the lived experience of Indian people, particularly those who had had little part in the initial processes of nation-building, or who in the particular circumstances of Indian independence felt threatened and potentially excluded. He used the metaphor of the journey the nation had before it, indicating that he recognized that forging the nation was a long term process of moulding attitudes, also of giving many disparate and previously disadvantaged groups a stake in the nation.
>
> (ibid., p. 223)

96 Anthony Parel makes this point while explaining the meaning which Gandhi attributed to *swaraj* in a monograph that included Gandhi's *Hind Swaraj*. Parel, op. cit., p. 73.

2 The Mahatma at the grassroots: the praxis of *ahimsa* or non-violence

1 M.K. Gandhi, *An Autobiography: or the story of my experiments with truth*, Jonathan Cape, London, 1966.
2 *Indian Opinion* was brought out by Gandhi in South Africa and *Young India* and *Harijan* were published in India.
3 Pyralal, *Mahatma Gandhi: the early phase*, Vol. I, p. 12.

4 While examining the role of Gandhi in galvanizing the masses into action in the 1920–2 Non-Cooperation Movement, Shahid Amin thus argues that

> there was no single authorized version of the Mahatma to which [the participants] may be said to have subscribed in 1921. Indeed, their ideas about Gandhi's 'orders' and 'powers' were often at variance with those of the local Congress–Khilafat leadership and clashed with the basic tenets of Gandhism itself. The violence of Chauri Chaura was rooted in this paradox.
>
> (See Shahid Amin, 'Gandhi as Mahatma: Gorakhpur district, Eastern Uttar Pradesh' in Ranajit Guha (ed.), *Subaltern Studies*, Vol. III, Oxford University Press, Delhi, 1984, p. 55)

The same pattern recurred in the context of the 1942 Quit India Movement in Midnapur (Bengal) where the location of the Mahatma image within the existing pattern of popular beliefs and the way it informed direct action was 'often at variance with the standard interpretation of the Congress creed'. See my *Local Politics and Indian Nationalism: Midnapur, 1919–1944*, Manohar, New Delhi, 1997, p. 198.

5 *Harijan*, 30 September, 1939.

6 Gandhi to Dharmadeva, *The Collected Works of Mahatma Gandhi* (*CWMG* hereafter), Publication Division, Government of India, New Delhi, 1958, Vol. 53, appendix III, p. 485.

7 W.H. Morris-Jones, 'Mahatma Gandhi: political philosopher', *Political Studies*, Vol. 3 (1) 1960, p. 17. According to Morris-Jones, Gandhi joins the company of Burke and others who have not escaped accusation of displaying the inconsistency of the opportunist politician.

8 Sushila Nayar, *Mahatma Gandhi's Last Imprisonment: the inside story*, Har-Anand Publications, New Delhi, 1996, p. 137.

9 For details, see Chakrabarty, op. cit.

10 *CWMG*, Vol. 51, p. 286.

11 Subhas Chandra Bose, *The Indian Struggle, 1920–42*, Asia Publishing House, London, 1964 (reprint), p. 293.

12 Central to Gandhism is *ahimsa* or non-violence which he conceptualized in the following manner:

> (a) Non-violence is the law of the human race and is infinitely greater than and superior to brute force. (b) In the last resort it does not avail to those who do not possess a living faith in the God of Love. (c) Non-violence affords the fullest protection to one's self respect and sense of honour, but not always to possession of land or movable property, though its habitual practice does prove a better bulwark than the possession of armed men to defend them. Non-violence in the very nature of things is of no assistance in the defence of ill-gotten gains and immoral acts. (d) Individuals or nations who would practise non-violence must be prepared to sacrifice (nations to the last man) their all except honour. It is therefore inconsistent with the possession of other people's countries, i.e., modern imperialism which is frankly based on force for its defence. (e) Non-violence is a power which can be wielded equally by all – children, young men and women or grown-up people – provided they have a living faith in the god of love and have therefore equal love for all mankind. When non-violence is accepted as the law of life it must pervade the whole being and not [be] applied to isolated acts. (f) It is a profound error to suppose that whilst the law is good enough for individuals it is not for [the] masses of mankind.
>
> (M.K. Gandhi, 'God of love, not war', *Harijan*, 5 September, 1936, *CWMG*, Vol. 63, p. 262)

13 Bhikhu Parekh, *Colonialism, Tradition and Reform: an analysis of Gandhi's political discourse*, Sage, New Delhi, 1999, p. 130. According to Parekh, Gandhi's definition of *ahimsa* as active and energetic love leading to dedicated service to fellow-men represented a radical departure from Indian traditions.

14 Gandhi's letter in *Modern Review*, October, 1916, reproduced in Raghavan Iyer, *The Moral and Political Thought of Mahatma Gandhi*, Oxford University Press, Delhi, 1973, pp. 179–80.

15 Gandhi defined *ahimsa* as 'infinite love' while elaborating the role of women in nationalism. M.K. Gandhi, 'What is woman's role?', *Harijan*, 12 February, 1940.

16 Jawaharlal Nehru, *An Autobiography (with musings on recent events in India)*, John Lane The Bodley Head, London, 1941, p. 540.

17 M.K. Gandhi, *Ethical Religion* (translated by A. Rmaiyer), S. Ganesan, Madras, 1922, p. 7, quoted in Thomas Pantham, 'Habermas' practical discourse and Gandhi's satyagraha', in Bhikhu Parekh and Thomas Pantham (eds), *Political Discourse: explorations in Indian and western political thought*, Sage, New Delhi, 1987, pp. 302–3.

18 Partha Chatterjee, 'Gandhi and the critique of civil society', in Ranajit Guha (ed.), *Subaltern Studies: writings on South Asian History and Society*, Vol. III, Oxford University Press, Delhi, 1984, p. 186.

19 Ibid.

20 M.K. Gandhi, 'Satyagraha – not passive resistance', *CWMG*, Vol. 13, p. 523. Gandhi further stated, '[w]e can … free ourselves of the unjust rule of the Government by defying the unjust rule and accepting the punishment[s] that go with it. We do not bear malice towards the Government. When we set its fears at rest … they will at once be subdued to our will.'

21 Ibid., p. 524.

22 Gandhi's speech on the *satyagraha* movement, Trichinoploy, 25 March, 1919, *CWMG*, Vol. 15, p. 155.

23 M.K. Gandhi, 'The duty of satyagrahis', *CWMG*, Vol. 15, p. 436.

24 M.K. Gandhi, *Autobiography*, *CWMG*, Vol. 39, p. 374.

25 Partha Chatterjee, 'Gandhi please stand up?', *Illustrated Weekly of India*, 15–21 January, 1984, p. 27.

26 Quoted in ibid.

27 M.K. Gandhi, 'Democracy versus mobocracy, *Young India*, 8 September, 1920, *CWMG*, Vol. 18, pp. 240–4.

28 Gandhi's press statement, 26 July, 1933, *CWMG*, Vol. 55, p. 299.

29 M.K. Gandhi, 'What are basic assumptions?, *CWMG*, Vol. 67, pp. 436–7.

30 Gandhi to Jawaharlal Nehru, 14 September, 1933, *CWMG*, Vol. 55, p. 428.

31 For Gandhi's evidence before the Hunter Committee, M.K. Gandhi, *Satyagraha*, Navjivan Publishing House, Ahmedabad, 1958, pp. 19–34; D.G. Tendulkar, *Mahatma: the life of Mohandas Karamchand Gandhi*, Vol. I, Ministry of Information and Broadcasting, Government of India, New Delhi, 1960.

32 Gandhi, *Satyagraha*, op. cit., p. 38.

33 Joan V. Bondurant, *Conquest of Violence: the Gandhian philosophy of conflict*, Princeton University Press, Princeton, 1958, p. 36.

34 B.R. Nanda, *In Search of Gandhi: essays and reflections*, Oxford University Press, New Delhi, 2004, p. 77.

35 M.K. Gandhi, 'Satyagraha – not passive resistance', *Young India*, 2 September, 1917.

36 *Satyagraha* has, argued Bhikhu Parekh,

> resonance in both Hindu and Christian religious traditions, but it has never been a part of either. It is basically composed of three important ideas, namely, the spiritual nature of human beings, the power of suffer-

ing love and the deliberate and skilful use of the latter to reach out to and activate the moral energies of others. The first metaphysical belief is common to both, indeed to all religions; the ontology of suffering love is unique to Christianity, and Gandhi himself said that that was where he derived it from; the idea that the soul is energy, that two souls can directly communicate by non-lingual means, and that they can influence and activate each other is an important part of Hindu epistemology and informs complex forms of yoga. Since by and large Christianity lacks the third and Hinduism the second element, one needed to be deeply familiar with both traditions, and to possess the creative capacity to discover and combine the two elements, to arrive at anything resembling the Gandhian concept of Satyagraha.

(Bhikhu Parekh, *Gandhi*, Oxford University Press, Oxford, 1997, p. 99)

37 J.J. Doke, *M.K. Gandhi: an Indian patriot in South Africa*, London, 1909, p. 135.
38 Anthony Parel (ed.), *Hind Swaraj and Other Writings*, Cambridge University Press, Cambridge, 1997, p. 90.
39 Identification of passive resistance with *satyagraha* was not acceptable to Gandhi. He defended *satyagraha* as being distinctly different from passive resistance, thus challenging the view that it approximated to the passive resistance practised in England by the suffragettes and by the opponents of the 1902 Education Act. What separates *satyagraha* from passive resistance is the fact that, while the former was compatible with mild forms of physical violence, these were an anathema to the latter. In his words,

> Burning of houses by [the women involved in the Suffragette Movement in England] and . . . fasting in prison . . . might very well be passive resistance, but they were not satyagraha. . . . The movement in South Africa is not passive but active. The Indians of South Africa believed that Truth was their object, that Truth ever triumphs, and with this definiteness of purpose they persistently held on to Truth. They put up with all the suffering that this persistence implied.

For a detailed account of this distinction, see M.K. Gandhi, *Satyagraha in South Africa*, Chapter 13 (*CWMG*, Vol. 29, pp. 93–7).
40 Parel, op. cit., p. 94.
41 *Satyagraha* was revolutionary in form and content. By his endorsement for 'resistance to unjust laws by soul force' Gandhi was seeking to inject 'manhood' among the Indians. He felt that 'it is contrary to our manhood, if we obey laws repugnant to our conscience. Such teaching is opposed to religion and means slavery. If the government were to ask us', Gandhi sarcastically argued, 'to go about without any clothing, should we do so?' Ibid., pp. 91–2.
42 Dennis Dalton, 'Gandhi's originality', in Anthony Parel (ed.), *Gandhi, Freedom and Self-rule*, Vistaar Publications, New Delhi, 2000, p. 74.
43 *Hind Swaraj*, op. cit., p. 91.
44 M.K. Gandhi, 'Some rules of satyagraha', *Young India*, 27 February, 1930. This speech is also reproduced in Rudrangshu Mukherjee (ed.), *The Penguin Gandhi Reader*, Penguin, New Delhi, 1993, pp. 157–60.
45 Bondurant, op. cit., p. 27.
46 Pantham, 'Habermas' practical discourse', op. cit., p. 303.
47 *Young India*, March, 1925, quoted in Iyer, op. cit., p. 287.
48 Ibid.
49 Ibid.
50 Iyer, op. cit.

51 M.K. Gandhi, 'India's case for swaraj', Yeshanand & Co, Bombay, 1932, p. 369, quoted in Iyer, op. cit., p. 287.

52 Gandhi, 'Was it coercive?', *Harijan*, 9 September, 1933, *CWMG*, Vol. 55, p. 412.

53 David Hardiman, *Gandhi in His Time and Ours*, Permanent Black, New Delhi, 2003, p. 65.

54 As Bondurant argues, 'civil disobedience is the direct contravention of specific laws' of the state. A *satyagraha* participating in civil disobedience challenges the state by refusing to obey the un-moral laws of the state. He may refuse to pay taxes; he may accept the consequence of violating the state laws by going to jail without qualms. Once the state's existence is continuously questioned by the civil resisters, the structure will crumble. Furthermore, his opposition to the state is strictly governed by *ahimsa* and a *satyagraha* never nurtures ill-feelings towards his opponents, even accepting the application of force by opponents while participating in *satyagraha* where violence is completely ruled out. Bondurant, op. cit., pp. 36–7.

55 Gandhi's talk to Travancore State Congress deputation, *Harijan*, 21 January, 1939, *CWMG*, Vol. 68, p. 133.

56 M.K. Gandhi, 'Was it coercive?', op. cit., p. 412.

57 *Harijan*, 11 March, 1939.

58 *Harijan*, 13 October, 1940.

59 Bondurant, op. cit., p. 37.

60 This is how Bhikhu Parekh described Gandhi's fast. See Parekh, *Gandhi*, op. cit., pp. 57–8.

61 M.K. Gandhi, 'Talk with ashram inmates', 22 March, 1934, *CWMG*, Vol. 57, p. 301.

62 Gandhi publicized 'Some rules of satyagraha' in *Young India* (27 February, 1930). These rules are as follows: *As an individual* (a) a *satyagrahee*, i.e, a civil resister will harbour no anger; (b) he will suffer the anger of the opponent; (c) in so doing he will put up with assaults from the opponent, never retaliate; but he will not submit, out of fear of punishment or the like, to any order given in anger; (d) when any person in authority seeks to arrest a civil resister, he will voluntarily submit to the arrest, and he will not resist the attachment or removal of his own property, if any, when the authorities seek to confiscate it; (e) if a civil resister has any property in his possession as a trustee, he will refuse to surrender it, even though in defending it he might lose his life. He will however, never retaliate; (f) non-retaliation excludes swearing and cursing; (g) therefore a civil resister will never insult his opponent, and therefore also not take part in many of the newly coined cries which are contrary to the spirit of *ahimsa*; (h) a civil resister will not salute the Union Jack, nor will he insult it or officials, English or Indian; (i) in the course of the struggle if anyone insults an official or commits an assault upon him, a civil resister will protect such official or officials from the insult or attack even at the risk of his life. The second set of rules is applicable to a *satyagrahee* when in prison: (a) as a prisoner, a civil resister will behave courteously towards prison officials, and will observe all such discipline of the prison as is not contrary to self-respect; as for instance, whilst he will *salaam* [show respect] officials in the usual manner, he will not perform any humiliating gyrations and refuse to shout 'victory to *Sarkar*' or the like. He will take cleanly cooked and cleanly served food, which is not contrary to his religion, and will refuse to take food insultingly served or served in unclean vessels; (b) a civil resister will make no distinction between an ordinary prisoner and himself, will in no way regard himself as superior to the rest, nor will he ask for any conveniences that may be necessary for keeping his body in good health and condition. He is entitled to ask for such conve-

niences as may be required for his physical or spiritual well-being; (c) a civil resister may not fast for want of conveniences whose deprivation does not involve any injury to one's self-respect. Rules are different for a *satyagrahee* when he is a part of a unit. In a unit (a) a civil resister will joyfully obey all the orders issued by the leader of the corps, whether they [are pleased] with him or not; (b) he will carry out orders in the first instance even though they appear to him insulting, inimical or foolish, and then appeal to higher authority. He is free before joining to determine the fitness of the corps to satisfy him, but after he has joined it, it becomes a duty to submit to his discipline, irksome or otherwise; if the sum total of the energy of the corps appears to a member to be improper or immoral, he has a right to sever his connection but being within it, he has no right to commit a breach of its discipline; (c) no civil resister is to expect maintenance for his dependents. It would be an accident if any such provision is made. A civil resister entrusts his dependents to the care of God. Even in ordinary warfare wherein hundreds of thousands give themselves up to it, they are able to make no previous provision. How much more, then, should such be the case in *satyagraha*? It is the universal experience that in such times hardly anybody is left to starve. Finally, there are also clear rules for a *satyagrahee* during communal fights involving Hindus, Muslims and other communities. In communal fights (a) no civil resister will intentionally become a cause of communal quarrels; (b) in the event of any such outbreak, he will not take sides, but he will assist only that party which is demonstratively in the right. Being a Hindu he will be generous towards Mussalmans and others, and will sacrifice himself in the attempt to save non-Hindus from a Hindu attack. And if the attack is from the other side, he will not participate in any retaliation but will give his life in protecting Hindus; (c) he will, to the best of his ability, avoid every occasion that may give rise to communal quarrels; (d) if there is a procession of *satyagrahees* they will do nothing that would wound the religious susceptibilities of any community, and they will not take part in other processions that are likely to wound such susceptibilities. Reproduced in R. Mukherjee, op. cit., pp. 157–60.

63 Vinit Haksar, *Rights, Communities and Disobedience: liberalism and Gandhi*, Oxford University Press, New Delhi, 2001, p. 110.

64 *Harijan*, 11 March, 1939.

65 *Young India*, 27 February, 1930, reproduced in R. Mukherjee, op. cit., p. 158.

66 Gandhi defended that, under certain conditions, non-cooperation with an evil state was the duty of a citizen. As he argued, 'you assist an administration most effectively by obeying its orders and decrees. An evil system never deserves such allegiance. Allegiance to it means partaking of the evil. A good man will therefore resist an evil system or administration with his whole soul. Disobedience of the laws of the evil state is therefore a duty'. M.K. Gandhi, *Non-Violent Resisitance*, Shocken Books, New York, 1961, p. 238, cited in Haksar, op. cit., p. 138.

67 My study of the Congress role in the strike in TISCO (Tata Iron and Steel Company) has shown that, as regards the national industries, the concerns of the Congress leaders, including Gandhi, were substantially different from those of the workers. By according priority to the struggle for *swaraj*, Gandhi always emphasized the cooperation between labour and capital in the Indian-owned industries. The argument flowed logically from his declared object to protect the native industries. The workers' experiences, however, demonstrated that national industry operated no differently from non-Indian industries in dealing with workers' demands or in its attitude toward trade unions. Thus the labourers found nothing to discriminate between the Bombay mill-owners who were Indians and the proprietors of, for instance, Ludlow Jute Mill at Changail

in Bengal. For details, see my *Subhas Chandra Bose and Middle Class Radicalism: a study in Indian nationalism, 1928–40*, Oxford University Press, Delhi, 1990, Chapter 3 (pp. 67–100).

68 I have pursued this argument in *The Partition of Bengal and Assam, 1932–47: contour of freedom*, RoutledgeCurzon, London, 2004, Chapter 1 (pp. 36–54). Stephen Henningham has also shown that Gandhi restrained the peasant-activists when they argued to defend a no-rent campaign in Champaran after the adoption of the 1918 Champaran Agricultural Act. Not only did he support the peasant campaign against the indigenous *zamindars* he also directed the Bihar Congress not to back the movement of the local peasants, led by Swami Viswananda against the unlawful demands of the oppressive Darbhanga Raj. Stephen Henningham, *Peasant Movements in Colonial India: north Bihar, 1917–1942*, Australian National University, Canberra, 1982.

69 Partha Chatterjee, *Nationalist Thought and the Colonial World: a derivative discourse*, Oxford University Press, Delhi, 1986, p. 125.

70 Ibid.

71 I borrow this phrase from Ranajit Guha's 'Idiom of dominance and subordination in colonial India', paper presented at the Subaltern Conference, Calcutta, 1986, p. 22.

72 *CWMG*, Vol. 3, pp. 113–14 and 119–20.

73 Ibid., p. 129.

74 I owe this point to Ranajit Guha who developed this in Guha, op. cit.

75 *CWMG*, Vol. 3, p. 152.

76 Tendulkar, op. cit., p. 53.

77 Bhikhu Parekh argues along this line. See his *Colonialism, Tradition and Reform*, op cit., p. 113.

78 Cited in R.K. Narayan, *Waiting for the Mahatma*, Indian Thought Publications, Chennai, 2003 (reprint), pp. 77–8.

79 Parekh, *Colonialism, Tradition and Reform*, op. cit., p. 114.

80 Ibid.

81 Ibid.

82 Gandhi's speech at Islamia College, Peshwar, 4 May, 1938, *CWMG*, Vol. 67, p. 63. Gandhi further argued that 'a handful of Indians fought the South African government with non-violence. [He returned] from South Africa with a clear conviction of the superiority of the method of non-violence to that of violence. In India also, we have used [it] for gaining our strength and we have achieved some measure of success.'

83 Ibid.

84 R. Duncan, *Selected Works of Mahatma Gandhi*, Hutchinson, New York, 1951, p. 53.

85 *Harijan*, 10 December, 1938, *CWMG*, Vol. 68, p. 106.

86 *Harijan*, 26 March, 1938, *CWMG*, Vol. 66, p. 406.

87 M.K. Gandhi, 'What is non-violence?', *Harijan*, 12 December, 1936, *CWMG*, Vol. 64, p. 152.

88 Duncan, op. cit., p. 55.

89 W.H. Morris-Jones, 'Mahatma Gandhi: political philosopher', op. cit., p. 27.

90 Ibid.

91 *Young India*, 16 June, 1927.

92 Ibid.

93 *Indian Opinion*, 19 October, 1899.

94 Gandhi's role in South Africa has received adequate scholarly attention. See, for details, R.A. Huttenback, *Gandhi in South Africa: British imperialism and the Indian question, 1860–1914*, Harvester Press, London, 1971; Judith Brown, *Gandhi's Rise to Power: Indian politics, 1915–1922*, Cambridge University Press,

Cambridge, 1972, pp. 1–15; Brown, *Gandhi: prisoner of hope*, op. cit., pp. 30–94 and Gandhi, *Satyagraha in South Africa*, op. cit.

95 For details, see Gandhi, *An Autobiography*, op. cit., pp. 362–7, and David Hardiman, *Peasant Nationalists in Gujarat, Kheda District*, Oxford University Press, New Delhi, 1981.

96 Brown, *Gandhi: prisoner of hope*, op. cit., pp. 109–27; R. Kumar (ed.), *Essays on Gandhian Politics: the Rowlatt Satyagraha of 1919*, Clarendon Press, Oxford, 1971.

97 Gandhi to P. Desai, 9 February, 1919, *CWMG*, Vol. 15, p. 88.

98 *Young India*, 20 September, 1920, *CWMG*, Vol. 18, pp. 270–3.

99 India Office Records London (hereafter IOR), Mss Eur 238/10, Reading Papers, Reading to the Secretary of State, 13 May, 1921. According to Reading, 'the non-cooperation movement, that is, non-violent resistance, had affected the administration adversely'.

100 For details, Judith Brown, *Gandhi: prisoner of hope*, op. cit., pp. 139–75; Brown, *Gandhi's Rise to Power*, op. cit., pp. 307–51; P.C. Bamford, *Histories of the Non-Cooperation and Khilafat Movements*, Imprint, Delhi, 1974 (reprint); G. Minault, *Khilafat Movement, 1919–22*, Oxford University Press, Delhi, 1982.

101 IOR, Mss Eur E 246/26, Chelmsford Papers, Frank Sly, the chief commissioner of the Central Provinces to the Viceroy, 11 January, 1921.

102 For details, see Bamford, op. cit., B.R. Nanda, *Gandhi, Pan-Islamism and Nationalism*, Oxford University Press, Bombay, 1989.

103 Ibid., p. 117.

104 *Young India*, 9 January, 1930, *CWMG*, Vol. 42, pp. 376–7.

105 For details, see R.J. Moore, *The Crisis of Indian Unity, 1917–1940*, Oxford University Press, Oxford, 1974; Judith Brown, *Gandhi and Civil Disobedience: the Mahatma in Indian politics, 1928–1934*, Cambridge University Press, Cambridge, 1977.

106 National Archives of India, New Delhi (NAI hereafter), Home-Poll 257/V & kw, a note by H. Baig, 13 June, 1930.

107 Chakrabarty, *Subhas Chandra Bose Middle Class Radicalism: a study in Indian nationalism, 1928–40*, Oxford University Press, Delhi, 1990.

108 Ian Talbot, *Punjab and the Raj, 1889–1947*, Oxford University Press, Delhi, 1988; Ayesha Jalal, *The Sole Spokesman: Jinnah, the Muslim League and the demand for Pakistan*, Cambridge University Press, Cambridge, 1985.

109 For details, see Amba Prasad, *Indian Revolt of 1942*, Impex, Delhi, 1958; F. Hutchinson, *Spontaneous Revolution: the Quit India Movement*, Manohar, New Delhi, 1971; G. Pandey (ed.), *The Indian Nation in 1942*, K.P. Bagchi & Company, 1982; N. Mitra (ed.), *The Indian Annual Register*, July–December, 1942 (this volume contains the government document entitled *'Congress Responsibility for Disturbances'*).

110 Bidyut Chakrabarty, 'Political mobilization in the localities, 1942', *Modern Asian Studies*, Vol. 26 (4), 1992.

111 Mitra op. cit., p. 112.

112 N. Mansergh *et al.*, *The Transfer of Power*, Vol. 2, p. 96, Gandhi's interview of 16 May, 1942, Her Majesty's Publications, London, 1982.

113 Mansergh *et al.*, op. cit., Vol. 2, p. 388.

114 Chakrabarty, 'Political mobilization in the localities, 1942', op. cit.; Biswamoy Pati, 'Storm over Malkan Giri: a note on Laxman Naik's revolt, 1942', in Pandey, op. cit.; Gail Omvedt, 'The Satara Prati Sarkar' in ibid.; Livi Rodrigues, *Rural Protest and Politics: a study of peasant movement in Maharastra*, unpublished PhD dissertation, University of London, 1984.

115 Chakrabarty, *Local Politics and Indian Nationalism*, op. cit.

116 Nehru Memorial Museum and Library (NMML hereafter), New Delhi, *Biplabi*

(a monthly journal, brought out by the Congress in Midnapur), Issue no. 51, 5 July, 1943.

117 NMML, *Biplabi*, Issue no. 56, 5 August, 1943.

118 Shahid Amin, 'Gandhi as Mahatma', *Subaltern Studies*, Vol. III, Oxford University Press, Delhi, 1984, pp. 51–2.

119 Quoted in Jacques Pouchepadass, 'Local leaders and the intelligentsia in the Champaran Satyagraha, 1917: a study of peasant mobilization', *Contributions to Indian Sociology* (new series), Vol. 8, pp. 82–3.

120 IOR, L/PJ/12/1, fortnightly Report for the first half of February, 1928.

121 IOR, Mss Eur E 238/10, Reading Papers, Viceroy to the Secretary of State, 13 October, 1921.

122 A detailed discussion has been pursued in my *Subhas Chandra Bose*, op. cit., Chapter 1.

123 Sumit Sarkar has broached this point in his *Modern India, 1885–1947*, Macmillan, Delhi, 1983.

124 Mark Juergensmeyer thus argues that the Gandhian model of 'conflict resolution' is not 'spatial', but 'transcendental' in the sense that *satyagraha* continues to evoke interest even in the contemporary era, presumably due to its relevance in harmoniously resolving conflicts between opposing forces. Mark Juergensmeyer, *Gandhi's Way: a handbook of conflict resolution*, Oxford University Press, New Delhi, 2003.

125 I owe this point to Thomas Pantham who referred to it in his *Political Theories and Social Reconstruction: a critical survey of the literature on India*, Sage, New Delhi, 1995, p. 110.

126 Ravinder Kumar, *Essays in the Social History of Modern India*, Oxford University Press, Delhi, 1983, p. 27.

127 This expression is quoted from Partha Chatterjee, 'Gandhi and the critique of civil society' in Ranajit Guha (ed.), *Subaltern Studies*, Vol. III, p. 189.

128 As the Mahatma himself admitted, it was not necessary for everyone joining the political campaign to accept *ahimsa* as a creed. It was possible to accept it merely as a political strategy, without its religious core. In his words, 'ahimsa with me is a creed, the breath of life. But it is never as a creed that I placed before India or, for that matter, before anyone except in casual or informal talks. I placed it before the Congress as political weapon, to be employed for the solution of practical problems'. Quoted in Chatterjee, 'Gandhi please stand up?', op. cit., p. 29.

3 Politics and ideology: critique of Gandhi

1 Claude Markovits hints at this possibility in his *The Un-Gandhian Gandhi: the life and afterlife of the Mahatma*, Permanent Black, New Delhi, 2003.

2 The vast literature on the partition of India dwells on the dialogical interaction between the two major architects of the freedom struggle in India. While Gandhi never approved of Hindus and Muslims being two nations, Jinnah defended his claim for an independent state for Muslims, i.e., Pakistan, on the basis of his well-argued two-nation theory. Some of the important works are: *Jinnah-Gandhi Talks*, July–October, 1944, *The Hindustan Times*, New Delhi, 1945; Stanley Wolpert, *Jinnah of Pakistan*, Oxford University Press, New York, 1985; Jalal, *The sole spokesman: Jinnah, the Muslim League and the demand for Pakistan*, Cambridge University Press, Cambridge, 1985; Anita Inder Singh, *The Origins of the Partition of India*, Oxford University Press, Delhi, 1987.

3 In contrast with other communist leaders, Roy appears to have received adequate scholarly attention. One of the most detailed accounts of his political

ideology is J.P. Haithcox, *Communism and Nationalism in India: M.N. Roy and Comintern policy, 1920–39*, Princeton University Press, Princeton, 1971; for a general study of the growth of the communist movement in India, see G.D. Overstreet and Marshall Windmiller, *Communism in India*, Perennial Press, Bombay, 1960.

4 Sudipta Kaviraj, 'The heteronomous radicalism of M.N. Roy' in Thomas Pantham and Kenneth L. Deutsch (eds), *Political Thought in Modern India*, Sage, New Delhi, 1986, p. 213.

5 M.N. Roy, *India in Transition*, Nachiketa Publications, Bombay, 1971, p. 210.

6 M.N. Roy 'On the national and colonial question', reproduced in Sibnarayan Ray (ed.), *Selected Works of M.N. Roy, 1923–1927*, Vol. II, Oxford University Press, New Delhi, 2000, pp. 305–6.

7 M.N. Roy, *The Future of Indian Politics*, Chapter 12, reproduced in Ray, op. cit., p. 513.

8 M.N. Roy, 'Original draft of supplementary theses on the national and colonial question', reproduced in Sibnarayan Ray (ed.), *Selected Works of M.N. Roy, 1917–1922*, Vol. I, Oxford University Press, New Delhi, 2000, p. 167.

9 Ibid., p. 168.

10 M.N. Roy, *India in Transition*, Chapter VIII, reproduced in ibid., p. 346.

11 Ibid., pp. 348–9.

12 Ibid., pp. 369–70.

13 Ibid., p. 368.

14 M.N. Roy, 'The cult of non violence: its socio-economic background', reproduced in Ray, *Selected Works of M.N. Roy, 1923–1927*, op. cit., Vol. II, p. 156.

15 Ibid.

16 Ibid., p. 154.

17 Ibid.

18 M.N. Roy, 'The release of Gandhi', in Ray, *Selected Works of M.N. Roy (1923–1927)*, op. cit., Vol. II, pp. 182–3.

19 Ibid., p. 182.

20 Ibid., p. 183.

21 M.N. Roy, 'At the crossroads', *The Vanguard of Indian Independence*, Vol. 1 (3), 15 June, 1922, reproduced in Ray, *Selected Works of M.N. Roy (1917–1922)*, op. cit., Vol. I, p. 541.

22 M.N. Roy, 'Appeal to the nationalists' – reproduced in Ray, *Selected Works of M.N. Roy, 1923–1927*, op. cit. Vol. II, p. 324.

23 M.N. Roy, 'Definition of swaraj', *The Vanguard of the Indian Independence*, Vol. II, reproduced in ibid., p. 101.

24 The 1922 Bardoli resolution, which suspended the Non-Cooperation Movement, included the following clauses:

> (1) The working Committee of the Indian National Congress deplores the inhuman conduct of the mob at Chauri Chaura in having brutally murdered constables and wantonly burned police station; (2) in view of the violent outbreaks every time mass civil disobedience is inaugurated, indicating that the country is not non-violent enough, the Working Committee of the Congress resolves that mass civil disobedience . . . be suspended, and instructs the local Congress Committees to advise the cultivators to pay land revenue and other taxes due to the government, and to suspend every other activity of an offensive character; (3) the suspension of mass civil disobedience shall be continued until the atmosphere is so non-violent as to insure the non-repetition of atrocities such as at Gorakhpur or of the hooliganism such as at Bombay and Madras on the 17th of

November and the 13th January; (4) all volunteer processions and public meetings for the defiance of authority should be stopped; (5) the Working Committee advises Congress workers and organizations to inform the *ryot* (peasants) that withholding of rent payment to the *zamindars* is contrary to the Congress resolutions and injurious to the best interests of the country; (6) the Working Committee assures the *zamindars* that the Congress movement is in no way intended to attack their legal rights and that even where the *ryots* have grievances, the Committee desires that redress be sought by mutual consultation and arbitration.

(B.P. Sitaramayya, *The History of the Indian National Congress*, 1935, Vol. II, S. Chand & Co., Delhi, 1969, pp. 377–98)

25 M.N. Roy, 'India's problem and its solution', reproduced in Ray, *Selected Works of M.N. Roy, 1917–1922*, op. cit., pp. 553–4.
26 Ibid., p. 554.
27 Ibid.
28 Ibid., p. 555.
29 Ibid.
30 Sudipta Kaviraj thus argues, 'Gandhi's politics were not wholly mystical; rather, even its mysticism was often deliberate, its irrationalities carefully thought-out'. Kaviraj, op. cit., p. 229.
31 For a detailed discussion of Tagore's socio-political views in general, see Radharaman Chakrabarti, 'Tagore: politics and beyond', in ibid., pp. 176–92.
32 With remarkable clarity of vision, Rabindranath Tagore succinctly wrote about his views on nation in a rather small piece, entitled *Nation Ki* (Bengali). During his lecture tour in America, 1916–17, he elaborated some of these points, including his views on nationalism in India. See *Nationalism*, Rupa, Delhi, 1994 (reprint of the collection, originally published in 1917), pp. 77–99.
33 Ibid., p. 89.
34 Rabindranath Tagore to Amiya Chakraborty, no date, in Sabyasachi Bhattacharyya (ed. and compiled), *The Mahatma and the Poet: letters and debates between Gandhi and Tagore*, 1915–41, National Book Trust, New Delhi, 1997, p. 172.
35 Ashis Nandy, *The Illegitimacy of Nationalism*, Oxford University Press, Delhi, 1994, p. 89.
36 Tagore, *Nationalism*, op. cit., p. 90.
37 Ashis Nandy thus aptly comments that Janaganamana 'could only be the anthem of a state rooted in the Indian civilization [and] not of Indian nation-state trying to be the heir to British-Indian empire'. Nandy, op cit., p. 88.
38 The Congress dismissed Jinnah's demand for parity because 'in numerical terms this meant the equation of minority with majority which was both absurd and politically impossible'. To this Jinnah retorted that 'the debate was not about numbers nor even about communities but about Nations. Nations were equal irrespective of the size'. For details of Jinnah's argument, see Diana Mansergh (ed.), *Independence Years: the selected Indian and commonwealth papers of Nicholas Mansergh*, Oxford University Press, Delhi, 1999, pp. 227–30.
39 Jinnah's Presidential address in the 1940 Lahore session of the All-India Muslim League. S.S. Pirzada (ed.), *Foundations of Pakistan*, Vol. II, National Publishing House, Karachi, no date, p. 337.
40 Jinnah always insisted that

there are two major nations in India. This is the root cause and essence of our troubles. When there are two major nations how can you talk of democracy which means that one nation majority will decide everything for the other nation although it may be unanimous in its opposition. . . . these two nations cannot be judged by western democracy. But they should be treated as equals and attempts should be made to solve the difficulties by acknowledging this fact.

(Jinnah's press statement, *The Dawn*, 1 August, 1946)

41 Ayesha Jalal, 'Nation, reason and religion:; Punjab's role in the partition of India', *Economic and Political Weekly*, 8 August, 1998, p. 2185.
42 Paul Brass, *Ethnicity and Nationalism: theory and comparison*, Sage, New Delhi, 1991, p. 94.
43 N.K. Bose and P.H. Patwardhan, *Gandhi in Indian Politics*, Asia Publishing House, Bombay, 1967, p. 7.
44 Central to the project of nationalism is, argues Manu Goswami,

> the naturalization of the nation form. This project entails the translation of local, regional, and transnational identities on a national-territorial scale, and the transformation of the abstract categorical conception of nation into a taken-for-granted frame of reference in everyday life. It involves the institution of a lived equivalence between the individual and the nation, and the forging of an interiorized relation between a particular national people, space, economy and state. The very durability of the nation form stems from the historically configured link between processes of nationalization and naturalization, or the production of an implicit and normatively presumptive national habitus.
>
> (Manu Goswami, 'Rethinking the modular nation form: toward a sociohistorical conception of nationalism', *Comparative Studies in Society and History*, Vol. 44 (4), October, 2002, p. 793)

45 As Tagore argued, 'we have no word for Nation in our language. When we borrow this word from other people, it never fits us'. Rabindranath Tagore, 'Reflections on non cooperation and cooperation', *Modern Review*, May, 1921, reproduced in Bhattacharya, The *Mahatma and the Poet*, op. cit., p. 55.
46 Nandy, op. cit., pp. x–xi.
47 For details of the Non-Cooperation Movement, see Judith Brown, *Gandhi's Rise to Power: Indian politics, 1915–1922*, Cambridge University Press, Cambridge, 1972.
48 Rabindranath Tagore, 'The call of truth', reproduced in Bhattacharya, *The Mahatma and the Poet*, op. cit., pp. 83–4.
49 Ibid., p. 81.
50 Tagore, 'Reflections on non cooperation and cooperation, op. cit., pp. 58, 62.
51 M.K. Gandhi, 'The poet's anxiety', *Young India*, 1 June, 1921, reproduced in ibid., *The Mahatma and the Poet*, ibid., pp. 67–8.
52 M.K. Gandhi, 'The great sentinel', *Young India*, 13 October, 1921, in ibid., p. 91.
53 Gandhi, 'The poet's anxiety', op. cit., p. 65.
54 Because of his involvement in the *swadeshi* movement, Tagore realized, reports Sumit Sarkar, that 'more than ninety percent of the lower classes have remained entirely indifferent towards the Swadeshi Movement'. Underlining the inadequate mass contact, Tagore thus felt 'the need for quiet work in the villages, but few heeded his words of warning and advice [because] young men found constructive work in villages dull and far less attractive than radical politics and eventually terrorism'. Sumit Sarkar, *The Swadeshi Movement in Bengal, 1903–8*, People's Publishing House, New Delhi, 1973, p. 286.
55 Ranajit Guha, *Dominance without Hegemony: history and power in colonial India*, Oxford University Press, Delhi, 1998, p. 121.
56 Cited in ibid. So bitter was Tagore, Guha further reports by quoting from his

views, that he hardly concealed his annoyance with the *swadeshi* activists by saying that 'to enforce unity on a person by twisting his neck can hardly be called an action of union; nor, by the same token, can the use of threat or journalistic slander to stop any public airing of disagreement be regarded as working for national unification'.

57 Although Tagore had reservations about Gandhi's views on the social and political goal of the Non-Cooperation Movement, he appreciated the Mahatma by saying that he 'has won the heart of India with his love; for that we have all acknowledged his sovereignty. He has given us a vision of the *shakti* of Truth; for that our gratitude to him is unbounded.' Rabindranath Tagore, 'The call of truth', reproduced in Bhattacharya, *The Mahatma and the Poet*, op. cit., p. 79.

58 Rabindranath Tagore, 'The cult of charkha', *Modern Review*, September, 1925, reproduced in ibid., pp. 101–2. On another occasion, Tagore remarked that Gandhi's insistence on *charkha* as complementary to *swaraj* was harmful to the campaign. In his words, 'a man like the Mahatma may succeed in getting some of our countrymen to take an interest in this kind of uninspiring nature for a time because of their faith in his personal greatness of soul. To obey him is for them an end in itself. To me it seems that such a state of mind is not helpful for the attainment of swaraj.' Rabindranath Tagore, 'Striving for swaraj', *Modern Review*, September, 1925, reproduced in ibid., p. 119.

59 Tagore, 'The cult of charkha', op. cit., pp. 104–5.

60 Tagore, 'Striving for swaraj', op. cit., p. 118.

61 Ibid., p. 115.

62 Ibid., p. 118.

63 Ibid., p. 121.

64 Ibid.

65 Gandhi, 'The poet and the charkha', *Young India*, 5 November, 1925, reproduced in Bhattacharya, *The Mahatma and the Poet*, op. cit., p. 123.

66 Ibid., p. 125.

67 Ibid., p. 124.

68 According to Gandhi

> *khadi* should be linked with liberty. All the time you are spinning, you would not think in terms of your own requirements, but in terms of the requirements of the nation. You will say, 'I want to clothe the whole nation that is naked and I must do it non-violently.' Each time you draw a thread, say to your selves, 'we are drawing the thread of swaraj'. Multiply this picture million-fold and you have freedom knocking at your door.
>
> (*Harijan*, 28 January, 1939, *CWMG*, Vol. 68, p. 133)

69 Gandhi, like the poet, also believed in the wider application of *charkha*. In his words,

> Round the charkha, that is amidst the people who have shed their idleness and who have understood the value of cooperation, a national servant would build up a programme of anti-malaria campaign, improved sanitation, settlement of village disputes, conservation and breeding of cattle and hundreds of other beneficial activities. Wherever charkha work is fairly established, all such ameliorative activity is going according to the capacity of the villagers and the workers concerned.
>
> (Gandhi, 'The poet and the charkha', op. cit., p. 126)

70 Gandhi's statement, 16 February, 1934.

71 Tagore's statement to the press, *Amrita Bazar Patrika*, 24 March, 1934.

72 Tagore to Mahatma, 28 January, 1934, reproduced in Bhattacharya, *The Mahatma and the Poet*, op. cit., p. 156.

73 Tagore's statement to the press, *Amrita Bazar Patrika*, op. cit.

74 M.K. Gandhi, 'Superstition vs. faith', *Harijan*, 28 February, 1934.

75 For a comprehensive discussion on Tagore and modern sensibility strictly from the literary point of view, see Bhabatosh Chatterjee, *Rabindranath Tagore and Modern Sensibility*, Oxford University Press, Delhi, 1996.

76 B.R. Ambedkar, 'Gandhism', reproduced in Valerian Rodrigues (ed.), *The Essential Writings of B.R. Ambedkar*, Oxford University Press, New Delhi, 2004, p. 165.

77 *Young India*, 19 January, 1921, reproduced in Mahatma Gandhi, *What Is Hinduism*, National Book Trust, New Delhi, 2001 (reprint), p. 115.

78 B.R. Ambedkar, 'Outside the Fold', in Rodrigues (ed.), op. cit., p. 331.

79 Gandhi's idea of village *swaraj* is that

> it is completely republic, independent of its neighbours for its own vital wants, and yet interdependent for many others in which dependence is a necessity. Thus every village's first concern will be to grow its own food crops and cotton for its cloth.... The government of the village will be conducted by a panchayat of five persons, annually elected by the adult villagers, male and female, possessing minimum prescribed qualifications. (M.K. Gandhi, *Harijan*, 7 July, 1942, *CWMG*, Vol. LXXVII, pp. 308–9)

80 Surinder S. Jodhika, 'Nation and village: images of rural India in Gandhi, Nehru and Ambedkar', *Economic and Political Weekly*, 10 August, 2002, p. 3346.

81 T.K. Oommen, 'Gandhi and village: towards a critical appraisal', in Subrata Mukherjee and Sushila Ramaswamy (eds), *Economic and Social Principles of Mahatma Gandhi*, Deep & Deep, New Delhi, 1998, p. 226.

82 Gauri Viswanathan, *Outside the Fold: conversion, modernity and belief*, Oxford University Press, Delhi, 1998, p. 238.

83 B.R. Ambedkar, *The Untouchables: who were they and why they became untouchables?*, Amrit Book Company, New Delhi, 1948, pp. 21–2.

84 Judith Brown, 'The Mahatma and modern India', *Modern Asian Studies*, Vol. 3 (4), 1969, p. 331.

85 Upendra Baxi, 'Emancipation as justice: Babasaheb Ambedkar's legacy and vision', unpublished paper presented at the inaugural oration at the Babasaheb Ambedkar Centenary Celebration, University of Madras, 5 March, 1991, p. 17.

86 B.R. Ambedkar, *Mr. Gandhi and Emancipation of Untouchables*, Bheem Patrika Publications, Jullander, 1943, pp. 196–7.

87 Gandhi's press statement. *Harijan*, 10 June, 1933.

88 Gandhi to Tagore, 9 May, 1933, reproduced in the *Amrita Bazar Patrika*, 10 May, 1933.

89 Bhikhu Parekh, *Gandhi*, Oxford University Press, Oxford, 1997, p. 18.

90 C.B. Khairmode, *Dr. Bhimrao Ramji Ambedkar* (in Marathi), Vol. 4, Sugava Prakashan, Pune, 1989, p. 42, quoted in M.S. Gore, *The Social Context of an Ideology: B.R. Ambedkar's political and social thought*, Sage, New Delhi, 1993, p. 137.

91 Ainslie T. Embree, *Imagining India: essays on Indian history*, Oxford University Press, Delhi, 1989, p. 171.

92 Gandhi had succeeded in avoiding the head-on collision. As a biographer thus noted, 'at Yerawada, the politician in Gandhi became successful and the Mahatma was defeated. So effective and crushing was the victory of Gandhi that he deprived Ambedkar of all his life-saving weapons and made him a powerless man as did Indra in the case of Karna'. Dhananjoy Keer, *Dr. Ambedkar: life and mission*, Popular Prakashan, Bombay, 1962, pp. 215–16.

93 The Poona Pact accorded reservation of seats for the untouchables in exchange

for Ambedkar's concession to joint rather than separate electorates. The 1932 Communal Award had granted untouchables seventy-eight seats in the legislature, along with the right to elect their own candidates as well as vote for general seats. Under the revised arrangement, they were granted 148 seats, with 18 per cent reservation in the central legislature. Only untouchables could contest these seats; however, their right to elect their own candidates was withdrawn, the disheartening implication for untouchables being that their representation would still remain in the hands of the majority community since their legislators would be chosen by the general electorate. For details, see Ravinder Kumar, 'Ambedkar, Gandhi and the Poona Pact, Occasional Paper on Society and History', No. 20, Nehru Memorial Museum and Library, New Delhi, 1985; and also, Gore, op. cit., pp. 136–9.

94 Tagore was critical of the Pact for its possible adverse impact on the electoral arithmetic in Bengal where Muslims constituted a majority. With the reservation for the *dalits* in the general constituencies, Hindus would soon become a thin minority in the legislature. Hence he argued: 'I am fully convinced that if [the Poona Pact] is accepted without modification, it will be a source of perpetual communal jealousy leading to constant disturbance of peace and fatal break in the spirit of mutual cooperation in [Bengal].' Tagore to the Mahatma, 28 July, 1933, reproduced in Bhattacharya, *The Mahatma and the Poet*, op. cit., p. 148. For a detailed discussion of the impact of the Poona Pact on representation in Bengal, see my 'The 1932 communal award and its impact in Bengal', *Modern Asian Studies*, Cambridge, Vol. 23 (2), 1989, pp. 518–23.

95 Mahatma Gandhi, for instance, insisted that the Scheduled Castes were a part of Hindu society and separating the two would be detrimental to the interests of the nation. Hence he opposed the plea for separate electorates for Scheduled Castes. He did, however, accept the idea of reservations through a system of joint electorates. One of the best literary works on both the socio-political background and the consequences thereof is Mulk Raj Anand's *Untouchable*, a novel that defended Gandhi against Ambedkar who, according to the novelist, sought to undermine the manifesto of political freedom on which the Indian nationalist movement was based. See *Untouchable* (preface by E.M. Forster), Penguin Books, London, 1940 (reprint). In her *Children of God*, Shanta Rameshwar Rao dealt with Gandhi–Ambedkar controversy on the issues raised in the Poona Pact. See *Children of God*, Orient Longman, Calcutta, 1992 (reprint). The occlusion of Ambedkar in both these novels is consistent with a certain tradition of writing about 'untouchability' that has its root in the antagonistic rhetoric of the Indian National Congress which responded to Ambedkar's threat of splitting the leadership with disdain and fear. Apart from literary works, the Poona Pact appears to be an under-researched subject. However, the following two articles are indicative of 'the mind set' that appeared to have significantly influenced the Pact and its critic: a) Kumar, op. cit.; and b) Valerian Rodrigues, 'Between tradition and modernity: the Gandhi-Ambedkar debate', in A.K. Narain and D.C. Ahir (eds), *Dr. Ambedkar, Buddhism Social Change*, B.R. Publishing, Delhi, 1994, pp. 129–45.

96 Viswanathan, op. cit., p. 123.

97 For an elaboration of this argument, see ibid., Chapter 7 (pp. 211–39).

98 Quoted in Bhagwan Das, 'Ambedkar's journey to mass conversion', in V. Grover (ed.), *B.R. Ambedkar*, Deep & Deep Publications, New Delhi, 1993, p. 595.

99 The 1932 Poona Pact seems to be a Gandhian challenge to 'the multiple nations' theory. Gandhi was opposed to Jinnah's 'two-nation' theory and characterized this as 'an artificial' way of conceptualizing the history of two organically linked communities. By preventing a further schism between the *'dalits'*

and the caste Hindus, the 1932 Poona Pact was a politically contrived solution to the growing chasm between the 'untouchables' and the rest of Hindu society.

100 In his 1940 Ramgarh presidential address, Abul Kalam Azad argues that

> [f]or a hundred and fifty years, British imperialism has pursued the policy of divide and rule, and, by emphasizing internal differences, sought to use various groups for the consolidation of its own power. That was the inevitable result of India's political subjection, and its folly for us to complain and grow bitter. A foreign government can never encourage internal unity in the subject country, for disunity is the surest guarantee for the continuance of its own domination.
>
> (Azad's presidential address at Ramgarh, 1940 in A.M. Zaidi and S.G. Zaidi (eds), *The Encyclopaedia of the Indian National Congress*, Vol. 12, S. Chand & Co., New Delhi, 1981, pp. 355–6)

101 Reiterating the famous 1940 Lahore resolution of the All-India Muslim League demanding an independent state for the Muslims since they constituted a separate nation, Jinnah always insisted that

> there are two major nations [in India]. This is the root cause and essence of our troubles. When there are two major nations how can you talk of democracy which means that one nation majority will decide everything for the other nation although it may be unanimous in its opposition.... these two nations cannot be judged by western democracy. But they should each be treated as equals and attempts should be made to solve the difficulties by acknowledging the fact.
>
> (Jinnah's press statement on 31 July, 1946, *The Dawn*, 1 August, 1946)

It is however debatable whether the highly publicized conflicting ideas and conceptions lay at the root of the Hindu–Muslim chasm at the grassroots since it has been amply demonstrated that

> explicit rivalries between the [principal] communities tended to exist [during the period preceding partition] at ... the level of organized politics at the top where Hindu and Muslim elites were rivals for influence with government and eventually for the control of government itself.
>
> (Ayesha Jalal and Anil Seal, 'Alternative to partition: Muslim politics between the wars', *Modern Asian Studies*, Vol. 15 (3), 1984, p. 415)

102 Sushil Srivastava, 'Constructing the Hindu identity: European moral and intellectual adventurism in 18th century India', *Economic and Political Weekly*, Vol. 16 (22), 1998, p. 1186. According to Srivastava,

> English writing on India that appeared after 1780 was preoccupied with the obligation to expound and glorify the literary and other achievements of the ancient past of the Hindoos. In this process, the *Brahminical* system and practices were naturally glorified and the newly discovered Sanskrit language was said to be the only source that could open the unknown mystifying world of *brahmans*. Sanskrit literature was alone distinguished as the sole source of knowledge that could unravel the mysteries of the glory that was India.

103 *The Star of India*, 24 March, 1940.

104 B.R. Ambedkar, 'Thoughts on Pakistan', in Mushirul Hasan (ed.), *Inventing Boundaries: gender, politics and partition of India*, Oxford University Press, Delhi, 2000, p. 48.

105 Francis Robinson, however, does not subscribe to the view that Muslims in

India constituted 'a nation'. His study of the Uttar Pradesh Muslims suggests that, by most of the standards applied to modern European nations, they were not a nation. Being Muslim, of course, argues Robinson, 'did not make them a nation'. Francis Robinson, *Separatism among Indian Muslims: the politics of the United Provinces, 1860–1923*, Cambridge University Press, Cambridge, 1974, p. 345. Robinson's argument does not appear to be tenable, since 'nation is always imagined into existence and never derivative'. In the context of colonialism, the Muslim 'nation' was constructed through a complex process of contestation involving the British, the Hindus and a particular type of imperial rule which unfolded with the partial devolution of power to the Indians in the beginning of the twentieth century.

106 B.R. Ambedkar, *Pakistan or the Partition of India*, Bombay, 1945 (second edition).

107 Ibid., p. vii.

108 Ibid., pp. 352–8. For a detailed analytical discussion of Ambedkar's argument in favour of the claim for Pakistan, see Partha Chatterjee, 'The nation in heterogeneous time', *Indian Economic and Social History Review*, Vol. 38 (4), 2001, pp. 414–15.

109 Notwithstanding his defence of the caste system, Gandhi held strong views challenging untouchability which Ambedkar failed to appreciate. His opposition to untouchability was based on the argument that it 'is not a sanction of religion; it is a device of *Satan*.... There is neither nobility nor bravery in treating the great and uncomplaining scavengers of the nation as worse than dogs to be despised and spat upon'. M.K. Gandhi, 'The sin of untouchability', *Young India*, 19 January, 1921, reproduced in Mahatma Gandhi, *What Is Hinduism*, National Book Trust, New Delhi, 2001 (reprint), p. 115.

110 B.R. Ambedkar, 'Annihilation of caste', reproduced in Valerian Rodrigues (ed.), *The Essential Writings of B.R. Ambedkar*, op. cit., p. 262.

111 Ibid., p. 275.

112 Ambedkar voiced his critique of caste in his address at the annual conference of the Jat-Pat-Todak Mandal of Lahore, later entitled 'Annihilation of Caste' in its published form. According to Gandhi, 'although this address is open to serious objection ... no reformer can ignore this because of its depth of analysis of Hindu scriptures. [On the basis of his analysis], Dr. Ambedkar', argued Gandhi,

> found that the vast majority of *savarna* Hindus had not only conducted themselves inhumanly against those of their fellow religionists whom they classed as untouchables, but they had based their conduct on the authority of their scriptures, and he began to search, he had found ample warrant for their belief in untouchability and all its implications. [He] had quoted chapter and verse in proof of his threefold indictment – inhuman conduct itself, the unabashed justification for it on the part of the perpetrators, and the subsequent discovery that the justification was warranted by their scriptures.
> (M.K. Gandhi, 'Dr. Ambedkar's indictment', *Harijan*, 11 July, 1936, reproduced in Gandhi, *What Is Hinduism*, op. cit., pp. 119–20.

113 *Harijan*, 11 November, 1935, *CWMG*, Vol. 62, pp. 121–2.

114 *Harijanbandhu*, 19 January, 1936, *CWMG*, Vol. 62, pp. 142–3.

115 M.K. Gandhi, 'Caste has to go', *Harijan*, 16 November, 1935, *CWMG*, Vol. 62, pp. 121–2.

116 M.K. Gandhi, 'Caste and varna', *Harijanbandhu*, 19 January, 1936, *CWMG*, Vol. 62, p. 142.

117 Judith Brown, 'The Mahatma and modern India', *Modern Asian Studies*, Vol. 3

(4), 1969, p. 330. In upholding *varnashrama*, Gandhi was, argues Judith Brown, 'compromising between the claims of orthodoxy and reform'.

118 Despite defending caste, Gandhi's attitude towards Hinduism was governed by a sense of 'openness' and 'catholicity' at the same time. He questioned the claim of priests to interpret the scriptures, disapproved of the practice of obscurantist rituals in the name of tradition and opposed the tendency to equate the knowledge of scriptures with spirituality. K.N. Panikkar, 'Assassination of the Mahatma', *The Hindu*, New Delhi, 28 October, 2004.

119 B.R. Ambedkar, 'Reply to the Mahatma', reproduced in Rodrigues (ed.), *The Essential Writings of B.R. Ambedkar*, op. cit., p. 318.

120 Ibid., p. 316.

121 M.G. Ranade (1842–1901) was a liberal politician who also became a member of the House of Commons. He was known for his critique of Hindu society, based on his understanding of the practices of Hinduism in contemporary India. Born in 1842 at Biphad in the Nasik district of Bombay presidency in a Chitpavan *Brahmin* family, MG Ranade was influenced by the pure monotheism of the *Upanishads*. He was famous for his views deprecating the caste system and untouchability. As a true liberal, he championed the cause of women and favoured widow-marriage. He was also an ardent supporter of industrialization, and emancipation of the *ryot* (cultivators holding land from the landlord on certain conditions) from the moneylender. As an editor of an Anglo-Marathi daily from Bombay, *Induprakash* (1864–71), Ranade published his views on social reform. A founder member of the Indian National Congress, Ranade was characterized as a 'modern *rishi*' (saint) by his Congress colleagues. He articulated his views in a) *Revenue Manual of the British Empire in India*; b) *Essays in Indian Economics*; and c) *Rise of the Maratha Power*. He also wrote *A Theist's Confession of Faith* in which he attempted to create an ideological basis for the *Prarthana Samaj*, a reformist organization. S.P. Sen (ed.), *Dictionary of National Biography*, Vol. III, Institute of Historical Studies, Calcutta, 1973–4, pp. 479–81.

122 C.B. Khairmode, *Dr. Bhimrao Ramaji Ambedkar* (in Marathi), Vol. 5, Maharastra Rajya Sahitya Ani Sanskrit Mandal, Bombay, 1987, p. 198, quoted in M.S. Gore, *The Social Context of an Ideology: Ambedkar's political and social thought*, Sage, New Delhi, 1993, p. 166.

123 Ambedkar quoted Ranade extensively to substantiate his argument against social orthodoxy. As Ranade, critical of both political radicalism and social toryism, argued,

> You cannot be liberal by halves. You cannot be liberal in politics and conservative in religion. The heart and the head must go together. You cannot cultivate your intellect, enrich your mind, enlarge the sphere of your political rights and privileges, and at the same time keep your hearts closed and cramped. It is an idle dream to expect men to remain enchained and enshackled in their own superstition and social evils, while they are struggling hard to win rights and privileges from their rulers. Before long these vain dreamers will find their dreams lost.
> (B.R. Ambedkar, 'Ranade, Gandhi and Jinnah', reproduced in Rodrigues (ed.), *The Essential Writings of B.R. Ambedkar*, op. cit., p. 124.

124 Ibid., p. 129.

125 Upendra Baxi elaborated this argument in Baxi, op. cit., pp. 35–7.

126 Viswanathan, op. cit., p. 216.

127 Ibid., p. 237.

4   Gandhi's writings in *Harijan*: discussion and interpretation

1   Gandhi outlined the philosophical basis of the *Hind Swaraj* in its foreword by saying:

> These views are mine, and yet not mine. They are mine because I hope to act according to them. They are almost a part of my being. But, yet, they are not mine, because I lay no claim to originality. They have been formed after reading several books. That which I dimly felt received support from these books.
>
> (Gandhi's foreword in *Hind Swaraj*. Anthony Parel (ed.), *Hind Swaraj and Other Writings*, Cambridge University Press, Cambridge, 1997, p. 10).

2   The thematic refers to 'an epistemological as well as ethical system which provides a framework of elements and rules for establishing relations between elements; the problematic consists of concrete statements about possibilities justified by reference to the thematic'. Partha Chatterjee has elaborated this distinction between 'thematic' and 'problematic' in his *Nationalist Thought and the Colonial World: a derivative discourse*, Oxford University Press, Delhi, 1986, Chapter 2 (pp. 36–43).

3   R.V. Shastri was a Poona-based social worker and freedom fighter actively associated with the activities of the *Servants of Untouchables Society*. Drawn to Gandhi and his ideology in the wake of the 1920–2 Non-Cooperation Movement, he took the initiative in the publication of *Harijan* on the advice of the Mahatma.

4   Apart from the reservation ensuring their political representation in the legislature, the Poona Pact, Gandhi believed, would also provide the *harijan* with an arrangement

> to take stock of their contribution towards their own purification and therefore the purification of Hinduism. But there is no doubt that by far the greatest responsibility rests on the shoulders of caste-Hindus. Reformers should make it a point of winning over the orthodox people to the movement by gentleness, humility, self-sacrifice and increasing purity of character.
>
> (*Harijan*, 22 July, 1933)

5   *Harijan*, 11 February, 1933.

6   M.K. Gandhi, 'To subscribers', *Harijan*, 9 February, 1934, *CWMG*, Vol. 57, p. 130.

7   Gandhi's favourite format of articulating views seems to be via 'dialogue'. The *Hind Swaraj*, for instance, was written in the form of a dialogue between the editor and reader. What is striking is that, by combining the role of an editor and reader, Gandhi addressed those significant issues which are not merely contextual but also transcendental since a large number of them continue to be relevant even after the expiry of ninety years of its first publication in *Gujrati* 1910.

8   Since separating the Scheduled Castes from the Hindus would be detrimental to the interests of the nation, Gandhi persuaded the Congress to accept the reservation for them *albeit* through a system of joint electorates which was articulated in the 1932 Poona Pact. As per the Pact, the election would be in two stages. The primary election would be through separate electorates: here the Scheduled Castes alone would elect their candidates. The result of this round would determine who was entitled to stand in the second and final election in constituencies reserved for the Scheduled Castes. Once the candidates had been chosen by the Scheduled Castes in the primary election, the winning candidate would be decided through joint electorates. Thus, the winner who would represent the Scheduled Castes would be elected by the Scheduled Castes and Hindus from among the list of candidates chosen by the Scheduled Castes.

9 Gandhi thus argued, '*Harijan* is not my weekly. So far as the proprietary rights are concerned, it belongs to the *Servants of Untouchables Society* and therefore I would like him [Ambedkar] to feel that it is as much his as ... any Hindus'. Gandhi's statement in *Harijan*, 11 February, 1933.

10 *Dr. Babasaheb Ambedkar Writings and Speeches*, [*Untouchables or the Children of India's Ghetto and Other Essays on Untouchables and Untouchability: Social, Political and Religious*] Education Department, Government of Maharastra, 1999, Vol. 5, p. 363.

11 *Harijan*, 11 February, 1933.

12 Ibid.

13 Ibid. In fact, on one occasion, he urged 'there would be only one caste known by the beautiful name Bhangi, that is to say the reformer or remover of all dirt'. *Harijan*, 7 July, 1946.

14 *Harijan*, 28 July, 1933. In his letter to Gandhi, Tagore further elaborated his arguments opposing the Pact by stating:

> if [the Pact] remains unaltered [it] will inflict a serious injury upon the social and political life in Bengal. Justice is an important aspect of truth and if it is allowed to be violated for the sake of immediate peace or speedy cutting of some political knots in the long run, it is sure to come back to those who are apparently benefited by it and will claim a very heavy price for the concession cheaply gained.... I look upon the whole thing from the point of humanity, which will cruelly suffer when its claim to justice is ignored.
> (Rabindranath Tagore to Gandhi, 8 August, 1933, published in Sabyasachi Bhattacharya (ed. and compiled), *The Mahatma and the Poet: letters and debates between Gandhi and Tagore, 1915–1941*, National Book Trust, New Delhi, 1997, p. 149)

15 This is how Bhikhu Parekh paraphrases Gandhi's notion of the Indian nation. See his 'Nationalism in a comparative perspective' in *Politisches Denken Jahrbuch*, Verlag J.B. Metzler, Stuttgart, 1994, p. 63. That Gandhi rejected the nationalist language was also underlined by Partha Chatterjee, who argued that:

> Gandhi does not even think within the thematic of nationalism. He seldom writes or speaks in terms of the conceptual frameworks or the modes of reasoning and inference adopted by the nationalists of his day, and quite emphatically rejects their rationalism, scientism and historicism.
> ('Gandhi and the critique of civil society' in Ranajit Guha (ed.), *Subaltern Studies: writings on South Asian history and society*, Oxford University Press, Delhi, 1984, p. 167)

16 *Harijan*, 28 October, 1939, *CWMG*, Vol. 70, p. 283.

17 *Harijan*, 11 November, 1939, *CWMG*, Vol. 70, pp. 334–5.

18 Rabindranath Tagore, 'The Congress', *The Modern Review*, July, 1939. Gandhi quoted excerpts from this article in defence of his arguments underlining the weaknesses of Jinnah's two-nation theory. See *Harijan*, 11 November, 1939, *CWMG*, Vol. 70, p. 332.

19 B.R. Ambedkar, 'A nation calling for a home', in *Dr. Babasaheb Ambedkar Writings and Speeches*, Vol. 8, Education Department, Government of Maharastra, 1990, p. 39.

20 *Harijan*, 5 August, 1939, *CWMG*, Vol. 70, p. 23.

21 Gandhi thus categorically stated that 'Communal differences have been used by the British Government to thwart India's aspiration. That the process is likely to have been unconscious does not make it less mischievous'. *Harijan*, 11 November, 1939.

22 *Harijan*, 2 December, 1939, *CWMG*, Vol. 70, p. 387.
23 *Harijan*, 6 April, 1940.
24 *Harijan*, 7 October, 1939, *CWMG*, Vol. 70, p. 212.
25 *Harijan*, 4 May, 1940.
26 Partha Chatterjee elaborates this argument with reference to his analysis of Gandhi on the basis of what he wrote in the *Hind Swaraj*. See his 'Gandhi and the critique of civil society', op. cit., p. 158.
27 *Charkha*, as Gandhi described 'is our ammunition – guns and artillery – and so we cannot afford to forsake it'. *Harijan*, 6 April, 1940, *CWMG*, Vol. 71, p. 383.
28 *Khadi*, as Gandhi characterized, 'is the chief village handicraft' and 'is a symbol of identification with the poorest in the land'. *Harijan*, 20 January, 1940, *CWMG*, Vol. 71, p. 103; *Harijan*, 30 December, 1939, *CWMG*, Vol. 71, p. 52.
29 *Harijan*, 4 November, 1939, *CWMG*, Vol. 70, p. 316.
30 'Is khadi economically sound', *Harijan*, 20 June, 1936, *CWMG*, Vol. 63, pp. 77–8.
31 'Village industries', *Harijan*, 16 November, 1934, *CWMG*, Vol. 59, p. 356. The opposition to the machine stems from his genuine concern for providing 'profitable employment' to all. He thus argued on another occasion

> We should not use machinery for producing things which we can produce without its aid and have got the capacity to do so. As machinery makes you its slave, we want to be independent and self-supporting; so we should not take the help of machinery when we can do without it. We want to make our villages free and self-sufficient and through them achieve our goal – liberty – and also protect it. I have no interest in the machine nor [do] I oppose it. If I can produce my things myself, I become my master and so need no machinery.
>
> (*Harijan*, 6 April, 1940, *CWMG*, Vol. 71, p. 383)

32 'Mills vs. charkha', *Harijan*, 12 August, 1939, *CWMG*, Vol. 70, p. 74.
33 *Harijan*, 29 August, 1936, discussion with Maurice Frydman on 25 August, 1936, *CWMG*, Vol. 63, p. 241. Maurice Frydman, a Polish engineer, interested in the village reconstruction movement, had met Gandhi earlier and was given the name Bharatanand.
34 *Harijan*, 29 September, 1940, interview to Francis G. Hickman, 17 September, 1940, *CWMG*, Vol. 73, pp. 29–30. The differences between Nehru and Gandhi may have had their roots in the former's insistence on the creation of a planning commission in the Soviet style as a mechanism to bring about radical changes in the economy. See, my 'Jawaharlal Nehru and planning, 1937–40', *Modern Asian Studies*, Vol. 26 (2), 1922.
35 Condemning the blind supporters of industrialism, Gandhi thus sarcastically stated that we deprive the villager of employment and, 'by way of compensation, give him lectures, magic-lantern shows and tinned music all at his expense, and pat ourselves on the back that we are working for his welfare. Can anything be more absurd?' 'Motor vs. cart', *Harijan*, 16 September, 1939, *CWMG*, Vol. 70, p. 118.
36 *Harijan*, 6 April, 1940, in *CWMG*, Vol. 71, p. 383.
37 *Harijan*, 27 January, 1940, *CWMG*, Vol. 71, p. 130.
38 'Meaning of the Gita', *CWMG*, Vol. 28, p. 317.
39 Gandhi was persuaded because, as he himself argued, 'We have also discovered through our progress that in the application of non-violence we have been able to reach the mass mind far more quickly and far more extensively than before.' *Harijan*, 24 February, 1946.
40 Gandhi wrote this piece entitled 'Satyagraha – not passive resistance' on 2 September, 1917, *CWMG*, Vol. 13, p. 523.

41 *Harijan*, 6 January, 1940, *CWMG*, Vol. 71, p. 62.

42 'What are the basic assumptions?', *Harijan*, 22 October, 1938, *CWMG*, Vol. 67, p. 437.

43 *Harijan*, 30 March, 1940, *CWMG*, Vol. 71, p. 360. The analogy of the army and its functioning is striking, given Gandhi's well-defined opposition to the Western military. He was probably inspired by the organized strength of an army which he sought to instil in the satyagrahees.

44 *Harijan*, 6 April, 1940, *CWMG*, Vol. 71, p. 378.

45 Gandhi on *khadi*, *CWMG*, Vol. 50, p. 211 and Vol. 56, p. 171.

46 *Harijan*, 11 February, 1939.

47 Ibid.

48 *Harijan*, 2 September, 1939.

49 *Harijan*, 11 November, 1939.

50 *Harijan*, 11 February, 1939.

51 *Harijan*, 2 September, 1939, *CWMG*, Vol. 70, pp. 117–18.

52 *Harijan*, 28 October, 1939, *CWMG*, Vol. 70, p. 280.

53 *Harijan*, 23 September, 1939, *CWMG*, Vol. 70, pp. 409–13.

54 'The only way', *Harijan*, 25 November, 1939, *CWMG*, Vol. 70, p. 363.

55 *Harijan*, 6 January, 1940, *CWMG*, Vol. 71, p. 63.

56 *Harijan*, 23 March, 1940, *CWMG*, Vol. 71, p. 345.

57 'Hindu–Muslim', *Harijan*, 8 June, 1940, *CWMG*, Vol. 72, p. 133.

58 *Harijan*, 28 October, 1939, *CWMG*, Vol. 70, p. 274.

59 Gandhi's letter to Ravishankar Shukla, 19 October, 1939, *CWMG*, Vol. 70, p. 277.

60 'One script for daughters of Sanskrit', *Harijan*, 5 August, 1939, *CWMG*, Vol. 70, pp. 46–7.

61 Gandhi's conversation with Sushila Nayar, reproduced in Sushila Nayar, *Mahatma Gandhi's Last Imprisonment: the inside story*, Har-Anand, New Delhi, 1996, pp. 97–8.

62 'My idea of a police force', *Harijan*, 1 September, 1940, *CWMG*, Vol. 72, p. 403.

63 Gandhi's ideological position on women-related issues was guided by his belief in a) equality between sexes; and b) differentiation of their social roles. For details, see Barbara Southard, 'The feminism of Mahatma Gandhi', in Subrata Mukherjee and Sushila Ramaswamy (eds), *Economic and Social Principles of Mahatma Gandhi*, Vol. 3, Deep & Deep Publications, New Delhi, 1998, pp. 311–31.

64 For details, see a) Karuna Ahmed, 'Gandhi, women's role and the freedom movement', Occasional Paper, Nehru Memorial Museum and Library, New Delhi, 1984; b) Madhu Kishwar, 'Women in Gandhi', *Economic and Political Weekly*, Vol. 20 (40 and 41), 5, 9 October, 1985; c) Devaki Jain, 'Gandhian contributions towards a theory of feminist ethic', in Devaki Jain and Diana Eck (eds), *Speaking of Faith: cross-cultural perspectives on women, religion and social change*, Kali for Women, Delhi, 1986.

65 Taking the example of Sita, Gandhi thus argued, 'Physically she was a weakling before Ravana, but her purity was more than a match even for his giant might. He tried to win her with all kinds of allurement but could not carnally touch her without her consent.' *Harijan*, 25 August, 1940, *CWMG*, Vol. 72, p. 392.

66 For an elaboration of this argument, see Anup Taneja, *Gandhi, Women and the National Movement, 1920–47*, Har-Anand, New Delhi, 2005.

67 Kumari Jayawardene has developed this argument in her *Feminism and Nationalism in the Third World*, Zed Books, London, 1986, pp. 260–82.

68 *CWMG*, Vol. 14, pp. 207–8.

69 *CWMG*, Vol. 17, p. 326.

70 *Harijan*, 24 February, 1940, *CWMG*, Vol. 71, pp. 207–8.
71 'Swaraj through women', *Harijan*, 2 December, 1939, *CWMG*, Vol. 70, p. 381.
72 'What is woman's role?', *Harijan*, 24 February, 1940, *CWMG*, Vol. 71, p. 208.
73 For a critical evaluation of Gandhi's views on women, see Sujata Patel, 'Construction and reconstruction of woman in Gandhi', *Economic and Political Weekly*, Vol. 23 (40), 20 February, 1988, pp. 377–87.
74 *Harijan*, 17 February, 1940, *CWMG*, Vol. 71, p. 197.
75 The distinction between the 'historical' and 'civilizational' Gandhi is purely analytical, seeking to convey the transcendental importance of Gandhi's social and political thought. The historical Gandhi was a finite being complete with common frailties and unique strength. His role in the nationalist movement was subject to criticism. His various political actions during the freedom struggle can be questioned. But the civilizational Gandhi, located in the social and political ideas of the Mahatma, continues to be relevant, since not only does it evoke academic historical interest, it also offers insights into contemporary human life and society. Rajni Bakshi, *Bapu Kuti: journeys in rediscovery of Gandhi*, Penguin, New Delhi, 1998, p. 10.
76 Ibid.
77 Ronald J. Terchek, *Gandhi: struggling for autonomy*, Vistaar Publications, New Delhi, 1998, p. 230.
78 *Harijan*, 28 March, 1936, *CWMG*, Vol. 67, p. 193.

5 Introducing the text

1 Only excerpts are reproduced here.
2 As expounded in his 1940 presidential address at Lahore defending the claim for Pakistan on the basis of his two-nation theory. Jinnah insisted that

> the Hindus and Muslims have two different religions, philosophies, social customs, literatures. They neither inter-marry, nor dine together, and indeed, they belong to two different civilizations which are based mainly on conflicting ideas and conceptions. Their aspects on life and of life are different. It is quite clear that Hindus and Mussalmans derive their inspirations from different sources of history. They have different epics, their heroes are different, and they have different episodes. Very often the hero of one is a foe of the other and likewise, their victories and defeats overlap. To yoke together two such nations under a single State, one as a numerical minority and the other as majority, must lead to growing discontent and final destruction of any fabric that may be so built up for the government of such a State.

The entire text of Jinnah's 1940 Lahore speech is reproduced in S.S. Pirzada (ed.), *Foundations of Pakistan, All India Muslim League Documents, 1906–1947*, Vol. 2, National Publishing House Ltd, Karachi, pp. 218–38.
3 The All-Indian Muslim League, meeting at Lahore, passed a resolution on 23 March, 1940 recording the view that no constitutional plan would be workable unless it was based on territorial readjustment and the creation of independent Muslim States.
4 Not translated here. The correspondent had been running a small craft-based school for the last two years. He wholeheartedly supported Gandhi's ideas on education on the basis of his own experience.

Conclusion

1 There are five different interpretations of the social and political thought which Gandhi articulated during his long association with India's freedom struggle.

They are: a) that Gandhian values and strategies are functional to the modernization of Indian traditions and to the traditionalization of (Western) modernity in India; b) that Gandhian values and strategies contribute to the political appropriation of the peasantry by/for the passive bourgeois-nationalist revolution, which defers or deflects the socialist revolution in India; c) that the programme of Gandhian *sarvodaya* must be revised and extended into a strategy of Total Revolution (as articulated later by Jayprakash Narayan); d) that some aspects of Gandhian thought serve the Hindu nationalist ideology; and e) that the Gandhian programme of *sarvodaya* through parliamentary *swaraj* and *satyagraha* is superior to the liberal and Marxist–Leninist paradigms of development and governance. For details, see Thomas Pantham, *Political Theories and Social Reconstruction: a critical survey of the literature on India*, Sage, New Delhi, 1995, pp. 102–25.

2 Jawaharlal Nehru, *The Discovery of India*, Oxford University Press, Delhi (centenary edition) 1985, pp. 451–2.

3 V.R. Mehta, *Foundations of Indian Political Thought*, Manohar, New Delhi, 1992, p. 211.

4 'What he did was', as Ainslie T. Embree argued, 'give the masses for the first time a sense of involvement in the nation's destiny while persuading the old leaders to accept his leadership.' Ainslie T. Embree, *Imagining India: essays on Indian history*, Oxford University Press, Delhi, 1989, p. 165.

5 Nehru, op. cit., p. 361.

6 Cited in Rajni Bakshi, *Bapu Kuti: journeys in rediscovery of Gandhi*, Penguin, New Delhi, 1998, p. 10.

7 Joan V. Bondurant, *Conquest of Violence: the Gandhian philosophy of conflict*, Princeton University Press, Princeton, 1958, p. 7.

8 *My Experiments with Truth* was written during Gandhi's imprisonment in the 1920s and first appeared serially in a Gujarati weekly known as *Young India*. The other three books that Gandhi wrote were *Satyagraha in South Africa*, *Hind Swaraj or Indian Home Rule* and *Key to Health*.

9 N.K. Bose and P.H. Pathwardhan, *Gandhi in Indian Politics*, Asia Publishing House, Bombay, 1967, p. 56.

10 Barrington Moore Jr, *Social Origins of Dictatorship and Democracy: lord and peasant in the making of the modern world*, Beacon Press, Boston, 1966, p. 173.

11 M.K. Gandhi, 'Masses and leadership', *Young India*, 3 November, 1920, *CWMG*, Vol. 18, p. 275.

12 Moore, op. cit., pp. 177–8.

13 Subhas Chandra Bose, *The Indian Struggle, 1920–42*, Asia Publishing House, London, 1964, p. 68. Bose further argued that, with the demise of CR Das, Lala Lajpat Rai and Motilal Nehru,

the entire intellect of the Congress has been mortgaged to one man [i.e. Gandhi] and those who dare to think freely and speak out openly are regarded by the Mahatma and his disciples as heretics and treated as such. [Furthermore], the promise of Swaraj within one year was not only unwise but childish. It made the Congress appear so foolish before all reasonable men. No doubt the Mahatma's disciples have tried subsequently to explain away the point by saying that the country did not fulfill the conditions and so Swaraj could not be won within one year. The explanation is as unsatisfactory as the original promise was unwise – because arguing in the same way, any leader can say that if you fulfill certain conditions you can be free in one hour. In making political forecasts, no leader worth the name should impose impossible conditions. He should estimate what conditions are likely to be fulfilled and what results are likely to be achieved in a given set of circumstances.

(Ibid., pp. 70–1)

14 Jawaharlal Nehru, *Jawaharlal Nehru: an autobiography*, John Lane The Bodley Head, London, 1941, p. 76. Despite being vague, Gandhi, Nehru argued, brought new vigour to the anti-British campaign. His presence was so electrifying that

> a demoralized, backward and broken-up people suddenly straightened their backs and lifted their heads and took part in disciplined, joint action on a country-wide scale. This action itself, we felt, would give irresistible power to the masses. We ignored the necessity of thought behind action; we forgot that without a conscious ideology and objective the energy and enthusiasm of masses must end largely in smoke.... [A] feeling that non-violence as conceived for political and economic movements or for righting wrongs was a new message which our people were destined to give to the world.

15 B.P. Sitamarayya, *The History of the Indian National Congress*, Vol. I (1922–35), S. Chand & Co., Delhi, 1969, p. 376.
16 R. Palme Dutt, *India Today*, Victor Gollancz Ltd, London, 1940, p. 307.
17 Judith Brown, 'The Mahatma and Modern India', *Modern Asian Studies*, Vol. 3 (4), 1969, p. 334.
18 R. Palme Dutt defined non-violence 'as an apparently common sense rule of expediency for at any rate the earlier stages of struggle of an unarmed people against a powerfully armed ruling enemy'. Palme Dutt, op. cit., p. 307.
19 Ibid., pp. 307–8.
20 E.M.S. Namboodripad, *The Mahatma and the Ism*, People's Publishing House, New Delhi, 1959, p. 61.
21 Partha Chatterjee, *The Politics of the Governed: reflections on popular politics in most of the world*, Permanent Black, New Delhi, 2004, p. 17.
22 Partha Chatterjee, *The Nation and Its Fragments: colonial and post-colonial histories*, Oxford University Press, Delhi, 1994, p. 6.
23 Ibid., pp. 121, 132.
24 Chatterjee, *The Politics of the Governed*, op. cit., p. 48.
25 Sumit Sarkar, *Modern India, 1885–1947*, Macmillan, New Delhi, 1983, p. 179.
26 Akeel Bilgrami however does not agree with this. On the basis of his reading of Gandhi's writings in *Young India*, he argues that the idea of Mill's tolerance does not cohere with Gandhi's fundamental thinking because

> a satyagrahi or a non-violent activist has to show a certain kind of self-restraint, in which it was not enough simply not to commit violence. It is equally important not to bear hostility to others or even to criticize them; it is only required that one not follow these others, if conscience doesn't permit it.

For Mill, tolerance is self-restraint and thus a negative act on the part of the tolerant, while a *satyagrahi* is not only tolerant but also translates his belief into acts despite adverse consequences. So the strength of a *satyagrahi* emanates not from truth, as emphasized by Mill, but from his moral values, which are critical in sustaining the tempo and spirit for the search for truth. The standard view that Gandhi was

> essentially applying Mill's argument for tolerance to an argument for non violence, is very wide of the mark. They exhibit diverging attitudes towards the concept of truth, and the epistemology it entails. Gandhi, like Mill, wants our own opinions to be held with modesty, but, unlike him, with an accompanying epistemology that does not discourage conviction or confidence. To that end, Gandhi rejects the notion of truth that Mill seems

to presuppose in his argument for tolerance. He replaces the entire argument ... with another that seems to have less to do with the notion of truth per se than with the nature of moral judgment.

(Akeel Bilgrami, 'Gandhi: the philosopher', *Economic and Political Weekly*, Vol. 38 (39), 27 September, 2003, pp. 4161, 4163)

27 Sarkar, op. cit., p. 180.
28 This discussion draws on Partha Chatterjee, *Nationalist Thought and the Colonial World: a derivative discourse*, Oxford University Press, Delhi, 1986, Chapter 4 (pp. 85–130).
29 Ibid., p. 110.
30 In a recent article, K.N. Panikkar argues that the real assassin of Gandhi was not Nathuram Godse, but Hindu communalism of which V.D. Savarkar was the most ardent ideologue and practitioner. (Savarkar was the progenitor of the idea of Hindutva, and the ideological mentor of the Rashtriya Swayam Sevak Sangh, or the RSS, one of the frontal 'cultural' organizations of the Bharatiya Janata Party (BJP), the leading partner of the erstwhile National Democratic Alliance-led government in New Delhi between 1999 and 2004). K.N. Panikkar, 'Assassination of the Mahatma', *The Hindu*, New Delhi, 28 October, 2004.
31 Gandhi was perceived by those involved in his assassination to be 'pro-Muslim' for he had suggested M.A. Jinnah as the prime minister of independent India and had undertaken a fast to ensure that India fulfilled its fiscal obligations to Pakistan arising out of partition. It is true, as Gyanendra Pandey has shown, that Gandhi's fast did accomplish something like 'a miracle'. The demand for driving every Muslim out of every part of Delhi lost its immediate appeal. Many Muslims were able to return to their homes and *mohallas* and, perhaps for the first time since late 1946, the people of Delhi began to return to the business of living and of rebuilding their lives, their uprooted city and their future. Gyanendra Pandey, *Remembering Partition: violence, nationalism and history in India*, Cambridge University Press, Cambridge, 2001, pp. 142–3. However to attribute the killing of Gandhi to the perceived notion of those identified as Hindu fundamentalists is too simplistic to capture the complex processes that were linked with the articulation of contradictory kinds of worldview, represented by Gandhi and V.D. Savarkar respectively. Whereas Gandhi's attitude towards religion was governed by universality and equality of faiths, Savarkar, who was Jinnah's alter-ego, insisted on the 'exclusivity' of Hinduism while defending the Indian nation strictly in terms of a 'nationalist language'. I have elaborated this argument elsewhere. Bidyut Chakrabarty (ed.), *Communal Identity in India: its construction and articulation in the twentieth century*, Oxford University Press, Delhi, 2003, pp. 10–12.
32 Nehru, *An Autobiography*, op. cit., p. 403.
33 In a recent book by Niall Ferguson, decolonization was attributed not to the nationalist movement but to the liberal democratic tradition of politics in Britain, which ultimately made it impossible for the British ruling class to sustain the anomaly of a despotic colonial empire and to resist the moral claim to national self-government by the colonized people. Niall Ferguson, *Empire: the rise and demise of the British world order and the lessons for global power*, Basic Books, New York, 2002.
34 Chatterjee, *Nationalist Thought and the Colonial World*, op. cit., p. 101.
35 Shahid Amin has dwelled on this process in his 'Gandhi as Mahatma: Gorakhpur district, eastern UP', in Ranajit Guha (ed.), *Subaltern Studies*, Vol. III, Oxford University Press, Delhi, 1984, pp. 1–61.
36 In a recent contribution, it has been shown how the popular Gandhian symbol of the *charkha* (spinning wheel) contributed to an understanding of the different

layers of politics of disjuncture which operate at many levels. *Charkha* was redefined in a way which was at variance with how Gandhian ideology and symbols were perceived by the Mahatma himself. In Gandhian discourse, the *charkha* signifies 'decentralization against centralized production', the sole remedy for the dwindling handloom industry and the traditional sector in general, a weapon for stopping the import of foreign goods, the only solution for hidden-mass unemployment of rural population'. The significance of the spinning wheel can be seen in Mahatma Gandhi's insistence that 'India as a nation can live and die only for the spinning wheel'. However, away from this, images of this popular symbol and Gandhian *swaraj* acquired various shapes in the domain of political culture. Sadan Jha, 'Charkha, "dear forgotten friend" of widows: reading the erasures of symbols', *Economic and Political Weekly*, Vol. 39 (28), 10 July, 2004, pp. 3113–20.

37 Bhikhu Parekh, *Gandhi*, Oxford University Press, Oxford, 1997, p. 92.
38 Sunil Khilnani, 'Gandhi and history', *Seminar* (India, 1997), Annual Number, No. 461, January, 1998, p. 114.
39 Ibid., p. 115.
40 Ronald Terchek, *Gandhi: struggling for autonomy*, Vistaar, New Delhi, 1998, p. 231.
41 I owe this point to Ronald Terchek. See ibid., p. 7.
42 Parekh, op. cit., p. 68.
43 Despite his critique of modern civilization, Gandhi did not dismiss it altogether and appreciated what he took to be its three great achievements. First, he admired its scientific enquiry; the second great achievement consisted in understanding the natural world and bringing it under greater human control; and third, by cultivating civic virtues, respect for rules, the capacity to subordinate the personal to collective interest, public morality, mutual respect and punctuality, the modern civilization made a unique contribution to human life. For details, see ibid., pp. 71–2.
44 Terchek, op. cit., p. 231.
45 Underlining the importance of decentralization, Gandhi's constructive programme offers new insights into the development process in a rural economy. For details, see Ajit K. Dasgupta, *Gandhi's Economic Thought*, Routledge, London and New York, 1996, pp. 178–81.
46 Akeel Bilgrami elaborated this point with reference to Gandhi's *Hind Swaraj*, which had articulated the Gandhian alternative vision of society, economy and polity. Bilgrami, op. cit., p. 4160.
47 Sarkar, op. cit., p. 181.
48 Although *swadeshi* was articulated during the 1903–8 *swadeshi* movement in Bengal, the ideas that inspired the movement became popular with the arrival of the Mahatma on the political scene. Ibid., pp. 178–81.
49 *Young India*, 17 September, 1925, *CWMG*, Vol. 50, p. 237.
50 Sabyasachi Bhattacharya, *Vande Mataram: the biography of a song*, Penguin, New Delhi, 2003, p. 94.
51 Embree, op. cit., p. 172.
52 Nehru, *An Autobiography*, op. cit., p. 548.
53 Sumit Sarkar elaborated this in Sarkar, op. cit., pp. 178–83.

Bibliographical notes

Gandhi's own writings are in themselves an endless but always rewarding study. He led an unusually active life and yet the quantity of his writings is enormous, touching almost all aspects of human life and existence. *The Collected Works of Mahatma Gandhi* are undoubtedly important compilations of Gandhi's writings on various issues including the specific literary tracts he wrote to illustrate his ideology. Moreover, there are numerous Navajivan publications which carry on the good work done earlier that deserve acknowledgement. It is difficult to pick and choose among the available publications, but no student of Gandhi and Indian freedom movement can do without *Young India* (1919–22), *Indian Home Rule* or *Hind Swaraj* (1919), *Speeches and Writings* (1922), *Satyagraha in South Africa* (1925), *The Story of My Experiments with Truth* (2 vols, 1927–9), *Indian Case for Swaraj* (1932), *Indian State Problems* (1941), *Economics of Khadi* (1941), *Women and Social Justice* (1947), *Gita – the Mother* (1947), *Delhi Diary*, being a collection of prayer speeches from 10 September, 1947 to 30 January, 1948 (1948), *Non-violence in Peace and War* (1949), *Hindu Dharma* (1950), *Towards Non-violent Society* (1951), *Satyagraha: Non-violent Resistance* (1951). These publications, some parts of which overlap, are illustrative, but are by no means exhaustive. These tracts, incorporated in *The Collected Works of Mahatma Gandhi* (100 volumes), published by the Publication Division, Ministry of Information and Broadcasting, Government of India (1958–84), are easily available and constitute an important source for any work on Gandhi.

Apart from his own writings, the following works are useful in conceptualizing Gandhi's ideas. *Mahatma Gandhi: His Own Story* (1930) and *Mahatma Gandhi at Work* (1931), both edited by C.F. Andrews; *Selections from Gandhi* (1948), edited by N.K. Bose; *Selected Writings of Mahatma Gandhi* (1951), selected and introduced by Ronald Duncan; *Teaching of Mahatma Gandhi* (1947), Edited by J.P. Chander; *The Mind of Mahatma Gandhi* (1945), edited by R.K. Prabhu and U.R. Rao; *Sarvadaya: Its Principles and Programme* (1951) edited by S.N. Agarwal; *The Wit and Wisdom of Gandhi* and *The Gandhi Reader* (1955), edited by Homer A. Jack.

Apart from academic works strictly on Gandhi and his political activities, there is a vast literature on India's freedom struggle, which informed

Gandhi's social and political ideas. So unlinking Gandhi from the context is neither appropriate nor theoretically justified. Seeking to identify the theoretical and empirical roots of *ahimsa* as an ideology, these works dwell on India's colonial context to grasp the complexity of what is generally known as Gandhism. Besides contextualizing Gandhi, they offer further elaboration of the processes behind the evolution of an ideology in contrast and in conjunction with competing ideologies which, however, remained peripheral so long as the Mahatma was on India's political scene. Gandhi is therefore not merely a story of a unique historical personality, but also of an organically evolved ideology with transcendental characteristics. The available literature is illustrative here.

One final point on this bibliography: colonialism had a determining role in the articulation of the nationalist response. Not only did colonialism provoke oppositional politics, it also shaped the nature of that politics in a strictly 'liberal' way. Studies of Gandhi and his ideas reflect this theoretical tilt. In other words, since liberalism was the ruling ideology and Gandhi's ideological response was built around this, the prevalent literature holds that bias though Gandhism was not 'strictly' a liberal response with roots in the political philosophy of the Enlightenment. Gandhi's social and political ideas were creative liberal responses to the contemporary issues. Apart from the obvious 'life and times' perspective, the available literature also dwells on this dimension of the Gandhian ideology, which was largely a contextualized articulation with transcendental theoretical importance. Keeping this in mind, the bibliography is structured accordingly: besides literature on Gandhi *per se*, it contains a large corpus of studies on India's freedom struggle that appeared to have set the empirical milieu for Gandhi to articulate his social and political thought.

Select bibliography

Alavi, Hamza, 'Social forces and ideology in the making of Pakistan', *Economic and Political Weekly*, 21 October, 2002

Alavi, Hamza, 'Misreading partition road signs', *Economic and Political Weekly*, 2–9 November, 2002

Ali, Chaudhuri Muhammad, *The Emergence of Pakistan*, Columbia University Press, New York, 1967

Ambedkar, B.R., *What Congress and Gandhi done to the untouchables*, Thacker & Co., Bombay, 1946

Ambedkar, B.R., *Dr. Babasaheb Ambedkar Writings and Speeches*, Vols I–VIII, Education Department, Government of Maharastra, 1999

Ambedkar, B.R., 'Thoughts on Pakistan', in Mushirul Hasan (ed.), *Inventing Boundaries: gender, politics and partition of India*, Oxford University Press, Delhi, 2000

Amin, Shahid, 'Gandhi as Mahatma: Gorakhpur district, eastern UP, 1921–2', in Ranajit Guha (ed.), *Subaltern Studies: writings on South Asian Studies*, Vol. III, Oxford University Press, Delhi, 1984

Amin, Shahid, *Event, Metaphor, Memory: Chauri Chaura, 1922–1992*, Oxford University Press, New Delhi, 1995

Ananthanathan, A.K., 'The significance of Gandhi's interpretation of Gita', *Gandhi Marg*, Vol. 13 (3), October, 1991

Bagchi, Amiya, *Private Investment in India, 1900–39*, Cambridge University Press, Cambridge, 1972

Bakshi, Rajni, *Bapu Kuti: journeys in rediscovery of Gandhi*, Penguin, New Delhi, 1998

Bandyopadhyay, Sekhar, *From Plassey to Partition: a history of modern India*, Orient Longman, New Delhi, 2004

Bandyopadhyaya, Jayantuja, *Social and Political Thought of Gandhi*, Allied Publishers, Bombay, 1969

Bhalla, Alok (ed.), *Stories about the Partition of India*, Penguin, New Delhi, 1994

Bhana Surendra and Goolam Vahed, *The Making of a Political Reformer: Gandhi and South Africa, 1893–1914*, Manohar, New Delhi, 2005

Bhattacharya, Sabyasachi (ed. and compiled), *The Mahatma and the Poet: letters and debates between Gandhi and Tagore, 1915–1941*, National Book Trust, New Delhi, 1997

Bhattacharya, Sabyasachi, *Vande Mataram: the biography of a song*, Penguin, New Delhi, 2003

Bhattacharyya, Buddhadeva, *Evolution of the Political Philosophy of Gandhi*, Calcutta Book House, Calcutta, 1969

Bilgrami, Akeel, 'Gandhi, the philosopher', *Economic and Political Weekly*, Vol. 38 (39), 2003

Birla, G.D., *In the Shadow of Mahatma: a personal memoir*, Orient Longman, Calcutta, 1964

Bondurant, Joan V., *Conquest of Violence: the Gandhian philosophy of conflict*, Princeton University Press, Princeton, 1958; also University of California Press, Berkeley, 1969 (revised edition)

Bose, Nirmal Kumar, *Studies in Gandhism*, India Associated Publishing Co., Calcutta 1962

Bose, Nirmal Kumar, *My Days with Gandhi*, Orient Longman, Calcutta, 1974

Bose, Subhas Chandra, *The Indian Struggle, 1920–42*, Asia Publishing House, London, 1964

Bose, Sugata, 'Nation, reason and religion: India's independence in international perspective', *Economic and Political Weekly*, 1 August, 1998

Bose, Sugata and Ayesha, Jalal, *Modern South Asia, History, Culture, Political Economy*, Oxford University Press, Delhi, 1998

Brown, Judith, 'The Mahatma and modern India', *Modern Asian Studies*, Vol. 3 (4), 1969

Brown, Judith, *Gandhi's Rise to Power: Indian politics, 1915–1922*, Cambridge University Press, Cambridge, 1972

Brown, Judith, *Gandhi and Civil Disobedience: the Mahatma in Indian politics, 1928–1934*, Cambridge University Press, Cambridge, 1977

Brown, Judith, *Modern India: the origins of an Asian democracy*, Oxford University Press, Delhi, 1985

Brown, Judith, *Gandhi: prisoner of hope*, Oxford University Press, Delhi, 1990

Brown, Judith, *Nehru: a political life*, Oxford University Press, New Delhi, 2004

Chakrabarty, Bidyut, 'Peasants and the Bengal Congress, 1928–38', *South Asia Research*, Vol. 5 (1), May, 1985

Chakrabarty, Bidyut, *Subhas Chandra Bose and Middle Class Radicalism: a study in Indian nationalism, 1928–40*, Oxford University Press, Delhi, 1990

Chakrabarty, Bidyut, *Local Politics and Indian Nationalism: Midnapur, 1919–1944*, Manohar, New Delhi, 1997

Chakrabarty, Bidyut, *Biplabi: a journal of the 1942 open rebellion*, K.P. Bagchi, Calcutta, 2002

Chakrabarty, Bidyut, 'Religion, colonialism and modernity: relocating "self" and "collectivity"', *Gandhi Marg*, Vol. 23 (3), 2002

Chakrabarty, Bidyut (ed.), *Communal Identity in India: its construction and articulation in the twentieth century*, Oxford University Press, Delhi, 2003

Chakrabarty, Bidyut, *The Partition of Bengal and Assam, 1932–47: contour of freedom*, RoutledgeCurzon, London and New York, 2004

Chakrabarty, Dipesh, 'Nation and imagination', *Studies in History*, Vol. 15 (2), New Series, 1999

Chatterjee, Margaret, *Gandhi's Religious Thought*, Macmillan, London, 1983

Chatterjee, Partha, 'Gandhi and the critique of civil society', in Ranajit Guha (ed.), *Subaltern Studies: writings on South Asian Studies*, Vol. III, Oxford University Press, Delhi, 1984

Chatterjee, Partha, 'Gandhi please stand up?', *Illustrated Weekly of India*, 15–21 January, 1984

Chatterjee, Partha, *Nationalist Thought and the Colonial World: a derivative discourse*, Oxford University Press, Delhi, 1986

Chatterjee, Partha, 'The nation in heterogeneous time', *Indian Economic and Social History Review*, Vol. 38 (4), 2001

Chatterjee, Partha, *A Princely Impostor? The kumar of Bhawal and the secret history of Indian nationalism*, Permanent Black, New Delhi, 2002

Chatterjee, Partha, *The Politics of the Governed: reflections on popular politics in most of the world*, Permanent Black, New Delhi, 2004

Chaudhuri, Nirad C., *The Autobiography of an Unknown Indian*, University of California Press, Berkeley, 1968

Chaudhuri, Nirad C., *Thy Hand Great Anarch: India, 1921–52*, Chatto and Windus, London, 1987

Choudhury, Khaliquzzaman, *Pathway to Pakistan*, Longmans, Lahore, 1961

Cohn, B., *Colonialism and Its Forms of Knowledge: the British in India*, Princeton University Press, Princeton, 1996

Dalton, Dennis, *Non-violence in Action: Gandhi's power*, Oxford University Press, Delhi, 1998

Darling, Malcolm Lyall, *At Freedom's Dawn*, Oxford University Press, London, 1949,

Das, Durga (ed.), *Vallabhbhai Patel Correspondence, 1945–50*, Vol. IV, Ahmedabad, 1972

Dasgupta, Ajit K., *Gandhi's Economic Thought*, Routledge, London and New York, 1996

Datta, V.N., 'Iqbal, Jinnah and India's partition', *Economic and Political Weekly*, 14–20 December, 2002

Doke, Joseph J., *M.K. Gandhi: an Indian patriot in South Africa*, London, 1909

Dutt, R. Palme, *India Today*, Victor Gollancz Ltd, London, 1940

Embree, Ainslie T., *Imagining India: essays on Indian history*, Oxford University Press, Delhi, 1989

Erikson, E., *Gandhi's Truth: on the origins of militant non-violence*, Faber and Faber, New York, 1970

Ferguson, Niall, *Empire: the rise and demise of the British world order and the lessons for global power*, Basic Books, New York, 2002

Fisher, Louis, *The Life of Mahatma Gandhi*, Harper and Row, New York, 1981

Fisher, Louis, *Gandhi: his life and message for the world*, New American Library, New York, 1982

Fox, Richard, *Gandhian Utopia: experiments with culture*, Beacon Press, Boston, 1989

Frank, Andre Gunder, 'Gandhi, the philosopher', *Economic and Political Weekly*, Vol. 38 (43), 2003

Freitag, Sandria B., *Collective Action and Community: public arenas and the emergence of communalism in north India*, Oxford University Press, Delhi, 1990

Gier, Nicholas, 'Gandhi, Ahimsa and self', *Gandhi Marg*, Vol. 15 (1), 1993

Gier, Nicholas, 'Gandhi, pre-modern, modern or post-modern?', *Gandhi Marg*, Vol. 18 (3), 1996

Gopal, S., *Selected Works of Jawaharlal Nehru*, 3 vols, Jonathan Cape, London, 1973–84

Gordon, L., 'Mahatma Gandhi's dialogue with Americans', *Economic and Political Weekly*, Vol. 37 (4), 2002

Gore, M.S., *The Social Context of an Ideology: Ambedkar's political and social thought*, Sage, New Delhi, 1993

Griffiths, Percival, *To Guard My People: the history of the Indian police*, Ernest Benn, London, 1971

Guha, Ranajit (ed.), *Subaltern Studies: writings on South Asian history and society*, Oxford University Press, Delhi, 1984

Guha, Ranajit, *Dominance without Hegemony: history and power in colonial India*, Oxford University Press, Delhi, 1998

Haksar, Vinit, *Rights, Communities and Disobedience: liberalism and Gandhi*, Oxford University Press, New Delhi, 2001

Haque, Azizul, *A Plea for Separate Electorate in Bengal*, Calcutta, 1931

Hardiman, David, *Peasant Nationalists of Gujarat: Kheda district, 1917–34*, Oxford University Press, Delhi, 1981

Hardiman, David, *Gandhi in His Time and Ours*, Permanent Black, New Delhi, 2003

Hardy, P., *The Muslims of British India*, Cambridge University Press, Cambridge, 1972

Hasan, Mushirul (ed.), *India Partitioned: the other face of freedom*, Vol. 1, Roli Books, New Delhi, 1995

Hasan, Mushirul, *Legacy of a Divided Nation: India's Muslims since independence*, Oxford University Press, Delhi, 1997

Hasan, Mushirul (ed.), *Inventing Boundaries: gender, politics and the partition of India*, Oxford University Press, New Delhi, 2000

Hashim, Abul, *In Retrospection*, Mowla Brothers, Dhaka, 1974

Henningham, S., 'The social setting of the Champaran satyagraha: the challenge of an alien rule, *Indian Economic and Social History Review*, Vol. 13 (1), 1976

Hodosn, H.V., *The Great Divide: Britain – India – Pakistan*, Hutchinson of London, London, 1969

Horsburgh, H.J.N., *Non-violence and Aggression: a study of Gandhi's moral equivalent of war*. Oxford University Press, London, 1968

Iyer, Raghavan, N., *The Moral and Political Thought of Mahatma Gandhi*, Oxford University Press, Delhi, 1973

Iyer, Raghavan (ed.), *The Moral and Political Writings of Mahatma Gandhi*, Clarendon Press, Oxford, Vols 1 and 2, 1986 and Vol. 3, 1987

Jha, Sadan, 'Charkha, "dear forgotten friend", of widows: reading the erasures of symbols', *Economic and Political Weekly*, Vol. 39 (28), 2004

Jinnah, Muhammad Ali, *Speeches*, Pakistan Publications, Karachi, 1963

Juergensmeyer, Mark, *Fighting with Gandhi*, Harper and Row, San Francisco, 1984

Juergensmeyer, Mark, *Gandhi's Way: a handbook of conflict resolution*, Oxford University Press, New Delhi, 2003

Kamath, M.V. and V.B. Kher, *The Story of Militant but Non-violent Trade Unionism: a biographical and historical study*, Navajivan Trust, Ahmedabad, 1993 (reprint)

Karunakaran, K.P., *New Perspectives on Gandhi*, Indian Institute of Advanced Studies, Shimla, 1969

Khilnani, Sunil, 'Gandhi and history', *Seminar*, No. 461 (Annual), January, 1998

Kripalani, Krishna, *Gandhi: a life*, National Book Trust, New Delhi, 1968

Kripalani, Sucheta, *An Unfinished Biography*, Navajivan Publishing House, Ahmedabad, 1978

Kumar, R., *Essays on Gandhian Politics: the Rowlatt Satyagraha of 1919*, Clarendon Press, Oxford, 1971

Leaves from a Diary: Shyama Prasad Mookherjee, Oxford University Press, Calcutta, 1993, pp. 105–7

Mahajan, Sucheta, *Independence and Partition: the erosion of colonial power*, Sage, New Delhi, 2000

Manor, J. (ed.), *Nehrus to the Nineties: the changing office of prime minister in India*, Hurst, London, 1994

Mansergh, Diana (ed.), *Independence Years: the selected Indian and commonwealth papers of Nicholas Mansergh*, Oxford University Press, Delhi, 1999

Markovits, Claude, *The Un-Gandhian Gandhi: the life and afterlife of the Mahatma*, Permanent Black, New Delhi, 2003

Mehta, V.R., *Foundations of Indian Political Thought*, Manohar, New Delhi, 1992

Menon, Dilip, 'Religion and colonial modernity: rethinking belief and identity', *Economic and Political Weekly*, 27 April, 2002

Menon, V.P., *The Transfer of Power in India*, Orient Longman, Madras, 1993 (reprint), Appendix X

Mitra, Ashok, *The New India, 1948–1955: memoirs of an Indian civil servant*, Popular Prakashan, Bombay, 1991

Moon, Penderel (ed.), *Wavell: the Viceroy's Journal*, Oxford University Press, Delhi, 1977

Moon, Penderel, *The British Conquest of Dominion of India*, Duckworth, London, 1989

Moore, Barrington Jr., *Social Origins of Dictatorship and Democracy: lord and peasant in the making of the modern world*, Beacon press, Boston, 1966

Morris-Jones, W.H., 'Mahatma Gandhi – political philosopher?', *Political Studies*, Vol. VIII (1), February, 1960

Mukherjee, Hiren, *Gandhi: a study*, People's Publishing House, New Delhi, 1991 (reprint)

Mukherjee, Rudrangshu, *The Penguin Gandhi reader*, Penguin, New Delhi, 1993

Mukherjee, Subrata, *Gandhian thought: Marxist interpretation*, Deep & Deep, New Delhi, 1997

Mukherjee, Subrata and Sushila Ramaswamy (eds), *Economic and Social Principles of Mahatma Gandhi*, Deep & Deep, New Delhi, 1998

Mukherjee, Subrata and Sushila Ramaswamy (eds), *Ethics, Religion and culture*, Deep & Deep, New Delhi, 1998

Mukherjee, Subrata and Sushila Ramaswamy (eds), *Non Violence and Satyagraha*, Deep & Deep, New Delhi, 1998

Mukherjee, Subrata and Sushila Ramaswamy (eds), *Political Ideas of Mahatma Gandhi*, Deep & Deep, New Delhi, 1998

Namboodiripad, E.M.S., *The Mahatma and the Ism*, People's Publishing House, New Delhi, 1959

Nanda, B.R., *The Nehrus: Motilal and Jawaharlal*, George & Allen, London, 1962

Nanda, B.R., *Gandhi and His Critics*, Oxford University Press, Delhi, 1985

Nanda, B.R., *Mahatma Gandhi: 125 years*, New Age International Publishers, New Delhi, 1995

Nanda, B.R., *Mahatma Gandhi*, Oxford University Press, Delhi, 1996 (reprint)

Nanda, B.R., *In Search of Gandhi: essays and reflections*, Oxford University Press, New Delhi, 2004

Nandy, Ashis, *The Illegitimacy of Nationalism: Rabindranath and the politics of self*, Oxford University Press, Delhi, 1994

Nandy, Ashis, *The Intimate Enemy: loss and recovery of self under colonialism*, Oxford University Press, Delhi, 1983

Narayan, R.K., *Waiting for the Mahatma*, Indian Thought Publications, Chennai, 2003 (reprint)

Nayar, Sushila, *Mahatma Gandhi's Last Imprisonment: the inside story*, Har-Anand, New Delhi, 1996

Nehru, Jawaharlal, *Jawaharlal Nehru: an autobiography*, John Lane The Bodley Head, London, 1941

Nehru, Jawaharlal, *The Discovery of India*, Oxford University Press, Delhi, (centenary edition), 1985

Orwell, G., 'Reflections on Gandhi', *Partisan Review*, 16 January, 1949

Pandey, Gyanendra, 'The prose of otherness', *Subaltern Studies*, Vol. VIII, Oxford University Press, Delhi, 1994

Pandey, Gyanendra, *Hindus and Others: the question of identity in India today*, Viking, New Delhi, 1997

Pandey, Gyanendra, *Remembering Partition: violence, nationalism and history in India*, Cambridge University Press, Cambridge, 2001

Pantham, Thomas, 'Thinking with Mahatma Gandhi: beyond liberal democracy', *Political Theory*, Vol. 11 (2), 1983

Pantham, Thomas, 'Habermas' practical discourse and Gandhi's satyagraha', in Bhikhu Parekh and Thomas Pantham (eds), *Political Discourse: explorations in Indian and western political thought*, Sage, New Delhi, 1987

Pantham, Thomas, 'Gandhi: *swaraj, sarvadaya* and *satyagraha*', in Thomas Pantham, *Political Theories and Social Reconstruction: a critical survey of the literature on India*, Sage, New Delhi, 1995

Pantham, Thomas and Kenneth L. Deutsch, *Political Thought in Modern India*, Sage, New Delhi, 1986

Parekh, Bhikhu, *Gandhi's Political Philosophy: a critical appreciation*, University of Notre Dame Press, Notre Dame, IN, 1989

Parekh, Bhikhu, 'Nehru and the national philosophy of India', *Economic and Political Weekly*, Vol. 26 (182), 1991

Parekh, Bhikhu, *Gandhi*, Oxford University Press, Oxford, 1997

Parekh, Bhikhu, *Colonialism, Tradition and Reform: an analysis of Gandhi's political discourse*, Sage, New Delhi, 1999

Parel, Anthony J. (ed.), *Hind Swaraj and Other Writings*, Cambridge University Press, Cambridge, 1997

Parel, Anthony J. (ed.), *Gandhi, Freedom and Self-Rule*, Vistaar, New Delhi, 2000

Pirzada, S.S. (ed.), *Foundations of Pakistan: All India Muslim League documents*, Vol. II, National Publishing House, Karachi, no date

Pouchepadas, Jacques, *Champaran and Gandhi: planters, peasants and Gandhian politics*, Oxford University Press, New Delhi, 1999

Prasad, Bimal, *Pathway to India's Partition: the foundations of Muslim nationalism*, Vol. I, Manohar, Delhi, 1996

Prasad, Bimal, *Pathway to India's Partition: a nation within a nation, 1877–1937*, Vol. II, Manohar, Delhi, 2000

Pyralal, Mahatma, *Gandhi, the Early Phase*, 2 Vols, Navajivan Publishing House, Ahmedabad, 1956 and 1958

Radhakrishnan, Sarvepalli (ed.), *Mahatma Gandhi: essays and reflections*, Jaico, Mumbai, 2003 (reprint)

Ray, Rajat K. (ed.), *Mind, Body and Society: life and mentality in colonial Bengal*, Oxford University Press, Calcutta, 1995

Ray, Rajat K., *Exploring Emotional History: gender, mentality and literature in the Indian awakening*, Oxford University Press, Delhi, 2001

Ray, Sibnarayan (ed.), *Selected Works of M.N. Roy*, Vol. I (1917–22), Oxford University Press, New Delhi, 2000

Ray, Sibnarayan (ed.), *Selected Works of M.N. Roy*, Vol. II (1923–7), Oxford University Press, New Delhi, 2000

Richards, G., *The Philosophy of Gandhi: a study of his basic ideas*, Curzon Press, Surrey, 1982

Rodrigues, Valerian (ed.), *The Essential Writings of B.R. Ambedkar*, Oxford University Press, New Delhi, 2004

Rolland Romain, *Mahatma Gandhi*, Allen and Unwin, London, 1924

Roy, M.N., *India in Transition*, Nachiketa Publications, Bombay, 1971 (reprint)

Roy, Ramashray, *Self and Society: a study of Gandhian thought*, Sage, New Delhi, 1985

Rudolph, L.I. and S.H. Rudolf, *The Modernity of Tradition: political development in India*, University of Chicago Press, Chicago and London, 1967

Sethi, J.D., *Gandhi Today*, Carolina Academic Press, Durham, 1978

Settar, S and Indira B. Gupta (eds), *Pangs of Partition: the parting of ways*, Vol. I, Manohar, New Delhi, 2002

Settar, S. and Indira B. Gupta (eds), *Pangs of Partition: the human dimension*, Vol. II, Manohar, New Delhi, 2002

Shaikh, Farzana, 'Muslims and political representation in colonial India: the making of Pakistan', *Modern Asian Studies*, Vol. 20 (3), 1986

Singh, Anita Inder, *The Origins of Partition of India, 1936–47*, Oxford University Press, Delhi, 1987

Sitaramayya, B. Pattabhi, *The History of the Indian National Congress*, Vols I (1922–35) and II (1935–47), S. Chand & Co., Delhi, 1969

Southard, Barbara, 'The feminism of Mahatma Gandhi', in Subrata Mukherjee and Sushila Ramaswamy (eds), *Economic and Social Principles of Mahatma Gandhi*, Vol. 3, Deep & Deep Publications, New Delhi, 1998

Spear, Percival, *The Oxford History of Modern India, 1740–1947*, Clarendon Press, Oxford, 1965

Tai, Yong Tan and Gynesh Kudaisya, *The Aftermath of Partition in South Asia*, Routledge, London, 2000

Taneja, Anup, *Gandhi, Women and the National Movement, 1920–47*, Har-Anand, New Delhi, 2005

Tendulkar, D.G., *Mahatma: the life of Mohandas Karanchand Gandhi*, Ministry of Information and Broadcasting, Government of India, New Delhi, 1961

Terchek Ronald J., *Gandhi: struggling for autonomy*, Vistaar, New Delhi, 1998

Tirmizi, S.A.I. (ed.), *The Paradoxes of Partition, 1937–47*, Vol. 1 (1937–9), Centre for Federal Studies, Jamia Hamdard, New Delhi, 1998

Van der Veer, Peter, *Religious Nationalism: Hindus and Muslims in India*, Oxford University Press, Delhi, 1996

Weber, Thomas, *Conflict Resolution and Gandhian Ethics*, The Gandhi Peace Foundation, New Delhi, 1991

Wolpert, S., *Nehru: a tryst with destiny*, Oxford University Press, New York, 1996

Zachariah Benjamin, *Nehru*, Routledge, London, 2004

Zaidi, A.M. and S.G. Zaidi (eds), *The Encyclopaedia of the Indian National Congress*, Vol. 12, S. Chand & Co., New Delhi, 1981

Ziegler, P., *Mountbatten: the official biography*, Collins, Glasgow, 1985

Index

Abani Mukherjee 52
absence of exploitation and *swaraj* 35
absence of poverty and *swaraj* 35
absolute and relative *dharma* 127
absolute truth 20
adjustment of communal quarrel 151
administration and non-violence 138
aggressive civil disobedience 132
Ahemedabad 77
ahimsa 13, 18; as a device for conflict
   resolution 60; as a mode of
   constructive political and social action
   38; in a negative form 59; as non-
   injury 59–60; in a positive form 59
ahimsa-driven nationalist struggle 16
Ahmedabad 4, 6–7
Ahmedabad textile mill strike 1918 6, 7
Ali brothers 150
Ali Imam 120
alien rule 35
All-India Village Industries Association
   152
Ambedkar BR 29, 84–5; critique of
   Brahminical way 114; and Gandhi
   103–11
Amrita Bazar Patrika 54, 89
anglicized elite 2
anti-British campaign 22; in India 30
anti-British counter offensive 71
anti-British sentiments 48, 82
anti-British struggle 52
anti-Rowlatt Satyagraha 59, 61
Arabic origin of languages 164
arguments for Constituent Assembly for
   India 125–6
artha 26
Asiatic Law Amendment Ordinance
   1906, 64
Atulanand Chakrabarti 149

August resolution 79
authoritarian societies 33
autonomy of individuals 175

Baba Ramchandra 81
Badshah Khan 79
Bal Gangadhar Tilak 44–5, 54
Bangladesh 32
Bardoli resolution 91
base of Indian nationalism 73
Basic Education Board 152
basic ingredients of nation 31
basic precepts of Gandhian thought 59,
   70
Bengali Muslims and Bengali Hindus
   148
Bettiah 4
bhadralok politics 52
Bhikhu Parekh 14
bifurcation of British India 85
Bihar earthquake as 'divine
   chastisement' 101
Bipin Pal 44
Biplabi 80
black hole of Indian civilization 103
blacksmith and economic development
   146
Bombay presidency 78
Bondurant JV 12
Brahminical texts 112
Brahma Satyam Jagatmithya 19
British administration 80
British capital 39
British rule: as an intimate enemy 24; in
   India 46, 67
British system of primary education
   126
British-Indian provinces and Gandhi
   23

Buddhist traditions in Gandhi's thought 74
bullock cart 146

capitalist path of development in India 1
cart driver and development 146
caste and *varna* 155–6
caste and *varnashrama* 110
caste has to go 154–5
caste system as a hierarchy 108
central legislatures 104
challenge to the age-old system of exploitation 131
Champaran 4, 6–7, 77, 80
charkha 39, 42, 92, 98–100, 121, 176, 177
charkha as an archaic tool 98
charkha-Ahimsa-Swaraj 140
Charles Taylor 33
Chaturvarnya 109–10
Chauri Chaura 12, 16, 78
Chengis Khan 141
Chittagong revolutionaries 53
Civil Disobedience Movement 10, 17, 62, 67, 71, 123, 176
civil disobedience and freedom 143
civil disobedience campaign 74
civil society 172
civilizational Gandhi 29, 166
civilizational identity of India 94
civilizational resources of Hindu religion and tradition 26
civilizational values and Gandhi 168
collaboration of indigenous capital 15
collectivist theory of state and society 174
colonial power and Indian society 16
colonialism 26; imperialism 24; and 'oppositional' politics 220
Communal Award, 1932, 105, 117
communal conflagration in India 137
communal division between Hindus and Muslims 50
communal identity 33
communal question and Gandhi 120
Communal unity 152
communities and cultural forces 94
compassion and *ahimsa* 73
compulsive disarmament 37
conceptualization of Indian society 1
conceptualization of non-violence 36
conceptualizing *swaraj* 34

Congress: agenda of the masses 92; flag as essential to freedom 143; as a platform for freedom 113; resolution of 1939, 125; volunteers 78; Working Committee 11
conquest of adversary 20, 21
constitutional means of protest 2
constitutionalism of the Moderates 168
constructive programme 152
contextual connotation of Gandhi's thoughts 20
contradictory nature of Gandhian thought 58
craft-based education 157
critique of Gandhi 113–15
critique of industrialism/western civilization 121–3
critique of Western civilization 24
custom of untouchability 101

Dadabhai Naoroji 39, 43
dalits 85, 104, 106, 111–12
Dandi March 134
daridranarayan 124
Das CR 52
debate between Gandhi and Ambedkar 111
Declaration of Independence 36–7
defensive civil disobedience 132
delegitimation of slavery 112
democracy and Gandhi 175
democratic institutions in India 44
democratization and *swaraj* 31
democratization as a process 112
Depressed Classes 118
Devnagari scripts 127
dharma 26, 38, 61
Dharmadeva 57
dhoti 2
dialectics between Gandhi and his critics 115
difference between Rabindranath Tagore and Gandhi 102
different nations and Gandhi 119
displacement of village labour 141
distinct Gandhian approach to nationalism 16
distortions of India's civilization 49
domain of sovereignty 171
dominion status 151
duragraha 21

economics and education 162

Edmund Burke 45
education 157–9; and future state 160–3; policy 162
elementary knowledge of history 158
Emerson 23
English educated lawyers 49
English nation 43
English rule in India 36
English speaking Indians 72
essence of Indian civilization 103
European history 2
European modular form of nation 94
European politics 2
exclusive domain of Hindu society 171
exclusivity of Islam 32
extremist phase 10
extremists 37

faith and reason in Gandhi's thought 26
famine in Kathiwar state 125
fasting as a self-purifying exercise 68
federal structure for India 124
foundational ideas of Gandhi's thought 19
free and compulsory education 162
freedom and justice as basis for Ambedkar's thought 114
freedom movment and *swaraj* 32
freedom struggle and *swaraj* 34
fundamental precepts of Gandhism 29
future social order 122
future state 124

Gandhi 1, 20, 22, 28; as an activist-theoretician 27; alternative vision 10; as a civilizational character 9; and classes 172; conceptualization of truth 19; contextualized response 9; critique of mill-production 141; explanation of non-violence 137; as 'fugitive' 166; and gender 128–9; as a great soul 12; idea of human development 131; and Indian villages 103; inter-cultural communication 14; and involvement of 'the peripheral' sections of society 93; as a liberal 66; as a loyalist 72; as mediator between various groups 170; and Mill JS 172; and Muslim League 121; not anarchic 66; as a paradox 103; as a political activist 57; political philosophy 14; as politically appropriate 113; and popular

initiative 171; *raj* 3; Rajkot statement 135; in South Africa 23; South African experiments 12; as a symbol of the weak and underprivileged 3; thought as multi-dimensional 166; as transcendental 220; and western civilization 131
Gandhian: conceptualization of *swaraj* 31; Congress 172; cosmology 10; intervention in *swaraj* 55; methods 22; mode of conflict resolution 66; movements at the grassroots 70
Gandhism as an ideology 75
Girni Kamgar Union 53
Gita 149
Gopen Chakrabarty 52
governance 151
Government of India Act, 1935, 104, 124
grammar of political mobilization 63
Great Divide 32
Gujrat Sabha 5

hand-spinning 176
Harijan 1, 23, 28, 56, 116; and *Hind Swaraj* contrasted 129, 131; as a text 130; as 'unrealistic' or 'obscurantist' text 176
Harijan Sevak Sangh 117
Harijan welfare 176
Harijanbandhu 132
Harijansevak 132
heterogeneous Indian civilization 32
hidden power in *ahimsa* 136
Hind Swaraj 1, 23, 64, 116
Hindi 164
Hindu dominance in united India 108
Hindu raj 107
Hindu traditions: in Gandhi's thought 74; and the Mahatma 14
Hinduized nationalist movement 103
Hindu-Muslim: amity 84; division 120; entangle 149; leadership in Non-cooperation and Khilafat Movement 48; schism 95, 107
Hindus against Muslims 106
Hindus and Muslims are not two nations 148
Hindustani 164
historical context of India's freedom struggle 30
historical Gandhi 166
history of the nationalist struggle 30

home rule 47
human actions in accordance with
  ahimsa and *satya* 28
hunger strike as a political weapon 68
Hunter Committee 63
hyper masculine world view 25

ideological changes and *Swaraj* 55
ideological route to freedom 70
imagined community 32
importance of the symbols 177
importance of truth and love in non-
  violent protest 13
incendiary manifesto 24
inclusionary character of Indian
  nationalism 47
India in Transition 90
India's socio-cultural traditions and
  non-violent protest 14
India's village economy 41
Indian: civilization 119; freedom
  struggle as nationalist 49;
  independence 29; nationalist
  movement 9, 70; nationhood 31;
  philosophy 23; religious traditions
  31; society 105
Indian National Congress 28, 47
Indian Opinion 56
Indianness of Gandhi's lifestyle 58
indigenous cultural traditions in India 2
indigenous roots of colonialism in India
  24
indigenous capitalism and India's
  economic future 53
indigenous combination of reason,
  morality and politics 27
industrial capitalism 24, 26
industrialism and modernity 40
industrialization and western
  civilization 25
industrialization as devastation 41
Infatuation about English language 154
Inner and outer domains of Hindu
  society 171
inter-marriage and inter-dining 110
involvement of various linguistic groups
  34
Iqbal as *brahminical* descent 121
irreligiosity and Gandhi 26

Jainist traditions in Gandhi's thought 74
Jawaharlal Nehru 8, 41, 60, 122; on
  Gandhi 167, 169

Jinnah 11, 85, 94, 102; two-nation
  theory 107
Judith Brown 10

kama 26
Karachi Congress, 1930 47
khaddar 91
khadi 22, 39, 41, 121, 176; as integral
  to swaraj 143; as a mission 142; and
  spinning 144; as swadeshi 142
Kheda 4, 6–7, 77
Kheda *satyagraha* 5, 6–7
Khilafat Movement 34, 84
Kitchlew 121
Koran 149
Kripalani JB 4

Lahore session of the Congress 49
language 164
language of nationalism 35
Legislative Council 51
Lenin's draft thesis on colonialism 87
literature on India's freedom struggle
  219
little and great traditions 94
Lord Reading 2
lovers of education 163
loyal constitutionalism 3

machine as dehumanizing 25
magical power (of the Mahatma) 9
Mahar 156
Mahatma *see* Ghandi
Malabar 145
mass actions as 'institutive' 168
mass civil disobedience 169
masses and Indian freedom struggle 22
massive bloodbaths in Bengal, Bihar
  and Punjab 12
material and spiritual domains 171
Maulana Mahomed Ali 143
Mazzini 45
mechanization: of human civilization
  122; as a menace 27
mediaeval syncretism 31
memories of oppression 32
merit of self-suffering 13
metropolitan manufacturers 39
militant nationalists 24
mill industry and colonialism 25
Mill JS 45
moderate era 10
moderate wing 43

moderate wing of the Congress 36
moderate-extremist critique of
   colonialism 40
moderates 76
modern civilization as a leveler 40
modern imperialism 25
Mohandas Karamchand Gandhi 1
Mohanlal Pandya 5
monolithic communities 33
Montague-Chelmsford Reform 51
moral and physical affinity with the
   masses 83
moral and truthful form of political
   action 38
moral courage and Gandhi 17
moral decline of India 24
moral issues and *satyagraha* 81
morality and passion 26
Motilalji 165
motor vs. cart 146
Muhammedan 35
municipal councils 51
Muslim League 28, 33, 51, 94, 151
Muslim League as a theocratic party 108
Muslim majority provinces 79
Muslim nationalists 150
Mussalmans and Gandhi 137

nation not derivative 173
nation, nationalism and national
   identity 119–20
national framework of politics 70
national independence and *swaraj* 35
national industries 53
nationalism 82; and *swaraj* 31
nationalist discourse 112; and Gandhi
   29
nationalist: language 32, 102; logic and
   Gandhi 171; movement and Gandhi's
   political ideas 21; thought 119; as a
   mob 62
nation-building and anti-imperial
   struggle 34
Nehru Report 49
new constituents of the national
   movement 47
Noakhali 12
non-cooperation: and Khilafat
   Movement 47–8, 49; non-cooperation
   movement 10, 17, 71, 76; non-
   cooperation movement as 'mobocracy'
   166
non-cooperation-Khilafat merger 129

non-violence 73; as cloak 89; *khadi* and
   satyagraha 123–4; on a larger national
   and international scale 134; as a
   means of political action 72; as a
   method 76; at the micro level 19;
   more than swordmanship 75;
   resolution of conflict 12; as a science
   82; as a strategy 74; who is a coward?
   133; who is a non-violent man? 135
no-revenue campaign 5
nyee talim 131

object of *satyagraha* 13

Pakistan 32, 102, 147
Pakistan and Constituent Assembly 150
Pakistan demand 51
Pakistan or the Partition of India 108
Palme Dutt R. 169–70
Panchayati raj 175
partition of India 102
passive national democratic revolution
   173
passive resistance 38
patidar peasants 5
peasant-communal moral critique 172
peasants and Workers' demands 53
Persian origin of languages 164
personal suffering and *satyagraha* 38
perspectives of *swaraj* 31
philosophical basis of *swaraj* 30
philosophical identities of nation 34
police force and Gandhi 138–9
policies of boycott and non-cooperation
   13
policy of appeasement towards Muslims
   173
political campaigns not one-dimensional
   64
political domination of man over man
   46
political freedom 15; and *swaraj* 37–8
political mobilization and Gandhi 30,
   177
political resources for governance 18
Political Sufferers' Conference 52
politico-cultural forces of nationalism
   71
politics and religion 147
politics defined in a 'liberal' way 220
Poona Pact 1932 106, 111, 118
post-enlightenment ethnocentric model
   15

post-enlightenment philosophy of
    nationalism 28
post-modernism 3
Prajadroha 44
Pratapgarh 81
primary education 161, 163
prohibition in caste system 110
promotion of communal harmony 67
protest movements in localities 8
provincial legislatures 104
Punjab 164
Purna swaraj or complete independence
    49, 50
Pyrelal 57

Quaid-e-Azam 148
question box 29, 117
Quit India Movement 9, 16, 17, 56, 71,
    79–80, 82

Rabindranath and *khadi* 98–9
Rabindranath Tagore 29, 42, 85; and
    Bihar earthquake 101; and boycott of
    English education 97; and *charkha*
    100; and constructive work 97;
    critique of religion-based nation state
    95; and economic boycott campaign
    96; and Gandhi 93–102; and *khaddar*
    102; and nation 95; and Non-
    Cooperation Movement 96; and
    non-nationalist philosophical
    framework 95; and *Swadeshi* 97; and
    swaraj 98
radical alternative to prevalent political
    discourses 19
Radical Democratic Party 87
radical humanism 87
Raghavan N Iyer 18
Raiyats 4
Raj 78
Rajendra Prasad 4
Rama the mythical hero 136
Rammonohar Lohia 122
Rashtrabhasa 154
regional-language-literate elites 3
Religion: and God 150; and man 150;
    and self-rule 147
republican state 91
revival of *khadi* 153
revolutionary terrorism 10, 16, 52
role of bargaining and pressure politics
    72
role of women 139–40

roots of *Swaraj* 54
Round Table Conference 111, 170
Rowlatt Satyagraha 77, 81
Roy MN 52, 85; and capitalist
    civilization 88; in the Communist
    International 87; and constructive
    programme 92; and Gandhi 86–93;
    and Gandhi's prejudices 92; the
    Marxist 86; on nationalism and
    colonialism 87; and non-violence
    89; the revolutionary terrorist 86; and
    Rowlatt Satyagraha 88; and Swaraj 90
rural Bengal 9
Ruskin 23

Saintly politics 2
Salt *satyagaha* 78
Satyagraha 4, 5, 20; as a bulwark 133;
    and Gandhi 64; as meaningful action
    62; not merely physical 65; as not
    merely a political doctrine 69; and
    persuasion 69; as a unique method of
    political change 173
Satyagrahee 39
Savarkar VD 107
Scheduled castes 106
scripts for Indian languages 126
self-determination in politics 43
self-rule: as *swaraj* 43; without self-
    determination 27
Servants of Untouchables Society 117
several Gandhis 82
Shankarlal Parikh 5
sharirbal (physical force) 27
Shastras 109, 157
silent social revolution 163
social and political implications of
    satyagraha 68
social reconstruction and vocational
    education 163
South Africa 175
South African experience 72, 76
South Asia 33
Spinners' Association 161
spinning 128
spinning wheel 2; vs. mills 144
spirit of ruthless competitiveness 26
sterile nationalist movement 83
Subhas Chandra Bose 53, 58
Subjects of Queen 72
Sudra 109
superiority of British civilization and
    ruling authority 15

suppression of women as denial of *ahimsa* 153
surnedranth Banerjee 37
swabhava (nature) 16, 37, 175
swadeshi 21, 27, 176–7; doctrine 35; movement 102, 113
swami Darshananda 81
swami Prajnananda 81
swaraj 10, 15, 18, 30; as a conceptual riddle 54; as a mental revolution 45; as a self-transformative activity 45; and *swadeshi* 21

takli (spinning wheel) 145, 158–9
taluks 145
tapas 63
tapasya (self suffering) 65
technological rationalism 26
Tej Bahadur Sapru 165
temple entry and *Harijans* 157
tension between Hindus and Muslims 68
The Bombay Chronicle 7
The Modern Review 98
The Statesman 135
The Times 7
theoretical-ideological foundation of Gandhism 29
Thoreau 23
three essential conditions for *satyagraha* 123
three Gandhis 84
tolerance and impartiality 31
Tolstoy 23
trans-cultural protest 25
Tripuri Congress 84
true democracy or *swaraj* 18
truth and non-violence 123
Tulshidas *Ramayana* 177
two Gandhis 12
two-nation theory 11, 78; and Gandhi 119

underprivileged and *satyagraha* 69

united action of Hindus and Muslims 135
universal adult suffrage 91
unorganized politics 51
untouchability and Hindus 152, 156–7
Untouchables 103; as a community 105; and political separatism 104
Urdu 127, 165
utility of industrialism as complementary to handicrafts 42
Uttar Pradesh 77

Vaishya 109
Vallabhbhai Patel 6
varnadharma 118
Varnas 109
varnashrama 109
vedanta ideal for spiritual unity 45
vernacular model of action 24
viceroy 56
village *ghani* 141
Village Industries Association 153, 161
village life and Gandhi 122
village sanitation and village life 153
violence and hatred 136
violence and *satyagraha* 69
violence in Western civilization 67
violent revolutionary action 172
Vittalbhai Patel 6
Vocational education 159–60
Vocational exercise and education 162
Voluntary federation 125

western educated elites 3
western industrial nations 26
western model of democracy 36
western modernity 175
western rationalism 175
woman as mistress of the house 139
women and household 128
women's contributive role 127

Young India 1, 56

Printed in the United States
154122LV00002B/39/P

9 780415 482097